W9-ARK-223

TSVETAEVA

By the same author

VORONEZHSKIE TETRADI
Osip Mandelstam
(Editor)

STIKHOTVORENIA I POEMY V PYATI TOMAKH
Marina Tsvetaeva
Compiled and Selected by Alexander Sumerkin
(Biographical Essay by Viktoria Schweitzer)

Viktoria Schweitzer

TSVETAEVA

Translated from the Russian by
Robert Chandler and H. T. Willetts
Poetry translated by Peter Norman

Edited and annotated by Angela Livingstone

Farrar, Straus and Giroux

New York

English translation copyright © 1992 by HarperCollins *Publishers*
First published in Russian by Sintaksis, Paris, in 1988, under the title
Byt i bytie Mariny Tsvetaevoy. Copyright © 1988 by Viktoria Schweitzer

Printed in the United States of America

First abridged, English language edition published in Great Britain
in 1992 by Harvill, an imprint of HarperCollins *Publishers*
First American edition, 1993

Library of Congress catalog card number 92-74436

TO THE MEMORY OF MY HUSBAND

ACKNOWLEDGEMENTS

On the occasion of the publication of the English edition of this book, I remember with love and gratitude my late husband and my parents, who always believed that I would succeed in writing it. I am also grateful to my daughter Marina, who always showed interest and who helped me in my work.

I am also enormously grateful to my first English editor, Carol O'Brien, for an enthusiasm and warm concern which helped me to complete the book, and to Syntaxis (Paris), who published the Russian edition.

I also wish to mention with gratitude Professor Lina Bernstein and Professor Andrew Kahn for their help in checking the English text.

Once again I thank all my friends and colleagues, both in Moscow and in the West, for their interest in my work and their help in finding materials.

I am also grateful to the Central State Archive for Literature and Art in Moscow, without which this book would be considerably the poorer: to the Deutscher Akademischer Austauschdienst; to The National Endowment for the Humanities; and to my colleagues and the administrators at Mount Holyoke and Amherst College, who encouraged me in my work on the book.

VIKTORIA SCHWEITZER
Amherst, March, 1992

CONTENTS

LIST OF ILLUSTRATIONS

Maria Aleksandrovna Tsvetaeva, the poet's mother, 1903
Ivan Vladimirovich Tsvetaev, the poet's father, 1890s
Susanna Davydovna (Tyo) and Aleksandr Danilovich Meyn

In the courtyard of the house on Tryokhprudny. Seated: Valeria, Marina, Maria Aleksandrovna with Asya. Standing: an unknown woman, Nadya Ilovayskaya, Ivan Vladimirovich Tsvetaev and Andrey Tsvetaev
Asya and Marina Tsvetaeva with Aleksandra Ivanovna Dobrokhotova, Nervi, 1903

The Tsvetaev family at their dacha in Tarusa

Asya and Marina Tsvetaeva with Vladislav Aleksandrovich Kobylyansky (Tiger), Nervi, 1903
Asya and Marina Tsvetaeva, 1905

Elena Ottobaldovna Voloshina (Pra), Koktebel
Maksimilian Aleksandrovich Voloshin, Koktebel
At the Voloshins' house in Koktebel, 1911. Sergey standing on the left, beside the wheel; Marina Tsvetaeva is sitting on the left; Max Voloshin is standing on the right

Sergey Efron and Marina Tsvetaeva, Autumn 1911
Anastasia Tsvetaeva, Sergey Efron and Marina Tsvetaeva in the drawing room of the house in Tryokhprudny, Moscow, Autumn 1911

Portrait of Marina Tsvetaeva by Magda Nakhman, 1913
In the Moscow flat of the poet Adelaida Gertsyk, 1915. In the foreground, seated: Adelaida Gertsyk with her son Nikita; to the right, beside the stove: E. K. Gertsyk; in the doorway: Marina Tsvetaeva; behind her: the philosopher, N. A. Berdyaev

Sofia Parnok, early 1900s
Osip Mandelstam, 1914
The autographs of Osip Mandelstam and Marina Tsvetaeva on a page from the album of the poet Malvina Maryanova, 1919–20

PUBLISHER'S NOTE

The publication of this occasionally abridged English edition of Viktoria Schweitzer's *Byt i bytie Mariny Tsvetaevoy* represents a truly collaborative effort: H. T. Willetts translated the prose for chapters 1–4 until ill health prevented him from continuing; Robert Chandler translated the prose for chapters 5–6 and the notes; Peter Norman translated all the poetry; and Dr Angela Livingstone, Professor in the Department of Literature, University of Essex, edited the translated and abridged text, also the biographical notes, and provided the footnotes and the bibliography.

In quoted material, omissions by the translators are shown in square brackets; omissions or additions made by the author are shown in round brackets and omissions of a line or one or more stanzas of poetry quoted in the text are shown thus: (. . .)

NOTE ON TRANSLITERATION

Russian names and other words have been transliterated according to System I as defined by J. T. Shaw in *The Transliteration of Modern Russian for English-Language Publications*, Madison and London, 1967.

Both e and з are rendered as "e" in English, but ё as "yo" or "o"; и is rendered as "i", both й and ы as "y" and both ый and ий as "y"; ия becomes "ia", ье– "ie".

Both ь and ъ are omitted (there is one exception, on p.248, in our following of this rule).

x is rendered as "kh".

Our one consistent variation on the system is that we have transliterated кс as "ks", rather than as "x". An exception is the short form of the name Maksimilian, which we give as Max. A few other names already familiar in a certain English spelling are given in that spelling; these include: Lydia (Chukovskaya), Mandelstam, Meyerhold, *Potemkin*.

Note to English-readers:

a) the letter e can represent either of two sounds: "e" (as in "egg") and "Ye" (as in "yes"), so that, for example, Elabuga, Elena and Elizaveta are pronounced with an initial sound of "ye", while Efron and Ellis have an initial sound of "e".

b) "Ya", "Yu" and "Ts" sometimes appear as initials – this is because each represents a single letter of the Russian alphabet.

EDITOR'S NOTE

The title of the original Russian edition of this book, *Byt i bytie Mariny Tsvetaevoy*, is, as the following attempt suggests, virtually untranslatable: "The Living and Being of Marina Tsvetaeva"? "Marina Tsvetaeva: Her Everyday Existence and Her Higher – or Inner – Being"? "Day-to-Day Detail and the Experience of the Real"? No English version can imitate the alliterative brevity of these two words, any more than it can reflect their range of connotation without becoming florid. They have therefore been abandoned as title or subtitle – with regret, since the distinction they point to was of the utmost importance to Tsvetaeva: Viktoria Schweitzer discusses it on p. 157.

ANGELA LIVINGSTONE
University of Essex, March 1992

God placed me all alone
Amid the wide world.
– You're no woman, but a bird.
Therefore: fly and sing:

MARINA TSVETAEVA

The spiritual disposition of a poet inclines to catastrophe.

OSIP MANDELSTAM

JOURNEY TO ELABUGA

Instead of a Preface

For years I had wanted to go to Elabuga, the town in which Tsvetaeva had spent her last days, to look at the town itself, the cemetery in which she is buried, and perhaps see people who knew her there. In the autumn of 1966, twenty-five years after her tragic end, my desire to go became overpowering, and I decided to retrace her steps: from Moscow to Elabuga by water, along the Volga, by way of Kostroma, Gorky and Kazan, and then along the Kama, by way of Chistopol.

I imagined that by following her route I could at least catch a glimpse of the river scenery as she saw it, and try to divine her thoughts and feelings. My hopes were disappointed. Not because everything had changed so much in a quarter of a century – even the river itself, with the disappearance of many ancient villages and the appearance of man-made seas, had changed. And not, I feel sure, because the jostling crowds on the quayside were no longer united by a common disaster – the war. But simply because it was impossible for me, on a comfortable river steamer, with a home and family and friends to return to, to put myself in the place of a homeless and lonely woman with a tragic life behind her and a hopeless future before her. All I could share with her was the water lapping against the ship's sides, the wooded river banks, and the frequently glimpsed churches, most of them derelict, many dilapidated, but all beautiful seen in the distance. What were Tsvetaeva's thoughts and hopes and memories as she gazed at the wake of the steamer, or the pinewoods, villages and churches along the banks? We passed through the mouth of the Oka near Gorky. Did she remember her childhood on the Oka, the hills and fields of Tarusa which she had loved? Or was she thinking only of the impossibility of finding any way of earning her keep in Elabuga, of the need to struggle on, if only for her son's sake, of the horrors of war? I do not know, but I felt sad and cold in my cosy cabin whenever I tried to imagine it.

When you approach Elabuga from the direction of Kazan, as Tsvetaeva did, the first thing you see is the sheer cliff looming over the quayside, which nestles precariously at its foot. The cliff is crowned by a white tower – a

I

remnant of the ancient Bolgar fortress known as Chortovo-Gorodishche [Devil's Town]. Some two or three kilometres from the quayside, you can see the town in silhouette – two-storey stone-built merchants' houses (Elabuga used to trade in cereals) on a hill overlooking the river and the water-meadows, beyond them rows of single-storey houses and cottages, and overlooking all of this three huge stone churches and a fire observation-tower. Also beautiful. When you drive into the town over the high embankment (tarmacked now, cobbled until a few years ago), built at the beginning of the century, and lined on both sides with luxuriant trees, the sun shining and the wind in your face, a feeling of happiness and peace steals over you. Tsvetaeva must have felt differently. Can she have had eyes for the beauty of the place?

I knew the address and quickly found the little three-windowed house on a quiet street not far from the centre, but I was not at all sure what sort of welcome an uninvited guest could expect, and hesitated to seek admission. I was, however, not the first to come in search of information about Tsvetaeva, and the occupants of the house took my arrival calmly, showing neither surprise nor enthusiasm. They were husband and wife, elderly pensioners, Anastasia Ivanovna and Mikhail Ivanovich Brodelshchikov.* Their children and grandchildren had left the district, or had houses of their own, and they lived alone. (This was in 1966.) But at the beginning of the war their six-year-old grandson Pavlik had been living with them. They proved to be likeable people, with an innate aversion to prying and to malicious gossip. All that I succeeded in learning from them they told me almost reluctantly, with no wish to censure or condemn. Anastasia Ivanovna did most of the talking, with Mikhail Ivanovich putting in a word or two from time to time.

They remembered Tsvetaeva, and the other evacuees who had lived with them after her, very well. Any new arrival in a quiet and uneventful provincial town is, of course, long remembered. And Tsvetaeva gave them something to remember . . . But the couple had had no idea that Tsvetaeva was a famous poet: she had registered as "writer and translator". For such a small town, Elabuga had rather a lot of evacuees – about a thousand grown-ups and roughly the same number of children. They were met by representatives of the local authority who took them around and installed them in their temporary homes. A group of fifteen were taken to the home of the Brodelshchikovs. As you enter their little house the kitchen is to the left

* A Russian's middle name is a patronymic, i.e. father's first name plus *-ovich* or *-evich*, *-ovna* or *-evna*. (The Brodelshchikovs happen to have had fathers of the same name.) People are usually called by their first name and patronymic.

of the hallway and the two best rooms to the right. As usual in country places, the rooms are separated by partitions which do not quite reach the ceiling, and there are curtains instead of doors, but still there is some privacy. Each room has three small windows. Tsvetaeva went in first and when she got to the second room said: "I'm staying here. I'm not going anywhere else." She and her son fetched their belongings and settled in. "I was quite upset," said Anastasia Ivanovna. "I didn't like the look of her at first: she was tall, round-shouldered, skinny, grey-haired, like a witch of some sort. Not at all attractive . . . But after a while it was all right, I got used to my lodger, and in fact we became quite friendly. We used to sit and smoke together. What was there to smoke in those days? Home-grown stuff. Rolled in newspaper if you could get it. I rolled cigarettes for her — Marina Ivanovna [Tsvetaeva] couldn't manage it herself — and we sat puffing away together."

From what Tsvetaeva's son says they arrived in Elabuga on 17 August. I do not know where they spent the first four days. They probably spent the nights in a school, as evacuees often did at that time, and Tsvetaeva went looking for somewhere to live in the daytime. She lived with the Brodelshchikovs for only ten days: they moved in on 21 August and on 31 August she was dead. And she was away from the house for some days in the meantime. "Perhaps," Anastasia Ivanovna said repeatedly, "if she'd lived a bit longer . . ." Perhaps they would have started talking to each other more freely, perhaps they would have become friends, perhaps . . . if she had lived . . .

Tsvetaeva must have liked the Brodelshchikov house. It was clean and quiet. She and her son had a room to themselves (even if it was only eight square metres), with a marvellous view from the windows: water-meadows down to the Kama, and woods and fields disappearing into the distance beyond it . . . "My sister's name and patronymic are the same as yours, Anastasia Ivanovna," Tsvetaeva told her landlady. "There was only one thing Marina Ivanovna didn't like," Mrs Brodelshchikov told me. "There was a distillery across the road and when it discharged the waste there was a very bad smell." To the Brodelshchikovs their lodger seemed old and unprepossessing, with her tired and worried look and her short hair combed back from her face. She was in fact not quite forty-nine. I showed them the photographs in Tsvetaeva's *Selected Works*, and not one of them seemed to them anything like the Tsvetaeva with whom they had lived at such close quarters. Not even the last one, copied from her Soviet passport, issued two years before she went to Elabuga. Much later, looking at the original of which this photograph was a retouched copy, I could see why. The photograph had been greatly "improved" for inclusion in the book: the hair had been slicked down, the eyebrows made more prominent, and, most striking change of all, the tragic lines at the corners of her mouth had been taken out, and a smile sketched in. She was shabbily dressed in a long dark frock, an old autumn coat, probably brown, and a knitted beret, pea-green in colour. "It always made me laugh," said Anastasia Ivanovna. "It was like a pea-flour pancake. In the house she always wore a big apron with a pocket. She had it on when she died."

She was very depressed. Most of the time she said nothing. Just smoked in silence. A Red Army regiment was stationed in Elabuga for training. Now and then soldiers marched through the streets singing. "They sing these victory songs," Tsvetaeva burst out, "yet the enemy's constantly advancing . . ." She left the house frequently looking for work, or for someone to buy what little was left of her silver cutlery. "Who could she sell it to?" said Anastasia Ivanovna. "Some people may have had money – the bourgeois, – but how could you know who?" There was no work to be had, and there were no buyers to be found. Tsvetaeva had brought some provisions with her – some meal and some sugar. But she evidently had neither the strength nor the heart to do any cooking.

"She didn't know how to do anything," Anastasia Ivanovna told me.

"How can you say that?" I said, almost annoyed. "She had had to do everything for herself, all her life."

"She couldn't do anything. I saw her, remember, we lived together. If I heated the water for her she would wash her hair. If she asked me to mop up for her I would. She'd say 'please mop the floor, Anastasia Ivanovna,' and I would. All she'd do herself was swish a floorcloth around and leave it at that. She never cooked a thing. She had food, but she wouldn't cook. I didn't have any kerosene, but there was a stove and firewood and frying pans and crocks – everything. She could have cooked . . ."

"What did they eat, then?"

"They went to the canteen. All you could get there at the time was some foul soup . . . Or else she'd ask me to sell her some fish. Mikhail Ivanovich is a keen fisherman and we always had fish. She'd buy some and say: 'I wish you'd clean it for me'. So I'd clean it, and then she'd say 'I wish you'd fry it for me'. So I'd fry it, it wasn't much trouble. When she died there was a whole big pan full of fried fish left over in the hallway."

In all that this simple woman told me about Tsvetaeva there was nothing to suggest that she condemned her for committing suicide. She only thought that Tsvetaeva had done so too soon, before she was really driven to it.

"They had a lot of stuff with them. A whole big sackful of food, for one thing – rice and pearl barley and different kinds of meal, all in little bags. About a stone and a half of sugar. She could have kept going longer . . . Something came over her, obviously . . . Still, she could have kept going longer . . . It would have been time enough when they'd eaten it all . . ."

Even before arriving in Elabuga Tsvetaeva had written to Kazan, to the Union of Writers of the Tatar Autonomous Republic as follows:

Dear Comrade Imamutdinov,

   This letter is written by Marina Tsvetaeva, writer and translator. I am one of the Litfond* group of evacuees to Elabuga on the Kama. I have a letter for you from Chagin, the acting director of the State Literary Publishing House, who requests your active assistance in helping me to establish myself here, and asks you to make use of me as a translator. I have no hope of establishing myself in Elabuga because I have no qualifications except as a writer. I also have a letter with the same signature to the Tatar Publishing House, with the same request. I shall shortly come to Kazan and present the above-mentioned letter to you.

   I earnestly beg you, and through you the Union of Writers, to do everything possible to help me establish myself and find work in Kazan. I am accompanied by my sixteen-year old son. I hope that I shall succeed in making myself useful as a translator of poetry.

Marina Tsvetaeva

She had not yet realized that going to Kazan was a practical impossibility. Wartime regulations strictly limited the movements of civilians. There was no reply to her letter. It is preserved in the archives of the Writers' Union of the Tatar Republic, with the words "action required" written across it. What action, we may wonder.

As soon as she had registered in Elabuga (without a permit you could neither settle nor move around) she travelled to nearby Chistopol, where there was a large colony of evacuated writers, in search of sympathy and help. She needed regular accommodation, work of some sort, and also – of great importance to her – someone to read poetry with. Once again she was unsuccessful. The literary authorities refused to support her application for a permit to reside in Chistopol, and seemed surprised that she wanted to move there. She was regarded with suspicion: it was only two years since she had returned from emigration, and her husband and daughter were both imprisoned. After much trouble and anxiety she was promised the necessary

* Literary Fund: an organization set up in 1859 in St Petersburg in order to help writers and their families who were in need. It closed down during the Civil War, but was revived in 1927.

document, but there was no hope of work in Chistopol either. She went back to Elabuga.

I myself stopped at Chistopol on my return journey. Although it is considerably bigger than Elabuga it had a depressing effect on me. A dusty, uncomfortable, unfriendly, God-forsaken town. She must have clutched at it as a drowning man clutches at a straw.

31 August 1941 was a Sunday. It so happened that Tsvetaeva was left alone in the house for the whole day. "If we hadn't gone out that day," Anastasia Ivanovna told me, "everything might have been all right. But we were ordered out to do some community service that day – cleaning up the airfield. Marina Ivanovna's son went instead of her. It would have been better if she'd gone herself. Nothing would have happened. At least she'd have been with other people."

Everybody who turned up for work that day was given a loaf of bread – that was something to remember it by. Mikhail Ivanovich didn't join in. He went off fishing with his grandson. "It was a lovely day. Pavlik and I decided to go fishing. 'We're off to do a bit of fishing, Marina Ivanovna,' I said to her. 'Will you be all right here by yourself?' 'Of course,' she said, 'of course I shall, off you go . . .' Almost as if she was glad we were going. If I'd had any idea what was going to happen we wouldn't have gone anywhere."

Anastasia Ivanovna got home first. As she went in she bumped into a chair and wondered what it was doing in the hallway. Then she looked up and saw her lodger hanging there. She ran out and called the woman next door, who rang for the police and the ambulance. They didn't dare cut her down. It took the doctor and the police two hours to get there.

"Why didn't you try to find out whether she was still alive as soon as you got back?" I asked. "Maybe there was still a chance of saving her?" "We should have looked," Anastasia Ivanovna answered. Mr Brodelshchikov was surprised by my question. "How could we cut her down?" he said. "When the police came they'd have wanted to know why we'd done it ourselves . . . It's lucky she left notes, or they might have thought we'd murdered her."

Tsvetaeva's body was taken to the hospital, and her room searched to make sure that nothing was missing. "They turned everything upside down," Anastasia Ivanovna said. Her son was there while they did it. It turned out that they only had four hundred roubles. Two letters were found as well. I don't know where they were lying, we didn't see them. One was to the writer Aseev, I think, asking him to look after her son, the other was just to say why she'd done it. The police and her son read them, we didn't."

I walked round Elabuga. A very clean, very green little town, comfortable enough in its provincial way, and somehow homely. But for some reason I was haunted by some lines addressed to Tsvetaeva by Osip Mandelstam half a century earlier.

> But in this wooden and dark
> Place, fit for fools in Christ,
> To stay with such a misty
> Nun portends disaster.

Portends disaster . . . Was that why Tsvetaeva was so desperately anxious to get out of Elabuga?

She was buried from the hospital. Nobody went to the funeral, her landlord and landlady told me. A homeless person stranded in Elabuga without friends or family, she was of no interest to anybody. Cemetery records were not kept in those days, so no one knows which is Tsvetaeva's grave.

I went uphill to a cemetery looking down on the town and far out over the Kama . . . The road had probably not changed in the past quarter of a century. It was deserted, and I seemed to see her borne along it on her last journey – a lonely human being, worn down by life, who was also one of Russia's finest poets. There were electric cables overhead, humming in the keen autumn wind. This noise accompanied me to the cemetery, as perhaps it had accompanied Tsvetaeva's body, instead of the tolling of a bell. It set some lines of hers buzzing in my head – an image of her whole life and work.

> The lyrical wires of my high tension
> Are humming . . .

These lines stayed with me all the way to the cemetery, and long afterwards.

The cemetery was surrounded by an old stone wall, and the heavy gate was fastened by a rusty bolt. A little chapel, no longer open, stood by the gate. The cemetery was carefully tended, green and neat. In its right-hand corner, at its highest point, between straight-stemmed, proud and solemn pines there were many unnamed graves: little mounds, some of them barely distinguishable, overgrown with withered grass and wormwood, and sprinkled with pine needles. I plucked some fronds of wormwood as a souvenir. It was 31 August. This was where evacuees were buried in 1941. Tsvetaeva's grave was said to be somewhere there. There was a view of the town, and beyond it of water-meadows, forests, the Kama. The deep silence was only occasionally broken by the noise of a motor vehicle or a tractor, muffled by the distance. Some years earlier Tsvetaeva's sister, Anastasia Ivanovna, had set up a small cross under one of the pine-trees, with a simple inscription:

On this side of the cemetery lies buried

MARINA IVANOVNA
TSVETAEVA

Born 26 September, Old Style,* 1892
in Moscow
✝ 31 August, New Style, 1941
in Elabuga

Tarusa, winter 1966–67

* The Julian calendar, which was twelve days behind the Gregorian calendar in the nineteenth century and thirteen days behind in the twentieth, was used in Russia until 14 February 1918, when the Gregorian calendar – used in Western Europe – was adopted. (Tsvetaeva disliked the "New Style" calendar. See p. 210 below.)

CHAPTER 1

PREHISTORY

Thus one begins to live by poetry.

BORIS PASTERNAK

HOW MUCH DO WE KNOW about our parents? Little or nothing. From their gestures, their looks, their actions, from words which it does not always understand, the child creates an image of its mother and father, seeks to understand them, to penetrate the secrets of their adult lives and their relationships.

> Thus one begins to understand.
> And in the noise of a spinning turbine
> It seems your mother is not your mother,
> You are not you, home is an alien land . . .*

In "The Egyptian Stamp"† Mandelstam echoes these lines of Pasternak: "Someone had attached me to a family of strangers . . ." Sometimes the feeling of "strangeness" remains forever, as it did with Pushkin.

Most women speak of their mothers as beautiful. But not Tsvetaeva. Nowhere does she describe her mother's appearance. What did appearance matter, when she knew that her mother was an extraordinary being, unlike anyone else? Tsvetaeva sees her mother as a romantic heroine. It was she who created the highly-charged atmosphere in the family. In her infatuation with music, literature, painting and later on medicine could be sensed a deep discontent. With what? Her children could not understand it, and most probably gave little thought to it, but in the "outpourings" of their mother's piano, which lulled them to sleep every night, could be heard a longing for some other life, a life denied to her. She tried to bequeath her

---

* From Pasternak's 1919 poem "Thus one begins . . .", about the development of a child who will be a poet; it ends with the line quoted as an epigraph to this chapter.
† Mandelstam's only piece of fictional writing, a modernist story set in St Petersburg, published in 1928.

unrealized dreams to her children. She was sure that the time would come when her children would understand. She was not mistaken. It was no simple matter. Things did not go easily and smoothly. But if their mother was strict and demanding this was just as it should be. Tsvetaeva could not imagine having any other mother. Would anyone else have read so many marvellous books with them, told them so many extraordinary stories, made them a gift of such beautiful music? Marina sensed that her mother had a secret. At twenty-one she told the philosopher Vasily Rozanov in a letter: "her tormented soul lives on in us, only what she concealed we reveal. Her rebellion, her madness, her longings we shout aloud."

Her father was a less vivid figure, who seemed to take little part in family life. He was associated with a word which the children did not quite understand and which they occasionally took to be somebody's name or title: the word "museum". In the spring of 1898, when visitors on business connected with the museum were particularly numerous, Ivan Tsvetaev made this entry in his diary: "The children heard the bell and the house echoed with shouts of 'Papa, Mama, Nanna, Museum's here again'." He was completely absorbed in his work of establishing Russia's first museum of classical sculpture. His was a remote world, inaccessible to his children. In Tsvetaeva's early poem "Boring Games" "playing at papa" is described as follows:

> Without rising from my chair
> I looked long into the book . . .

Her father's good nature, equable temperament and gentleness offset her mother's passionate intolerance. With the years came recognition of the "quiet heroism" concealed beneath her father's aloof and placid exterior. But I am not sure that Tsvetaeva ever fully understood what a remarkable person her father was. Her mother undoubtedly overshadowed him. Her mother's pictures hung on the walls, her mother's music, her tempestuous character, her brilliance commanded her children's attention and fascinated them. What attraction could their father's quiet reserve hold for them? And of course their mother was closer to them, since their father's life was spent for the most part away from home, and they felt that the atmosphere in the house depended on her.

Somewhere in the background loomed a grandfather, or rather two grandfathers: their mother's "Papa", Aleksandr Danilovich Meyn, whose wife their mother for some reason called "Aunty", and "Grandpa Ilovaysky", who always came visiting alone, and for some reason was only the grandfather of the older children, Marina's sister Valeria and her brother Andrey. Her "own" grandfather was kind, he brought presents for all the children, and sometimes took them for rides in his own carriage. Grandpa Ilovaysky did not bring presents, and seemed to notice little of what went on around him: at any rate, he could never distinguish Marina from her sister Asya (Anastasia), although they were quite unlike each other. Why were there two grandfathers and why were they so different? Why did their mother have in her room a picture of her own mother, quite young, and not of Aunty, while in the best drawing-room there was a picture of Valeria's and Andrey's mother? At a still greater remove there was someone known by the strange word "Mamaka" – someone's great grandmother, a Romanian, who had died in Marina's room. It was from her that Valeria had inherited some white silk lace, and learnt to dance the "barynya". Who were all these people? What was the connection between them?

Gradually, from chance remarks and vague hints, from the division of things into "ours" and "Valeria's" or "the Ilovayskys'", Marina began to get a picture of the history of her home and family.

Long ago her father had had another wife, the mother of Valeria and Andrey, young, beautiful and an excellent singer – she may have performed in public. She had died quite young, like Marina's own grandmother, whose portrait hung in the dining room. (That explained Aunty.) Valeria was only eight at the time, and Andrey a new-born baby. Then Marina's mother – a young and remarkable woman – had married her father, a far-from-young and quite unremarkable professor. Her mother had longed to perform heroic deeds, and gratified her longing by sacrificing herself for the sake of another woman's children. Then Marina and Asya were born.

Was it really like that? The surprising thing is that Marina understood the high moral tone of her family home and the nature of the relationships within it so early and so accurately. In her "Reply to a Questionnaire" (1926) she writes:

> the dominant influence was that of my mother (music, nature, poetry, Germany). The passion for heroic action. One against all. Heroica. My father's influence was less obvious but no less powerful. (His passion for work, the absence of careerism, his simplicity, his singlemindedness.) Father's and mother's influence fused in a Spartan attitude to life. Two leitmotifs in one house – music and the museum. The atmosphere of the house was neither bourgeois nor intellectual – it was "chevaleresque".

It would be difficult to imagine two people less alike in temperament and aspirations, in origin and upbringing, than Marina's parents. Ivan

Vladimirovich Tsvetaev* had made his way in the world entirely by his own efforts. He was born on 4 May 1847 in the Vladimir province in the family of a village priest, and he never forgot his origin and the poverty of his family. When at the end of his days he was given the title of Honorary Trustee, and was forced to have an expensive uniform made, he confessed in a private letter that "there is something almost outrageous in this expense for the son of a priest who earned a hundred and twenty roubles a year to begin with, then three hundred, then after forty years service five hundred, collecting them moreover a kopek or two at a time." According to family tradition Ivan Tsvetaev and his three brothers were all educated in a church school. He then went to the Vladimir seminary, but at nineteen abruptly changed his plans, and left for St Petersburg† to study at the Academy of Medicine and Surgery. That same autumn however saw him enrolled in the Faculty of History and Philology at the University of St Petersburg. There he found his vocation. The diploma which he obtained four years later gave him "all the rights and privileges bound up with the degree of Candidate in accordance with the laws of the Russian Empire". This meant, amongst other things, that Ivan Tsvetaev had transferred from the priestly to the gentry estate, had become a "gentleman of the bell tower", as he once rather ironically put it. More important, he was awarded a gold medal for his dissertation, "A Critical Examination of the text of Tacitus's *Germania*", and kept on by the university to train for a teaching post. While doing so he taught Greek for a year in the Third St Petersburg Girls' High School. His official curriculum vitae, compiled seven years after he left university, shows that he had wasted no time. Remembering what was said above about his father's earnings, we see that Ivan Tsvetaev had shot ahead. His income was by then made up of

Salary	900 roubles
Board	150 roubles
Rent allowance	150 roubles
Total	1200 roubles

There follows in chronological order a list of Tsvetaev's achievements over the preceding years. He had successfully presented his master's thesis on the *Germania* of Cornelius Tacitus at St Petersburg, taught Latin Literature at

---

* Occasionally referred to, in this translation, by his first name and patronymic (Ivan Vladimirovich); his wife will be regularly referred to in this way (Maria Aleksandrovna).
† Then (and until 1918) Russia's capital. Named "Petrograd" from 1914 to 1924 and "Leningrad" from 1924 to 1991. Now, again called St Petersburg.

the Universities of Warsaw and Kiev, and most important of all, spent more than two years abroad, collecting material for his doctoral thesis. He was interested in the ancient Italic languages – he was one of the pioneers in this field. The excavations at Pompeii, which brought to light inscriptions in an unknown language, had begun in earnest only fifteen years earlier. It proved to be the language of the ancient Samnites, who lived in the second millennium BC, and had subsequently merged with their Roman conquerors. Tsvetaev collected and studied the surviving inscriptions in the language of the Samnites (Oscan). In Italy he came under the spell of ancient art and architecture.

By 1877, when he was elected to a lectureship in Latin Literature at Moscow University, his interests went far beyond language and literature, and when a few years later he was invited to take charge of the Engravings Room, and then to become Curator of the Department of Fine Arts and Classical Antiquities in the Public and Rumyantsev Museums in Moscow, he readily accepted. After his appointment to the chair of the Theory and History of Art in 1889 his dream was to establish a museum of ancient art within the university, and he began busily supplementing the collections in his care. His plans gradually became more ambitious, and this work absorbed almost a quarter of a century of selfless and loving labour.

For ten years Ivan Vladimirovich Tsvetaev was married to Varvara Dimitrievna Ilovayskaya, daughter of his friend, the well-known historian. Her grandmother was the "Mamaka" who outlived her to spend her last days in what was by then the home of Ivan Vladimirovich's second wife. Had his first marriage been a happy one? It appeared that it had, although family tradition maintained that Varvara Dimitrievna had loved another and married Ivan Vladimirovich only in obedience to her father. However that may have been, she brought warmth and gaiety into Tsvetaev's home, he loved her all his life and it was many years before he recovered after her sudden death. The wound in his heart had still not healed when he married for the second time in spring 1891.

Maria Aleksandrovna Meyn, born in 1868, was twenty-one years younger than her husband. Her father was rich and well-known in Moscow, and although she was no beauty she could certainly have made a more brilliant match. Her romanticism must have been the explanation for her marriage to a widower twice her age with two children of his own.

She herself had lost her mother when she was nineteen days old. Was that perhaps the reason why she took on the role of mother to little Andrey Tsvetaev, orphaned in early infancy? Her own mother, Maria Lukinichna Bernatskaya, who had died at twenty-seven, came from a very old but impoverished Polish family. This was excuse enough for Marina to identify herself with Marina Mniszek (the Polish wife of the Pretender Dimitry*). Maria Aleksandrovna's father, Aleksandr Danilovich Meyn, was of Baltic German descent, with a dash of Serbian blood. He had begun his career as a teacher of general history, had served, according to Valeria Tsvetaeva's memoirs, as head of Chancery to the Governor-General of Moscow, edited the *Moscow Provincial News*, and by the time of his daughter's marriage had risen to be director of the Land Bank. He was not without artistic interest. He collected books and antique casts – all of which he subsequently presented to the city of Moscow. His house was luxuriously furnished, and Maria Aleksandrovna had a very good piano. She had grown up under the tutelage of a Swiss governess, Susanna Davydovna, whom she called "tyotya" ("aunt"), and her children Tyo†. Apparently Susanna Davydovna never learnt to speak Russian correctly and referred to herself in the third person as "la tante", or "tyo". Tyo was extremely kind, sensitive, a little eccentric, and utterly devoted to the Meyns, father and daughter. In his old age Aleksandr Danilovich Meyn married Susanna Davydovna, and she became "Madame General Meyn", the name by which some old people in Tarusa still remember her. This "family international" may help to explain Tsvetaeva's unqualified contempt for all forms of nationalism and chauvinism. The family was, however, Orthodox, and observant.

Maria Aleksandrovna Meyn had a lonely childhood. She was not sent to boarding school or even to a local high school. Her paternal home was austere and unsociable. She had no young friends or companions. Her father took in a little girl called Tonya, but it was perhaps too late – the girls were eight years old, and Maria Aleksandrovna already had very definite interests of her own. They grew up and were educated together, their clothes and hairstyles were identical, but there seems to have been no real intimacy between them.

Maria was a very unusual person, clever and with great artistic talents. Lonely and motherless, she took refuge in books: they were her friends, mentors and comforters. Books and music became her whole life, a substitute for reality. She was given an excellent education at home, became fluent in four European languages, had an excellent knowledge of history and literature, wrote verse in Russian and German, and translated from and into the various languages she knew. She had great musical talent. Her piano teacher was one of Nikolay Rubinstein's best pupils. She also had artistic ability and had lessons from the well-known genre painter Mikhail Klodt.

* See note to p. 114.
† Pronounced like the second, third and fourth letters in "at York", softening the "t".

She was a passionate nature-lover. In her childhood and adolescence she seemed to have all that her heart could desire, but something very important was missing: the ease, affection and understanding which are so essential to a developing personality. Her father worshipped her, but was demanding and tyrannical. The kindly but limited Susanna Davydovna could not share the young girl's intellectual and artistic interests, nor could she shield her from her father's heavy-handedness. "My mother," wrote Marina Tsvetaeva, "lived a shut-in, unhealthy, bookish life, no life for a child. At seven she knew a great deal about world history and mythology, she was an obsessive hero-worshipper, she was a magnificent pianist . . ." She had a yearning for unusual emotions and experiences, but tradition decreed that her life must roll along a comfortable groove, conform to a pattern which was perhaps admirable but which was not of her choosing. Maria Aleksandrovna found an outlet for her turbulent emotions and her dreams in music and in her diary – her only friends. Her character gradually became reserved and aloof.

Her father played a fatal role in her life. "Grandpa Meyn", remembered with affection by both his grand-daughters, twice disrupted his daughter's life. At sixteen or seventeen Maria Aleksandrovna fell in love as only a romantic dreamer can. There were assignations, there were horseback rides by moonlight. But the man she loved was married. Her father was outraged and demanded that their meetings should cease. Divorce in his eyes was a sin and he would not hear of it. His daughter complied, but it was years before she stopped remembering and loving the hero of her girlish romance. An entry in her diary says that "I shall never again love as I loved him, and I owe it to him that I have anything to remember my youth by: though I paid for my love in suffering I have loved in a way that I would never have believed possible! . . . Papa and Aunty, Papa especially, do not understand me. They still imagine that I am a child . . . Papa, for instance, is sure that my love was only the first flaring of passion in an inexperienced heart, and that I have long ago forgotten all about it . . . If only he knew that my feelings have lived on for more than two years, deep hidden, but still alive . . ."

Maria Aleksandrovna was a remarkable pianist ("an enormous talent", wrote Marina). She felt that music was her vocation, and found in it an outlet for the sorrow and the turbulence in her soul. She might have become a concert pianist, but once again she had chosen a path which her father could not approve. In his circle there was something almost indecent in the idea of an emancipated woman-artist. Maria Aleksandrovna submitted. Was this a manifestation of daughterly love or of a meekness inculcated by her upbringing? Probably both. Marina is probably right when she speaks of "my grandfather, who ruined my mother's life and whom she adored to his and her last breath".

The roots of Maria Aleksandrovna's character are perhaps to be found in her twice-shattered dreams. A difficult, imperious, impatient character. A hint of hysteria under her superficial reserve can perhaps be traced to the need to conceal her exalted passions.

Her only escape was marriage. But it was not a prospect which held any hope of happiness for her. She thought of her inevitable marriage almost with revulsion. Her diary has preserved her bitter thoughts: "The time will come when I shall, whether I like it or not, have to abandon my ideals and put my hand to the broom . . . Once the petty cares of workaday life begin, and I find myself stuck in the mud, I shall no longer have time for reading. I shall have to live on the stock which I am now laying in. I must just take good care that there is enough to spare for the rest of my life. I shall go on living for my ideals as long as I can." This goes a long way towards explaining Maria Aleksandrovna's "strange" marriage and her subsequent behaviour as wife and mother. It is conceivable that she chose the middle-aged and unattractive Professor Tsvetaev not only "with the express purpose of providing his orphaned children with a mother", as his oldest daughter thought, but because she knew that he too "lived for his ideals". Perhaps the young girl expected to become his helpmeet in his life's work: she undoubtedly felt herself capable of much more than merely "putting her hand to the broom".

One thing is clear: Tsvetaeva's mother hoped to get over her emotional drama by marrying. Did she succeed? The situation in which she found herself was an unfavourable one. Young and inexperienced as she was Maria Aleksandrovna could not know this before her marriage. She could not know that her husband still grieved for his dead wife and was not even able to conceal his grief. She was jealous of her predecessor, and struggled unsuccessfully to overcome this feeling. "We were married over her coffin," she wrote in her diary.

Many years later Marina painstakingly analysed a similar situation in "The House at Old Pimen" – the marriage of "Grandpa Ilovaysky" and *his* second wife, Aleksandra Aleksandrovna Ilovayskaya, who was twenty years his junior. She had married a widower with children, under parental pressure, or for his money, or perhaps because she was attracted by the idea of becoming the mistress of a famous man's house. Perhaps – who knows? – there was an unhappy love affair, like that of Tsvetaeva's mother, in the background of this marriage too. But that is the one possibility which Tsvetaeva does not mention . . . She describes this marriage between an old

man and a young beauty as "the cohabitation of jailor and prisoner . . . Little
by little life pinned the beautiful creature down. When you know that
never, never will you escape you make the best of life where you are. You get
used to your cell. What seemed to you an offence against reason and law
when you first entered becomes the norm. The jailor, seeing your docility,
relaxes, gives way a little, and an unnatural, but genuine alliance is
concluded between jailor and prisoner, the unloved and the unloving." Did
it ever cross Tsvetaeva's mind that her parents' marriage also began as an
unnatural union of two broken and grieving hearts? Had she any idea of the
drama enacted in her own family? I think that with the heightened
sensitivity of the poet she could not have failed to feel it. She read her
mother's diaries in her youth – so she knew. But prying into your parents'
secrets is frightening. You cannot sit in judgement over them. Tsvetaeva
observes a respectful daughterly silence about this side of her parents' lives.
She did, just once, after her father's death reveal a family secret to Vasily
Rozanov. "Mama and Papa were completely unlike each other. She and he
had both been badly hurt. Mama had her music, her poetry and her
longings, Papa had his scholarly work. Their lives were lived side by side,
without even merging. But they loved each other very much . . ." That was
written in 1914, to a man she had never seen. It was like someone confiding
his most intimate secret to a stranger met by chance on a train. She had been
shaken by the uninhibited candour of Rozanov's "The Solitary" and her
first insight into her mother's inner self. Rozanov seemed to her a person
more capable than anyone of understanding her mother's story. This is the
one and only occasion on which she speaks of "Mama" and "Papa" –
afterwards it was always "Mother" and "Father". When she tries to
recreate the world of her childhood in her later prose works Tsvetaeva
paints an almost idyllic picture of home life, although we know that Maria
Aleksandrovna fell in love with at least two other men in the course of her
marriage. Casual phrases such as "the beautiful Varvara Dimitrievna, my
father's first love, whom he went on loving and mourning eternally", or
"the portrait of Andrey's mother, which played such a fateful role in *our*
mother's life" (the portrait, commissioned by Ivan Tsvetaev, went on
hanging in the drawing room after his second marriage) tell us that she knew
about the drama in the past lives of her parents, and passed no judgement on
them. Writing about her family and relations between its members, as
always in her prose writings, she tries to "elicit" what seems to her most
important – in this case what united her parents and held the family
together: this was their mutual respect. Ivan Vladimirovich Tsvetaev could
never have become, could never have wished to become, his young wife's

"jailor". Nor could Maria Aleksandrovna ever have allowed herself to become "a prisoner"; to submerge her individuality in another person's life. Their life together was built on a compromise: each showed tolerance and understanding of the other partner's inner life. It is to Maria Aleksandrovna's credit that she never turned into her husband's "housekeeper", never departed from the ideals of her youth, but continued to live for music, literature, and the beauties of nature, and brought up her daughters in the same way.

Ivan Tsvetaev was completely absorbed in his many duties: teaching and administration in the University, responsibility for the departments of Fine Arts and Antiquities both in the University and at the Rumyantsev Museum. At various times he combined all this with work at the Ethnographic Museum, and gave lectures in other learned institutions in Moscow as well as at the University. When he was appointed Professor of the Theory and History of Art Tsvetaev's burning ambition was to create a museum of ancient art at the University for the benefit of his students. As he became more and more at home in the world of ancient and medieval sculpture his original conception grew into a much more ambitious plan for a comprehensive museum, which would satisfy the most exacting requirements of contemporary scholarship. He spent some twenty-five years of his life working to make this dream a reality. Only his fanatical belief that what he was doing was right and necessary gave him the strength to move mountains and to complete his life's work: Tsvetaeva portrays her father as a hard and enthusiastic worker, a heroic scholar, but fails to see that he was also a poet: the museum was his poem. A poet, however, compelled to occupy himself with the most prosaic matters, money matters above all, since the University had practically no funds to purchase exhibits, let alone a building to house them. Money had to be obtained from voluntary donors, and the task of obtaining it called for enthusiasm, skill in dealing with people, and eloquence. To judge by results, Ivan Tsvetaev possessed all the necessary qualities. "I wandered round Moscow all by myself begging money for the museum", "I went hunting for donors", "I became adept at kissing ladies' hands in my quest for money for the Museum" . . . Such remarks occur from time to time in his letters. Money worries, which sometimes pushed his creative plans into the background, remained with Ivan Vladimirovich till the day the Museum* opened. After a committee to further the project had been set up, and the building plan approved, Ivan wrote to the architect, R. I. Kleyn, urging him to "make every pillar and

---

* Officially opened as the Alexander III Museum of Fine Arts in 1912, it is now known as the Pushkin Museum of Fine Arts.

every prominent detail sing a request for alms". In a will written when he was seriously ill he gives an itemized account of expenditure on the museum. It is evident from his letters that he used not only his own but "the children's money" (interest on the capital left to his older children by their mother) to cover current construction costs. There was no sacrifice which he would not have made for the museum. "Tasks of historical significance are not accomplished without self-denial, without the renunciation of mundane, routine interests and amenities . . ." No, Ivan Tsvetaev was not the unworldly and dispassionate academic his daughter thought she saw in him, it was just that his flame burnt within him, inconspicuously. Perhaps this was what Marina's mother had understood and admired in him before their marriage? She must have felt close to the purity and idealism of his ambitions.

Luckily for both of them Maria Aleksandrovna wholeheartedly accepted her husband's dream, was drawn into it, began studying art and museum lore to put herself on an equal footing. Soon after their marriage they began travelling abroad together, looking round museums and selecting exhibits. It was Maria Aleksandrovna who produced the preliminary plan on which the design for the present building of the Museum of Fine Art was based. She became Ivan's right hand, kept journals and notes on their visits to Western European museums, dealt with foreign correspondence, gave him useful advice. "There were probably very few women in our country as knowledgeable in the field of classical sculpture as she was," Tsvetaev wrote in his report on the creation of the museum. Their common interest cemented their family life. Marina Tsvetaeva was wrong when she wrote that "their lives ran side by side but never merged . . ." True, his wife's romanticism was foreign to Ivan Tsvetaev, but he did not fight against it. The music flooding the house did not disturb him, although he himself was unmusical. He trained himself not to hear it. "He was so good at not hearing it," Marina noted, "that he didn't even shut his study door." Maria Aleksandrovna's romanticism flourished unhindered, to flood down, in time, on the heads of her children.

Marina's mother and father were both fanatically devoted to their own worlds — she to the world of music, romance, poetry, he to that of his museum. This fanatical devotion to their ideals formed the basis of their morality.

Such was the family which saw the beginning of one of the Russian poets most fanatically devoted to poetry: Marina Tsvetaeva.

CHAPTER 2

THE HOUSE IN
THREE PONDS LANE

Lovely house, our wonderful house
In Tryokhprudny — now turned into poems!
MARINA TSVETAEVA

IN THE VERY CENTRE of Moscow you can still find Tryokhprudny
[Three Ponds] Lane — not even the name has changed! Walk from Pushkin
Square along Bolshaya Bronnaya Street in the direction of the Nikita Gate,
and the second turn to the right is Tryokhprudny Lane. It does not lead to a
main street, but loses itself in a network of other back lanes. But it is a
stone's throw from the Pushkin monument, the Tverskoy Boulevard, the
Nikita Gate and Patriarch's Ponds.

But it is no good looking for the old-fashioned, chocolate-coloured house
which once stood on the site of No. 8. It is more than sixty years since the
house in which Marina Tsvetaeva was born ceased to exist. We have a
description of it given by Marina's older sister Valeria.

The house has eleven rooms. Behind it there is a grassy yard with poplars,
an outbuilding with seven rooms, a coach house, two cellars, a shed with
stalls, a separate kitchen across the yard, and next to that a spacious room
that used to be called "the laundry". Between us and the house next door
there was a covered well with a wooden pump, surrounded by a solid
fence. Boardwalks ran across the yard from the gate to the house and the
kitchen. In summer the yard was overgrown with thick grass, and it was
sad to see it crushed by the wheels of the watercarrier's cart. Besides the
poplars and the acacias there was a white lilac tree by the outbuilding and a
snowball-tree by the back door.

In those days we had a yardman called Lukyan, a Ryazan peasant who
was homesick for his native village. He kept ducks in the yard — they
waddled about round the well, and he built little pigeon houses under the

20

roof of the shed. The pigeons were quite tame and would settle on his shoulders. The outbuilding was let at the time (1888) to a family with a shop on Tverskaya Street. They kept a cow, and a cowherd used to come blowing his horn every morning to drive it with the others out to Petrovsky Park. There was a hundred-year old silver poplar by the gate, its heavy branches hung out over the street.

The entrance to the house was from the yard. The front porch was enclosed, and painted in red and white stripes. Dark steps led up to a heavy door with a bronze bell-pull. The best rooms in the house were the spacious high-ceilinged white hall with five big windows, and the large drawing room, all dark red. Then came father's study, with a big, heavy desk, a big sofa, and book-lined walls. The other rooms were not so high, because there was a mezzanine above them, with four rooms looking out on the courtyard. Seen from the street the house appeared to have only one storey.

In this house Marina Tsvetaeva was born, and here she lived for nearly twenty years, until she got married. She "loved it and sang its praises" (her words). She had other "places of my own" (Tarusa and Koktebel), but Tryokhprudny Lane was dearest of all to her.

It is difficult to picture such a house in the centre of a big capital city less than a century ago. It was more like a country gentleman's estate. Valeria Tsvetaeva remembered the house as it was before Marina's birth, but nothing much changed in the intervening years. They stopped keeping a cow in Marina's childhood, and the caretakers changed. But when Marina left home there was still no electricity.

Marina was born on 26 September (Old Style) 1892. Her arrival was a great disappointment to her mother, who had dreamed of a son and had already chosen a splendid name for him – Aleksandr. She had a succession of wet-nurses, one of them a gipsy. She grew up a strong and healthy child. Her pet names were "Marusya" and "Musya".

When she was two her sister Anastasia ("Asya") arrived. Maria Aleksandrovna's hopes for a son had been disappointed for the second time. She fed Asya herself, but the child was weak and often ill. This may have been why her mother worried more about her younger child and – so Marina thought – loved her more. By the time Marina started noticing her surroundings, at the age of two, so she tells us, the pattern of family life in Tryokhprudny Lane was fixed. This had not been achieved easily in a home which had so recently had another mistress, which was still run as she had run it, and which housed her eight-year-old daughter. Probably because she handled the situation badly Maria Aleksandrovna failed to win her stepdaughter's affection, and indeed aroused her hostility. Valeria

Tsvetaeva's recollections of her stepmother's arrival are subjective, though she shows some desire to be fair.

> She was loyal and straightforward, but sharp-tempered, hasty and intolerant. I was never subjected to crude and humiliating punishment, but there was no warmth or affection either. We grew further apart from each other, and I began to run wild. Later on I realized that Maria Aleksandrovna had led a very sheltered life till she was twenty-two, and had taken on a task beyond her powers – that of mothering someone else's children, and being a good wife to a man twice her age whom she hardly knew. She began at once frantically trying to destroy her predecessor's nest and remake it completely.

The house was in fact reorganized along Tsvetaev-Meyn rather than Tsvetaev-Ilovaysky lines. The Ilovaysky regime may well have been easier and more cheerful – the house had not then known death. In Varvara Dimitrievna's day the house rang with songs, romances, operatic arias; now it was filled with the strains of Haydn, Beethoven, Schumann and Chopin. Lightheartedness and simplicity forsook the house in Tryokhprudny Lane forever with the arrival of the new mistress.

Valeria was sent to the Catherine II Institute for the Daughters of Gentlemen. Young Andrey stayed at home and grew up with his half-sisters. Maria Aleksandrovna treated him as she did her own daughters, or perhaps rather more indulgently.

I said that Marina Tsvetaeva never described her mother's appearance, but that is not quite true. In her essay "Mother and Music" there is a lightly sketched description of her at the piano. "Her head, with its short wavy hair, was never bent, even when she was writing or playing, but thrown backwards, supported on a neck as long and straight as the candles to either side of her." It is a psychological portrait: inflexibility was her mother's most salient characteristic, and the piano was the great passion of her life.

This inflexibility determined the character of her relations with her children and the way they were brought up – which was left entirely to her. She was reserved, and gave no outward signs of affection. This does not mean that she was indifferent to her daughters. She loved them dearly, and transferred her own unrealized hopes to them. But their upbringing was governed by fixed and rigidly applied rules. These were by and large those of her own strict and narrow upbringing in her father's house, but reinforced by her passionate nature and her own disappointments. Her dream was that her daughters would inherit her own love of the arts and her own sublime ambitions, but instead of suffering her fate would go out into the world of the arts, in which her circumstances had prevented her from setting foot.

Marina showed exceptional musical talent, and her mother intended her to become a pianist. She had perfect pitch, she had big, supple hands and she was conscientious. Although she was not fond of practising she never tried to dodge it or to cut short the time which her mother decreed should be spent at the keyboard. Tsvetaeva wrote later that her own "exercises" at the piano had never given her pleasure, because she had learned very early to love music in her mother's excellent performance. Nonetheless she made very good progress, and confessed that she would have become a pianist if her mother had lived longer. Marina was four when her mother began giving her lessons. She learnt to read at the same age, and also took to making up rhymes. All children do it, but her mother made a prophetic entry in her diary: "my four-year-old Marina walks round and round me putting words together and making them rhyme. Perhaps she will be a poet."

Once and for all the principle was established that only the things of the spirit mattered: art, the enjoyment of natural beauty, honour and honesty. Religion was not forced upon the children. Marina's father was religious, but without a trace of sanctimoniousness. Her mother believed in God in some way of her own. The family attended the university church. The children grew up knowing of God's existence, and that was thought sufficient.

They were provided with everything that could further their intellectual and spiritual development – governesses to teach them languages, books, toys, music, visits to the theatre. They began learning to speak three languages – Russian, German and French – more or less simultaneously. "No expense was spared", as the saying goes, and their mother devoted a great deal of her own time to their education. She gave her daughters their first music lessons, read them books in the languages which they were learning, and talked to them about all the things which were dear and important to her. But "other children" on the boulevard where the little Tsvetaevs were taken for walks, or even those who lived in their own garden house, were strictly forbidden. Their mother hardly ever visited other families, and no one brought children to their house. Maria Aleksandrovna was afraid of infectious infantile diseases, but still more afraid of "bad" influences.

She would go up to their nursery or call them down to her own room, and spend hours reading to them or telling them stories. Those were unrepeatable and unforgettable evenings, when Marina and Asya snuggled up to their mother and listened to her stories about her childhood, their grandfather's place in the country, her travels abroad with him, the books which she had once read and which they would some day read, heroes of days long gone, poets . . . On such evenings her mother instilled in Marina a nostalgic love of things which had been and would never return. "All my life my way of loving was to say goodbye," she would write later. Those hours of intimacy with their mother, when they all snuggled up together under a heavy fur coat and fused into a single being, the girls remembered all their lives. Their mother read them the books of her own childhood. *Evening Pastimes* and *The Spring* were bought specially for them. Marina was carried away by writers now scarcely remembered: E. Sysoeva, Eugénie Tour, the Comtesse de Ségur. But her mother also read them Chekhov, Korolenko, Mark Twain and Hector Malot's *Sans famille* in French – years later Marina still grieved for its heroes. They read fairy stories too: Perrault, the Brothers Grimm, Hoffmann, Andersen. Marina's favourite story was "The Snow Queen". She wanted to be, she imagined herself, as free and daring as the little Robber Girl. Their mother introduced them to Pushkin, Dante and Shakespeare at an early age. But closest to their hearts were Germany and the German romantics, with their predilection for the middle ages and knight errantry, for the heroes of history and legend. Marina made their acquaintance first in translation, then in the original. Undine, Lorelei, the Erlking* became part of herself.

Maria Aleksandrovna had once dreamt of laying in enough intellectual "material" to last her for life, and now she eagerly imparted it to her children, "provisioning" them in their turn. She was anxious to inculcate in them her own philosophy of life. Marina greedily absorbed her mother's stories, though at that age there was much she did not understand.

> Mother was in such a hurry, with notes of music, with letters of the alphabet, with Undines and Jane Eyres and Anton Goremykas,† with contempt for physical pain, with Saint Helena, with the one against the many or the one without the many, as if she knew that she would run out of time, so here, at least this, and this, and this . . . So there'd be something to remember her by! So as to feed us for life at one go! How, from the first moment to the last, she gave and gave to us – even crushed us with giving! . . . It was as though she had buried herself alive in us – to live on there eternally. And what good fortune that all this was not science but Lyricism – that of which there is always too little . . . Mother gave us to drink from the opened vein of Lyricism.

* Undine: a water sprite who falls in love with a human (subject of a German verse-tale by La Motte Fouqué, also a verse-tale by the Russian poet Zhukovsky); Lorelei: siren whose beautiful singing lures sailors on the Rhine to their death (poem by Heine); Erlking (Erlkönig): the King of the Alders, who lures children to their death in the forest (poem by Goethe).

† *Anton Goremyka*: a novel (1847) by D. V. Grigorovich about the sorrows of the peasantry.

Things external and material were considered base and unworthy, and Maria Aleksandrovna tried to inspire contempt for them in her daughters. That the family was well off and wanted for nothing only made this easier. "Money is filth," she would say, and Marina inherited this attitude. The children wore simple and unostentatious clothes, as their mother had in her own childhood. They were taught not to want highly flavoured food and sweet things. Cakes and fruit did appear on the table, though, and their mother sometimes treated them to a pastry with hot chocolate or fragrant tea in a confectioner's shop. But at home sweets were kept under lock and key; the children were not forbidden to ask for them but they never did so. Knowing from an early age that their mother's reply would be a scornful and indignant look, they took it for granted that asking for things was shameful and demeaning. The rules by which her mother lived left a deep imprint on Marina's character. "It was a house of unspoken commandments and prohibitions," she recalled. The children silently yearned all the more for what was forbidden. But the Spartan ways inculcated by their mother helped them to endure the deprivations which fell to their lot in later life.

Childhood sped by leaving behind a memory of happiness. Winter was spent in Moscow. In the house they were born in, where they knew every nook and cranny and could distinguish the creak of every door and every step of the stairway up to their own quarters. And yet it was full of mystery, it changed from one time of day and night to another, it held endless possibilities of discovery. There were daily walks, to the Tverskoy Boulevard and the Pushkin monument, or to Patriarch's Ponds. Marina preferred the first, because she had loved the Pushkin monument before she knew anything about the poet himself. Sometimes there were outings with her mother to buy books, pictures, drawing books, paints, pencils. There were occasional visits to the theatre. The cries of pedlars, knife-grinders and rag-and-bone men or the plangent strains of a barrel organ could be heard from the street. Then there were the holidays. Especially Christmas, with presents round the tree which always came as a surprise when at last the children were allowed to see it, with its brilliant decorations, its candles already lit, and sweets hanging from its branches. Never again would Tsvetaeva enjoy warmth and comfort like that of her childhood home.

Summer meant semi-rural Tarusa. A little town in the Kaluga Province, near the clear and quiet waters of the Oka, at the very heart of Russia. A typically Russian town – stoutly built, roomy houses, the massive cathedral church of the Assumption, the market square, the "town gardens" along the river bank, the church of the Resurrection looking down from its high hill. There were well-stocked stores and shops. There was the placidity and the unhurried pace of provincial life. The surrounding countryside was also typically Russian: a lonely birch-tree or a clump of pines in the middle of a field or a meadow, copses of birch, windbreaks, and beyond – endless forest. Marina became a tireless walker, like her father. The field paths, the little streams, the gentle hills, restful and soothing, lured the walker on and on into the distance. You cannot think of Tarusa without remembering Tsvetaeva's lines:

> Blue hills near Moscow,
> In the air, slightly warm – dust and tar.
> All day I sleep, all day I laugh, that means,
> I am coming to from winter . . .

There was a little less than twelve miles to go from Tarusa station. The Tsvetaevs were met by the Tarusa cabby, Medvezhatkin, in his best conveyance – "the carriage with lamps". After dark, with the lamps lit, it was a romantic journey. Marina was always travel-sick, in the train and in the carriage, but the joy of arrival made up for all discomforts. Once they crossed the Oka by ferry they could take the upper road through the town or the lower road along the river. The dacha which Professor Tsvetaev rented from the municipality stood by itself, less than a mile beyond Tarusa. A very comfortable little wooden house with a mezzanine, a wide terrace and a small first floor balcony, it offered the children a great variety of possibilities for enjoyment. From the balcony they could see far beyond the Oka, and catch glimpses of reflected light from the river through the treetops.

In Tarusa they saw a great deal of the Dobrotvorsky family, whose big wooden house with its ornate carvings still stands on the main street. Ivan Zinovievich Dobrotvorsky ("Uncle Vanya" to the children) was a doctor in the service of the district council, and is still remembered with respect in Tarusa, although he died many years ago. His wife, Olga Aleksandrovna, was Ivan Tsvetaev's cousin. The two families were very close. There would be visits, always holiday occasions for the Tsvetaev children, to the comfortable house in Tarusa to which Tyo had moved for the rest of her days after Grandpa Meyn's death. Now and then they would go to see Vasily Polenov, the artist, whose estate was four or five miles further down the Oka. There they would find many young people, and all sorts of jollifications were arranged.

It was a simple, uneventful country life: boating, bathing, gathering mushrooms and berries, expeditions to favourite places. Here, too, the house was filled with their mother's music. Sometimes she and Valeria sang duets, and the sound of their voices floated with the river into the distance. The children were closer to their mother here than in Moscow. They saw more of their father too. He took walks and bathed with them. He could not bear inactivity. If he was not at his desk he had to be working in his garden. Every member of the family found special reasons for loving Tarusa. In autumn there would be sad goodbyes and promises not to forget "my birch-tree, my nut-tree, my fir-tree when I leave Tarusa". One fir-tree really was Marina's very own: her father had rented the dacha for many years on end, and had planted a fir-tree to mark the birth of each of his children. To Tsvetaeva, who was never to travel much inside Russia and hardly knew the Russian countryside, "my country" was a concept embodied in the words "Tarusa" and the "house in Tryokprudny".

Hers was an enviably happy but not entirely cloudless and uncompli-cated childhood. Relations between the children themselves, and between them and their mother, were far from simple. Tsvetaeva once let slip her wish that "my mother might have behaved as naturally with me as other mothers did with other little girls", but she said it without bitterness or self-pity. She accepted and loved and delighted in her mother just as she was. But growing up with such a mother had its difficulties. Maria Aleksandrovna was not only strict and demanding, she was also abrupt, scornful, unpredictable. "Despotic in her behaviour and compassionate at heart," Anastasia Tsvetaeva calls her mother in her early book *Smoke, Smoke, Smoke*. Maria Aleksandrovna lacked the patience and equability which anyone in constant contact with children needs. She thought that her children ought to know and understand much more than they possibly could at their age. Marina was afraid not only to ask *for* things but even to ask questions. She once asked her mother what Napoleon was. "'You mean you don't know about Napoleon?' 'No, nobody's told me.' 'Nobody has to be told things like that!' I shall never forget how deeply and hopelessly ashamed I felt."

Still, not being able to ask forced her to seek answers of her own and aroused her imagination. The punishment for naughtiness was to be shut in a dark lumber-room. That did not worry Marina. Much harder to bear was her mother's nagging, her loud lamentations – "To think that my children . . .", "to think that Grandpa's granddaughters could do such a thing!" Marina had no wish to upset her mother, but at times this scolding had the opposite effect from that intended – resentment impelled her to do what was forbidden. Anastasia Tsvetaeva asserts that the ideas of good and evil changed places in her sister's mind. It would be truer to say that she knowingly overstepped the limits of the good. She writes about this herself in "The Devil". Whatever was generally approved was alien to her. Even in childhood she had her own peculiar view of the world, in which reality and fantasy were so closely interwoven as to be indistinguishable. Her detailed and inspired account of her childhood relationship with the Devil – even if it is only a matter of poetic licence – ends by convincing the reader that her encounter with him was beneficial. Before she ever heard of Faust she came to think of the Devil as "part of that power that endlessly does good". It perhaps seems strange that the child of a family in which religion enjoyed respect should indulge such fancies – but who can control a child's imaginings? It took very little to set Marina's imagination racing.

Take "Mother and Music": what extraordinary associations the names of notes, musical notation and the hated metronome awakened in the child's mind. The musical signs come to life as sparrows, each hopping from its twig onto the keys, the piano becomes a hippopotamus, the metronome a coffin in which lives "immortal / long dead / Death" itself. And then there was poetry! Not wanting and not daring to ask for explanations Marina filled the gaps in her understanding from her imagination. What made it easier was the ready grasp of poetic meaning which she had shown from early childhood. Every line, indeed every word held a whole hidden world which the child's own poetic imagination brought to life. These childish imaginings were Tsvetaeva's first poetic creations. This was how the poet was born in little Musya – or rather forced a way through childish preoccupations and mischief, through games and musical studies. Tsvetaeva knew – her mother had impressed it on her at a very early age – that any talent, including the gift of poetry, is inborn, something bestowed in advance, and that its possessor has done nothing to deserve it. "I learnt, never to forget it, that I myself didn't count, that my ear was God-given. This saved me both from conceit and from self-doubt, from any sort of egoism in art."

Marina's character did not make life easy either for herself or for those around her. She was proud and shy, stubborn and headstrong, the need to protect her inner world from intruders showed itself far too early. It tended to isolate her from her surroundings. She probably did wrong not for the sheer enjoyment of it but simply because she did not realize that it was wrong. But repentance was made difficult by her irascible obstinacy, and the unconquerable shyness which she sometimes sought in vain to conceal by deliberate brusqueness.

This shyness made it difficult for her as a child to admit that she was at fault, even when she was conscious of it: it was easier for her to submit to punishment. "Fear and pity, anger and longing, were the passions of my childhood." She was always ready to protect a mistreated cat and dog, but might strike a nurse or a governess. The children came to blows with or without excuse, and every argument was settled by fighting. Marina's method was biting, Andrey's pinching, while Asya, the weakest, scratched and squealed horribly. She squealed anyway at difficult moments, and her brother and sister squealed to tease her. There was a great deal of teasing and jeering. Quarrels between the sisters were usually caused by determination to be the sole possessor of something or other — not necessarily something material. Marina was the main culprit here: whatever she loved she wanted all to herself. Everything had to be divided into "yours" and "mine": pictures, toys, pencils, trees, clouds, books, heroes . . . "That's mine" meant that something was taboo, and that the other sister must not even dare to covet it secretly, let alone ask for it. Marina could not even stand Asya reading the same books as herself or admiring "her" literary heroes. Bartering went on incessantly: I'll give you this, if you'll give me that for it. Often the operation was purely theoretical, since what was exchanged was a disembodied concept. The only things unexchangeable, according to Anastasia Tsvetaeva's reminiscences, were two ballads by Zhukovsky: "Undine" (after La Motte Fouqué) belonged to Marina, while "Sohrab and Rustum" (in imitation of Rückert) was Asya's property. Marina ferociously defended her right to love, admire, dream and yearn alone, her right to an inner world inaccessible to others.

> Novels pleased her from her youth;
> For her they stood for everything . . .

wrote Pushkin, to distinguish his Tatyana from the people around her. Pushkin's Tatyana was the ideal of several generations of Russian girls, for whom books "took the place of all else." Maria Aleksandrovna Tsvetaeva was one of them. And Marina was another. As soon as she had learnt to read she devoured indiscriminately everything she could find: books which her mother gave her, books which her mother forbade her to read, books which Andrey, her senior, was supposed to but did not read, books from her half-sister Valeria's bookcase, which, like everything belonging to the Ilovayskys, was out of bounds to her. She read the books of her mother's childhood and those of Valeria's childhood. At the age of five she came across Pushkin's works in Valeria's bookcase. It was a "grown-up" Pushkin. She knew that her mother would not allow her to read it and would be angry if she saw her with it, so she read it furtively, with her head inside the bookcase. Pushkin was her first poet, the poet whom she had known long before she learnt to read, from his monument on the Tverskoy Boulevard, from the picture showing his duel, which hung in her parents' bedroom, and from her mother's stories. He was the first poet whom she read by herself. And he would always remain for her the first of Poets. If we take her word for it — and why shouldn't we? — her mother, Pushkin and the Devil between them determined her whole outlook and her future. Marina read avidly throughout her childhood. She lived in and for books. She had difficulty in tearing herself away from them and taking notice of the world about her. "She's vanished into a book," Maria Aleksandrovna used to say. Between the ages of seven and nine, however, she plunged just as enthusiastically into the "musical literature" which her mother had banned — the songs and romances on Valeria's shelves. All that she read she eagerly absorbed, storing up the incomprehensible until she could make sense of it.

O childhood! The scoop of the soul's depths!

This line of Pasternak's was one of Tsvetaeva's favourites. Her heart and mind were amazingly receptive in these years of accumulation. All that her mother taught her she hid away and faithfully preserved. Maria Aleksandrovna should have been pleased her daughter had made her dream come true, realized not in music but in poetry. Love for her mother and gratitude to her never cooled in Marina's heart. The hours they had spent together she remembered as an incomparably happy time. It is doubtful whether she ever again had such a deep and intense relationship with anyone. Even her mother's strictness, her rigidity, her Spartan principles, which at first sight look like barriers, in fact brought them closer together, since they became part of Marina's own nature. The mother transferred her own character, her own cast of mind to her daughter. Sharing an aversion to sentimentality and the open expression of emotion, they understood each other without a word spoken, for Marina already dwelt in her mother's high romantic world. That is what she means when she calls the house in Tryokhprudny Lane "the land where all was understood".

What Maria Aleksandrovna perhaps understood and approved least of all was Marina's early attempts at verse. It is easy to find excuses for her. Her dream was that her daughter would become a pianist, and she could see that Marina's playing was good and her verse bad. It probably did not occur to her that there are no Mozarts in the history of literature, and that the infant Marina's verses should not have been compared with those of Pushkin or Goethe. Marina's clumsy doggerel looked absurd beside the great poetry which was the breath of life to her mother.

Marina began writing early. At the age of seven, before starting school, she had already filled one exercise book — the first she remembers — with poems. None of her earliest verse has survived. The scattered fragments quoted by the adult Tsvetaeva are clumsy and derivative, with echoes of everything that she had read. She could not stop writing. In her "History of a Dedication" she quotes the final quatrain of her first manuscript book of poems.

> This is the end of my dear writings,
> I'll scarcely take them up again,
> I'll remember them, oblivious,
> I love them.

This is followed by an exchange with an imaginary reader: "'Did you never write bad verses?' 'Of course — but all my bad verse was written before I started school.' Bad verse is like measles. Better to get it over in infancy." Maria Aleksandrovna was upset by this "infantile illness", not realizing that her daughter was "doomed" to be a poet. She did not live to read the poems which would have convinced her of it.

As for Marina's father, he was preoccupied with his own efforts, and remained aloof from the day-to-day doings of his household, relying on his wife to look after the children. One day he emerged from his study as Marina's mother was scolding her yet again for reading Valeria's love-songs. She appealed to him for support: "'I can't actually lock the bookcase just to keep her out of it,' my mother said to my father as he walked rapidly past towards the hall carrying a briefcase and with an attentive but uncomprehending look on his face." This one sentence of Marina's defines her father's place in the house. He was kind, he was affectionate and, like Valeria when she was at home, he could often mollify Maria Aleksandrovna, but most of the time he was simply absent. The children were always hearing about the museum, and knew that their mother was no less devoted to their father's dream than he was, but they could hardly be expected to understand how much energy and hard work he put into his brain-child. To them their father was old and dull, their mother young and fascinating. But her father's loyalty to his idea, and his tireless industry, had their effect on Marina's character.

Marina had been attending music classes since she was six, so that starting school at nine changed her life very little. The only real difference was that she looked forward to holidays more than ever. So things continued until 1902, when a storm burst over the house in Tryokhprudny Lane. Ivan Vladimirovich Tsvetaev and his wife had travelled to the Urals that summer, to order marble for the museum. The children eagerly awaited their return, hoping that they would bring back a Ural cat. There was no

31

cat, but their parents brought lots of specimens of Ural stone, and still more interesting stories. Then, that autumn, their mother suddenly fell ill. The doctors diagnosed tuberculosis and recommended that she should go to Italy. The whole family set off to spend the winter there, except Andrey, who stayed behind with Grandpa Ilovaysky to continue his schooling in Russia.

ABROAD

Marina's first feeling when she heard the news was one of joy. We're going to the seaside! It was the realization of a secret dream. All through the summer she had been under the spell of Pushkin's "To the Sea".

Farewell, free element! . . .

These lines were like a spell, the key to a huge world in which she was mistress. She did not stop to ask herself whether what she saw and imagined in them was their generally accepted meaning. She felt and responded to the most important thing in the poem – the inseparability of love and sorrow. She learnt something else from it that she would never forget: that the only "free element" is poetry, that there is no other. Marina learnt "To the Sea" by heart, and copied it out over and over again into little books she made for herself, to carry it around with her, wrote it as neatly as she could, without blots or corrections, so as "to have written it myself". Now she would soon be seeing the sea with her own eyes.

She could not yet understand the gravity of the disaster which had befallen the family, could not understand that her old life, the wonderfully happy life of Tryokhprudny Lane and Tarusa, was over forever. True, her mother declared as she left that "I shall never come back to this house, children". Strange words, of the sort that children scarcely hear at the time, but keep at the back of their minds to remember many years later. Their eager thoughts were fixed on the new experiences awaiting them. A quick succession of new countries, strangers, "other people's" children, flashed before their minds. In the next three years the girls found themselves in three different countries.

By November 1902 the Tsvetaev family was at Nervi near Genoa. Maria Aleksandrovna felt quite ill, and there had been times when her husband feared that he would not get her as far as Italy. For the first month at Nervi she did not leave her room, resisting all attempts to take her down to the sea. "The sound of waves makes her depressed and tearful," Ivan Tsvetaev wrote. The children had never seen their mother like that. Her illness gave them their freedom. Their daily routine now depended more on Valeria, who was easy-going and fond of them in those days, and let them do many things which their mother would not have allowed. Marina learnt what freedom was for the first time: she had never before realized that she was not free. The owner of the *Pension Russe* in which the Tsvetaevs were staying had two motherless sons, aged eleven and sixteen. Marina and Asya quickly made friends with Volodya, the younger of the two. He taught them to climb the cliffs, to light bonfires and bake fish in the embers. The girls sampled their first cigarette in his company. They spent whole days in the open air together – in the gardens, on the cliffs or on the sea. As soon as Maria Aleksandrovna felt better she hired a piano, and music lessons began again. A teacher came in to give the girls Russian lessons, so that they would not forget their own language. (Marina could already speak and read Italian.) But there was still plenty of free time left over, and the most important thing in life was her friendship with Volodya. She included some lines commemorating that friendship in her early published work.

> He was blue-eyed, with ginger hair
> (Like gunpowder during a game!),
> Affectionate, wily. But we
> Were two small blond-haired sisters.
>
> Night had come down upon the cliffs,
> At sea a bonfire smokes,
> And Volodya wearily leans
> His head on the sisters' shoulders.
>
> But the sisters angrily argue:
> "He's mine!" "No. He's mine!" "But why?"
> Volodya decides: "You both!
> You're my wives, I'm your husband, a Turk."
>
> (. . .)
> Skirts catch on the edges of the rocks,
> A pocket is torn by the pebbles.
> We are smoking pipes, like grown-ups,
> He's a chieftain and we are the thieves.

Marina had never known until then such enjoyable companionship with other children. For the first time she broke away from the world into which her mother had introduced her, and plunged into enthralling games: robbers, smugglers, pirates . . . The sisters escaped from the boring supervision of grown-ups, lured irresistibly by "wild freedom" – the title which Tsvetaeva gives to one of her poems in remembrance of that time.

The grown-ups around them in Nervi were no less interesting. The Russian émigré revolutionaries living in the *Pension Russe* made an enormous impression on Marina. Meeting them, she writes in her "Reply to a Questionnaire", was "one of the important spiritual events" of her life. She had never previously known anyone like them. They rejected God, marriage and the family. There were no husbands and wives amongst them, only "friends". They argued incessantly – about political parties, the revolution, the people – while remaining on good terms with each other. They were all "for the people", "for the oppressed" and against the Tsar. Marina eagerly absorbed their discussions, anxiously trying to understand it all. According to her sister she wrote poems about them. None of these have come down to us, but we may suppose that they were written in the spirit of the revolutionary songs which she sometimes heard them sing in the evening. The revolutionaries paid calls to enjoy Maria Aleksandrovna's music, the comfort with which she surrounded herself, and Russian tea. Marina's mother, seeing how she was intrigued by these people, listened apprehensively to all that was said. The freedom of the cliffs and the freedom of which the revolutionaries talked so fervently held Marina in thrall that winter. For the three of them, Marina, Asya and Volodya, freedom gradually became licence. As Valeria Tsvetaeva writes in her memoirs, "they got completely out of hand . . . Their games became mischievous pranks which offended other people." All four children ran wild and lost all sense of proportion. This could not go on for long.

That winter Maria Aleksandrovna fell in love with Vladislav Aleksandrovich Kobylyansky, whom Marina nicknamed "The Tiger". He was not her first amour. Two years earlier she had been attracted to Andrey's tutor, whom Valeria also liked, and the young man had to leave the house. Valeria's opaque comment on this is: "my father did not know that his removal would make little difference." The last entry in Maria Aleksandrovna's diary, mentioned by Anastasia Tsvetaeva, evidently refers to this: "'I am thirty-two, I have a husband and children, but . . .' after which a number of pages have been neatly cut out. Somebody, Valeria perhaps, told us that papa had cut them out." Does that "but", and the destruction of those pages, so that the children would not read them, testify to a drama in the Tsvetaev family? In any case, the younger children, Andrey, Marina and Asya, had noticed nothing at the time. But their mother's feelings for "The Tiger" were no secret to the little girls, who adored him themselves! He was a revolutionary and an exile! An extraordinary person, unlike anyone they had ever known! Proud, ironical, a mocker, an odd man out even amongst his revolutionary comrades, refusing to recognize "petit bourgeois" rules of behaviour, he was friendly, attentive and considerate with Maria Aleksandrovna and her daughters. A photograph taken at Nervi shows "The Tiger" holding Marina and Asya by the hand. With his long, narrow face framed by a pointed beard, his keen, ironical gaze, and the curious black ribbon he wore instead of a tie, he looks like a romantic hero, or perhaps just a little bit like Mephistopheles. We can see why Marina mentioned "The Tiger" in "The Devil". How could they help loving him? It was only when he returned from abroad many years later, after the Revolution, and sought her out in Moscow, that Marina learnt of his great love for her mother, of her mother's readiness to abandon her family and share her life with "The Tiger", and of how at the last moment she could not bring herself to damage her husband's and her children's lives. But, although Marina and Asya knew nothing of this at Nervi, the emotional upheaval that their mother experienced inevitably affected her relations with her daughters; illness was not her only distraction.

Towards the end of winter it became obvious that Maria Aleksandrovna could not return to Russia, and it was decided that she should live abroad until June 1904. Ivan Vladimirovich had to find somewhere to put the girls. They could no longer be left without proper supervision and regular schooling: Marina was really beginning to resemble Andersen's little Robber Girl. He found a boarding school in Lausanne which agreed to take them. Tyo, who arrived in Nervi to get them ready, found that they had run completely wild and felt that she ought to discipline them, but ended by spoiling them as she always had. Maria Aleksandrovna by then felt strong enough to visit various Italian cities with her husband and Valeria.

In May, Tyo took Marina and Asya to Lausanne, tearing them away from Nervi, the sea, their new friends, and their new-found freedom. They hated the Lacaze boarding school in Lausanne in advance. What sort of substitute could it possibly be for the wild life they had been leading, for Volodya, for their revolutionary friends? But when they got there they were warmly received. There was an atmosphere of good will and family comfort, the boarders were on friendly terms with one another. The intervals between lessons, the walks in town or in the school's little garden, and even study periods were enjoyable. There was no resisting it, and Marina and Asya plunged headlong into yet another new life and into the French language. Asya proved to be the youngest child in the school, but the older girls admitted Marina to their circle, because though not yet eleven she was as clever and mature as any of them. She found school-work easy and

35

pleasant, and her strict music teacher was well satisfied with her progress. Her short-sightedness made it difficult for her to read music and small print, and while she was in Lausanne she began wearing glasses. She read a lot as she always had, but now it was in French. Her day was full to the limit with lessons, music, reading, games, friends, letters to her parents . . . Their mother came for short visits. As always, the girls were thrilled by her presence, their conversations, the memories they shared, their walks with her. She belonged to them, only to them, all over again. It was all too short, as holidays always are.

> Looking into the depths of our souls,
> Our mother used to hold our hands.
> Oh, this hour, on the eve of parting,
> Oh, this twilight hour in Ouchy!

In vacations the school went to the Alps, to Mont Blanc. The sisters saw that majestic scenery for the first time. There were walks along mountain tracks, with meals in wayside inns. They visited the Castle of Chillon, of which they knew from Zhukovsky's ballad. Nervi was receding farther into the past and becoming a dream. Anastasia Tsvetaeva writes that she and her sister had given up religion altogether at Nervi, and adopted the atheism of their grown-up revolutionary friends. In the Lacaze school Marina was, to begin with, very militant in defence of her new convictions. She found, however, that no one sympathized or supported her. Instead, the cheerful, friendly atmosphere of this Catholic school, its high moral tone, with no trace of sanctimoniousness, and her talks about God with the headmistress and her spiritual adviser, brought about a revolution in Marina's heart. In "Reply to a Questionnaire" she mentions "Catholicism at the age of eleven" among the most important events in her spiritual life, together with "Revolution". Anastasia tells us about their lengthy bedtime prayers, the exaltation they felt as they entered the church which so recently they had mocked, and their efforts to behave as Christians. In this they seem to have made little progress. They might, perhaps, control their natural impulses, wait till the other girls had taken their pick and make do with the worst cakes – but then, they had been trained not to be greedy at home in Moscow. Marina and Asya spent more than a year in Lausanne, and were happy there. Appropriately, a plaque in honour of "Marina Tsvetaeva, Russian poet" on the building which housed the Pensionnat Lacaze, 3 Boulevard de Grancy, was put up in 1982.

The picture changes once again. The girls were taken away from the Pensionnat Lacaze and the whole family went north, to the Black Forest, which they knew so well from fairy stories. Maria Aleksandrovna hoped to accustom her lungs to a harsher climate in preparation for her return to Russia in a year's time. The children were to spend the winter in a Catholic boarding school at Freiburg, so they would speak yet another language like natives. Their mother would settle somewhere quite near so that they could see her regularly. Late summer they spent with their parents (it was so long since all four of them had been together) in the village of Langackern, in the hills outside Freiburg. The hotel "Zum Engel" still stands, surrounded by the same forests and hills and little villages. Even the enormous lime-tree under which the Tsvetaev family liked to eat lunch and drink tea is still there in front of the house. The hospitable innkeepers and their children, Karl and Marile, did not resemble Volodya in the least, but they and the Tsvetaevs became firm friends. Maria Aleksandrovna felt almost well, and her husband was happy to see her much better. The whole family went walking along the beautiful forest paths. They could not know that this was their last happy and carefree time together. Marina fell in love with the Black Forest, as she was bound to – Germany, after all, was her ancestral homeland, and her mother had taught her to love the country as passionately as she did herself. "How I loved the Black Forest, loved it with a love that hurt, loved madly," she recalled in 1919, that time of famine and devastation. "The golden valleys, the menacing embrace of the sounding forest, not to mention the village with its inn signs – 'Zum Adler', 'Zum Löwen' . . ." Ancient German stories and legends came to life again. The black summits of the firs reminded her of medieval castles. Her mother read them Wilhelm Hauff's *Lichtenstein* in German. Germany and the German language became dear to Marina. She knew German as well as she knew Russian, and loved the spirit of Germany as though it was her native land. She adored Greece, but knew it only at secondhand, from German sources. Her knowledge of Greek mythology, for instance, came from Gustav Schwab's *Most Beautiful Legends of Classical Antiquity*. Tsvetaeva lived her whole life in the belief that "I have many souls, but the most important of them is the Germanic."

Summer was over all too soon. Their father went home to Russia, the girls moved into a boarding school kept by the Brink sisters at Freiburg and their mother took an apartment in the mansard of a venerable house a block away from them. For Marina and Asya life in Freiburg had one bright spot – the possibility of seeing their mother frequently. The Brink boarding school was a grim place, especially after their marvellous summer in the Black Forest, and the free and easy life of the Pensionnat Lacaze. Discipline and obedience were what the Brink establishment required of its pupils. The boredom of the place made the sisters mischievous and perverse. The threat of black marks was no deterrent. Meals were dull and meagre, walks always followed the same tiresome route up the Schlossberg, the mountain that hangs over the town. It can only have been because the Brink sisters lacked imagination. Ivan Tsvetaev arrived from Moscow to visit his family in January, and complained in a letter with what for him was uncharacteristic harshness that "yesterday both our little girls came back from their walk up the mountain covered with blood: their idiot of a teacher had taken them up there although there was ice under foot, and as they were coming down a steep path they fell over each other, so that the little one broke her nose and the older one barked her knee." We can easily imagine the desiccated teacher, the pupils miserably trooping two by two along the icy path, and Marina and Asya, never notably well behaved, pushing and jostling each other to relieve their boredom. Even God became such a tedious and unpleasant subject in the Brink establishment that Marina reacted by gradually losing the devoutness acquired in Lausanne.

The only joy that Freiburg held for them, their meetings with their mother, came to an end in February. She caught a chill, her condition deteriorated suddenly, and she had to go into a sanatorium at St Blasien. After seeing her installed there, their father went back to Russia. Without mother, life in the boarding school seemed still harder to bear. This sad time coincided with other sad events in Moscow. Grandpa Ilovaysky's children by his second marriage both died of tuberculosis, first Seryozha, then Nadya. They were roughly Valeria's age, and she and Nadya were friends. Long ago, as a child of five or seven, Marina had been in love with Seryozha, and he had been the only "grown-up" to show any interest in her verses. It was not very long since the Ilovayskys had lived together with the Tsvetaevs in the *Pension Russe* at Nervi. Nadya was the most beautiful of all of them – people turned to look at her in the street, and Marina had acted as postman for her and a certain young man. The news that Nadya was no more had a devastating effect on Marina, which she kept secret for more than twenty years. She first mentioned it only in 1928 in a letter to Nadya's friend, Vera Bunina, and subsequently described it in "The House at Old Pimen".

This was the first mystical experience in her life – her story about the devil was a feat of her childish imagination. Now, at the age of eleven, when she heard of Nadya's death she felt her absence like an empty space in the world ("the end of a rope, suddenly left in my hand") and an intolerable yearning to turn time backward, so that this death would not have happened, would never happen, a yearning to see Nadya again, gaze upon her, tell her how much she loved her. Mentally, she revisited all the places where Nadya might be, and understood for the first time in her life that this parting is forever, that death means being nowhere, that Nadya no longer existed. She could not reconcile herself to this calamity and she began stubbornly looking for Nadya, flying to some lonely spot to which intuition told her Nadya might come, fearful only that intruders might come and frighten her away. She implored Nadya to wait for her, she thought of cunning tricks to take her by surprise. There was room for nothing else in her life except this obsession. She felt that Nadya was somewhere near, beside her, walking behind her, that Nadya needed her love . . . Never once did she see her – which may be why the "spell" lasted so long: "For two years on end I loved her, *saw* her in my dreams – I remember those dreams – and why I didn't die, didn't break away and follow her, I do not understand."

As a grown woman, Marina often saw the dead poet Aleksandr Blok as though he were still alive. "After Blok's death I kept meeting him on Moscow bridges at night. I *knew* that he wandered there, and that although he did not know me I was his greatest love, the great love ordained for him and never realized." After the funeral of A. A. Stakhovich she wrote in her diary "there is no wall between 'dead' and 'alive', between 'was' and 'is'. There is a mutual trust. He knows that I *am*, in spite of my body, I know that he *is*, in spite of his coffin! There is a compact, a contract, a conspiracy of friends. And with every person who departs, some part of me, of my longing, of my soul, takes leave and goes – *there*! . . ." In 1905 Marina was too young to have such thoughts. What stirred in her and kept alive so long this obsessive desire to meet someone no longer of this world? Its origin may have been a deep dread, denied admission to her consciousness, of her mother's death. Could she, after she had seen so many sick people at Nervi and so many graves there, after she had witnessed the death of a consumptive German youth with whom the family had made friends, avoid thinking of the terrible threat hanging over her mother? Banishing this thought to the depths of her mind, from which it could never escape, she must have transferred her anxiety for her mother, still alive, to Nadya, already dead. The coincidence in time – she heard of Nadya's death as she was parting with her mother – intensified the horror of what was inexorably approaching. Though the parting with her mother was only temporary – St Blasien was so near to Freiburg that they would all be there together for the summer – it seemed to Marina as eternal as her parting with Nadya. And perhaps Marina sought reassurance: seeing Nadya again would be a sign that her mother too would not go away, leaving nothing of herself behind. Her admission in a letter to Vera Bunina that "Nadya's death overshadowed that of my mother" does not mean that she was callous. It is simply that, in the year and a half between the two deaths, in her grief for Nadya she had also been mourning for her mother.

Nadya did not appear, but there were "signs", or what Marina chose to recognize as signs, of her: in a cloud which reminded her of Nadya's flushed cheeks or the oval of her face, in the scents of a flower shop, which revived memories of the "battle of flowers" at Nervi, in weak coffee resembling in colour Nadya's eyes. In the same way, she would later see a sign from her dead mother, as she wrote to Ellis in summer 1909. She saw her mother in a dream and asked her "to make it so that we can meet in the street, if it's only for a minute, *please*, Mama!" "That isn't possible," her mother had said, sadly, "but remember, if you sometimes see something strange and lovely in the house or in the street that will be me, or sent by me!" and with that she vanished. In the same dream Marina saw a tree in a tub, and knew that it was her mother! Tsvetaeva's thoughts on sleep and dreams should be the subject of a special study. Sleep was for her the mystical junction between life and death. Dreams opened the door to the beyond, to eternity.

The mystical experiences first provoked by the death of Nadya Ilovayskaya were no less powerfully repeated in 1926 after the death of Rainer Maria Rilke, whom Marina had never seen, but whose greatness as a man and as a poet she thought comparable with that of Pushkin or Goethe. But when she heard of his death she did not rush out into the streets of Paris hoping to meet him. By that time she had a magic wand – poetry. She addressed Rilke, in the other world, directly, in her verse letter "A New Year's" (about which Joseph Brodsky has written so well*) and in the article "Your Death". When in "A New Year's" she writes

> . . . because the other world,
> ours – at thirteen, in the Novodevichy,†
> I understood – is not without language, but has all languages.

her thoughts have gone back to Nadya, and to her own quest for the other-worldly so many years earlier. She visited Nadya's grave in the Novodevichy cemetery after her return to Russia, and after her mother's death, and it is this again that she has in mind when she writes in "Your

---

* "Footnote to a Poem", translated by Barry Rubin, in Joseph Brodsky, *Less Than One: Selected Essays* New York, 1985, and Harmondsworth, 1986, pp. 195–267.
† "New Virgin" Monastery in Moscow, in whose cemetery many famous persons are buried.

Death" of "all our dead, whether they lie in Moscow in the Novodevichy, or . . .". Nadya's death was the first she experienced, her first encounter with the mysterious and alluring world beyond, the first to give her a glimpse of eternity. The first in the series of deaths of which she wrote: A. A. Stakhovich, Aleksandr Blok, Rainer Maria Rilke, Vladimir Mayakovsky, Nikolay Gronsky . . . After Nadya there seems to have been nothing enigmatic about life and death for Marina – she saw this world and the next as an unbroken unity, and at times, as for instance in her lines addressed to Rilke, felt that she was more at home in "the other" world than in this one. The idea which was to become the stimulus and the underlying theme of her poetry – that of "parting" – crystallized from her childhood experiences. "Parting" meant separation from friends or loved ones, the break with your homeland, death. The concept of parting grew wider and deeper, until it became at last a tragic rejection of life. But it was this too that drove her to write, because by writing she could overcome it.

The school term ended, and their father took the girls to St Blasien for the summer, to be near the sanatorium where Maria Aleksandrovna was receiving treatment. Once again, they roamed the country roads and forest paths of the Black Forest, but this time their mother was too weak to accompany them. There had been no improvement in her health after a year in the miracle-working forest. What had Marina gained from her year in Freiburg? Above all, her perfect command of German, her feeling of kinship with Germany, her memories of her German friends Marile and Karl, children of the owner of Hotel "Zum Engel", and her mother's last active summer in the "fabulous Schwarzwald". And her visual memories of the medieval city with its incomparable cathedral. Yet, strange as it may seem, it was there in Freiburg that she conceived the two great passions of her life: for Napoleon and for Russia. What she felt for Russia was not nostalgia but anxiety and hurt. Her father's letters, with news of Russia's defeats in the war with Japan, filled her with agitated concern and pain for Russia. Her feeling for her "homeland" was awakened by Russia's débâcle.

It was time to go home. The family had never intended to stay abroad for ever, and Asya's Russian was getting shaky. Home, however, did not mean Moscow. Maria Aleksandrovna was forbidden to live in the north and together with her daughters she made her home in Yalta, on the Black Sea.

The life of the household was governed by the gravity of her illness. Its daily routine was made up of doctors' visits, taking the invalid's temperature and worrying whenever it had risen by a degree, fetching medicines from the pharmacy and administering them. In time they got used to it. A teacher was hired to prepare the girls for a Russian school. Maria Aleksandrovna began giving Marina music lessons again, was pleased with her progress, and still cherished the hope that she would become a pianist. But something new erupted in their lives – revolution! As 1905 drew to a close the country was in uproar, on strike, up in arms . . . The mutinies on the *Potemkin* and the *Ochakov*, the treachery of the *St George*, the arrest of Lieutenant Shmidt, the Tsar's manifestos:* stirred by these exciting events Marina eagerly awaited the newspapers. The Tsvetaevs in Yalta were concerned not only for the fortunes of Russia but for their family in Moscow: Ivan Vladimirovich, Andrey and Valeria were at home in Moscow when the rising began in December. It was clear from the newspapers that Tryokhprudny Lane was cut off by barricades. Marina listened intently to the political arguments which broke out at the common table in their Yalta pension. There are two entries for 1905–1906 in her "Reply to a Questionnaire". She remembers first her "second encounter with revolution – in 1905–1906. Yalta Socialist Revolutionaries". A family of SRs (Socialist Revolutionaries), who were neighbours of theirs, aroused Marina's interest, and she used to call on them, although her mother forbade it. She was attracted by their belief in the cause, as she had been by the émigrés at Nervi a year earlier. She wrote revolutionary verses, but this time did not show them to her mother. They were growing apart. Marina had reached the difficult age as her mother was dying. Maria Aleksandrovna was preoccupied with her illness, Marina with her own interests and feelings, and their previous intimacy no longer existed. Marina's revolutionary enthusiasm, however, had little connection with reality. She reacted to what was happening with feverish excitement, listened eagerly to the discussions of those around her, was thrilled by and grieved for Lieutenant Shmidt and Maria Spiridonova,† but all this was in the mind. She was too young to join the revolutionaries, and they would not have taken her seriously. As she drifted farther away from her mother she became more and more isolated.

Marina's short-lived passion for the revolution reflected the feelings of many people in the circle to which the Tsvetaev family belonged, but not those of her parents. Her mother was conservative, and looked askance at

---

* The battleship *Potemkin* (*Potyomkin*) was temporarily taken over by mutinying sailors in June 1905. The mutiny on the *Ochakov* was led by Lieutenant Pyotr Shmidt, who was executed. At the end of the year the Tsar issued manifestoes promising constitutional government.
† Idealist Socialist-Revolutionary who shot the tyrannical General Luzhenovsky in 1906, and was himself shot in 1941.

what was going on and at her daughter's infatuation. Her father had always remained aloof from politics, and now, with his wife's illness and the practical problems it created to worry about, he seems not even to have felt a need to understand the situation. The museum, and his family, were all that he could manage. In a letter to R. Kleyn in April 1906 his normal reserve in discussing family matters gave way to a cry of despair: "All my thoughts have been concentrated on my sick wife, on ways of treating her complaint, and places where she might find them, on medicines and doctors in various parts of Europe . . . Family grief has put everything else out of my mind . . . Weighed down by private grief I feel no interest in matters of anxious concern to Russia at this time . . . If anything outside the circle of family worries and griefs claims my attention and serves as a focus for my thoughts and desires it is our museum as it moves on towards completion."

Marina's stubborn attachment to the revolution may in part be explained by an urge to resist parental influence and reject parental views, quite normal in people of her age. Father and mother take no interest in the revolution – so I shall do so. However that may be, she had completely outgrown her interest in "ideologies" and in "society" by the age of sixteen, and never went back to them. Such enthusiasms, like measles and bad verses, are something we must experience, and recover from, for ourselves, and the sooner the better. A quarter of a century later Marina remembered how at the age of thirteen she had asked an old revolutionary: "Can one be a poet *and* a party member?" and he had unhesitatingly answered "no". At sixteen, Marina began writing seriously: she was herself – and by herself – again.

In mid-March 1906, Maria Aleksandrovna had a haemorrhage. She took to her bed and ate practically nothing. Ivan arrived from Moscow. They both realized that she was dying, but he did all he could to keep her spirits up. In May, the best doctors in Yalta met to discuss her case, and tried to "suggest" to her that her condition was not hopeless. "Since then she seems rather better," wrote Ivan. "After two months in bed the patient gets up, walks across the room to the terrace, and makes an effort to swallow, though it is very difficult for her. Before the consultation I was beginning to give up hope that M.A. would ever return to her own part of the world. Now we are seriously thinking of setting off for Tarusa in twenty days' time. Our dacha there is being repaired." The devoted Tyo appeared, to take her Manya home. By the beginning of June they were at Tarusa. Marina has not told us what revisiting the scenes of her childhood meant to her. Her mother's imminent death probably overshadowed everything else. Maria Aleksandrovna was dying painfully but bravely. A week before her death Ivan wrote that "my sick wife's condition becomes steadily worse. Fever-reducing medicines no longer have any effect, and she is burning terribly in the very high temperature which goes with continual inflammation of the lungs and the bronchial tract. All that we call the body is eaten away and has vanished."

Maria Aleksandrovna grieved as she lay dying that she would never see her daughters grown up. She made a will, under which until they were forty Marina and Asya were to receive only the interest on the capital she was leaving them. She is supposed to have said in explanation "otherwise they'll spend it all on the revolution!" When she felt that death was near she said goodbye to her daughters and gave them her blessing. Valeria Tsvetaeva notes in her memoirs that her stepmother did not send for her to say goodbye, and adds "I was grateful for her honesty at that dreadful moment." Nor did she send for a priest to administer the last rites. On 6 July she was no more. Her body was taken to Moscow, carried past the house in Tryokhprudny Lane and buried in the Vagankov cemetery, beside the graves of her parents. Two months later Ivan Tsvetaev had a stroke. He was ill in hospital for a long time.

Marina's childhood was over.

A CONTROVERSIAL CHILDHOOD

Why should there be controversy about Marina Tsvetaeva's childhood? Is there really anything unclear or mysterious about it? I doubt whether we know as much about the childhood of any other Russian poet. Marina herself wrote on the subject twice: in the verses of 1908–1910 included in her first books, and in her later prose, dating from the mid-thirties. Anastasia's memoirs of her own and Marina's childhood ran into three editions. What can there be left to argue about? There is, however, room for differences of opinion on one very important question: how truthfully and accurately has Tsvetaeva portrayed her childhood world?

The argument grows, and will continue, as new information on Tsvetaeva continues to appear. The content of Tsvetaeva's letters is compared with passages in her prose writings, and the poet is found guilty of revising reality if not of perfidy. We see the same words again and again: true story, legend, true-to-life account, artistic truth, poetic truth. The controversy has gone beyond the bounds of Tsvetaeva's prose writing on her childhood, and extended to her recollections generally. Here I shall

44

concern myself only with the theme of childhood in Tsvetaeva. Reading Anastasia Tsvetaeva's *Memoirs* and Marina's "childhood" prose side by side, the Leningrad scholar Irma Kudrova has come to the conclusion that Marina's childhood was not the "land of unqualified happiness" which her younger sister portrays. Kudrova analyses passages from Marina's prose to show that those around the young Marina, even her mother, failed to understand her, and not only did not sympathize with but made fun of her attempts to write poetry. Kudrova accuses the household in Tryokhprudny Lane of failing to show her sufficient warmth, affection and kindness so that "the feeling that she was rejected took an ever firmer hold on the child." She asserts that there was no openness, no understanding, no tenderness in Maria Aleksandrovna's relations with her daughter, and sees in this the roots of Marina's feeling that life is tragic.

Anastasia Tsvetaeva rushed to the defence of her family and her mother with truly Tsvetaev vigour – she found Kudrova's conclusions insulting, and to protect the "honour of the family" she was ready to reject what appeared to be the meaning of Marina's autobiographical prose. She confesses that when she was reading it she had been saddened to note how distorted were the pictures drawn in it, of her mother, of herself, the younger sister, and of the whole spirit of the house in Tryokhprudny Lane . . . "Until I suddenly realized that Marina wasn't 'distorting' us, she was portraying something else! At the centre of these stories is Marina. And her – the poet's – loneliness amongst non-poets." "The poet amongst non-poets" is certainly one of the major themes that runs through her autobiographical prose. But does this give us grounds for questioning her truthfulness? For saying that the house on Tryokhprudny Lane "is no more than a stage set", necessary for the creation of a legend which has no relation to reality, and that the family was a battlefield on which she fought – against whom, and for what? We should be left with an unpleasant feeling that Marina Tsvetaeva traduced her family and her childhood to heighten her own "unusualness". A feeling aggravated by the fact that in the same article Anastasia Tsvetaeva calls her sister's essays on Maksimilian Voloshin, Andrey Bely and Osip Mandelstam "portraits of high artistry and striking fidelity . . . Marina resurrected the days she spent with them. By force of memory and by love." To ask whether Tsvetaeva's memories of her earliest home, her mother and her childhood were fainter than those of her poet friends, and her love for them less, would be a rhetorical question. Let us ask ourselves instead what made it possible for Kudrova to doubt the "unclouded happiness" of Tsvetaeva's childhood, and for Anastasia to accuse her sister of deliberately and grotesquely distorting the truth. There are several reasons. Kudrova is right in saying that there was no "unclouded happiness". But who has ever claimed that childhood ever is cloudless? Even Boris Pasternak, who was psychologically as unlike Tsvetaeva as he could be, a man capable of deriving happiness from anything and everything, wrote about the terrors that beset childhood – notably in "The Childhood of Lyuvers"* of which Tsvetaeva was so fond. And also in these lines:

> . . . It seems your mother is not your mother,
> You are not you, home is an alien land.

> What can terrible beauty do,
> Sitting down on the bench of lilac,
> If not to steal away children?
> Thus do suspicions come about.
> Thus fears ripen . . .

Let us ponder this testimony from a fellow poet – and its final words: "Thus one begins to live by poetry."

Perhaps that poignant feeling of orphanhood which welled up in Marina long before her mother's death came from the same source as this poem? In her prose about her childhood she always seems something of a "stepdaughter". She is jealous of her younger sister, whom their mother loved more. Anastasia does not deny it: she was a weak child, and sometimes seriously ill, and Maria Aleksandrovna showed her more affection and looked after her rather more carefully. This was enough to awaken in Marina the uneasy feeling that "your mother is not your mother, you are not you, home is an alien land". She too was a poet.

Kudrova is right about something else: there was nothing simple about the character of Maria Aleksandrovna, her relations with Marina, or the whole situation in the house on Tryokhprudny Lane. Marina's autobiographical prose provides the best evidence that there was nothing simple about herself as a child. Simplicity, like talent, is a gift of nature. Maria Aleksandrovna would perhaps have liked to be a simple person: her complex character brought her no happiness. She may have hoped that her daughter would be simpler and happier, but there was nothing she could do about that. She probably found Anastasia simpler and more straightforward, and so easier and pleasanter to deal with. No doubt she tried not to show it, but Marina felt it just the same. Does this explain her childish fantasy about "a different family", in which "there would be no Asya, and I would be the only and dearly loved daughter"?

* Also known in translation as "Zhenya Luvers' Childhood" (see Boris Pasternak, *The Voice of Prose*, vol. 1. ed. C. Barnes, Edinburgh, 1986).

Marina was much more difficult to live with. Nonetheless, Kudrova seems to me to have things the wrong way round. Marina did not withdraw into herself because others did not understand her or would not take the trouble to understand her: she was more difficult to understand and to deal with than other children because from too early an age she lived in a distinct world of her own, which no one else could enter. Kudrova is, I think, mistaken when she says that "the mother could not recognize herself in her older daughter". On the contrary, she thought that she could discern in Marina a passionate and complex personality like her own. And what she probably felt bound to fight against, for the sake of Marina's future happiness, was herself reborn, not her daughter's poetic gift. She strove to suppress her own nature in her daughter. But that there was a loving intimacy between them is obvious from everything that Marina says about her mother in her poetry, her prose and her letters. Without deep affection Maria Aleksandrovna could not have influenced so powerfully her daughter's whole future as a poet.

Anastasia Tsvetaeva's main mistake is her insistence on the "twin sisterhood" of herself and Marina. This has made it difficult for her to penetrate the inner meaning and the truth of Marina's autobiographical prose. I do not dispute that the sisters had identical voices. But this is not enough to allow us to say that they were "remarkably similar in spiritual make-up"; let alone that "their reactions were identical, like those of identical twins". This was not and could not have been true: one sister was a poet, the other was not. If Anastasia Tsvetaeva had accepted this it would have been easier for her to understand not only her sister's writings but her life and death. A way of perceiving, a particular kind of mentality, is what makes the poet a poet and distinguishes him or her from ordinary mortals. If she had looked at her sister's prose just once with the eyes of a sympathetic reader and not those of a "twin", Anastasia would have seen that Marina never "distorted" or "embroidered", that she had no intention of painting a grotesque picture of her family life. What she describes is how she *felt* in her childhood home – and how she would always feel in the world. "The loneliness of the poet amongst non-poets" was not retrospective "embroidery": it was what Marina had *experienced* in her childhood.

In this polemic Kudrova ignores the poems about childhood in *Evening Album* and *The Magic Lantern*, whereas Anastasia Tsvetaeva treats them as reliable documentary evidence. Such pieces as "At Ouchy", "To Mama", "Kurlyk", "Reading Lichtenstein", of course convey Tsvetaeva's recollections of her prematurely interrupted childhood, her mother, and the warmth of her mother's presence in her young life. They are sketches of childhood scenes and feelings, made close to the events described in them, and closer still to the pain and grief of loss.

> Sadness, it seems, you left as a legacy
> To us, O mother, your little girls: . . .

These poetic reminiscences are rose-tinted – as indeed are Tsvetaeva's first volumes of collected verse generally. In their rapturous celebration of the poet herself and the world around her, their "mad delight in the trivia of existence" (Nikolay Gumilyov, speaking of her first book), they are close to Anastasia Tsvetaeva's memoirs. There is nothing resembling them in Marina's prose writings on the same theme, and this has led some people to speak of a contradiction between these and the early poems. Are we to suppose that Marina's attitude to her childhood changed? Did she project backwards her disillusionment with life as a whole? Not at all. The contradiction is merely superficial. It would be strange if a woman of forty, with the insights which hardship and suffering had brought her, repeated what she had written as a girl of seventeen or eighteen just embarking on life. Such repetition would have been senseless. Her early poems are simple, artless, naïve. This childlike artlessness and naïvete is missing in her prose. Here she has set herself a different task – that of "RESURRECTING. Seeing for myself and making others see." Not allowing that vanishing world which she so loves and to which she feels inseparably tied to vanish for ever.

Significantly, it is in poems written simultaneously with her prose reminiscences of childhood and addressed to "the other place", to "the departed", to "The Fathers" that Tsvetaeva defined precisely her conception of the Poet and of Poetry.

> You, who inspired a child
> Doomed to be a poet
> To revere all things,
> Save sounding brass . . .

"The child doomed to be a poet" – that is the inner theme, the sub-text of Tsvetaeva's prose writing about her childhood. Here she is engaged not in mythopoeia, not in social history, but in research. The world of childhood – very much a closed world, one would think – has been incorporated in the cycle of her main intellectual preoccupations in those years: with the Poet, the Poet and Time, the poet's place in time and relationship with the world outside.

The chronological evidence supports this statement. In 1932 Tsvetaeva was writing works of a literary-philosophical character: "The Poet and

Time", "Art in the light of Conscience", "Epic and Lyric of Contemporary Russia: Mayakovsky and Pasternak". She began writing in prose about childhood in 1933 and continued until 1937, the year of her "Pushkin" essays. As she finished "My Pushkin" she wrote to her friend Anna Tesková (a Czech translator from Russia) that "this is my early childhood: 'Pushkin in the nursery' – amended to read in *my* nursery". This amendment is most important to our understanding of Tsvetaeva's attitude to her childhood, and why it was so different from "everybody else's". Tsvetaeva's last literary essay, "Pushkin and Pugachov"* – which she could equally well have called "My Pushkin and my Pugachov" – is at the same time chronologically her last memoir of her childhood, for here, as in "My Pushkin", literary criticism, philosophy, psychology and childhood impressions are woven into one unbroken fabric. Thus, Tsvetaeva's prose writings about her childhood not only coincide in time with works which seek to define the Poet and Poetry, but are dovetailed into some of them.

What is the Poet? What is the Poet's role in the world? These "eternal" themes exercised Tsvetaeva's creative imagination. The foundation of her own outlook is an instinctive feeling that the Poet stands in opposition to the world. The Poet is the prisoner of his or her gift and time. Her conception is identical with that formulated later by Pasternak:

> You're a hostage of eternity,
> Held prisoner by time . . .

And in this is the key to her understanding of her childhood. "The creative state is a state of enchantment . . . The creative state is a state of dreaming . . ." as she puts it in "Art in the Light of Conscience". This, surely, describes the somnambulistic state in which the little Marina encounters the Devil, or copies out Pushkin's "To the Sea" time after time after time? Tsvetaeva's prose writings about her childhood are not memoirs – she never referred to them by that name. She has no interest in "childhood", or even in "the formation of personality" as such. She sets out to investigate a particular phenomenon – the incarnation of the Poet in the child: convinced that Poetry is akin to Eternity, unchanging from the beginning to the end of time, Tsvetaeva sets out to discover why a particular child comes to be "branded" Poet. Note that from the child's point of view the process is a passive one, indeed one of suffering. Almost from the day she was born her mother taught her insistently that "Your ear is God-given. Only the effort is your own".

In her enquiry into the phenomenon of the child poet, Tsvetaeva uses

* Emelyan Pugachov: leader of the peasant uprising of 1773–4 and Pretender to the Throne.

her own childhood as research material, because she knows it best. And that is all there is to it. Looked at from this point of view, her prose about her childhood reads differently. There is no invention in it: it is no less true than what emerges from her early poems. She once said of her writing about other people: "I never interfere with the facts, I merely interpret them." But "facts" mean nothing until they are interpreted. The "truth" in Tsvetaeva's autobiographical prose is the truth as she experienced it and relived it. What Anastasia writes about their childhood together is most probably also the truth – the truth as she, Asya, knows it. Its divergences from Marina's truth merely reflect the dissimilarity between the two sisters, their way of seeing the world, and their self-awareness. Marina's "negative" statements about her family, which are the subject of dispute between Kudrova and Anastasia Tsvetaeva, were not made out of a desire to get her own back because she was insufficiently loved and insufficiently understood as a child – even if she felt that to be so at the time. She never stopped loving and feeling grateful to the house on Tryokhprudny Lane. When she was working on her "childhood" prose she confessed in a letter to Anna Tesková that she ("as I dare say you do") loved *only* her childhood, only" what *was, then*". But she shows us how lonely she was from the beginning, even with such an unusual mother, in such a highly intellectual family, and in such a truly happy childhood. Anastasia Tsvetaeva's reminiscences create the impression that Marina cultivated her loneliness. In reality she was imprisoned in it – in her "emotional solitude", from which the only escape was into poetry. A transparent wall separates the one "doomed to be a poet" from other people, a wall which they perhaps do not see, which can be approached but not passed. Scrutinizing her childhood self through the magnifying glass of maturity Tsvetaeva analyses and interprets her feelings, experiences and thoughts at that time. This has nothing to do with her problems in emigration, which Soviet writers are so fond of invoking. Kudrova, for instance, writes that "in the thirties Tsvetaeva came to understand clearly the breakdown in her relations with the world, and felt painfully that her connection with it was out of order". The whole of Tsvetaeva's autobiographical prose, more so even than her theoretical works, cries out against this viewpoint. It bears witness that there was no "breakdown", that if she had any "relationship with the world" it was negative to begin with. How could a "connection" be "finally disrupted" when it had never existed at any time in her life? If her own mother could not – and Marina convincingly shows that she could not, not that she did not wish to – understand the poet-to-be, what could be expected of outsiders who did not even try to understand?

The poet has introduced us to the world of her childhood in order to show us how the "free element" overwhelmed her, separated her from other people and carried her away on the tide of poetry.

Her childhood was cut short, but life did not stand still. She had to get used to *real* orphanhood – the life of an adolescent girl without a mother. Neither her older sister Valeria nor any other female relative showed willingness to take over the upbringing of Marina and Asya. The task may have seemed too difficult: they were not like other girls in their circle. They now had only their father to protect and care for them, but he had no influence on Marina. His tact and tolerance were unlimited, but there was little he could do for young girls at an age when what they needed above all was a mother's help and understanding. Housekeepers followed one another in quick succession. Not one of them affected Marina's life in any way. The year after Maria Aleksandrovna's death Valeria went away to teach in a school at Kozlov, and when she returned set up house by herself. The family was falling apart. Tsvetaeva confided later on that she had "grown up without a mother, in other words I took every knock there was to take. The awkwardness of all who grow up motherless has remained with me. It is mostly internal. And the feeling of being an orphan." The feeling of orphanhood grew worse over the years. During the first year after her mother's death she lived and was educated at the Von Derwies boarding school on Staraya Basmannaya Street, going home only on Sundays and holidays. She was still drawn to revolutionary ideas and revolutionary literature – and, most unusual for such an establishment, she found her schoolfellows talking about revolution. The school authorities, however, were disinclined to tolerate the "free thinking" that Tsvetaeva brought with her. She was expelled in early spring, before the school year ended. Schoolwork no longer interested her. In the next three years she continued her education at two other schools, but it was a formality. She could not give up school without distressing her father, for whom education was a duty and a matter of the greatest importance. Marina "retired" from the school after the seventh grade. The eighth was meant to be a training course for teachers, and Marina was quite certain that this was something she would never be. After her mother's death she also gradually cut down and finally gave up piano playing: there was no longer anyone for whom she could make an effort, no one she could please or upset by her performance. Did her expulsion from the Von Derwies boarding school have a sobering effect? This was approximately the time which she singles out as another stage in her chronicle of "spiritual events":

16 years old. Break with ideology, in love with Sarah Bernhardt
("L'Aiglon"), outburst of Bonapartism. From 16 to 18 – Napoleon, Victor
Hugo, Béranger, Frédéric Masson, Thiers,* Memoirs, cult. French and
German poets.

Marina immersed herself in the age of Napoleon, lived in his world, reacted
to the victories and the failures of this genius of his age, and to the dramatic
fate of his son the Duke of Reichstadt, as though she was experiencing these
things herself. She surrounded herself with books, engravings, and portraits
connected with him, and even put Napoleon's portrait where the icon
should have been in her bedroom. This was plain sacrilege, but when her
father noticed it and tried to talk her out of it he was harshly rebuffed.
Marina fought for her intellectual freedom with a strength beyond her years.
She hardly ever went to school. In the morning she would hide in the attic
until her father left for his office, then go down to her room and lose herself
in the age of Napoleon. Having survived, but not outlived, this passion she
wrote to Rozanov in 1914: "at the age of 16 I fell madly in love with
Napoleon I and Napoleon II, and spent a whole year in my little room, away
from other people, alone in a vast world of my own . . .". The world which
had opened up before her was vast indeed: the world of history and
literature. Marina collected and read everything written about Napoleon in
the three languages she knew — memoirs, historical documents, mono-
graphs, poetry . . . What Marina loved was not so much the real Napoleon as
the Napoleonic legend. Whereas Pushkin was intrigued by Napoleon's
duality, the coexistence in a single person of "genius and wickedness" —

> Why was it you were sent and who sent you?
> Of what, of good or evil, were you the faithful perpetrator?
> Why did you fade away, why shine,
> You, wondrous visitor on earth?

— what stirred Tsvetaeva was Napoleon's extraordinary fate, his majestic
rise and — above all — his grievous fall. True to character, she inevitably
loved above all the prisoner of St Helena. She confesses in her diary that
"knowing myself, I know that I would have had the courage to fall in love
with Napoleon on the day of his fall." Curiously enough, Tsvetaeva did not
devote a single poem to Napoleon — probably because she had no wish to
compete with her great predecessor. She chose as her hero the young Duke
of Reichstadt, Rostand's *Aiglon*. In the noble and exalted youth, dreaming

* Sarah Bernhardt – the famous actress. Other names – all French figures of the nineteenth-
 century: Hugo and Béranger – poets, Masson – historian, Thiers – politician.

of his father's feats and his father's glory, but deprived of freedom, she saw the embodiment of her romantic ideals.

Inevitably, with her passion for Napoleon, she yearned for France, and fell in love with the ageing but still great Sarah Bernhardt in her role as L'Aiglon. It also inspired her first serious literary effort – she began translating Rostand. She could not wait to see Paris, and with her father's permission, she made her way there in the summer of 1909, a girl of sixteen, all by herself. Her excuse was that she wanted to study old French literature at the Sorbonne, but in reality she longed to pay homage at places connected with Napoleon, to breathe, "his" air, to see Sarah Bernhardt as L'Aiglon. The nostalgia for the past which had been with her since childhood fused with adolescent unease about the present and the future. Reality hardly existed for her, life seemed an insubstantial mirage. She lived surrounded by beloved ghosts. Paris did not alter this. She wrote, in Paris:

> The houses touch the stars, the sky is lower,
> The fume-laden earth is close to it.
> In immense and joyous Paris
> The same secret longing lingers.
>
> The evening boulevards are noisy,
> The last ray of sunset has faded,
> On all sides are couples, couples,
> Quivering lips and saucy glances . . .

She lived surrounded by beloved ghosts. She was eager to convince herself that it is possible to live without other people, that the bole of a chestnut tree can take the place of a friend's bosom (her affection for trees never left her).

> I am alone. It is so sweet
> To nestle my head against the chestnut's bole!
> And in my heart the verse of Rostand weeps
> As it wept in the Moscow I have left.
>
> Paris by night is alien and sad,
> Past madness is dearer to my heart:
> When I go home, the sadness of violets
> And someone's tender portrait are there,
>
> A brotherly, sorrowful countenance
> And a tender profile on the wall.
> Rostand and the martyr Reichstadt
> And Sarah – I shall dream of them all! . . .

But just a few months later Marina would begin to feel that trees and photographs were not enough, and that she needed human, masculine, love and friendship.

> By day I hide it, by day I'm silent.
> The moon is risen – I can no more!
> On these moonlit nights I desire
> To lean against the shoulder that I love.

Paris gave her a feeling of being much more grown up and independent, but also aggravated the pain of loneliness. True, the sisters had acquired two new friends before Marina went to Paris – Lidia Aleksandrovna Tamburer, a dentist who moved in Moscow literary and artistic circles, and the poet Ellis (Lev Lvovich Kobylinsky), the first real live poet Marina had met. Lidia Aleksandrovna became a friend of the whole Tsvetaev family, and is mentioned, though not by name, in Marina's essay on Voloshin and in her reminiscences of her father. How badly she needed an adult woman friend! Lidia Aleksandrovna could not, of course, take her mother's place, but she was fond of Marina and her verses, she was someone with whom it was possible to talk about literature, someone who could give advice on problems spiritual or mundane. Marina called her "the she-dragon", and the nickname caught on in her circle of friends. Years later Marina remembered her as "our common friend – friend of my old father's museum and of my juvenile verses, friend of my grown-up brother's vigils with rod and line and of my younger sister's first adult conquests, a friend to each of us singly and to the family as a whole, the one in whose friendship we found shelter when we no longer had a mother . . .". With the she-dragon around life was simple and cheerful, and she helped Marina through many trials in her adolescence.

Ellis flashed by like a meteor on the horizon of the Tsvetaev sisters, briefly illuminating worlds previously unknown to them, and disappeared leaving no mark on their minds. Marina remembered him as "the translator of Baudelaire, one of the most passionate early Symbolists, a chaotic poet, but a man of genius . . .". Ellis was indeed a remarkable man, a strange figure even at a time rich in unusual people. Rather than drawing on the recollections of some other literary figure I shall quote from N. Valentinov, a Marxist revolutionary who was in close contact with Symbolist circles in Moscow in 1907–1909. In his "Two Years with the Symbolists" he writes as follows:

> Ellis is unforgettable and, like A. Bely, unrepeatable. This strange person with intensely green eyes, a face of white marble, a little beard as black as if it had been lacquered, bright red "vampire" lips, turned night into day and day into night, living in a darkened room with the blinds always down

and candles burning before a portrait of Baudelaire, or later on a bust of Dante, had the temperament of a fanatical agitator, created extraordinary myths, produced all sorts of parodies and was an astonishing mimic. Bely used to say that Ellis was in thrall to "mediumism" . . . Combining Baudelairian propaganda with aspirations to the "infinite", and his *aspiration à l'infini* with occultism, he began entertaining me with splendid inventions in which contacts with other worlds, demoniac flights into the abyss, all sorts of *paradis artificiels*, Love and Death and Sin and Beauty were woven into a single chaotic and fantastic tapestry.

It is easy to imagine how interesting and attractive such a man must have seemed to the adolescent Marina and the barely adolescent Asya. Especially to Marina, who had already exhibited her hankering after "other worlds". Valentinov goes on:

> Ellis took it into his head to depict the "path to Eternity" for my benefit in Symbolist fashion. To reproduce the picture he knew of our (his and my) journey through the corridor of Eternity is quite beyond my powers. He conjures up the darkness, then the mysterious greyish-yellow and reddish-black spots of unknown provenance like birds beating against the luminous glass walls of the "corridor". We walk on and on, the path is endless. There are fires on every side of us, under us, above our heads, flickering out and flaring up again from one moment to the next. The grey gloom thickens. No end to the corridor can be seen. There is and can be no end. And in the infinite distance there is something frightening, unknown, tormenting. Or perhaps not something but someone. "Look there, look, right down the corridor, can you see it – isn't there something or someone barely visible there?" Ellis, in a spiritualistic trance, asks in agitation.

Valentinov, a grown-up and sober positivist, had no difficulty in breaking away from Ellis's spiritualistic spells. Not so Marina and Asya: they longed for the unusual. They set out with Ellis on fantastic voyages, but to his credit he did not whisk them off along the scary corridors of Eternity, but to fabulous worlds more appropriate to their age. Ellis describes one of these vigils in a poem dedicated to Marina and called "Into Paradise".

> The children settled on a couch,
> It was cold and night time out of doors,
> And above them, in a portrait
> Mother slept her final rest.

(There was in fact a picture of Maria Aleksandrovna in her coffin in Ivan Vladimirovich's study.)

(. . .)

Well then, whither shall we travel?
A hundred roads lie there before us,
And to which of our neighbours
Will the Unicorn then whirl us?

So once again we shall devise
To what we'll dedicate the night:
To the giants or to the pygmies,
As of wont we shall take flight . . .

For a time the sisters looked on Ellis as a wizard, and for him the house in Tryokhprudny Lane was one of many nests in which his disorderly, footloose life periodically landed him. Ivan Tsvetaev looked kindly on Ellis, as an educated man: he had graduated in economics from Moscow University, and had been invited to stay on, but his infatuation with Symbolist ideas had destroyed all interest in economics, and in Marxism, which he had found attractive in his youth. He had given up the idea of a career, lived on occasional literary earnings, and often went hungry. His ambition in life was to bring about the spiritual regeneration of the world, to combat the Spirit of Evil, which, according to his theory, had spread far and wide because of the corruption of man's nature. He thought that he found views identical with his own in Baudelaire, and was a passionate propagator, interpreter and translator of that poet's work. Ellis had studied a variety of social and economic theories, and had rejected them all, convinced that only a spiritual revolution would help mankind to overcome the Spirit of Evil. Dante and Baudelaire were his idols. Such was the man with whom Marina and Asya spent their evenings – and sometimes their nights! – listening to his inspired monologues, trying to keep up with his unbridled imaginings, making up stories of their own for him, and confiding their dreams for him to interpret. It was often almost daylight when they left the house to see him home through the quiet streets of Moscow. Valeria Tsvetaeva recalls that her father used to remove their coats from the entrance hall to prevent them doing this. But they didn't let it stop them. Asya would ride off on the box of a cab forgetting all about coats and with her hair flying in the wind . . . What use was scolding? When they parted from Ellis the girls found it hard to come down to earth again – to school and lessons and the prose of day-time. This friendship was at its warmest in the spring of 1909, when Ivan went to an archaeological congress in Cairo, and Marina and Asya found themselves free from any control at all.

What can have drawn Ellis to two girls who had only just left childhood behind them? He was, of course, flattered by their acceptance of his domination over their hearts and souls, but he evidently also had an intelligent appreciation of Marina's talent and her independent spirit. She read her verses to him – and her translation of *L'Aiglon*. [She discovered after completing it that it had already been translated by T. Shchepkina-Kupernik. She concealed the text, or destroyed it, and never mentioned it again.] Ellis listened with rapt attention and approval. No one had ever seriously discussed her work with her before. Even more important in reinforcing her self-assurance: Ellis, a real poet and critic whose work was published, read his own verses and translations to her! He wrote poems for both sisters – "Into Paradise" and "Guardian Angel" for Marina, "To the Former Asya", for Asya. These were subsequently included in his *Argo*.

Ellis opened up the world of contemporary Russian poetry for Marina, introduced her to the ideas and the debates of the Symbolists, recited their verses magnificently. It was then that Tsvetaeva fell in love "passionately but briefly" with the poetry of Valery Bryusov. With Ellis as her friend Marina, still a wild, shy, painfully awkward little girl, was entering adult life too soon. Anastasia Tsvetaeva tells us that when their friendship *à trois* was at its height Ellis without warning proposed to Marina, still barely seventeen. We can hear a vague allusion to this in her poem "A Mistake". He was, of course, refused: "at that time the word 'suitor' seemed indecent, and 'husband' (the word and the thing) simply impossible," Marina recalled, speaking of the relationship between Andrey Bely and his future wife Asya Turgeneva. Fortunately this episode did not spoil relations with Ellis. He introduced Marina, still a schoolgirl, to the Moscow literary circle at the centre of which his own life was spent. Early in 1910 he joined in founding the Musaget* publishing house, which became one of the focal points of literary and intellectual life in Moscow. Tsvetaeva became an habituée and also visited K. Krakht, in whose house the members of the "junior Musaget" assembled. She confessed later that she was completely incapable of understanding the papers and debates on literary theory, and treated them as she did maths lessons at school. It cost her an effort to break out of her voluntary isolation and move amongst other people. In her essay on Andrey Bely she stresses that she remained silent at gatherings in Musaget, out of shyness and "continually wounded pride".

That, of course, was true. But two pages later she contradicts herself and quotes a remark of her own which shows that in spite (or because?) of her shyness she could put on airs even in those days. "I don't like

---

* Moscow Publishing House of "junior" Symbolists.

Vyacheslav Ivanov, because he told me that my poems were like squeezed lemons. Just to see what I would say. What I said was 'you're absolutely right!' Gershenzon was very angry with me, simply furious the moment I said it." All the same, at Musaget and in the Free Aesthetics groups she saw and heard remarkable people, and found the atmosphere of creative fervour congenial. Ellis took some verses of hers for the proposed Musaget anthology. For Marina it was a great honour to appear in print side by side with the "Olympians" – Blok, Vyacheslav Ivanov, Andrey Bely, Mikhail Kuzmin, Nikolay Gumilyov . . . She was the youngest contributor to the collection.

The *Anthology* appeared in summer 1911, but unknown to her father, and although as a schoolgirl she was not supposed to do so, Marina had already brought out a volume of her own verse, *Evening Album*, in autumn 1910. Ellis was behind it. It was he who introduced the sisters to his friend Vladimir Ottonovich Nilender, the young Marina's first love. She would have been annoyed by that last sentence, since she always maintained that love was an emotion with which she had been familiar ever since she could remember, and that she would be hard put to it to decide who had been her first love "in earliest childhood, in pre-childhood". Nevertheless, Nilender was the first young man of flesh and blood to make Marina desire meetings, yearn, weep and write poems. She was seventeen, he was twenty-six. He, like her, lived for poetry, but his passion was for remote antiquity – he was a classical scholar, an investigator and interpreter of the ancient world. Ancient Greece was his spiritual home. At the time of his friendship with Tsvetaeva he was engaged in translating Orphic hymns and the "Fragments" of Heraclitus of Ephesus. Tsvetaeva's copy of the *Fragments*, published in 1910, has survived, with her marginal notes. The philosophical views of Heraclitus were congenial to Tsvetaeva, and became part of her mental furniture. As late as 1933 she used one of Heraclitus's most important tenets ("no one has ever stepped twice into the same river") as the epigraph to her article "Poets with History and Poets without a History". It was through Nilender too that she discovered Orpheus. Variations on the Orpheus theme would appear repeatedly in her verse.

"I first heard of Orpheus with the ears of my soul, not those of my head, from the man who was – or so I supposed at the time – my first love". The qualification – "so I supposed at the time" – need not worry us: Tsvetaeva never forgot Nilender, and refers to him several times in her prose though not by name. Apart from these references, and what we can deduce from her early poems, we know little about their relationship. According to Anastasia, Nilender was captivated by Marina, but their romance came to nothing. The time had come for her to long for love, to seek for an escape from her loneliness, but not yet to find it. She and Nilender decided not to meet any more. And "instead of a letter to the man with whom it was impossible for me to have any other contact", Tsvetaeva collected the poems she had written as a fifteen- and sixteen-year-old and brought out *Evening Album*. Publication in Russia was simplicity itself at that time – you had only to pay the printer. "Instead of a letter": these words defined the character of the book. Things which it had sometimes been difficult, and was now impossible to say face-to-face, she put into verse which "he" would read alone, as though it were a letter or a diary. This was the easy way to open her heart, without embarrassment or awkwardness or fear of using "the wrong words". We can understand why Marina read and re-read the diary of Marie Baschkirtseff and dedicated *Evening Album* to her "brilliant memory". A diary, like a letter, is conducive to greater candour and outspokenness than any other genre. The collection makes us think of a cosy evening in the light of an oil lamp, with girls whispering in the corner of a sofa and writing verses in each other's albums. Tsvetaeva's book was even printed on thick "album" paper and clad in a stout green binding.

What is the book about? You could say that it is about nothing in particular and at the same time about many things. The verses record the initiation of an adolescent soul into the world. First impressions of life crowd in on the poet's wide-open eyes and ears and heart. The happiness of being with her mother, the warmth of a comfortable home, the joyous discovery of nature, the disappointments of first love, friendship, school, books – it is all here. From this collection we can picture the author's feelings, her moods, even her daily routine. The *Album* has three parts. "Childhood" is the sisters' common childhood, before they became separate beings and each began to think of herself as "I" and not as part of "we". There are lovingly detailed memories of their games together, their friends, their grief for their mother. The reader cannot help being struck by the naturalness of Tsvetaeva's narrative and equally by her confidence that whoever reads her verses will understand her.

The section entitled "Love" is addressed to Nilender. In "Childhood" she had told him about her past: here she speaks of her present, her love, the pain of parting and of loneliness. We can see Marina and Asya growing apart: the verses to Ellis the Wizard are written in the name of both sisters, but in those connected with Nilender the "I" is Marina herself.

> You will be memorable to me, like the tenderest note
> In the awakening of the soul . . .

or:

> Our hall is yearning for you,
> – You scarcely saw it in the dark –
> Those words are yearning for you
> Which I didn't tell you in the dark . . .

In the section "Only Shadows", addressed to the "beloved shades" of Napoleon, the Duke of Reichstadt and his beloved, the "lady with the camellias", and Sarah Bernhardt, Nilender makes an appearance at the end, also transformed into a shade in the Elysium of Tsvetaeva's soul. The verses in *Evening Album* seem to me now extremely naïve and sentimental, and rather weak. Nonetheless, the book was a great success on its first appearance. M. Voloshin in *Morning Russia*, V. Bryusov in *Russian Thought*, N. Gumilyov in *Apollon*, and (in faraway Rostov-on-Don) the budding poet Marietta Shaginyan in *Priazovsky Kray*, all reviewed it warmly. They were struck above all by the freshness and intimacy of Tsvetaeva's verse. Voloshin wrote that it was sometimes uncertain and off key, like a child's voice, but able to convey nuances beyond the reach of "more adult" verse. Bryusov singled out Tsvetaeva's book from amongst the tremendous spate of verse collections by beginners who, as he put it, live in "a fantastic world of their own creation and seem to know nothing of what happens around us, of what we find ourselves saying and thinking, day in and day out . . . Marina Tsvetaeva's verses, by contrast, always set out from some real fact, something actually experienced." Gumilyov noted that Tsvetaeva's first book had brought something new into Russian poetry: "a new and bold, sometimes excessively bold, intimacy; her themes, infantile love for instance, are new, her undisguised, mad enthusiasm for the trivia of existence is something new." He wrote about the "inner talent" and the "inner originality of the young poetess: a poet wearing an expression unlike that of anyone else", had appeared on the horizon of Russian poetry. It was evident that Tsvetaeva was not susceptible to the influence of others. When she and Ellis were friends she had succeeded in resisting his "inculcation" of Baudelaire. When she was fascinated by Blok and Bryusov, and frequented Musaget, the headquarters of the Moscow Symbolists, she had remained untouched by Symbolist influence. She was from the very beginning one of a kind, different from all the others.

When a little while later, Voloshin, contradicting the poet Adelaida Gertsyk, undertook to discover literary influences of some sort in Tsvetaeva's work, he had the worst of the argument. Seizing on a few words in his review which displeased her, Marina charged into battle with the "maître", Valery Bryusov. Her behaviour looked like impertinence, a desire to "épater", but she effectively displayed her reasons for rejecting Symbolist poetics.

> One has to sing that all is dark,
> That dreams are hanging over the world . . .

— thus she defines that poetics, adding ironically:

> That is now the fashion.

She insists that the symbolist predilection for the nebulous is alien to her. By addressing this poem directly "to V. Ya. Bryusov" and including it in her second collection, Tsvetaeva declared war on him and incurred his hostility for many years to come.

Vladislav Khodasevich, writing much later about Nina Petrovskaya, one of the Moscow group of Symbolists, defines the essence of that literary movement in an extremely interesting way: "the Symbolists refused to separate the poet from the mass, his life in literature from his personal life. Symbolism refused to be merely an artistic school, a literary trend. It strove continuously to become a life-creating method . . . It was a succession of attempts, at times truly heroic, to find the philosopher's stone of art, a way of fusing life and art." In the struggle between "the writer" and "the man" in every Symbolist Khodasevich finds the explanation of the fact that their creative powers were to some extent squandered on "making poems out of the poet's personality". If, as I believe, this view of Symbolism is sound we can see that its theories were bound to be uncongenial to Tsvetaeva. I am not talking about her attitude to the poetry of the Symbolists, or her relations with some of them. She worshipped Blok, delighted in Bely, was friendly with Balmont and Voloshin, was ready to "sit at the feet" of Vyacheslav Ivanov. It is not a question of attraction to, or aversion from, this or that individual, but of different ways of apprehending the world. In Tsvetaeva's case there could be no question of "creating a poem out of her own life". She was a creature of duty — duty to poetry, and duty to her family. Her life was devoted to the fulfilment of those duties, and she very rarely defaulted. She was not engaged in "constructing" her life, but in living it according to a pre-arranged plan.

This may sound strange in relation to the adolescent girl whom we are considering in this chapter. At the time Tsvetaeva gave no thought at all to such matters. She was wild and wilful, careless of the opinions and concerns of those around her. At seventeen she started smoking, and conceived a passion for rowanberry liqueur, taking care that her father, whom she loved and respected, in spite of the worries she caused him, should not find out. Valeria remembers Marina throwing a liqueur bottle out of the window, without stopping to think that it would fall near the porch and might hit someone on the head. She remembered, too, an occasion on which her father arrived home in the evening to find the yardman firmly removing someone from the yard, " 'Who's that?' he asked. 'What's going on?' It turned out that Marina had advertised for a potential husband in the *Matrimonial Gazette*, giving her address. It was just a silly practical joke."

Mischievousness, refusal to study, contempt for generally accepted rules of conduct . . . Was she seeking relief from, compensation for, her overpowering feeling of loneliness? She was able to shut herself off from the world about her, and work tirelessly reading, composing, translating . . . At eighteen she had already translated *L'Aiglon* and published her first collection of verse. At nineteen she was the author of a second book. Perhaps, without realizing it, she was already following the path of duty. Did that make things any easier for her family? A year after her father's death she confessed that "he had no idea what to do with us and we caused him a great deal of suffering". The situation in Tryokhprudny Lane became more and more difficult: the family had no focal point and no common interests, every member of it went his or her own way. Ivan Tsvetaev's thoughts and efforts were wholly devoted to the museum, the completion of which was postponed from year to year. His health was deteriorating and he began to fear that he would leave his life's work unfinished. Moreover, from early 1909 onwards he was at loggerheads with the Minister of Education, his classmate at university, A. N. Shvarts. The theft of some engravings from the Rumyantsev Museum, of which Ivan Tsvetaev was still director, gave the minister an excuse to send in a series of investigating commissions in search of evidence to support accusations of negligence and malfeasance against the director. Shvarts three times applied to the Senate for permission to bring criminal charges against Tsvetaev, undeterred by the fact that the thief had been apprehended and many of the engravings recovered soon after their disappearance. The Senate examined the case three times and ended by dismissing it for lack of evidence. This "moral victory", however, cost Tsvetaev dear. Nicholas II read Shvarts's report without knowing about the Senate's decision and agreed to dismiss Tsvetaev, without regard to his twenty-eight years of service, and without granting him a pension. Where could he look for support and consolation now that Maria Aleksandrovna was no longer at his side? However sorry his children were for him, it was not in their character to show such feelings openly. He had so little in common with them, and no authority over them.

The youngest daughters had got into the habit of deceiving him, though they may only have told white lies so as not to upset him. Not one of his children would or could live by his "archaic" rules. With the unfairness characteristic of her years, Marina gives us an unkind portrait of her family in her poem "The Dining Room". Its members are "alien to each other in all things", indeed "enemies", and their life together in Tryokhprudny Lane is at best "peace for a plate of soup". Bryusov must have had this poem in mind when he wrote in his review of *Evening Album* that "as you read her book you feel embarrassed at times, as though you had indiscreetly peeped through an open window into someone else's home and witnessed a scene which outsiders were not supposed to see . . .". Valeria noted in her diary that

> things are not as they should be in Tryokhprudny Lane. It will all come right in the end, but we should be better off without all these clashes . . . .
> As I see it Marina doesn't close her eyes to it all. She is just organically unaware of other people, even those closest to her, except when she needs them. Some of her keys are mute. You can't call her either good-natured or mean. She is a creature of ungovernable impulses. She is capable of disregarding everything except herself. She is pig-headed. She is very clever, very talented. When she is working at something she really wants to do, it isn't work to her but sheer enjoyment. And she's still only an adolescent . . . Time will tell what will become of her. I just feel that I am losing touch with the Marina to whom I felt close when she was younger. Without a word spoken. It is just happening.

This entry in Valeria's diary is important because it describes Marina at what was for her the exceptionally difficult transitional period between girlhood and young womanhood. Her older sister seems to have seen how unusual Marina was, and understood her merits and her faults, yet to have had no wish to penetrate beneath the surface. For the older sister it was easier to "lose touch" than to enquire into what was happening to Marina. Yet Valeria was perhaps the only person who could have replaced her mother and given her the feminine sympathy and affection she so badly needed. True, Marina and Asya were closer in those years than at any time, but Asya was too young for Marina to confide in completely and needed help with her own inner storms.

In 1910, towards the end of winter, Marina apparently tried to commit suicide. Our only evidence for this is from the memoirs of Anastasia Tsvetaeva. The romance with Nilender had ended before it began, and Marina felt that there was no escape from her loneliness. Spring was on the way, and Asya was with Tyo at Tarusa. Marina had stayed behind: Sarah Bernhardt was visiting Moscow on tour, and she had bought tickets for every performance. Asya sensed before she left Moscow that her sister had some sort of plan in connection with *L'Aiglon*. When Marina appeared at Tarusa a little later she let slip the phrase "it didn't come off". What didn't? Asya decided later from hints her sister dropped that she had intended to shoot herself during a performance of *L'Aiglon*, but that the revolver had not gone off. Was this true? It seems likely that Anastasia remembered and understood these hints thirty years later when she received at third-hand an old letter written by her sister before a suicide attempt. Unfortunately the letter is lost, and there are serious inconsistencies in Anastasia's recollections. Perhaps there was no suicide attempt after all? Perhaps Marina found relief from unbearable tension in writing her farewell letter? Writing was always her way out of life's tight corners. But even if there was only a suicide note, and no suicide attempt, we can still see how troubled Marina's mind was as she reached adolescence, how oppressed she was by loneliness and her − at first sight − self-afflicted, bookish seclusion.

Her friendship with Nilender had been still-born. Ellis's visits to the house in Tryokhprudny Lane had ended after the scandal in spring 1910 when he had cut pages out of books in the Rumyantsev Library. His association with the Tsvetaev sisters was not broken off, but the friendship became less intense, and a faint tinge of irony crept into it. Marina would write in autumn 1911 that she did not like the idea of asking Ellis to introduce her future husband to Musaget. And in her narrative poem "The Sorcerer" (1914), recalling the ecstatic love which she and Asya had felt for him, Marina is frankly ironical both about her former self and about the hero of the poem. Aleksandr Blok once said of Ellis, in a letter to Andrey Bely: "I am afraid of Ellis. There is something alien and horrible in him . . . when I suddenly catch sight of him and he turns one of his many faces towards me." Blok was not alone in saying that Ellis could be horrible and terrifying, but he never showed those "faces" of his to the youthful sisters. They were shown only his "nice" side − the excitable enthusiast, the ebullient fantasist always full of enthusiasm and antipathies, and in retrospect, just a little comic . . . The Ellis epoch in Marina's life was over.

It was followed immediately by the Voloshin epoch, ushered in by his article about her *Evening Album*. The friendship which sprang up between them was at first purely literary. Voloshin tried to interest Tsvetaeva in the books which preoccupied him at the time, and she in turn told him what she liked best. In the first period they were "feeling each other out". In spite of Voloshin's good will towards her and her work Tsvetaeva did not immediately commit herself to this new friendship. As she wrote at an early stage of their acquaintance:

> Are you desperately grown up? Oh, no!
> You are a child and you need toys,
> That is why I fear a trap,
> Why my greeting is restrained . . .

But in spite of the great difference in age between them (Voloshin was the older by sixteen years) it was not long before they found a common language. As early as spring 1911, in letters written from Gurzuf, Tsvetaeva is opening her heart to Voloshin as a trusted friend. She speaks of the sea, but we can hear in her words her longing for a Human Being: "I gaze upon the sea – from afar, or close by, dipping my hands into it, but it is never mine, and I never belong to it. There is no way of merging with and dissolving in it." This – the impossibility of "merging and dissolving" – was to be a constant theme in Tsvetaeva's work. In a letter dated 18 April 1911, she half-jokingly calls Voloshin "Monsieur mon père spirituel", but the contents of the letter are serious: it is, as she emphasizes at the end of it, almost a confession. In spite of the naïveté of some flat statements ("The doctor cannot understand the poem! He must be either a bad doctor or an insincere man . . ."), Marina is clearly capable of analysing and soberly assessing her condition: "The fault lies with books and with my deep mistrust of real, everyday life . . . I can forget myself only when I am alone, and only in a book, over a book! I have got more from books than from people. Memories of people always pale in comparison with memories of books – I am not speaking of childhood memories, only about adults!" She imagines that she has lived through it all in her mind, and life seems to her flat and coarse. "Does this mean that I can never be happy?" she asks Voloshin, and herself. And, finally, a confession that would remain significant through the years ahead: "I am left with a feeling of utter loneliness, for which there is no cure. Another person's body is a wall, preventing me from seeing the soul within. Oh how I hate that wall!"

> Assuage my soul! (Without touching lips,
> We cannot assuage our souls!) By clinging to lips
> We also cling to Psyche, flitting guest of lips . . .
> Assuage my soul; and thus assuage my lips.

These verses, written twelve years later, surely echo her girlish letter. All her life, Tsvetaeva wanted to rise above the body and mingle with others only on the spiritual plane. Here, in 1911, she expects from Voloshin "a human answer, not one out of a book".

When we think of Tsvetaeva in early youth we see a spell-bound soul wandering lost in a forest of books, in a kingdom of shadows. She lived in the enchanted world of her loneliness, unable to find her way out of it. Her first book ended with a prayer:

Give me to understand, oh Christ, that not all is merely shadow,
Let me, at last, not a mere shadow embrace!

CHAPTER 3

"SUN – NOT BLOOD – SWELLS MY VEINS"

THE SPELL WAS BROKEN – as it was supposed to be, according to her childhood fairy tales – by a beautiful prince. His name was Sergey Efron. He found Marina at Koktebel on 5 May 1911 – and delivered her from the realm of shadows.

What is this strange word – Koktebél? Its origin is a matter of controversy, but some scholars interpret it to mean "Blue Height". It lies, indeed, in a hollow amongst the mountains on the southeastern coast of the Crimea. Its story goes back into the forgotten past. Traces of the Scythians and the Pechenegs, as well as of medieval Italian and Armenian settlements, are still to be found in Koktebel's soil. The modern development of Koktebel began no more than a quarter of a century before the event which I am about to relate. It was no easy matter: the region was waterless, and uninhabited except for a tiny Tatar-Bolgar village, the landscape was weird and rather frightening – created millions of years ago by an eruption of the Kara Dag (Black Mountain) volcano, long since extinct, now forming the western end of the Gulf of Koktebel. It is easy to imagine that the eruption happened only yesterday, that nothing has changed since, that the earth has not yet cooled (in summer it is always red-hot from the sun, and burns the soles of your feet through light summer shoes), that all those wrinkles and folds in the earth's surface, still bare of vegetation, record a recent battle of the elements. Only a very unusual mentality could take a liking to that "tragic landscape" and want to settle there.

Maksimilian Voloshin's mother, Elena Ottobaldovna, was one of Koktebel's first inhabitants. She bought a plot right by the sea and began building while her son was still at school. She spent a large part of the year in Koktebel, and Max would return there from all his wanderings. Gradually, after visiting many other lands, he came to love Koktebel and the Eastern Crimea, which he identified with the ancient Cimmeria, Homer's land on the rim of the world and at the gate of Hades:

. . . The sorrowful land of the Cimmerians, for ever covered
In damp mist and hazy cloud . . .

Cimmeria was a link with the Mediterranean — you could people it with myths. The fantastic landscape conjured up associations with ancient Greece and with biblical history. This is how Voloshin, who was the first to find in Koktebel a subject for art — as poet and as watercolourist — describes it:

Eurydice's feet have trodden the wide stone staircases in those rocky gorges and left no trace. A crowded and chaotic landscape — a jumble of ridges heaped up by earthquakes, valleys like the vale of Jehoshaphat on the Day of Judgement, glades with a covering of fine mountain grass, the Cyclopean walls of phantom cities, stairways to Hades . . . And this extraordinary jumble is so monochrome that after a dozen steps you feel hopelessly lost in a labyrinth without exit. At midday when the sun stands vertically over Opuk (the mountain on which, according to ancient tradition, the city of Cimmericon stood — V.S.) and mirages begin to float in in the mist over the distant plains, you can imagine that here as on Sinai, the ground beneath your feet is "paved" with sapphires and burns like the blue sky. At such a moment the visitor really does experience the "noonday panic".

Over the years, the Voloshins' home at Koktebel began to "sprout" people. Koktebel could never become a fashionable resort — it was very much an acquired taste. It lacked the luxuriant evergreen vegetation usual in the Southern Crimea; there was no shade, no promenade, none of the usual pleasant walks to stretch the holidaymaker's legs, no restaurant. Just sun, mountains, and sea. Elena Ottobaldovna charged next to nothing for rooms in her house. The guests clubbed together to feed themselves, or else walked over a mile to the one and only eating house, kept, as Tsvetaeva recalls, by "the best-natured woman in the world". Luxury was provided by the one café — a sort of wooden shed decorated by the painters and poets of Koktebel, where you could eat a hot roll, drink real Tatar or Turkish coffee, and buy chocolate. If you were hard up, ample credit was available at the Voloshins', at the eating house and at the café. People more interested in the strange landscape and in cheerful and friendly company than in the comfort and glamour of actual resorts began to frequent Koktebel. Voloshin wrote later: "We made only one condition: every new arrival must be welcomed as our own personal guest."

The previous winter, Voloshin had invited Marina and Asya to spend the summer of 1911 at Koktebel. After a month of solitude at Gurzuf, after a journey of eighty kilometres — "a whole day's travel in a creaking cart through the wilds of the Eastern Crimea" – Marina found herself in that land unlike any other, fabulous and fantastic Koktebel. Asya was to join her later.

One of the first people Marina met there was Sergey (Seryozha) Efron.

SERYOZHA

> He is slim with the slimness of young branches.
> His eyes so beautifully useless!
> Under the wings of his brows, flung widely open,
> Are two bottomless depths . . .

He was still just a boy, not yet eighteen, a year younger than Marina, tall and thin, with a slight stoop. Huge, luminous eyes brooded in his beautiful, sensitive poetic face.

> There are enormous eyes
> Of the colour of the sea . . .

"Efron eyes": Seryozha's sisters, and later on Tsvetaeva's daughter, had them too. "Someone you don't know comes into the room, you see those eyes, and you know at once that's an Efron", I was told by an artist who had known them all at Koktebel.

Maybe everything really began from the pebble of Koktebel? Many semi-precious stones lay hidden on the Koktebel beaches. People dug them up, made collections of them, showed off their finds to each other. Elena Ottobaldovna even used them to ornament the kaftans she made for herself, for her friends or for sale. In Tsvetaeva's memory her first meeting with Seryozha was associated with one of these pebbles.

> 1911. I had had measles, and my hair was cropped short. I was lying on the beach, digging, and Max Voloshin was digging beside me.
> "Max," I said, "the only man I can marry is the one who guesses which of all the stones on the beach is my favourite."
> "Marina," said Max in his honeyed voice, "I dare say you know already that people in love grow stupid. So if the man you are to love brings you a cobblestone, you will quite sincerely say that's your favourite!"
> "No, Max! Everything that happens to me makes me cleverer! Even love!"
> What I had said came true. Almost on the first day we met, S. Ya. Efron dug up and presented to me a Genoan cornelian bead, which I still have by me to this day.

That was written in 1931, but their daughter still had the pebble at the beginning of the seventies.

Marina and Seryozha took to each other at once, and forever. Eagerly, ecstatically she immersed herself in his family history. Everything in it was out of the ordinary, reminding her of books she had loved since childhood, and therefore unbearably dear to her. His was a strange ancestry: his maternal grandfather, a handsome and brilliant captain of lifeguards, came from the aristocratic Durnovo family, his maternal grandmother was of merchant stock. On his father's side Seryozha's forebears were Jewish, and his great-grandfather may have been a rabbi.

> In his visage tragically there merged
> Two ancient races . . .

Elizaveta Petrovna Durnovo and Yakov Konstantinovich Efron had met at a clandestine gathering of revolutionary populists. Both were active members first of the "Land and Freedom" party, then of its "Black Partition" faction. Both were in favour of terrorist methods. Yakov Efron is known to have taken part in at least one political assassination.

The revolutionary N. A. Morozov describes Elizaveta Durnovo as a "tall, stately young lady, with a pale face and enormous luminous eyes." A sister revolutionary remembered her as a "beautiful, energetic, vivacious woman, who stood out amongst the half-hearted and excessively reasonable Muscovites." Liza (Elizaveta) Durnovo was one of those idealistic Russian girls of good family whom compassion for the sufferings of the "simple people" led along the road of revolutionary struggle and in the end to terrorism. She owed her conception of "the people" to the verses of Nekrasov: "Until I read them I thought that the educated were far superior to the common people. Reading them convinced me that the educated lose the most precious thing of all — spiritual purity." From the 1860s on successive generations of Russian youth followed the strange and tragic path that began with the quest for truth, freedom and spiritual purity, and ended in hatred and the justification of political murder on moral grounds.

Liza Durnovo became a revolutionary populist at the beginning of the 1870s. Though there is no evidence that she herself took part in terrorist acts, we know that she not only approved of terror, but became, during the first Russian revolution [1905], a member of the most extreme terrorist organization, the Maximalists.

She devoted her whole life to the revolution, even though she had nine children. (Three of them died in infancy.) The older Efron children also joined the revolutionary movement. The family home in Moscow, and their dacha at Bykovo, were always full of underground people, revolutionary literature and even weapons. There was endless political debate, because, tight as their family ties were, the mother and her daughters had different political allegiances: the daughters belonged to the Socialist Revolutionary Party. Letters reflecting these disagreements found their way into Elizaveta Durnovo-Efron's dossier in the Tsarist secret police archives. One of the daughters wrote of her mother: "she is now a fanatical Maximalist, and believes in it with such passionate sincerity . . . I have tried arguing with her, but it's no good." Seryozha most probably took no part in these arguments. He was one of the two youngest children, and there was a gap of five to ten years between them and their older siblings. But he listened, and like any adolescent had views of his own.

There would seem to be nothing in common between Seryozha's background and that of Marina: the conservative and loyalist Tsvetaev family bore no resemblance to the fanatically revolutionary Efrons. Their interests and way of life were entirely different. But Seryozha and Marina did have one thing, and a very important thing, in common. They had both been left motherless at an early age.

Seryozha's mother was arrested in summer 1906. (Her second arrest – the first had been in 1880.) She was to have been tried with the eighty-six members of the "Moscow Opposition", but relatives obtained her release on bail nine months later, in view of her poor health. She was now over fifty, but, just as she had done twenty-seven years ago, she escaped abroad, this time not alone, but with her son Kostya, who was two years younger than Seryozha. Seryozha, at fourteen, was left in the care of his older sisters. In effect he was orphaned at the same age as Marina, and also lost his beloved brother and playmate. The separation was painful to him. True, he spent one summer with them in Switzerland. But in January 1910 Kostya came home from school in Paris and hanged himself. The reason for his suicide remains uncertain. The newspapers at the time said that the boy was upset by a dressing-down from a teacher. I have read somewhere that he hanged himself accidentally while playing at "the revolutionary's execution". Elizaveta in despair hanged herself that same night. She was buried together with her son. Luckily for him, Yakov Efron had died earlier in Paris, in the summer of 1909.

Their meeting gave Tsvetaeva all that her heart had longed for: heroism, romance, self-sacrifice, unusual people, exalted feelings. And Seryozha himself was so beautiful, so young, so pure, and so powerfully drawn to her, as though she alone, and no one and nothing else, could bind him to this life. Years after that summer at Koktebel, in her last cycle of love

poems, to Anatoly Shteiger, "Poems to an Orphan" – that word again! –
Tsvetaeva gave a precise definition of her attitude to people:

> At long last I have met
> The one I need:
> Someone has a desparate
> Need of me . . .

She was mistaken on that occasion, as she almost always had been in the
past. But with Seryozha her hopes were realized: he was the only one in her
life who needed her "as he needed bread". They rushed into each others'
arms to overcome their loneliness by merging each into the other. And not
every poet is so lucky – Seryozha liked at once, and never ceased liking,
Marina's poetry, understood that she was a genius and could not be "like
everybody else". Very shortly after their first meeting, not later than the
end of 1911, he wrote his story "The Enchantress", a faithful portrait of the
young Tsvetaeva. There is no doubt that Mara, the heroine of the story, is
Marina. Mara's appearance is that of Tsvetaeva between the ages of sixteen
and eighteen: "A big little-girl in a navy-blue sailor suit, with short light
hair, a round face, green eyes that looked straight into mine . . ." Mara's
words – "I am no good at proving things. I don't know how to live, but my
imagination has never betrayed me, and never will" – are surely Marina's.
Mara quotes lines from Marina's poems as though they were her own, and
recounts episodes from "her" childhood with which we are familiar from
Tsvetaeva's autobiographical prose.

Sergey Efron gives us two contrasting versions of Mara – one sarcastic,
one ecstatic. The "sober view" of her is that of the older members of a family
with whom Mara is staying as a guest. They find her a strange and awkward
young woman, far too self-assured for her age, behaving and speaking in a
deliberately provocative way. Mara's (Marina's) awkwardness was
probably the result of the shyness that tormented her all her life. In the
story, Mara loses her shyness with children. In the nursery at night with
two little boys (one of them, Kira, a self-portrait of Seryozha) she can be
herself, make up stories with them, tell them about her own childhood and
about the things that are most important to her . . . They adore her, and
understand that she is not mad, as the grown-ups suppose, but an
enchantress. The boy with the "aquamarine eyes" –

> (. . . Aquamarine and chrysoprase
> Of his greeny-blue and bluey-grey
> Constantly half-closed eyes . . .)

– never lost this certainty through all the ups and downs of their life together.

What was Sergey Efron himself like? To Tsvetaeva he was a paragon, a phenomenon from another age, her knight without reproach. Others who met Efron often saw him in the same light. He had charm and a sense of humour. People talked about his chivalry, his exceptional dignity, his unquestionable honesty, his impeccable manners. Tsvetaeva was not the only one who thought that he resembled a medieval knight. I have, however, met people who found him weak and spineless, not particularly clever or able. He was a dilettante. He studied for a while in a drama school, appeared in a few plays, dabbled in literature, tried his hand at art history. A woman who had known both of them well in emigration told me that "he was a nice man, but weak – you could do whatever you liked with him." But even those who spoke of him in this way cast no doubt on his honesty and nobility.

Tsvetaeva was aware of a certain "incompleteness" in Seryozha. A strange comparison makes a fleeting appearance in a manuscript from 1913:

> Were he a girl – few moons would he
> Have met, sitting at a weaving-frame . . .
> A brush, a sword or strings
> Fingers ask for.

For the present he is only a boy with whom she stands on the threshold of life:

> Dearest, dearest, we're like gods:
> The whole world lies before us!

But she has confidence in him and in his future: his honesty and nobility guarantee it. She expects miracles from him. For years Sergey Efron was to be the romantic hero of Tsvetaeva's poetry. I emphasize the word romantic. The poems addressed to him as her husband are not love lyrics in the ordinary sense – there is no passion, no jealousy, there are none of the usual amorous protestations. More than twenty of Tsvetaeva's poems are addressed to and dedicated to Efron, or connected with him in some way – and there is not a single erotic note anywhere in them. Does this tell us something about the character of the relationship which developed between them? Soon after their first meeting she begs him:

> Do not hinder me in my surprise,
> Be in the terrible secret, like a boy,
> And help me to remain,
> Although a wife, a little girl.

Her verses to her husband are never night verses. Even when after a five-year separation she found him, and, as she herself thought, her life again, the poem celebrating their reunion ends with these lines:

> Life: the wide-open joy of greeting
> Each other in the morning!

I would not, even it if were possible, wish to pry into the details of Tsvetaeva's intimate life with her husband. One researcher has detected a hint in Sofia Parnok's ironical lines: "Not you, O youth, released her from her spell". But wide-open joy is not easily discounted — and Tsvetaeva never addressed such radiant words to anyone else. There would be no one else in her life like Seryozha. It was as though the "wall of the body" had collapsed, and their lives had been built anew on foundations of spiritual affinity.

Now, at the beginning of the path, she hastened to recast her hero in a mould created by her imagination. She projected onto Seryozha the reflected glory of the heroic young generals of 1812, and of the knights of old. She was not just assured of his high destiny. The earliest of her poems addressed to Seryozha have an imperious ring: Tsvetaeva seems to be conjuring destiny, to be saying "I will have it so".

> I wear with challenging pride his ring
> — Yes, in Eternity a wife, not just on paper.
> His inordinately narrow face
> Resembling a sword . . .

These are the first lines of a poem in which she paints a romantic portrait of Seryozha and predicts his future. Each line is a step leading upwards to the pedestal — or the scaffold? — of the concluding words:

> In him I am faithful to chivalry.
> To all of you who fearless lived and died.
> In fateful times such people
> Compose verses — and ascend the block

She could not know that the "fateful times" were not so far away. Then Seryozha turned into the White warrior and the White Swan of her *The Camp of the Swans*, *Parting* and *Craft*. At the same time she refashioned her earlier poems dedicated to him, making her comparisons more precise and raising her hero to new heights:

> Of your regiment — a dragoon,
> Decembrists and men of Versailles:

> And one cannot know – he is so young –
> Whether his fingers ask for a brush,
> A sword or strings.

The reference to "the men of Versailles "is significant – Seryozha was by then in the White Army.

Only a flawless human being could have lived up to the demands which Tsvetaeva's poems to her husband made on him. Of no one else – except perhaps herself – would she expect so much. No one else would she elevate to such heights. She was searching for her ideal romantic hero, whom she would later find embodied in the concept of the Poet.

There can be no doubt that Tsvetaeva felt herself an adult person beside this stripling. And he gladly accepted her seniority: significantly, in his story Mara is seventeen and Kira only seven years old! Marina may, without realizing it, have begun by adopting Seryozha as her son. In all Marina's attachments, passion and maternal sentiment went together. In her relationship with her husband, love, concern and tolerance went with an urge to direct his life along the channel of her choosing.

Ilya Erenburg, who knew them both in his early years, and helped them to find each other after the Civil War, shared with me his idea that it was Marina who "moulded" Sergey Efron's personality and set the pattern of his life. "She was a poet," Erenburg said, "so he started writing . . ." That is true. The poetic force-field round Tsvetaeva was so strong that those closest to her – her sister, her husband, her younger daughter – all began writing. Anastasia Tsvetaeva published in 1915 and 1916 two prose works (*Royal Reflections* and *Smoke, Smoke, Smoke*) with philosophical pretensions and obviously influenced by Rozanov. *Childhood*, a collection of stories by Sergey Efron appeared in 1912. Alya Efron, Marina's daughter, was not much more than five years old when she began keeping a diary and writing verse. "Tsvetaeva wrote monarchist poems," Erenburg went on, "so Efron joined up – what, you may wonder, could the White Army mean to a Jew like him?" What indeed? Given the Efron family tradition the logical place for him was in the ranks of the "Reds", and it may be that his break with that tradition had a fatal effect on his whole subsequent career. But his mixed origins, as well as Marina's influence, were of importance here. Though half-Jewish he was baptized in the Orthodox church.

> In his visage tragically there merged
> Two ancient races . . .

Why "tragically"? Was he himself conscious of the ambiguity of his position as a "half-breed", and did he suffer as a result? Was it this that gave a more painful resonance to the word "Russia"?

> What a handsome man: A half-breed!
> By whom baptized? In what font? . . .

Tsvetaeva asked this question of another Sergey – but it could equally well have been addressed to Efron. The Volunteer army and the struggle to save monarchist Russia were to be his second baptism. The tragedy was that the choice he made was not final. He was tossed from side to side. As an émigré he very shortly abandoned the cause of the White Volunteers, began to feel guilty towards the new Russia, and embraced "Eurasianism"* with a more and more pronounced pro-Soviet bias.

Erenburg worked out his theory to its logical conclusion. "In emigration Tsvetaeva wrote her 'Homesickness', and Efron organized his 'Association for Return to the Motherland' . . ." This is true, but susceptible to more than one explanation. Homesickness for the lost motherland is a natural feeling for any exile. In Tsvetaeva it went with an outright refusal to accept what had happened and was happening in Russia. To enter the service of yesterday's enemy was for her something unnatural and sacrilegious. Efron was torn between his wife's moral (and political – though she was outside and above politics) clarity and firmness, and the amoral tradition of his family. Family tradition prevailed, and he began collaborating with the Cheka,† just as half a century before his father had participated in at least one political murder. Efron's youthful indecision, which Tsvetaeva sensed but was not fully aware of, meant in fact that he had no fixed centre. The metamorphosis of the "knight errant", the "Decembrist",‡ the "hero of Versailles", into a common-or-garden Chekist had tragic results for Efron and for his whole family.

As long as he lived Sergey was not only her husband but her son, and the most difficult of all her children. The roots of this relationship were in their early orphanhood, and in Marina's intuitive understanding of any human being's need of a mother. But, as so often happens, the son did not take the path chosen by his mother: even love was helpless there. The gulf between them opened up along a political line of cleavage. Their relationship reached its logical limit – and should have ended – but it would not die. Tsvetaeva would remain to the end a dutiful wife and friend, true to the vow she had made to herself and before the altar.

---

* Many émigré intellectuals in the 1920s and '30s embraced this view of Russians as half-Asian and of the Soviet régime as a manifestation of the Asian half: savage, but dynamic and creative.
† Secret Police, set up by Lenin in 1917 to fight "Counter-Revolution".
‡ Participant in the December 1825 uprising against the tsarist autocracy.

But that was all in the distant future. For the time being, in summer 1911, the future was a fairy tale with a happy ending. For the first time Marina loved and was loved. She had found someone who needed her. She began fussing over Seryozha from the moment they met. He was still a schoolboy, and had suffered from tuberculosis since early adolescence. She worried about his health, his diet, his comforts, his school-leaving exam, his university entrance – and, later on, his army service. Her "seniority" made her free and independent. She wrote to Voloshin shortly before her wedding to say: "I have coped with many things that used to seem impossibly difficult, and I shall go on coping. I must be very strong, and must believe in myself, otherwise life will be impossible! It's strange, Max, to feel suddenly quite independent. It comes as a great surprise to me – I always assumed that someone else would arrange my life."

She was barely nineteen. Happiness lay before her and Seryozha.

> First and genuine happiness
> Not from books!

Koktebel took its visitors back to the primitive. The harshness of the place gave them no choice. Tsvetaeva recalls "the bare rocks, the moraine shore, not a bush, not a spring, nothing green except high in the mountains (peonies there big as a child's head), otherwise nothing but steppe-grass, wormwood, the sea, the wilderness . . .". The landscape dictated the Koktebelians' dress, which shocked the few "normal" summer visitors (not guests of the Voloshins). Max himself wore a long and roomy canvas smock, knee-length drawers and sandals without socks. His "forest" of hair was bound with a leather strap, or a wreath of wormwood. Elena Ottobaldovna – whom her friends and even her friends' children always called "Pra", meaning "Pramater" [original mother] – walked around in a kaftan, Turkish trousers and soft Tatar slippers. The other women also wore Turkish trousers: more convenient for scrambling over the rocks and climbing mountain tracks! This form of dress, and the long poetry readings far into the night on the high open terrace of the Voloshin house, gave rise to any amount of malicious gossip. Anything different is always evil and menacing to your "normal" citizen.

Even drinking water was in short supply at Koktebel (it had to be brought from a distance), and food was not as plentiful as you would expect in a resort. "The only milk was thin and bitter (from goats fed on steppe-grass and wormwood), there were never any warm home-made rolls, in fact there were no rolls at all, only dry Turkish pretzels, and even those were in limited supply . . . But still . . . it was a place in which inspiration thrived. You felt that you were cheek by jowl with the elements. Fire, a sun that baked the earth until it cracked and burnt your feet through the soles of summer shoes. Earth, newly emerged from chaos, but already ancient in its wrinkled bareness. Air, which together with the sunbaked earth sometimes created fantastic mirages. Water, the sea, coming and going like a living creature, eternally talking in a language of its own, forgotten by man . . ."

> . . . And now Homer is silent,
> And the Black Sea, in its oratory, roars
> And with heavy thunder approaches my pillow.*

Tsvetaeva, who had always lived in the company of the Greek gods and heroes, and had recently heard "with the ears of her soul" the Orphic hymns from the lips of Nilender, entered effortlessly into the legend of Cimmeria created by Voloshin. Ancient myths came to life again: Orpheus had come to this place to descend into Hades in search of Eurydice; on this shore Odysseus had met the shade of his dead mother, and the Amazons had prepared for battle . . . It may seem strange that Tsvetaeva wrote hardly any poems dealing directly with Koktebel, though we cannot be entirely sure of that because one volume of verse written in those years was never published and has disappeared. We may nevertheless suppose that Koktebel sank into her consciousness, to surface again from time to time throughout her creative life. When she turned to subjects and images from antiquity, it was the unique landscape of Koktebel she saw with her inner eye; her whole body throbbed with the memory of its mountain tracks, its rocks, its deserted beaches.

Koktebel became a little world of its own — a world of union with nature, friendly fun and unconstrained freedom. There were so many jokes, pranks, innocent or less innocent mystifications of which Max himself was the heart and soul. Bathing, collecting pebbles, mountain rambles, trips to Stary Krym or Feodosia, the frugal but always noisy communal meals, tea-drinking at the big unpainted table on the Voloshins' terrace — everything became a festival. But no one was ever idle. All had work of their own to do in the afternoon. The artists wandered off to make sketches, while others sought solitude in the mountains, by the sea, or in their rooms, and wrote. It was in Koktebel, in summer 1913, that Magda Nakhman painted her

---

* From "Sleeplessness . . ." (1915) by Osip Mandelstam.

portraits of Marina and Seryozha. One of the habitués of Koktebel told me that Nakhman always prettified her subjects, but in my view she has depicted the soul of the "enchantress", as Efron called her. This, the only portrait for which Tsvetaeva ever sat, still exists in Moscow. Nakhman's portrait of Efron hung on Anastasia Tsvetaeva's wall, and disappeared when she was arrested. Only a photograph of it survives.

In the evenings – which sometimes went on till next morning – they gathered under the open sky on Max's turret to "worship the moon", reciting verse, listening to the sea, arguing about art, discussing each other's paintings, sketches, and writings . . . They were mad about callisthenic dancing. Vera Efron, Sergey's sister, who had studied "plastic dance" in Rabenek's "school of rhythm and grace", directed them, and even Pra and Max, all six poods* of him, joined in. Voloshin's "Sonnets of Koktebel" humorously record some of the livelier moments. Tsvetaeva is mentioned in two of them. In "Morning", "Marina sleeps and dreams of nonsense" – no idle joke: dreams were enormously important to her all her life. In "Gaydan", Marina is seen through the eyes of one of the innumerable Koktebel dogs with whom she was on the friendliest of terms. Gaydan tells of his love:

> As I walked with them, I got to know them.
> There were many of them, but I went with one.
> She slept alone in the dust with me,
> And I knew not what name to call her.
>
> With her shaggy locks she resembles
> Our women. Of a night under the moon
> I howled for her, bit my straw mattress
> And in her tobacco smoke sensed her presence . . .

The shaggy locks were of course Marina's. (Her hair was just growing again after repeated razor-cuts: she hoped that it would start curling, and in the end it did.) Marina was devoted to dogs, and she lived in the smoke of her everlasting cigarettes. In a group photograph taken at Koktebel she is squatting on her heels, with her arms round a big dog – perhaps Gaydan?

From that summer right up to the Revolution Tsvetaeva frequently visited Koktebel. She spent one or two months there almost every year, in spring or summer. The winter of 1913–1914 she spent with her family in Feodosia, where Seryozha obtained his school-leaving certificate as an external student at the local high school. Koktebel delivered her from her

---

* 216 lbs.

bookish seclusion and helped others to discover her. It was in a sense a substitute for the house in Tryokhprudny Lane, and the now completely disrupted Tsvetaev household. She began to think of Koktebel, with Pra and Max, as a fortress in which she could take shelter from any of life's storms.

All this – Cimmeria, the noisy, merry, motley, youthful company, to which she was so unused, love, Seryozha, his sisters – had happened so suddenly. She and Seryozha, just the two of them, went on from Koktebel to the Ufa steppe, to drink *kumys* [mare's milk]. Asya and her lover – she was not yet seventeen, he was eighteen – left from the Feodosia station the same day for Moscow, and on to Finland. The two sisters were beginning to drift apart.

All this was carefully concealed from Ivan Vladimirovich Tsvetaev. Letters and money from home were forwarded from Koktebel. His illness was one reason for their secrecy. At the beginning of September, on one of his regular trips abroad for the museum, Ivan Vladimirovich landed in hospital. "My heart has become weak," he wrote to a colleague in the museum. "I only noticed after I had made the round of all the towns on my itinerary that I was having to hold on the walls of houses, and sit down frequently on the boulevards for fear of falling. Well, perhaps I shall pull out of it before it gets too bad." He did "pull out of it", and was back in Tryokhprudny Lane early in October. A surprise awaited him: Marina was getting married, and she and Seryozha, together with Lilya and Vera Efron, had already rented an apartment in a new building on Sivtsev Vrazhek. We can imagine that Ivan Tsvetaev was less than delighted: his little girl, after running away from school herself, was now about to marry a youth who had not yet left school! The presence of the Efron sisters went some little way towards reassuring him: they were older than Seryozha, and took his mother's place. But they too thought the marriage premature. Ivan could not foresee the blow that awaited him in the near future: Asya, barely seventeen, Asya, whose delicate health had caused him so much anxiety, was also on the threshold of marriage. Late that autumn it emerged that she was expecting a child, but this was concealed from her father for the time being.

According to Anastasia Tsvetaeva's memoirs, relations between Marina and Seryozha remained platonic for quite a time. But this made no difference – they were in any case determined never to part. Ivan Vladimorovich had to be told. Marina reproduced in a letter to Voloshin what must be one of the world's most hackneyed dialogues:

My talk with Papa ended peacefully, in spite of its stormy beginning. He was doing the storming; I behaved well and kept calm. "I know that none of you in our day" (our day – poor Papa!) believe in listening to anybody. But you didn't even consult me. You just came along and said 'I'm getting married!' " "But Papa, how could I consult you? You'd only have tried to dissuade me." First, he said: "I shan't be at your wedding, of course. No, no, no!" . . . Then, afterwards: "Well then, when are you thinking of having the wedding?"

The time to leave the house in Tryokhprudny Lane had arrived – so abruptly. As she said goodbye to it Marina reviewed the memories it held for her.

> In these last and final moments
> All grew dear to me, as of old . . .

And strangely – or perhaps it is not strange, but what we would expect of a poet – on the threshold of happiness she foretells like the Sibyl of old the end of that world of hers. Her hand is guided by feelings of gratitude, but someone seems to whisper at her back: "make haste, make haste, this is the beginning, but it is also the end." Not so long ago she had thought that "it is stupid, and even indecent, to be happy. Stupid and indecent to think 'today is mine' ", as she writes in a letter to Voloshin. Now she had discovered that happiness was possible and necessary, indeed a duty. She was happy for the first time since her childhood.

> Oh, how sunnily, how starrily
> Life's first volume is begun,
> I implore you, before it is too late,
> Do come and see our house!
>
> Soon that world will be destroyed,
> Take a look at it in secret,
> Whilst the poplar is not yet felled
> And our house is not yet sold.

She was mistaken only about the details. The house would not be sold but dismantled for firewood in the cold winter after the Revolution. Why was Tsvetaeva so certain that the whole world she had known would soon vanish forever?

> This irretrievable wondrous world
> You will yet find, only hurry!
> Call in on Tryokhprudny Lane,
> Enter this soul of my soul.

Did she, when she wrote those lines, realize what she was prophesying? I doubt it.

Tsvetaeva and Efron were married at the end of January 1912. One of the witnesses was Pra, who flouted the proprieties by "scrawling over a whole page of the church register 'the inconsolable widow of Kirienko-Voloshin'", bringing a breath of Koktebel's free and easy ways into the solemn ceremony.

A number of other joyous events happened around the same time. Marina now won her first — and only — literary prize in the Pushkin competition of the Society for Free Aesthetics with her poem "In Paradise". Then her second collection of verse *The Magic Lantern* and *Childhood*, a volume of stories by Efron, were published with their own imprint. (They could afford this: money left by their parents had made them independent.) Life had become a fairy tale — so they called their publishing house after Andersen's "Ole-Lukøie" [Ole Shut-eye] who visits children to tell them stories at night. The fabulous imprint appeared on only two other volumes: Tsvetaeva's *From Two Books* and Voloshin's *Repin*, before it ceased to exist. A third collection of verse by Tsvetaeva, "Maria Baschkirtseff", was announced but never appeared, and we do not know what became of it.

The Magic Lantern was not overlooked by reviewers, but unlike *Evening Album* it was not unanimously approved. Tsvetaeva had foreseen this in a letter to Voloshin: "Max, I'm sure you won't like my second collection. You say that it ought to be better than the first, or it will be bad: 'en poésie, comme en amour, rester à la même place, c'est reculer'.* These are fine words, capable of inspiring me but powerless to change me!" She herself said later on that *Evening Album* and *Magic Lantern* were "in spirit — a single book". The usual comment on the second collection was to the same effect: the poet was weakly repeating herself. That more was expected of her should have been encouraging, but Tsvetaeva was aggrieved by such criticism. A year later she published *From Two Books*, which contains a mere fifty poems from her first two collections. She was in no hurry to see her next volume in print. Nothing from 1912 was published at the time. Though she defiantly puts the date 1912 at the beginning of her "Youthful Poems", the collection includes only one item from that year. Perhaps she did not feel like writing while she was so distracted by new experiences and the practical demands of a new life, with her pregnancy and the birth of her first child.

Marina and Seryozha went on their honeymoon at the end of February. They spent some time in Italy and France, visited the Black Forest, lived in

* "In poetry, as in love, to stay in the same place is to go backwards."

Paris. Marina saw Sarah Bernhardt in *L'Aiglon*, as she had three years earlier. Seryozha wrote to his sister that he was "amazed by her acting. Her voice is that of an old woman, her step is infirm, and it is nonetheless beautiful". Early in May they returned to Moscow – she wanted to be present at the opening of the Alexander III Museum of Fine Arts.

Ivan Vladimirovich Tsvetaev had brought his life's work to a conclusion: the museum to which he had devoted half a century was opening at last. This, alone of his children, gave him unclouded joy in his old age. Valeria Tsvetaeva remembers her father saying "I have been unsuccessful with my family, but not in serving my country."

The ceremonial opening took place on 31 May 1912. The Emperor Nicholas II was present, together with his mother and his daughters. Marina imagined that the Emperor had looked at her and she had peered into his "pure, transparent, icy, utterly childlike eyes".

Only twenty years later, when she came to write an essay about her father, his museum, and its opening did Tsvetaeva fully realize what an unusual man her father had been, how much fanatical enthusiasm and capacity for self-sacrifice his unremarkable appearance and modest manner concealed. As she described the occasion in her essay, he stood on the steps at the entrance to the museum, "a vision of absolute tranquillity". But tranquillity proved fatal to Ivan Vladimirovich: the tension to which he had so long been accustomed had given him the strength to live. His health was precarious, and although he remained in his post and thought of writing another book, this was not enough to sustain him. He died barely a year after the opening ceremony. That last year was gladdened by the birth of his grandchildren: Asya's son Andrey in August, Marina's daughter Ariadna (Alya) on 5 September 1912. Both sisters thought themselves lucky – Asya had very much wanted a son, and Marina a daughter. Ivan stood godfather to both children, and Voloshin's mother, Pra, was invited to act as godmother to Alya.

ALYA

Marina chose her daughter's name from Greek mythology. Ariadne was one of her favourite heroines, and later was a subject of her poems and of a tragedy. Many people found the name strange, but Tsvetaeva did not let that worry her: "I called her Ariadna in spite of Seryozha who likes Russian names, and friends who thought it affected."

The christening was on 20 December. Marina recorded that "Pra turned up to the christening in female dress — i.e. in a skirt instead of her Turkish trousers. But the white caftan embroidered with gold, and the aquiline features, so reminiscent of Goethe, were the same as ever. My father was visibly embarrassed. Pra radiated resolution, as always, and I — as always — was crazy with fear and thanked Heaven that mothers are not present at christenings. The priest remarked to Vera afterwards that 'the mother keeps running up and down stairs, and has short hair like a boy, and the godmother is obviously a man'."

The birth of a first child is a tremendous event — especially in such a young family: Marina was not yet twenty, and Seryozha not yet nineteen. But we know little about the occasion. Tsvetaeva merely recorded in her diary that Alya [Ariadna] was born at 5.30 a.m., with the bells of Moscow ringing for the early service. The Efrons were living in Ekaterinsky Lane, in a house of their own, bought with money given by Tyo as a wedding present. Marina had chosen it because it resembled the house in Tryokhprudny Lane, and she did her best to reproduce her old home in the arrangement and furnishing of the rooms. There was a shaggy dog like a lion, called Osman. Alya (so she herself told me) probably learnt to walk hanging on to his tail. There was an old nurse, who had been in the family of Tolstoy's son at Khamovniki for many years. Marina loved her stories. It was a comfortable, cheerful, happy house.

Marina made a slow recovery after childbirth, but fed Alya herself to begin with. Then there was a rapid succession of nurses. Alya was a pretty child, with golden hair, and huge, luminous eyes, "Seryozha's eyes", except that they were light blue. The young mother was delighted with her little girl's looks, and rapturously recorded every new stage in her development.

Feodosia, Tuesday 12 November 1913.
Alya is one year and two months old . . . So far she knows 16 words . . . She now has 11 teeth. If you say "hold my hand, Alya" she mischievously hides hers behind her back . . . Lately she's acquired another charming habit. Seryozha keeps stroking my head, and saying "Mama, this is Mama! Nice Mama, nice Mama! Stroke her, Alya!" And Alya has started stroking me herself lately, and saying "mi-mi" for "milaya" (nice) . . . Her eyes: when we were living in Yalta, the woman in the next room, a café singer, said with a sigh whenever she looked at Alya: "those eyes will be the ruin of so many people".

Tsvetaeva wrote these lines at about that time:

The beauty of two enormous eyes,
Their menace, their danger,

Alya

Inaccessibility, pride
And passion . . .

Feodosia, 5 December 1913. Wednesday.
Alya is one year three months today. Has 12 teeth. Can't say new words,
but if you ask her where's the picture? the horse? the cat? eyes? mouth?
nose? ear? she points in the right direction – and looks under my hair for
my ear . . . She has been walking from the age of 11½ months, not very well,
I have to admit, unsteadily and too quickly. She's very afraid of falling, and
walks with her legs too far apart.

Feodosia. New Year's Eve 1913. Tuesday.
A year ago today we had the Christmas tree at Ekaterinsky Lane. Papa was
there – his last Christmas tree! Alya was brought down in a pink satin
coverlet – mine once, from my grandfather . . . Some days after Seryozha
had gone into hospital I was sitting in his room with her and she kept going
up to his bed, lifting up the quilt, looking around and saying over and over
again "Papa! Where Papa?"

Like any other mother Tsvetaeva dreamed of a splendid future for her first-
born. She visualized Alya as a great beauty, surrounded by admirers, and
endowed with talents which she would – of course! – use to the full.
Tsvetaeva's first poem to Alya was written when she was barely a year old,
and until 1920 she regularly reappeared in her mother's verse. Their
relationship changed quite quickly: it ceased to be that of a mother to a new
human being and became a reciprocal relationship *between* a mother and a
growing girl. The change is reflected in Tsvetaeva's poetry, but the
leitmotif remains the same: her delight in her wonderful daughter.

Alya was indeed exceptionally gifted. She could read at four, write at
five, and began keeping a diary at six. What should have been her early
school years coincided with the Revolution, and Tsvetaeva taught Alya
herself, making her write down the events of the past day instead of copying
things out of textbooks or taking boring dictations. Some of these childhood
jottings survived, and Ariadna [Alya] Efron has included some of them in
her memoirs, among them a vignette called "My Mother".

My mother is very strange. My mother is not at all like a mother. Mothers
always think their own children are wonderful, and other children too, but
Marina doesn't like little children. She has light chestnut hair, curly round
the sides. She has green eyes, a hooked nose and red lips. She has a good
figure, and hands that I like. Her favourite day is Annunciation Day. She is
sad and quick and she likes Poetry and Music. She writes poetry. She is
patient, she gets angry and is loving. She is always hurrying somewhere.
She has a great soul. A kind voice. A quick walk. Marina's hands are all
covered with rings. Marina reads in the night. Her eyes are nearly always

mocking: she doesn't like people bothering her with stupid questions, it makes her angry. Sometimes she walks round as if she is lost, then suddenly seems to wake up, starts talking, and then seems to go off again somewhere.

The child saw Marina as *she* saw herself in the mirror: the eyes, the hair, the hooked nose, the voice, the hands, the rings, the walk are as we know from Tsvetaeva's self-portraits in verse. Alya looks at her with the eye of an artist-to-be. But her view may have been influenced by poems she had heard her mother recite. The entry is dated December 1918, when Alya was only six years and three months old, but she was barely seven when she became her mother's regular auditor and enthusiastic appraiser. The surprising thing about her description is the combination of a child's vision with serious understanding.

Realizing that her mother is "very strange", "not like other mothers", she is neither irritated nor censorious. Alya is sure that her mother's peculiarities are connected with something extraordinary, something lofty, perhaps mysterious. We feel that Alya is proud of Marina. And Marina was proud of her daughter. Even before Alya learnt to write and began keeping a diary, Marina delighted in her way of talking, the childishly quaint way of looking at the world. Maria Ivanovna Grinyova (Kuznetsova), then a young actress and acquaintance of the Efrons, recalled that "Marina too sometimes became animated . . . and would launch on one of her serious and inimitably idiosyncratic accounts of comic and moving conversations and arguments with her daughter, three-year-old Alya. Marina's dialogues would be relayed next day at the Kamerny Theatre — and peals of helpless laughter would be heard from the dressing rooms . . .".

The insights shown by the infant Alya, her understanding of adults, the very form and language of her juvenile diaries, have made some readers doubt their reliability. But, any suspicion that they are an adult's attempt to counterfeit a child's style is refuted by archival materials, and by the fact that Tsvetaeva intended in the early twenties to make out of Alya's diaries a second volume of her own (alas, never completed) prose work "Omens of the Earth". Ariadna Efron herself, in a letter to Pavel Antokolsky in 1966, says that her childhood diaries "narrate with the precision, the circumstantiality, and the infantile solemnity of medieval chronicles . . .". It is to be hoped that these "medieval chronicles" will some day be published.

Alya was her mother's daughter. At seven she was writing verse, drawing, exchanging letters with Anna Akhmatova, Konstantin Balmont, Voloshin and Pra. Her development would perhaps have been less rapid if she had lived in the normal milieu of a pre-revolutionary intellectual family, with servants, nursemaids, governesses, high school. But she grew up as Tsvetaeva's daughter, when all that had vanished. Through the years of Revolution Alya and her mother were alone together. Not only were there no servants or governesses – she did not even go to school. She went out with her mother "hunting" for food, visited friends and attended literary gatherings with her. Marina, just as her own mother had done, tried hard to provide all the spiritual nourishment she could. In "Poems to my Son", later on, she confessed that:

> I have instilled into you – all Russia,
> All Russia – as if by a pump!

In the same way, she pumped into Alya Poetry, Music, Romanticism, Nature, Love. And Alya, unlike Marina as a child, was eager to take in everything that came from her mother. This may be partly because there was in Alya less of the creative artist's individualism, with its automatic resistance to interference from outside. But it was mainly the result of the passionate attachment of daughter and mother in Alya's childhood and adolescence. Alya was Tsvetaeva's alter ego. They formed an indivisible whole, and Marina was evidently not always aware of the age difference between herself and her daughter, at six or eight or ten.

This made her love for the child all the more demanding – she tried to fashion Alya not in her own image but to an ideal model invented for her. Had not Maria Aleksandrovna demanded something like this from her daughters? Marina got her way. Alya was a brilliant child, very grown up, capable of sharing her mother's interests and her feelings. She never knew what it was to be a child. She had no friendships with girls of her own age. She lived in an adult world, and became an organic part of it. She was always hearing poetry – and she loved and understood it. When she was nine she wrote to her godmother, Pra, "Marina and I are reading mythology. My favourite is Phaeton, who wanted to drive his father's chariot, and set the seas and rivers *on fire*! And Orpheus is like Blok – pitiful, but able to move stones . . .". She saw the world through Marina's eyes – as far as her years permitted, of course. She felt Seryozha's absence as painfully as Marina did, felt for her in all her amours, was friends with her friends and hostile to her enemies. Alya's one idea was to be the shield-bearer of her poet-mother. This was her one ambition throughout her childhood and early girlhood. The turning point came when she was twelve. She rebelled and struggled to break free of her mother's oppressive influence, to reconstruct her life on lines of her own. For a short time relations between mother and daughter almost reached the point of mutual hatred. Alya resented her mother's attempts to arrange her life for her, and Alya's "rebellion" terrified Marina.

When, many terrible years later, the family returned to the Soviet Union, imprisonment, torture, the camps, banishment, would be Alya's lot. When she was released from prison-camp after seventeen years, not a single member of her family was still living. She went to live in Tarusa, which her mother had loved, went home to Tsvetaeva's manuscripts, Tsvetaeva's poetry, Tsvetaeva's cause. She devoted her remaining years to them.

Of her own choice, Tsvetaeva's life in those years was confined to her family, her friends, her favourite books. She was unselfconsciously egocentric, as such young people can be, and as yet unable to see other people clearly. However, even when she was fully adult she insisted — and no doubt she was right — that egocentricity is a normal characteristic of poets. "There is no such things as spiritual egoism. There is egocentricity, but what makes all the difference is the capacity of the ego, hence the dimensions of the 'centre' itself. Egocentrics — and that includes all poets and philosophers — are as a rule the most detached and unselfish people in the world. It is simply that they . . . make no distinction between everyone else's pain and their own." However that may be, the young Tsvetaeva's ego had no room for anyone else's pain, perhaps because for once in her life she had no pain of her own.

When Tsvetaeva's poetic powers "came back" to her at Koktebel in spring 1913 they were conspicuously more mature. The tone of her verse had changed. Her diction was now more austere and restrained. This was no longer schoolgirl verse. The sentimentality, the cloying diminutive suffixes had disappeared. The poet's thoughts were now focused on her immediate, day-to-day experience. *From Two Books* was prefaced with a sort of manifesto, calling for the fixing of every fugitive moment in verse: "Do not despise the external! The colour of your eyes is just as important as their expression, the upholstery of a sofa no less important than the words spoken on it. Write more precisely! There is nothing that is not important!" To "fix the moment" she dated this preface very precisely: Wednesday 16 January 1913. But the declaration came too late. Tsvetaeva's poetry had outgrown it: the "upholstery of the sofa" had ceased to interest her as a poet. Only the beginning of her declaration was of any relevance to her future: "All this actually happened. My verses are my diary, my poetry is a poetry of proper names." Her poetry would remain a diary recording her inner life. When at a later date she published a volume of poems written in 1913–1915 she called it simply "Youthful Poems", thus stressing her break with the "childishness" which had captivated reviewers of her first book. She stood on the threshold of new discoveries and her "youthful poems" were the bridge by which she approached them.

The three and half years after she first met Sergey Efron were the happiest and most serene in Tsvetaeva's life. She underwent a transformation and her poetry changed with her as it absorbed what was for her the amazing experience of carefree happiness. It flooded her being, and taught her to rejoice in life: the sun, the wind, the logs crackling in the fireplace, the ringing of church bells, talking to friends, her daughter's prattle, a felicitous rhyme . . . Two letters she wrote to Vasily Rozanov registered this happiness.

> Dear, dear Vasily Vasilievich,
> My whole being is now filled with a sort of exultation, I have become kind, I say nice things to everybody, instead of walking I want to run, no, not to run but to fly . . . .

> Dear Vasily Vasilievich,
> This is such a joyous time, such sunshine, such a cold wind. I ran along the broad garden path, past the slender acacias, the wind ruffled my short hair, and I felt so light, so free . . . .

What had become of her shyness, her aloofness, her remoteness from all around her? It was as though she had been born again. With it came a new awareness of her appearance. At the age of twenty she blossomed and grew prettier. The actress Maria Grinyova has this to say about her first meeting with Tsvetaeva, who had been invited to read her poems to drama students on a winter's evening in 1912/13:

> The mirror was already occupied! A shapely young woman stood looking into it while she undid the ribbons of her bonnet. When they were finally untied and the bonnet removed I saw a mass of golden hair. Standing behind her I caught my breath at the sight of her dress! Such an unusual, such an enchanting dress, of golden brown silk, full-skirted, ankle-length, nipped in at her narrow waist by an old-fashioned corsage. She was showing just a little of her neck, and wore a cameo brooch. An enchanting girl from last century! I myself felt pathetic – a badly-dressed creature in a short, narrow slit skirt ("like everybody else!"). At that moment she turned round from the mirror, and again I was rooted to the spot: her face was a delicate pink but her look severe. Her lips were pursed. Her head held high – showing her faultlessly regular features. But her eyes – light, unmoving eyes, somehow lost to the world about them, bewitching eyes.

Maria Grinyova's memoirs, written half a century later, may exaggerate what she felt at the time, but Tsvetaeva herself was not unmoved by the change in her appearance. In childhood and adolescence she had always been painfully aware of her plumpness, her clumsiness, her excessively high colour (as she thought it to be), but now she began to feel pleased with her looks. She took note of her vivid green (gooseberry-coloured) eyes, her luxuriant golden hair, which was beginning to curl at the ends, her figure, now slender and shapely, her light and rapid step. Sketches for a self-portrait began to appear frequently in her verse.

> I was endowed with a pleasant voice
> And an entrancing curve of brow . . .
>
> And the green of my eyes, and my tender voice,
> And the gold of my hair . . . .

She began to take an interest in clothes and ornaments, but in this as in other things she tried to develop a style of her own. People who met her were surprised to see her wearing not only defiantly unfashionable dresses, but as many silver bracelets and rings, as a gypsy. She had a particular fondness for such things and sang their praises more than once.

> A bracelet of antique turquoise
> On a flower stem,
> On this my narrow, this my long
> Hand . . . .

Turquoise, amber, amethyst, Bohemian glass – these were her favourite ornaments; she had no use for gold or diamonds.

The heroine of "Youthful Poems" is presented in such a variety of guises and situations that the reader cannot help thinking: this young woman is trying herself out in new and strange poses and circumstances to see which suit her best. It is something of a game. She plays one part after another, for herself and for the reader, to see how she will look in each of them. She fixes the image in verse as though in a snapshot, studies it herself and offers it to the reader to examine and admire. Here she is wandering about the streets at night, in a fit of youthful sadness – for no particular reason, except perhaps that another day of her life has gone by.

> This spring-like day has faded
> Forever over Theodosia,
> And everywhere shadows lengthen
> In this magnificent twilight hour.
>
> Choking with sadness,
> I walk alone, with not a thought,
> Both my slim arms I've dropped
> And let them hang.

> I walk along the Genoan walls,
> Meeting the kisses of the wind,
> And the silken streams of my dress
> Flutter about my knees.
>
> And the edge of the ring is modest,
> And a bouquet of several violets
> Right by my face itself
> Is touchingly small and frail.
>
> I walk along the ramparts,
> In the sadness of evening and spring,
> And the evening lengthens the shadows,
> And hopelessness seeks for words.

Hopelessness? Why? About what? The rhythm of the verse is so smooth and calm, the words so ordinary and unremarkable, the heroine is so observant of details, that no feeling of sadness and hopelessness results.

At times Tsvetaeva obviously enjoys a stylized old-world effect: she seems to see herself as a figure in a picture by [the turn-of-the-century Russian artist] Konstantin Somov.

> In a vast garden of lime-trees,
> Both innocent and ancient,
> I walk along with a mandoline
> Wearing a very long dress.
>
> (. . .)
>
> My curls divided by a parting . . .
> The rustling of the silk so tight,
> A deep and low-necked bodice
> And skirt in sumptuous pleats.
>
> My gait is delicate and weary,
> And figure like a supple rod . . .

Is she being deliberately provocative? Of course not. Or if there is a trace of provocation it is not at all like the yellow blouse worn by Mayakovsky to tease the public, or the elaborately painted faces and the carrot in the buttonhole of the dinner-jacket favoured by other Futurists. But Tsvetaeva's affectations did not go unremarked. Grinyova's story about the poetry reading at the drama school goes on like this: "A friend to the left of me whispers: 'she must be the only one in all Moscow who wears anything like that, I saw things just like it in my stepmother's clothes chest'. I hear from my right: 'her grandmother's dresses'. 'What enchanting audacity,' I whisper delightedly, 'to dress up like that for a social occasion.'"

It is not difficult to imagine how much Tsvetaeva, who not so long ago "felt awful" (her own word) in company, must have enjoyed this whispering behind her back, the admiring attention which her verses and she herself attracted. Tsvetaeva was interested in her own personality as she had never been before, and admired herself as she never would again. It was not a matter of narcissism or conceit: she was looking for her true self, taking pleasure in getting to know her changing self.

> Sun — not blood — swells the veins
> On my hand already brown and tanned.
> I am all alone with my great love
> For my soul, my own soul.
>
> I wait for a grasshopper, count a hundred,
> Break off the stalk and start to chew . . .
> It's strange to feel so strongly, so simply
> The fleetingness of life — of my life too.

She catches a glimpse of the bottomless depths of the human soul, tries to peer into them and to understand. She is, as it were, investigating the whole world in her own person. She reaches no great depth as yet, but we see here a presage of her tragic future. Joy in discovering the world is accompanied in "Youthful Poems" by constantly recurring thoughts of death — unsurprisingly: yourself as a living creature goes with reflection on the perishability of all earthly things, and on the possibility of your own death. "Possibility" is the word in Tsvetaeva's case, for there is no doom-laden sense of its inevitability in these poems. In a letter to Rozanov she speaks of her lack of religious belief and says "hence my despair, my horror of old age and death." This may very well have been a transitory mood, but the "horror" finds no expression in Tsvetaeva's verse at the time. She went on to say that she was "by nature totally incapable of prayer and resignation. I have a mad love of life, a convulsive, feverish lust for life . . .". And later — "if you write to me don't try to make a Christian of me. At present life has a very different meaning for me."

It is noteworthy that Marina enclosed her verses about death in this letter to the philosopher. If Rozanov read them carefully, he must have seen that his young correspondent's heart held neither horror nor despair, but a thoroughly pagan protest against the very possibility of death.

> Listen! — I don't accept it!
> This is just a trap!
> They won't lower me into the ground,
> Not me . . .

And again:

> To be tender, mad and noisy,
> – To thirst for life so much –
> To be fascinating and clever,
> To be enchanting!
>
> Tenderer than all who are or were,
> To know no blame . . .
> Oh, indignation, that in the grave
> We are all the same!
>
> To become one that no one loves,
> Oh, to become like ice!

When she returned to this theme a lifetime later her tone was quite different. In these later verses, written in autumn 1936, we meet not rebellion but reflective acquiescence.

> In my thoughts of something other,
> And, like treasure, undiscovered,
> Poppy after poppy, step by step,
> All the garden I've beheaded.
>
> Thus, at one time or another,
> In dry summer, by a field's edge,
> Death with unheeding hand will
> Strike off a head – my own.

What it is that she has failed to find she does not tell us. It is as though these two quatrains were not so much a poem (Tsvetaeva did not publish them) as an answer to a long-suppressed question of her own. There is one escape from her reverie – death. She does not ask for death, she has no foreboding of it, she is simply sure of its inevitability, and apparently unmoved by that thought: it will come "who knows when". The words "at the edge of the field" inevitably remind us of the folk saying "living a life isn't crossing a field". For the present Tsvetaeva is concerned with something else: some day death will come along, as absent-minded as she herself in the present reverie, and will give her no time to think, to answer the supremely important question that is always in her mind. What was the riddle she was trying to solve? She has left us no hint. Perhaps, as in Aleksandr Blok's "Free Thoughts", it was one to which the answer comes only at the moment of death?

> And in that moment – all thoughts passed through his brain,
> The only ones he needed. They passed –
> And died . . .

She was now living an enviably happy, settled life, and there was every reason to believe that it would continue to flow quietly along in its appointed channel. She had the devoted and ecstatic Seryozha at her side, Alya, surrounded by solicitous nurses, was growing, and her beauty and cleverness were a joy. The young Efrons were welcomed in the literary and theatrical societies and salons of Moscow. Sergey and his sisters were connected with Khalyutina's Drama School, and with the recently opened Kamerny Theatre. All three of them wanted to go on the stage, but Sergey was still an external student working for his school-leaving certificate. Marina's reputation was growing, she gave a number of public readings and her poetry was well received. We have a number of firsthand accounts of Tsvetaeva's recitals. Maria Grinyova remembered the impression she made on teachers and students at the Drama School: "the first thing that struck us was her delivery, which was unlike anything we had heard or been taught. She spoke her verse in an unexpectedly simple and modest fashion. There was a rare unity of intonation and meaning, as if there was no more than a minute between the creation of the verse and its recitation . . . The intermission was consumed by argument. Some went into raptures, others were more guarded and said that Tsvetaeva's way of reading verse was all very well at home, amongst close friends, but . . . ."

In my view, nothing helps us more to interpret a poem than to hear the poet read it. Being heard was probably very important to Tsvetaeva: the intimacy of her rendering emphasized the intimacy of her subject matter. She did not like the sort of histrionic delivery that "loud-pedals" the meaning at the expense of the melody. In those days she and her sister often recited together, in unison. They had identical voices, which harmonized on the same note. Anastasia Tsvetaeva writes that "in our verse we used the voice naturally, avoiding that detestable emotional over-emphasis that actors go in for. We spoke simply and distinctly. In a sing-song? Ask those who remember. Rhythmically, at any rate." Alas! Everyone remembers differently. Here is Nikolay Elenev on Marina's recital, in 1914, of lines (evidently not preserved) in honour of M. Petipa. "Marina began to recite her verses in a flat, rather comical voice. Marina never sang her verse. She had an uncompromising love of the word, its distinctive meaning, its architectonics."

In other words, she *spoke* her verse: she did *not* sing it. But Vera Zvyagintseva, who heard Tsvetaeva in 1919–1921 and again in 1939–1941, seems to contradict Elenev: "She recited verse of all kinds, however frivolous, or however tragic, in a singsong, repeating the same melodic figure over and over again. Her expressive range was too limited for verse-reading." Perhaps Tsvetaeva's manner had changed? Regrettably, we have no recordings of her voice, and must please ourselves which version we accept. What matters is that her readings in those early days were always a success, which must surely have been gratifying to her.

The Efrons spent spring and summer 1913 in Koktebel. Ivan Vladimirovich Tsvetaev died on 31 August. Luckily, Marina had travelled to Moscow two weeks before that to let her house. She got there in time to see her father alive and in good heart, and to be present at his end. As it happened all his other children were also in Moscow. After the funeral Marina and her family settled in Yalta where Seryozha was receiving treatment in a sanatorium. At the end of autumn they moved to Feodosia, to be closer to Max and Koktebel. Anastasia Tsvetaeva, already divorced, and her little Andrey were living not far away. There were lots of people, lots of life, lots of fun. Seryozha was still working for his school-leaving exam, but that did not prevent him from joining the others in the evening, and even producing a humorous "newspaper", the *Koktebel Echo*. Literary evenings were organized regularly, on one pretext or another. They were by now well known in Feodosia, and the Efrons and Asya were welcome guests in every cultivated household in the town.

Marina, Asya and Seryozha saw the New Year, 1914, in at Max's place, in a completely deserted, wintry, storm-swept Koktebel. Tsvetaeva has given us a marvellous description of the occasion in her essay on Voloshin, "A Living Word about a Living Man". That night, she tells us, a fire broke out in Max's studio, and he extinguished it by force of will, by "casting a spell".

The war that would turn the world upside-down found Tsvetaeva in Moscow, hard at work on a cycle of poems addressed to Pyotr Efron, Seryozha's older brother. He had come back from abroad to die of tuberculosis, and had died at the end of summer. Marina had been attracted to him, and still fancied as much as two years later that she "could have loved him madly! No, it wasn't passion – there is no sign of it in the verses – it was "a cloud of tenderness and sadness", "on the brink of the abyss" – of all situations the most favourable to Tsvetaeva's muse. She confessed on several occasions that in life and in love partings meant more to her than meetings. Here the shadow of the eternal parting hung over them from the very first day. How could Tsvetaeva remain indifferent, how could she fail to reach out impulsively to one who bore such a resemblance to Seryozha, to this young life (Pyotr was thirty years old) receding, fading while she watched? In comparison with this what significance could she attach to the dim and distant war that had just broken out? A poem about the war was literally "wedged" into the cycle dedicated to Pyotr Efron.

> War, war! Censing in front of icons
> And the jingling of spurs.
> But the Tsar's affairs do not concern me,
> Nor the people's quarrels.
>
> It seems that on a frayed tightrope
> I am a tiny dancer.
> I am a shade of someone's shade, sleep-walker
> Of two dark moons.

She defiantly proclaims that those dark moons, the eyes of her dying friend, are more important to her than any world catastrophe. Just as defiantly a few months later, when chauvinist anti-German feeling had reached fever pitch, she wrote her declaration of love for Germany:

> You are persecuted by the world,
> To your enemies there is no end.
> So how can I abandon you.
> So how can I betray you.

On the one side — patriotic hatred of Germany: on the other side, Tsvetaeva's love of that country, with which she feels a blood tie, and of all that German legends, German art, German philosophy mean to her.

> I am delighted by your songs,
> I hear not the spurs of officers,
> When in Freiburg, on the Schwabentor,
> Saint George to me is sacred.
>
> (. . .)
>
> Nothing is more magical nor full
> Of wisdom than you, fragrant land,
> Where the Lorelei combs her golden locks
> Over the eternal river Rhine.

The war, at first, did not affect the Efrons, and they had no thought of other storms ahead. Seryozha got a place in the History and Literature Faculty of Moscow University — how delighted Ivan Tsvetaev would have been had he lived to see it! They had not felt like going back to Zamoskvorechie, and on their return from the Crimea they rented an apartment at No. 6 Borisoglebsky Lane, off the Arbat, the most ridiculous and inconvenient two-storey apartment there ever was, one room of which was lit only by a skylight, while the window of Sergey's attic opened onto the roof. Nobody else would have wanted it, but Tsvetaeva immediately

took a liking to the place, arranged it to suit herself and lived there until she
left Russia.

A "FRIEND" OR A "MISTAKE"?

The threat to the young family's happiness came from a most unexpected
quarter. In autumn 1914 Marina met the poet Sofia Parnok, who was nine
years older than herself, and had lived openly as a lesbian since separating
from her husband in 1909. It seems to have been love at first sight. Marina
confessed that:

> My heart spoke at once, "My dearest!"
> At random I forgave you everything,
> Though knowing nothing, even your name!
> Oh, do love me, do love me!

We cannot be sure what made Tsvetaeva rush into this passionate
relationship. Dissatisfaction? She discusses such encounters in "Lettre à
l'Amazone" (Letter to the Amazon), a short prose work written by her in
French.

> Et voici que la jeune fille souriante qui ne veut pas d'étranger dans son
> corps, qui ne veut pas de lui et du sien, qui ne veut que du *mien*, rencontre
> au tournant d'une route une autre *moi*, une *elle*, qu'elle n'a pas à craindre,
> dont elle n'a pas à se défendre, car l'autre ne peut pas lui faire du mal . . .
> Pour le moment, elle est heureuse et libre, libre d'aimer de coeur, sans
> corps, d'aimer sans avoir peur, d'aimer sans faire mal . . . .*

The words "fear" and "pain" recur several times on this page of Tsvetaeva's
work. But she was married and a mother, although she was only twenty-
two, when she and Sofia met. A year later Parnok wrote some lines to Sergey
Efron:

> Not you, O youth, released her from the spell.
> Marvelling at the flame of those loving lips,
> O you who were first, it will not be your name
> The lover jealously recalls, but mine.

---

* "And this is how the smiling young girl who does not want a stranger in her body, who does
not want a him or a his, but only a *mine*, meets at a turning in the road another *me*, a *she*, in
whom there is nothing to fear, against whom she does not need to defend herself, for the
other cannot harm her . . . For the moment, she is happy and free, free to love with the
heart, not the body, to love without being afraid, to love without doing harm . . ."

Perhaps Parnok had learnt things about her friend's intimate life that made it possible for her to triumph in this way over a rival.

Or was it perhaps that Tsvetaeva found a tranquil life uncongenial, and longed for storms and cataclysms? Sated with quiet happiness, did her nature demand change? We are reminded of her words to Rozanov: "my convulsive, feverish lust for life". In her first poem to Parnok she defiantly proclaims:

> I love you. Like a storm-cloud
> Above you, lies sin . . .

Perhaps curiosity, an invariable characteristic of genius, lured her onto that unknown, mysterious and dangerous path? Does not "Letter to the Amazon" hint at this? "I was always afraid that I would never love again, never learn anything new." The air of the theatrical and literary salons in those days was heavy with the scent of forbidden love . . . It gave piquancy to art. Such liaisons were more or less openly acknowledged, and were not for the most part viewed with disapproval. But I should not be surprised to learn that the thought of Sappho, and nothing more, impelled Tsvetaeva to behave as she did.

I shall pass over the ups and downs of the relationship, which dragged on for some eighteen months. I might have ignored it altogether, had it not played a disastrous part in Tsvetaeva's life, and left conspicuous traces in her writings. During their intimacy, and at the time of their estrangement, Tsvetaeva wrote about twenty poems. She returned to the theme of Sapphic love many years later in "Letter to the Amazon", which is certainly an attempt to interpret her own experience. The theme underlies and gives a lyrical colouring to her last prose work, "The Story of Sonechka".

When she was putting together her volume of "Youthful Poems" in the winter of 1919–1920, Tsvetaeva included a cycle of seventeen poems addressed to Parnok. She called it "The Mistake", and the word accurately expressed her feelings about this episode in her life. Later on the title seemed too explicit, and she replaced it with the neutral "The Friend". There is no denying either Tsvetaeva's infatuation with Parnok, or the affection she felt for her. The poems testify to that.

> I repeat on the eve of parting,
> Towards the end of loving,
> That those possessive hands of yours
> I used to love,
>
> And those eyes (upon whom
> Did they not deign to rest!)

Demanding a reckoning
For every casual look . . .

She swears eternal fidelity to her friend:

Under the sun all eyes are burning,
No day is like another.
I am telling you this in case
I should prove false.

Whoever's lips I might be kissing
At a lover's tryst,
To whoever I might dreadfully swear
At some black midnight hour,

One ought to live, as a mother bids her baby,
And flower like a tiny flower
And never in anyone's direction
Cast a sidelong glance . . .

Do you see the cross of Cypress?
— It is known to you —
Everything will reawaken, should you whistle
Under my window.

However, the first of the above-quoted poems continues with the words:

And, wearily, I'll also say,
— Don't hurry to listen! —
That your soul has come to stand
Athwart my soul . . .

When twenty years later, in "Letter to the Amazon", Tsvetaeva tries to understand the essential significance of lesbian relationships, and the reasons for what she thought to be their inevitable collapse, she traces their origins to a "quest of the Soul". As she saw it, the older of the two friends, the seeker, is "a snare for the soul". The younger, Tsvetaeva writes, "veut aimer — mais . . . elle aimerait bien — si . . . et la voilà dans les bras de l'autre, la tête contre la poitrine, où réside l'*âme*."*

Parnok was the older, Tsvetaeva the younger partner in their relationship. In one of the poems she has drawn a picture of herself with her head on her friend's breast:

* ". . . wishes to love — but . . . she would like it — if . . . and there she is in the arms of the other, her head against the other's breast, where the *soul* resides . . ."

99

> How you hugged my head against you,
> Caressing every curl,
> How the flower of your enamel brooch
> Made my lips go cold . . .

And then, very soon, "your soul stood athwart mine" – and the whole poem ends with a despairing cry:

> Happy is he who has not met you
> On life's path.

If we compare the poems addressed to Parnok and "Letter to the Amazon", we are left with the impression that it is the soul which has failed in its quest, that the soul, not the body, resists this love.

Tsvetaeva wrote to her husband's sister Lilya in 1915 that "Sonya loves me very much and I love her – and this is for ever, I can never leave her". She and Parnok were living at the time in a villa at Svyatye Gory in the Kharkov province. Alya and her nurse were with them. Before this they had all – sisters included – spent two months at Koktebel. Marina's husband was serving as a nursing orderly on a hospital train and had been away from home for some months. Marina was torn between him and Parnok. There were many strands in her feeling for Sonya – including daughterly sentiment, the need for a mother after so many years of motherlessness. Her last poem to Parnok, written after their final breach, speaks of the mother-daughter aspect of their relationship:

> In bygone days you were to me like a mother,
> I could call you in the night . . .

Parnok's lines to Tsvetaeva confirm this:

> "You seemed to me an awkward little girl"
> Oh, Sappho pierced me with the arrow of a single line!
> By night I fell a-thinking of that head with curly hair,
> And I changed the passion of my heart's tumult for a mother's care . . .

I shall not deal here with the theme of the Child (Tsvetaeva spells it with a capital letter). This, for her, is the stumbling block, the beginning of the end of most lesbian relationships. She writes with understanding and great compassion of the older woman who takes the initiative in forming such a union: "L'île. L'éternelle isolée. La mère perdant une à une ses filles, les perdant pour l'éternité."*

* "The island. The eternally isolated. The mother losing her daughters one by one, losing them for eternity."

This island makes a shadowy appearance in some lines addressed to Parnok:

> You are no flower – you are a stem of steel,
> More evil than evil, sharper than sharp,
> From what island were you taken away?

Her question answers itself: the island is Lesbos. Once again, "the island" is a symbol for life-long, eternal loneliness, outlawry, for a sorority of lepers, for exclusion from the world of nature, for a solitary old age and a lonely death:

> Saule pleureur! Saule éploré! Saule, corps et âme des femes! Nuque éplorée du saule. Chevelure grise ramenée sur la face, pour ne plus rien voir. Chevelure grise balayant la face de la terre. Les eaux, les airs, les montagnes, les arbres nous sont donnés pour comprendre l'âme des humains, si profondément cachée. Quand je vois se désespérer un saule, je comprends Sapho* (Concluding words of "Letter to the Amazon".)

I began by saying that Tsvetaeva's love affair with Parnok had a disastrous effect on her life. Yet it stimulated her writing in prose, and inspired her to write verse. But right from the beginning she saw something frightening in it, and associated love itself not with happiness, but with struggle. Their friendship was two weeks old when Tsvetaeva described a night together:

> The outline of your face
> Is very frightening.
> (. . .)
> – Have you surrendered? – is the question.
> – I didn't struggle . . .

And a little later:

> The mouth is innocent, dissolute,
> Like some monstrous flower.

In her relationship with Parnok, Tsvetaeva senses something sinful, repulsive, offensive to woman's nature. In "Letter to the Amazon" she speaks frankly: "Mais qu'en dira, qu'en dit la nature, la seule vengeresse et justicière de nos écarts physiques? La nature dit: non . . . Hors-nature."†

---

* "Weeping willow! Willow full of tears! Willow, body and soul of women! Willow's nape full of tears. Grey hair pulled over the face so as to see nothing more. Grey hair sweeping the face of the earth. Water, air, mountains and trees are given us to understand the human soul, so profoundly hidden. When I see a willow in despair, I understand Sappho."
† "But what will nature – sole avenger and arbiter of our physical deviations – say, what does she say? Nature says: no . . . it's outside nature."

Even at the height of her passion something in Tsvetaeva protests against it so strongly that side by side with professions of love, protestations of loyalty, outbursts of jealousy and resentment, we become aware of her desire to break off the relationship. Her soul yearns to escape. She begs her friend to leave her:

> Why do you want, why do you need
> The soul of a Spartan child?

And she ends the cycle with a plea that sounds almost brutal:

> And now go . . . You too,
> And also you, and you.
>
> Cease to love me, Cease to love me all of you! . . .

It does not matter which of them "had the honour" of the breach. Each of them probably felt the urge to break away at times — Parnok to move on to her next affair, Tsvetaeva to free herself from the spell of this almost unbearable passion. They parted with hard feelings. The relationship, difficult in itself, had also been clouded by the wrong they were doing to Seryozha. Tsvetaeva was fully conscious of it, and suffered. When she wrote to her husband's sister from Svyatye Gory confessing her love for "Sonya" she also had this to say of Seryozha:

> I shall love him all my life, he is dear to me, I shall never leave him for anyone. I write to him every day, or every other day, he knows all there is to know about me, except that I try not to write about the saddest thing too often. There is an everlasting weight on my heart. I go to sleep with it and wake up with it.

"The saddest thing", and the "weight" refer of course to her relationship with Parnok. She knew that her family and friends were worried about her and Seryozha. Her contemporaries generally avoid speaking about this dark episode in Tsvetaeva's life, but Elena Voloshina [Pra] in her letters to the artist Yulia Obolenskaya — one of the Koktebel circle — speaks quite frankly about the Efrons' family affairs. Pra was fond of Seryozha and Marina, she was little Alya's godmother, and she was worried about their future as a family. She first mentions Marina's "romance" on 30 December 1914, as something generally known: "The news about Marina is pretty terrible. She and Sonya have gone off somewhere or other for a few days, she tried to keep it a deep secret. This Sonya has now quarrelled with the woman she used to live with and taken a separate apartment on the Arbat. Lilya and I are embarrassed and very worried by all this, but it's beyond our power to break the spell."

"This Sonya" emphasizes Pra's hostility to Parnok as someone alien and destructive. She is afraid for Marina, and also feels a certain shame for her, but she takes a sober view of the matter: the "spell" is proof against any attempt at rational dissuasion. Only three weeks later we are surprised to discover from another of Pra's letters that Seryozha too had had an affair. "Seryozha's affair has ended with no harm done, Marina's is developing with an irresistible force that nothing can check. It will have to burn itself out, and Allah alone knows how it will end."

What was this affair of Seryozha's? Three weeks earlier there had been no hint of it, yet now it has "ended satisfactorily". I have no information about it, but can imagine that Seryozha's response to Marina's infatuation with Parnok was to *invent* an affair of his own – hoping perhaps to ease his wife's conscience and to make her friends judge her less harshly. His adoration of her was proof against any of her aberrations or betrayals. The Parnok affair was the first such experience in their life together, and Seryozha's weakness showed itself: he was incapable of resisting, or struggling, he could only withdraw, bide his time, while Marina's passion burnt itself out. I had the good fortune to talk to Konstantin Rodzevich, the hero of Tsvetaeva's "Poem of the Mountain" and "Poem of the End". When I asked him about Sergey Efron's reactions to Tsvetaeva's affair with Parnok, Rodzevich replied "he just got out of the way and gave her her freedom". When, in spring 1915, Efron left the University to join the army as a medical orderly it was probably, more than anything, in order "to get out of the way". Tsvetaeva must surely have found this painful.

The final break between Marina and Parnok came in February 1916. Tsvetaeva had "burnt out", "broken the spell", but in that year and a half something had snapped in her, something had gone never to return. She called this "romance" her "first catastrophe". For it was not her relationship with Mandelstam, as I first thought, but that with Parnok that would bring out the "vagabond" in her, the "hellraiser", the Tsvetaeva of "partings". Her youth ended with Parnok. Here are the concluding lines, written in December 1915, of "Youthful Poems".

> I was endowed with a pleasant voice,
> And an entrancing curve of brow.
> Fate kissed me on my lips,
> Fate taught me to be pre-eminent.
>
> To lips I paid handsome tribute,
> On graves I scattered roses . . .
> But as I hurried, the heavy hand of Fate
> Seized me by my hair.

Perhaps Tsvetaeva was thinking of the hatred of the younger partner for the older, with which, as she says in her "Letter to the Amazon", all such unions end. "(Avale, avale, avale encore, ravale tout — pour tout ce que tu m'as fait!) . . . Et dans les yeux — cette haine! Haine d'une servante enfin affranchie. Volupté de mettre le pied sur un coeur."*

After this brush with fate everything seemed permitted, nothing seemed forbidden. No new passion, no new "sin", was impossible. One thing remained unchanged — her relationship with her husband. This contained the "higher" truth which does not necessarily coincide with day-to-day living. The day after her last reminiscence in verse of Parnok, Tsvetaeva offered her husband her repentance.

> At a black midnight hour I came to you,
> For the last time seeking aid.
> I am a vagrant with no memory of kin,
> A sinking ship.
>
> (. . .)
>
> By imposters, predatory dogs,
> I am plundered to the end.
> At your palace, veritable king,
> I stand — a beggar!

Did she have other lesbian liaisons? I think not. In "Letter to the Amazon" there is the sentence: "on ne l'y prendra plus."†

This "blow of Fate" left its mark on Tsvetaeva's writing. The epigraph to her 1916 poems reads

> Birds of Paradise are singing,
> We may not enter Paradise . . .

The way into Paradise was henceforth barred to Tsvetaeva's verse — if Paradise is thought of as a realm of peace and light. Henceforth she was possessed by the spirit of unquiet, of anxiety and eternal seeking.

It was not a rational process. A poet can hardly decide to "write entirely differently as from January the first". But when we pass on quickly from "Youthful Poems" to *Mileposts: Part I*, we have the impression of a dizzy

---

* "(Swallow, swallow, swallow more, choke everything down — for all that you have done to me!) . . . And in your eyes — this hatred! Hatred of a servant girl finally liberated. Pleasure of setting your foot on a heart."
† "She won't be caught that way again."

leap, though the first of these collections ends on 31 December 1915 and the second begins in January 1916. The biggest change is in the lyrical heroine's apprehension of herself and of the world. Gone is the pink and golden girl in carefully chosen out-of-fashion frocks, given to admiring herself in the mirror; gone are the pensive walks in avenues of limes. She has broken out to the new freedom of unexplored roads. She feels the wind and the glow of camp fires by night on her face – she is ready for chance encounters and instant passion. Landscape and interiors have changed. Her verse will never return to the drawing room. "The soul of a Spartan child" is also a thing of the distant past. Tsvetaeva's lyrical persona feels itself to be free from the conventions and obligations of her previous life, steps over the bounds set by religion, family, and habit. Something arcane and forbidden has been revealed to her and has carried her away.

> Like a cat I crept out upon the steps
> And turned my face towards the wind.
> The wind blew softly and the birds soared by . . .

Those are the first lines of her adult volume. Her poetry would pass through other phases, but there would be no other turning point so important and at first sight so surprising.

In 1913, addressing her sister, Tsvetaeva could boldly claim:

> We alone in the market of the world
> Are without sin . . .

but now she is conscious of her sinfulness, and is not shy of admitting it. She does not set out to shock, like the young Mayakovsky, does not write confessional verse like Akhmatova, does not withhold herself like Mandelstam. She bares her soul, inviting her readers to share her experience, but often at the risk of antagonizing them. The figure closest to her former lyrical persona is that of the "seeker of adventures": her other masks are quite unlike the old ones. She is the vagabond, the "tavern queen":

> Having wined and danced our fill at the crazy feast,
> We would roll, my friend, a little in the wind of night . . .

She is the "convict princess":

> Who in the wind is a beggar?
> Anyone on the great highway
> Is a prince in disguise!
>
> (. . .)

> Thus in the world's desert,
> Abandoning earth's pasture
> And shunning habitation,
>
> The convict princesses
> And the convict princes
> Live by begging and reign . . .

Or she is the apostate — the necromancer, the sorceress, the witch. The unbelief to which Tsvetaeva had confessed, writing to Rozanov, had not previously intruded on her verse, but now it is openly voiced:

> By now all know
> To which saints I pray
> In all sorts of chapels,
> In all sorts of green ones . . .

The theme of apostasy, of the "parting" with God, is heard now and then in *Mileposts: Part I*.

> Thieves' maw in the night:
> Shame will swallow you and bereave you of God.
> But then it will teach you
> To sing, smiling in someone's face, and steal . . .

Tsvetaeva recognizes that she is only now learning to "sing". She realizes how strange is the path her verse has chosen, and is aware that there is no turning back.

> Only in a fairytale the prodigal son
> Returns to his father's house.

She seeks fellow-travellers for the journey. Meetings and partings — more partings than meetings — the quest for travelling companions, for a Companion, a kindred soul, became Tsvetaeva's *idée fixe*, in her life and in her verse. Her fellow-wayfarers had, of course, changed. She was surrounded now with adventurers, vagabonds, thieves — the people of the high road. Tsvetaeva's lyrical heroine tries to move amongst those who reject and are rejected. She is drawn to them and feels close to them. For the first time she needs not family and friends but simply people. This one line was to put forth many shoots:

> Hands have been given me — to stretch out both to all . . .

to everyone in whom she catches the slightest glimpse of kinship with herself. For the present they are "confederates", "accomplices in crime".

The heroine of *Mileposts: Part I* wears a dark halo of sin – and wears it defiantly.

> I walk down the street –
> People stand to one side.
> As if from a robber,
> As if from a corpse

The reader will not, I trust, take all this literally. Tsvetaeva did not of course take to roaming the roads or wandering from alehouse to tavern. She did not give up her beloved apartment in Borisoglebsky Lane, and she continued to do her best as housekeeper, wife and mother. Her verse reveals not the details of her day-to-day existence but the inner experience of a soul that had severed its ties with ordinary life. Yet there are still vague but persistent rumours that Tsvetaeva was no stranger to evildoing. She was, it is said, capable of doing wrong "for no particular reason": stealing, appropriating another person's treasures. Her contemporaries have, understandably, preferred to withhold details.

With the change in her outlook all else changed too: diction, colouring, rhythm. In "Youthful Poems" the key words are "game", "mischievousness", "merriment", "laughter", "tenderness". In *Mileposts* they are displaced by words connoting anxiety, instability, restless movement – words like "road", "milestone", "wind", "night", "sleeplessness", "weeping". I have tried to compare descriptions of dress, ornaments and interiors in the two books. In "Youthful Poems" there are hints of luxury everywhere: a magnificent frock of gold-threaded faille, a jacket with a winged collar, a straw hat, a shawl from Turkish lands, a fur coat, a muff, an opal ring, a turquoise bracelet, a chaise-longue, a fire-place, Sèvres figurines. In *Mileposts* there is simply nothing comparable. Tsvetaeva had lost interest in such things. There are no descriptions of dress, her own or anyone else's, exquisite or otherwise. There are no interiors, because Tsvetaeva's verses have migrated from confined rooms to open fields, the bazaar, the outskirts of the city, the streets and squares of Moscow.

In "Youthful Poems" light colours dominate: white, pink, gold. In *Mileposts* dark colours prevail: grey, blue-grey, black, blue-black, black-blue, darker and darker shades, until we reach coal-black (eyes, and nights). The heavy, dark strokes reinforce the feeling of anxiety that suffuses the book. Darkness from which escape is difficult interacts with the headlong rhythm in which *Mileposts* is written. A tornado seems to snatch up the heroine and her reader, whirling them from page to page. Every page is a blind corner round which something unexpected awaits. The wind and the birds play the main parts – nowhere in Russian poetry is there such a gathering of different birds. The familiar nightingale from "Youthful Poems" now has to compete with crows, swans, turtledoves, eagles, even owls and quails. The collocation of wind and birds — the incessant beating of wings in the wind — creates a feeling of haste and anxiety. In *Mileposts* even the wind is no longer what it was in "Youthful Poems". "The kisses of the wind" are no longer possible: this wind neither caresses nor plays jokes, it tyrannizes the personages of the poems, presaging the "Russian draught" that Tsvetaeva called on to "blow my soul away" during the Civil War. The press of verbs gives the poems in *Mileposts* a particular intensity, hurries the theme, and the rapt reader with it, through the book. The novelty and richness of the rhythms and intonation go some way to account for the surprise we feel. Out on the highroad, Tsvetaeva has drawn for the first time on a source previously foreign to her — folklore. She does not imitate, she reproduces the voices of the world into which she has flung her heroine. It has many more voices than her previous world, and it is unfamiliar. Here is a pedlar crying his wares:

> Goods for sale: Goods for sale:
> Hurry, good gentlefolk!
> Golden goods I am selling,
> Clean goods, goods not worn,
> Not threadbare, not dyed,
> I'm not asking too much!

A brazen, devil-may-care, merry voice that rings on in every reader's ear. Here are two similar but distinct voices. The first is that of a sorceress. She wraps her words in mystery, which Tsvetaeva conveys not in her choice of words — the diction is unremarkable — but in the structure and strange rhythm, the juxtaposition of lines with sharply differentiated accentuation:

> You will depart with the first storm-clouds,
> Your way will be through primeval forests and hot-burning sands.
> You will cry out your soul,
> You will weep out your eyes.

The second reads palms, and makes much more precise predictions.

> Downfall from a woman. That,
> Young man, is the sign on your palm.
> Turn your eyes down! Pray! Beware! The enemy
> Keeps vigil at midnight.

Diction, syntax, rhythm — all are different from those of the preceding poem. And here is a third voice — that of a witch invoking the aid of the forces of night:

Black as the pupil of an eye, like an eye sucking
The light – I love you, vigilant night.
Give me a voice to sing your praises, O first mother
Of songs, whose hand holds the bridle of the four winds.

Voloshin said with good reason that at least ten poets co-existed in Marina, and that she harmed herself by excess. He half-seriously suggested that she should publish her poems as the work of ten different poets. "But Max! What would that leave *me* with?" "Everything, Marina! Everything that you have yet to be!" There were indeed new departures ahead. But she had discovered her most important themes: Poetry itself, Russia, Love.

Darkness suffuses the book – twilight, night, menacing skies. But the darkness within is still more intense – a sense of apostasy, unrighteousness, sinfulness, vacillation between intoxication with such feelings and a sudden longing to break out towards the light is characteristic of Tsvetaeva's lyrical heroine. Two poems are devoted to the Annunciation, Tsvetaeva's favourite church feast, when caged birds are traditionally released. Ordinary religious practice seems never to have held much appeal for her, but she describes an Annunciation service in the cathedral of that name with joy and spiritual exhilaration. Her description ends with a demonstration that in spite of everything she has not forgotten how to pray. The poet begs the Mother of God to protect her daughter from the temptations to which she herself had yielded.

> The faces of the saints shine
> In black sleeplessness,
> The window-frames are icy
> In the black cupola.
> Like a golden bush,
> Like a family tree,
> The chandelier droops.
> Blessed be the fruit of thy womb,
> Beloved
> Virgin!
>
> From hand to hand a candle
> Has gone a-wandering.
> From mouth to mouth the word
> Has gone a-wandering:
> "To the Mother of God."
> The candle is lit,
> It's bright, it's hot.

109

> To the Sun-Mother,
> Lost in the shade
> I also appeal and rejoice!
> O Mother,
> Pray preserve for a mother
> Her daughter of the light blue eyes!
> In radiant wisdom
> Enlighten her, send her
> Along the lost path
> Of goodness . . .

This is a prayer from a transgressor who has lost her way, but not all hope: the "accursed places" have not yet taken over her whole soul.

> Grant health to her,
> To her bedside
> Send the Angel,
> Which has flown from me.
> Keep her from verbal exuberance,
> That she should not become predatory,
> Like me, a necromancer.

The only "light" themes in *Mileposts* are her daughter, and Poetry — always to Tsvetaeva the most important theme of all.

In her essay "Hero of Labour" Tsvetaeva states that in the years 1912—1920 she "lived outside the literary life". This is not quite true. She published no new collection after *From Two Books* (1913), nor did she run around in a flock of young poets and poetesses. "I never did and never shall belong to any poetic school", she said emphatically in her "Reply to a Questionnaire" in 1926. Nonetheless, she was part of Moscow literary life and of Russian poetry. Firmly rooted as she was in German romanticism, infatuated though she was in her youth with Napoleon, Rostand and Hugo, modern Russian poetry was still, whether she liked it or not, the medium in which Tsvetaeva had her being, the air she breathed. As though it went without saying, critics have annexed Tsvetaeva to the world of "women's poetry", the very existence of which she would later deny outright. She found the word "poetess", applied to herself, insulting. But although Tsvetaeva had nothing in common with most of the Russian women poets of her time she must have known their work, and she took a lively interest in three of them: Adelaida Gertsyk, Cherubina de Gabriac and Anna Akhmatova. After Ellis, Voloshin had been Tsvetaeva's second Virgil. He had bestowed on her not

Maria Aleksandrovna Tsvetaeva, the poet's mother, 1903

Ivan Vladimirovich Tsvetaev, the poet's father, 1890s

Susanna Davydovna (Tyo) and Aleksandr Danilovich Meyn

In the courtyard of the house on Tryokhprudny. Seated: Valeria, Marina, Maria Aleksandrovna with Asya. Standing: an unknown woman, Nadya Ilovayskaya, Ivan Vladimirovich Tsvetaev and Andrey Tsvetaev

Asya and Marina Tsvetaeva with Aleksandra Ivanovna Dobrokhotova, Nervi, 1903

The Tsvetaev family at their dacha in Tarusa

Asya and Marina Tsvetaeva with Vladislav Aleksandrovich Kobylyansky (Tiger), Nervi, 1903

Asya and Marina Tsvetaeva, 1905

Elena Ottobaldovna Voloshina (Pra),
Koktebel

Maksimilian Aleksandrovich
Voloshin, Koktebel

At the Voloshins' house in Koktebel, 1911. Sergey standing on the left, beside the wheel; Marina Tsvetaeva is sitting on the left; Max Voloshin is standing on the right

Sergey Efron and Marina Tsvetaeva, Autumn 1911

Anastasia Tsvetaeva, Sergey Efron and Marina Tsvetaeva in the drawing room of the house in Tryokhprudny, Moscow, Autumn 1911

Portrait of Marina
Tsvetaeva by Magda
Nakhman, 1913

In the Moscow flat
of the poet Adelaida
Gertsyk, 1915. In the
foreground, seated:
Adelaida Gertsyk with
her son Nikita; to the
right, beside the stove:
E.K.Gertsyk; in the
doorway: Marina
Tsvetaeva; behind her:
the philosopher,
N.A.Berdyaev

Sofia Parnok, early 1900s

Osip Mandelstam, 1914

The autographs of
Osip Mandelstam and
Marina Tsvetaeva on a
page from the album of
the poet Malvina
Maryanova, 1919-20

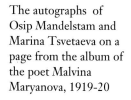

only his friendship but his whole immense and immensely varied circle of art-obsessed friends. His first present was Adelaida Kazimirovna Gertsyk, a poetess twenty years Tsvetaeva's senior. To give the reader some idea of Marina's older friend I shall quote what contemporaries had to say about her. Here are some lines from a sonnet by Vyacheslav Ivanov, written in 1907.

> Be it the rustle of a snake, the whisper of the Sybil,
> Or the crackle of autumn in dry thorns.
> Your magical verse instills fear
> Of the presence of the unseen power of things.
>
> (. . .)
>
> Thus you slip by, a stranger to the fun of girls,
> Closing your lips to love and anger,
> Like a deaf-mute and secret shadow,
>
> Heeding with your heart the roar and song
> Of profound and sleepless sources,
> Suddenly to sob at the fetters of earth's prison.

Voloshin wrote in a poem dedicated to Gertsyk after her death in 1925:

> She could not lie, but one never happened
> To hear the truth from her lips:
> That hackneyed, public, lack-lustre truth,
> With which man is stupefied.
> In her speeches the austere foundations
> Of the world's home-spun hemp was transformed
> Into sacred, sparkling cloth –
> The shroud of Isis . . .

When Gertsyk's sister Evgenia objected to the opening lines Voloshin insisted that they were essential. "That was as a rule the first thing that struck people about Adelaida Kazimirovna [Gertsyk]. Take for example the way she reported things she had heard. Her way of seeing and hearing was so different, that this was the first impression her unusual character made on people." Voloshin's description of her verse closely resembles that of Vyacheslav Ivanov:

> The uneven lines of her poems,
> Whistling like the rustle of ancient grasses
> She would whisper with a prophetic expression,
> Like a village spell against the evil eye . . .

Gertsyk's verse attracts these two poets because it is unmodern, timeless, obsessed with the remoter regions of nature, the soul and time. We can understand why Voloshin called her poems "ancient threnodies". She sought new forms in the diction and rhythms of Russian folklore, and it is possible that Marina first met poetry of that sort in Gertsyk's "Lament".

> Whither do you go, O soul, as you mournfully wend your way?
> Why, burning, do you tremble, why do you grieve?
> Oh, one may not deck you out
> In bright vestments,
> Psalms and songs may not be
> Sung over you! . . .

Remembering how Voloshin had "presented" or "lost" Gertsyk to her, Tsvetaeva confided that "he drew me a picture of her: she was deaf, ugly, ageing and irresistible. She liked my poetry and was hoping to see me. I went – and found only that she was irresistible. We became passionate friends." What could friendship with a woman old enough to be her mother mean to Tsvetaeva? She promised to write a special piece about Gertsyk, "since she was an event in my life as important as Max", but went back on her word. Nor have their sisters, Anastasia Tsvetaeva and Evgenia Gertsyk, filled the gap. Did Marina like Gertsyk's poems? What probably impressed her was Gertsyk's ability to preserve and protect a poetic world of her own, her quest for untrodden ways, her deliberate recourse to the speech of the common people – all that would be so important to Tsvetaeva's own work.

> Suffering's spells were loosened,
> Earth was soothed by torment.
> The hours for silence had arrived,
> Both for forgiveness and oblivion . . .

– wrote Adelaida Gertsyk. And are not Tsvetaeva's poems, too, nourished by "suffering's spells"?

It is difficult nowadays to imagine what readers found in Gertsyk's verses three-quarters of a century ago. To us they seem technically flawed and somewhat monotonous. Nonetheless, we can discern in her verse the strivings of a pure and sincere soul towards light and faith, a soul torn between the need to suffer and a longing for the blissful quiet born of the earth's whispers and the rustlings of the steppe. Her efforts to find simple ways of expressing thoughts and feelings not at all simple, the absence of affection, the "Genius of the heart" – these are other qualities in Gertsyk which could well attract Tsvetaeva. Gertsyk's love of the "charms of suffering" was not a modish affectation. The phrase expressed her reactions

to the joys and pains of living. The Gertsyk family spent the Civil War in the Crimea, which changed hands several times. When the years of hunger, of imprisonment by the Reds, of hovering between life and death, were over, and life was returning to normal, Gertsyk confessed that the "absence of the pathos of disaster seems to have deprived me of the strength to live".

Gertsyk's "Poems", presented to her by the author, Tsvetaeva bound together with Voloshin's in a single volume. She wrote later that "they are forever bound together in my grateful memory". Tsvetaeva attended the literary and philosophical soirées of the Gertsyk sisters and Adelaida's husband Dmitry Zhukovsky. The Revolution separated them – Gertsyk and her husband were in the Crimea, Tsvetaeva in Moscow – but did not end their friendship. When she learnt of the miserable position of the Voloshins and of Gertsyk's family after the occupation of the Crimea by the Red Army Tsvetaeva hastened to aid them. Impractical as she was in her own affairs, she went along to the Kremlin, told Lunacharsky what the situation was, and herself took up a collection amongst Moscow writers for the starving writers in the Crimea. Voloshin informed his mother in December 1921 that he had "written a desperate letter to Marina about the Gertsyks' situation, asking her to set everything in motion in Moscow". "They raised a real storm there . . . This week I received $2\frac{1}{2}$ million for the Gertsyks." Marina also sent the Gertsyk sisters her new volume. In her last letter to a friend in the West Gertsyk wrote: "Tell Marina that her *Mileposts*, which she left for us when she went away, is the best that remains of Russia."

Tsevtaeva was deeply moved by the story of Cherubina de Gabriac, although she never met Elizaveta Ivanovna Dimitrieva (to give the poet her real name). An extraordinary story at first sight, but very much in the spirit of the times, tragic yet farcical.

"Cherubina de Gabriac" was a literary hoax perpetrated by Max Voloshin, before Marina met him. Her name and her poems flashed like a meteor across the pages of the Petersburg magazine *Apollon* and vanished below the literary horizon forever. Tsvetaeva, who knew the whole story from Max, wrote that "Cherubina was cast down from the tower of her castle and smashed to smithereens on the paving-stones of her previous existence". The poetess for whom Voloshin invented this exotic and high-sounding pseudonym, and a mysterious entourage to go with it, was a modest and mousy schoolteacher. Her dealings with *Apollon* were conducted through letters and telephone calls. No one was allowed to see her. Voloshin had, of course, tried to involve Tsvetaeva in a hoax of the same sort when he suggested that she should publish her work under a number of different names. "His mythopoeia," Tsvetaeva wrote, "came to grief on the rocks of my German Protestant honesty, and the lethal pride that makes me put my name to everything I write." Dimitrieva did accept Max's suggestion. Her poems were well reviewed, and the editors of *Apollon* were in love with their unknown contributor. Everybody was eager to see "Cherubina", and in the end Voloshin's hoax was exposed. The poetess ceased to exist and Elizaveta Ivanovna Dimitrieva left Petersburg soon afterwards. Intrigued by Dimitrieva's story, Tsvetaeva wrote to her, sent her own poems, and received a reply. What most interested Tsvetaeva was the connection (or apparent lack of connection) between the poetic gift and its possessor. There was such a contrast between Dimitrieva's person and her high-flown romantic verses. According to Voloshin "she was lame from birth, and from childhood on was used to thinking of herself as a freak". But her soul was that of a rebel. Tsvetaeva wrote of her "no poet rejects any elemental emotion – including the urge to rebel". The pupils of this remarkable and unjustly forgotten poetess, who was also a history teacher, were once asked by the district superintendent of schools "who is your favourite Tsar?" and, not surprisingly, answered with one voice "Grishka Otrepiev".* This incident delighted Tsvetaeva: her own favourite "Tsar" was Pugachov. Odd lines by "de Gabriac" she remembered for years, and she quoted some of them in her essay "A Living Word about a Living Man":

> And the image of shameless orchids
> I hate in worldly faces!

"The image", wrote Tsvetaeva, "is Akhmatova's, the beat is mine, but the lines were written before anything of Akhmatova's or of mine. Which shows the truth of my contention that all the verse there is or ever was or will be is written by one (anonymous) woman."

Tsvetaeva was in love with Akhmatova and her poetry for many years. In love with the image of the woman-poet which she created from Akhmatova's verse, and embodied in her own, though the two met only once, after Tsvetaeva's return from emigration.

In Tsvetaeva's eyes Akhmatova's poetry stood out from the spate of "women's lyrics" and raised her above other women-poets. In 1921 Tsvetaeva wrote to Akhmatova: "you are my favourite poet; long, long ago,

---

* Grigory (Grishka) Otrepiev, a runaway monk who claimed to be (the dead) Tsarevich Dimitry, thus later known as the "False Dimitry", briefly gained the Russian throne at the beginning of the seventeenth century, the so-called "Time of Troubles", taking the place of the disputed Tsar Boris Godunov. The wife of Grishka Otrepiev and Tsaritsa was the Polish princess Maryna Mniszech (Marina Mniszek). All this became the subject of Pushkin's play *Boris Godunov*. See also p. 49 above and p. 132 below.

six years ago, I dreamt of you, and your book to be, in a dark green morocco binding with silver lettering, called 'Golden Words' . . . and when I woke up I knew that you would write it." This dream prompted her to write her first poem to Akhmatova, which is dated 11 February 1915, and ends with this verse:

> At a sleepy, morning hour,
> – It seems it was four-fifteen –
> I fell in love with you,
> Anna Akhmatova.

The poem contains one striking visual image. Drawing the portrait of a woman she had never seen, Tsvetaeva reaches for a painter's brush or pencil:

> You can be conveyed by a single
> Broken, black line . . .

These lines seem to reproduce in words Modigliani's well-known 1911 drawing of Akhmatova, which Tsvetaeva could not have known at the time. With a single, sinuous black line Modigliani sketched the figure of a semi-recumbent woman with bowed head. Reserve and introspection are expressed in her unselfconscious immobility. Tsvetaeva, similarly, finds:

> Cold in your gaiety, heat
> In your misery.

She writes:

> It's no trouble for you
> To attract any mortal!
> And your innocent verse
> Aims straight for the heart . . .

Tsvetaeva's lines and Modigliani's sketch convey the same feeling of strength and vulnerability. At the time of his friendship with the young Akhmatova, Modigliani did not know her poetry: "He greatly regretted that he could not understand my verses, and suspected that marvellous things were concealed there, though in fact these were only timid first attempts." This makes the close similarity between Modigliani's portrayal of Akhmatova and that of Tsvetaeva all the more remarkable. Akhmatova's words seem to suggest that she read her verse to the artist, who listened and regretted that he could not understand it. But her appearance, his conversations with her, the rhythm and melody of her lines enabled him to divine the poet's nature, as it revealed itself to Tsvetaeva in those same early verses. The art historian Nikolay Khardzhiev wrote of Modigliani's drawing: "we have before us not a portrait of Anna Andreevna Gumilyova" (Akhmatova's married name) "as she was in 1911, but a timeless image of the poet listening to her inner voice." Both in the drawing and in Tsvetaeva's poem we catch a prophetic glimpse of Akhmatova's future career.

Tsvetaeva spent the end of December 1915 and the beginning of January 1916 in Petersburg, by then renamed Petrograd. She met several Petersburg poets, but not Blok, Akhmatova or Gumilyov. Akhmatova was not in town. Tsvetaeva's work had begun to appear in the Petrograd journal, *Severnye Zapiski*, she frequented literary salons, and herself gave readings. Literary Petrograd regarded her as a representative of literary Moscow. She got the impression that she was being compared and contrasted with Akhmatova. In her "Otherworldly Evening", dedicated to Mikhail Kuzmin (whom she saw and heard only once), she resurrected one of those literary soirées in Petrograd: "I recited everything I'd written in 1915, and it wasn't enough for them, they still wanted more. I was well aware that I was letting Moscow down, that I must raise Moscow's reputation to Akhmatova's level." Tsvetaeva had an extraordinary gift for appreciating other people's talent. She regarded poetry as something supra-personal, and so was entirely free from envy. In 1916 she wrote a cycle of eleven poems to Akhmatova — poems of rapturous, adoring eulogy. The selfless generosity of Tsvetaeva's raptures is as startling as their extravagance.

> O Muse of weeping, most magnificent of muses!
> O you, chance progeny of a white night!
> You send down upon Russia a black blizzard,
> And your wailing pierces us, like arrows.
>
> And we start back and emit a dull: ah!
> A hundred thousand swear an oath to you: Anna
> Akhmatova! That name is an immense sigh,
> It falls into the depth that knows no name.
>
> We are crowned for we tread upon the same earth
> As you and the heavens above us are the same!
> And he who is mortally wounded by your fate
> Descends to his deathbed already immortal.
>
> In my melodious city the domes are ablaze,
> And a blind beggar glorifies the radiant Saviour . . .
> And I bestow on you my city of bells,
> — Akhmatova! — and my heart I give in addition.

The visit to Petrograd, during which Akhmatova's name followed her everywhere, was one of the experiences that impelled Tsvetaeva to write her cycle. But she did not begin work on it till six months later, so there may well have been others. There is a strange sentence in "History of a Dedication": "Summer 1916 – I am reading Akhmatova for the first time." This surely cannot mean that Tsvetaeva had not seen Akhmatova's *Evening*, in the preface* to which her own name is mentioned. Nor that the many poems by Akhmatova which appeared in periodicals had never come to her notice. Perhaps she meant that she first held a copy of *Rosary* (which then was in its fourth edition) in her hands in the summer of 1916? Tsvetaeva reiterated her statement in a letter to Akhmatova in 1926: ". . . I have loved you for ten years now. Since summer 1916, at Aleksandrovskaya Sloboda." We must, I think, take Tsvetaeva to mean that just as she had earlier, under Nilender's instruction, "heard Orpheus for the first time with the ears of my soul", so now in summer 1916 she first read Akhmatova with the "eyes of her soul". She most probably owed her new insight into Akhmatova to Osip Mandelstam, her guest in Moscow and at Aleksandrov that summer. He was Akhmatova's friend, her colleague in the Poet's Guild and the Acmeist† movement, and a great admirer of her work.

Tsvetaeva and Mandelstam probably talked about Akhmatova and read her verses together. I hear echoes of these conversations in their similar interpretation of that poetic phenomenon, Akhmatova. The similarity becomes particularly clear if we compare Tsvetaeva's cycle with the poems addressed to Akhmatova by Mandelstam in the years 1910–1920 and his article "On Contemporary Poetry (on the occasion of the publication of *Almanac of the Muses*)." Both Mandelstam and Tsvetaeva had ears for the tragic-prophetic notes in Akhmatova's poetry, the hurt and indignation beneath her outer composure.

> An ominous voice – bitter drink –
> Unfetters the depths of the soul:
> Thus – like indignant Phaedra –
> Rachel once stood . . .

as Mandelstam puts it in his "Half turned away, O grief" (1914). And Tsvetaeva echoes him:

---

* In his Preface to Akhmatova's *Vecher* (Evening), published in St Petersburg in 1912, Mikhail Kuzmin linked Tsvetaeva with Mandelstam and Akhmatova as poets who enjoyed every moment of life.

† The Acmeists were a group of poets (including Akhmatova, Gumilyov and Mandelstam) who, from 1909, opposed both the Symbolists and the formal inventions of the Futurists and who were thought to be more conservative, both in poetry and in general outlook.

. . . you, whose voice — O depths, O darkness: —

and again:

> This tender youthfulness is guided
> By pride and bitterness . . . .

She intensifies and carries to their logical extreme the implications of Mandelstam's words "unfetters the depths of the soul" and "indignant Phaedra", crying out, not to avert the spell but to bring it down upon herself:

> You, who tear off the shroud
> From catafalques and cradles,
> Rouser of the fury of the winds,
> And initiator of snow-storms,
>
> Of fevers, of poems and of wars . . .

Her Akhmatova "unfetters" not only souls, but the elements and the forces of destiny. She is a necromancer, with magical powers. The image of the sorceress appears again, this time not victorious but in torment, in her poem "Akhmatova", written at the end of 1921. Both Tsvetaeva and Mandelstam remarked on the songlike character of Akhmatova's verse, its imitation of folk lament. Tsvetaeva extolled the "Muse of weeping" and her "wailing" (as ritual lamentation was called in peasant speech), while Mandelstam wrote that "Akhmatova's verse is close to folksong not only in structure but in substance, since it invariably has the character of ritual lamentation". Anticipating Akhmatova's further development as a poet, Mandelstam prophetically remarked that "the note of renunciation grows ever stronger in her verse, and it is now close to becoming one of the symbols of Russia's greatness". Tsvetaeva has similar things to say, in verse:

> No one do you imitate . . .

And:

> I can hear passionate voices —
> And one that is stubbornly silent . . .

The whole cycle pays homage to Akhmatova's greatness:

> To golden-tongued Anna — of all Russia,
> To her words of atonement,
> May my voice be borne by the wind.

Why does it seem to me so important that Mandelstam and Tsvetaeva were at one about Akhmatova? Mainly because they all belonged to the generation which had superseded the Symbolists and initiated a new epoch in Russian poetry, and yet the three of them were so dissimilar. Tsvetaeva and Akhmatova were opposites in their behaviour as human beings, in their poetic personalities, and in their poetic manner. That was, I believe, what attracted Tsvetaeva to Akhmatova: she loved in her qualities which she lacked herself – above all, restraint and harmony. Akhmatova's outward reserve, concealing the fires within, distances the poet from her verse: in this she is the opposite of Tsvetaeva, whose lines are as turbulent as her nature. In Akhmatova's poetry things at first sight incompatible are harmoniously combined – necromancy and Christian prayer, for instance. Whereas Tsvetaeva is a poet of extremes, of disharmony embodied in lines that don't just weep but sob, forever crying out in pain – even when her voice is not raised above a whisper. Mandelstam spoke of Akhmatova's "hieratic solemnity" and this quality amazed and captivated Tsvetaeva. She exalted Akhmatova's poetry, and the impossibility for her of writing like Akhmatova only heightened its attraction. But Akhmatova would never find Tsvetaeva's poetry congenial, was unmoved by her eulogies, and did not respond to "Poems to Akhmatova". The spring and summer in which she wrote those verses, Mandelstam's visit to Moscow, their long walks together, their talks about Akhmatova, their verse readings – all lived on in Tsvetaeva's imagination as a blissful holiday. In "An Otherworldly Evening" she says "I am indebted to Akhmatova for the poems about Moscow written after my visit to Petersburg". At least two of the nine poems in the Petersburg cycle, however, are addressed to Osip Mandelstam.

MANDELSTAM

Their intimacy perhaps began on that January evening, which Tsvetaeva called "otherworldly". They had taken little notice of each other the previous summer at Koktebel. "I was going down to the sea, as he was coming back from it. We passed each other at the garden gate." And that was all, though they were in Koktebel simultaneously for nearly three weeks in summer 1915. Tsvetaeva then had eyes for nobody except Sofia Parnok, with whom she went on from Koktebel to the Ukraine.

Then, in Petrograd, Tsvetaeva and Mandelstam first heard each other's verse. She remembers him "declaiming, his camel's eyes half-closed":

"Sun — Not Blood — Swells My Veins"

> Let us go to Tsa-arskoye Se-elo,*
> Free and gay and drunken,
> The Uhlans there are smiling,
> Leaping into their strong saddles . . .

The censorship changed '*pyany*' (drunken) to '*ryany*' (dashing): no drunken Uhlans at Tsarskoe Selo, only dashing ones!" Mandelstam recited the uncensored version of his poem, but Tsvetaeva was not to be outdone — she recited for the very first time her "Warring Germany" and "I know the truth! All previous truths begone!" These poems were a declaration of love for Germany and a cry of protest, at the very height of the war.

> People should not fight other people on earth . . .

Mandelstam seemed to have been waiting for this to spur him on: the feelings expressed in Tsvetaeva's verses were close to his own, and he began working on the same theme. 10 January 1916 is the date inscribed in the presentation copy of his new volume, *Stone* ("To Marina Tsvetaeva — a remembrance-stone"). And his "Dithyramb to Peace", an uncompromisingly anti-war poem, entitled in the published version "The Menagerie", is dated 11 January:

> We have learnt how to die,
> But is this what we wanted? —

he asks in one of the early variants. "The Menagerie" is, of course, a profounder work than Tsvetaeva's anti-war poems: she could not yet match Mandelstam's range of cultural-historical and philosophical reference. For the time being she can only defiantly proclaim that:

> Germany is my madness!
> Germany is my love!
>
> (. . .)
>
> . . . I swear to you, O Germany,
> I am in love with you till the grave.

Whereas Mandelstam seeks the roots of this love, and of the ancient kinship of Russia and Germany.

> And I sing the wine of ages —
> The origin of Italic speech —

---

* Tsarskoe Selo ("Tsar's Village") is the imperial residence and estate just outside St Petersburg (renamed Pushkin).

And Slavonic and Germanic flax
In the proto-Aryan cradle!

Later, a maturer Tsvetaeva would call these lines of Mandelstam's "an inspired formulation of the union between ourselves and Germany from the cradle and for all time".

That was how their intimacy began. In "History of a Dedication" Tsvetaeva remembered that "the whole period, from the 'Germanic-Slavonic flax' to 'We walked in the cemetery' [i.e. the poem "Not believing in the miracle of resurrection"] belonged to me, those wonderful days from February to June 1916 when I made Mandelstam a present of Moscow." We know little about the details of their relationship. When Tsvetaeva went home to Moscow from Petrograd on 20 January Mandelstam followed her and stayed there about two weeks. After his departure Tsvetaeva wrote her first poem to him — by way of farewell.

No one has taken anything away!
It's delightful that we are apart.
I send you a kiss — across hundreds
Of separating versts . . .

"I didn't know that he was coming back," she noted on one manuscript. He returned to Moscow that February, and the succession of "arrivals and departures, raids and retreats," as Tsvetaeva put it, continued into the summer. He travelled to Moscow so frequently that he occasionally thought of taking a job and settling there. Connections of his old friend Sergey Kablukov tried to find him employment in which he could use his knowledge of languages — in the Universal Library publishing house, or in a bank. Nothing, of course, came of it, or could come of it, Mandelstam being the man he was. Who can imagine him working in a bank? The lady who was trying to find him a place wrote to Kablukov: "Since he goes backwards and forwards between Moscow and Petersburg so often perhaps he ought to take one job there and another here? Or is he perhaps working with the railway? He's more like an aeroplane than a man."

Kablukov himself asked Vyacheslav Ivanov to get Mandelstam on to the staff of *Russian Thought*. It all ended suddenly. Early in the summer Mandelstam was Tsvetaeva's guest at Aleksandrov, where she was staying with her sister. And from there he beat his final retreat, never to return. Tsvetaeva wrote about it with understanding, humour and affection. But in a letter to Elizaveta Efron written immediately after the event and published only recently, Tsvetaeva speaks of it in quite a different vein — ironically, almost mockingly. I am, however, inclined to trust the poems she and Mandelstam wrote, and the "History of a Dedication", rather than the letter, in which Tsvetaeva was probably disingenuously turning a serious and deeply emotional relationship into a joke. She was, after all, writing to her husband's sister about her first affair since Parnok. Besides, the liaison had only just ended, and Tsvetaeva was probably smarting from Mandelstam's defection. That is all we can say about the facts, but there is something much more important — the verse.

> There remains to us only the name —
> A magical sound, for a long time.
> Please accept from me the sand
> Which I pour from palm to palm . . .

Mandelstam wrote this to Tsvetaeva from Koktebel after his "retreat". A complex chain of associations leads from it to a poem written three years before he met Tsvetaeva, with the line:

> And eternity is like sand from the sea . . .

And Tsvetaeva would say a little later:

> With me, in my hand — almost a handful of dust —
> Are my poems! . . .

The poems which Mandelstam and Tsvetaeva addressed to each other bear no dedication, but Tsvetaeva lists the most important of them in "History of a Dedication", and not long before she died she marked her poems to Mandelstam in a copy of *Mileposts: I* belonging to Aleksey Kruchonykh. Those poems which form part of the "dialogue" but were not mentioned by her can be identified by their context and date of composition.

As I have said, their dialogue begins at what looks like the end — with Tsvetaeva's farewell verses:

> No one has looked at you departing
> More tenderly, more irrevocably . . .
> I send you a kiss across hundreds
> Of separating years.

There is nothing here by which we can identify Mandelstam the man. Even her endearments are for the Poet. Tsvetaeva was the first to point out his poetic descent from the great and grand Derzhavin, contrasting his verse with her own — "unmannerly", remote from all poetic schools, born of the chaos within her.

> I know that our gift is unequal.
> My voice for the first time is quiet.
> What are they to you, young Derzhavin,
> My unmannerly verses!

In the first line of the next stanza her eulogy of Mandelstam is interrupted by a jarring note.

> I bless you on your terrible flight:
> Fly away, young eagle!
> You suffered the sun without blinking –
> Is my young glance so heavy?

All perfectly clear, but ... Why does she ask "Is my young glance so heavy?" And how is this connected with the word "terrible"? Can a young woman's glance seem "terrible"? She obviously has in mind what is called "the evil eye": she fears that her praise may bring ill-luck to Mandelstam, and takes comfort in the thought that she does not have the evil eye. That her glance is not "heavy" echoes the colloquial expression "I shan't put the evil eye on you, I have a light eye".

In this poem Tsvetaeva first showed an anxiety for her friend's future which she herself could not have explained at the time. She could not know that her prophecy would come true. She said in a letter to Aleksandr Bakhrakh* fifteen years later: "I do know that spells can be cast inadvertently, and that they nearly always bring misfortune! But – thanks be to all the gods – misfortune for oneself! I am not afraid of myself, I am afraid of my verses." She was wrong: in her verses to Mandelstam she had wished on him – or perhaps only foretold – all his misfortunes.

To rid herself of her troubled premonitions she writes this adjuration:

> Seeing my loved ones off on a journey,
> I sing them songs for them to remember ...

But instead of addressing herself to a loved one or loved ones she calls on the forces of nature (like Prince Igor's Yaroslavna† in her lament for her lost husband) – on the wind, the road, the cloud, and after that on the snake, and on people, begging them to be kind and to help those from whom she is parting:

> Throw away, robber, your fierce knife.

---

* A young critic and journalist living in Berlin in the 1920s, with whom Tsvetaeva corresponded in the summer of 1923 after he had reviewed her books *Craft* and *Parting*.

† The twelfth-century *Lay of the Host of Igor* tells the tale of Prince Igor's raid against the nomad Polovtsy; the lament of his wife Yaroslavna is a particularly fine and famous passage.

> You, passing beauty,
> Be to them a joyous bride . . .

— and ends with a prayer:

> O Mother of God in the heavens,
> Remember those of mine that pass!

In the next month Tsvetaeva wrote two other friendly and affectionate poems to Mandelstam, and received one in the same vein from him . . . Then, suddenly, the disaster theme returns — this time not as a foreboding, but as a certainty.

> Downfall from a woman. That,
> Young man, is the sign on your palm.

Even the poet's widow, Nadezhda Mandelstam, failed to see the significance of these lines, and took their first words literally. From the third line onwards Tsvetaeva forgets about the "woman", and "someone" (unnamed and undefined) makes his appearance:

> . . . Enemy
> Is on watch at midnight . . .

She sees no hope of salvation.

> No salvation, neither
> From the heavenly gift of song, nor haughty curl of lip.
> You are liked,
> Since you are from heaven.

Liked by whom? And who is the enemy? The enigmatic character of the lines is explained largely by the vagueness of the poet's prophetic knowledge, but also by their form: they are written as though spoken by a fortune-teller, whose whole art consists in speaking in vague hints into which everyone can read something of relevance to himself. The next strange stanza gives a faithful portrait of Mandelstam (everyone who ever saw him mentions the half-closed eyes and the haughty tilt of his head) and at the same time, a glimpse into the future. The twice repeated "ah!" conveys the dread which her words inspire in the speaker herself:

> Ah, your head thrown back,
> Eyes half-closed and hiding — what?
> Ah, your head will be thrown back —
> In a different way.

The first lines, apart from their photographic quality, are also a picture of the poet's inner self. They link up with the opening of a poem written three days later:

> A strange malaise struck him down,
> And a most sweet fear came upon him.
> He would stand and gaze heavenwards,
> And the youth with his far-sighted eye
> Would see neither stars nor morning glow.

Tsvetaeva is describing the poetic trance, the "sweet fear" when, with "eyes sleepily closed" and "mouth half-open", staring and seeing nothing, the poet sinks into himself, concealing his poetic thoughts under his eyelids. At such moments – and a poet's life is made up entirely of such moments, – he is quite defenceless. We know now exactly what happened to Mandelstam on the night of 1–2 May 1938: how *they* came to the godforsaken sanatorium, cut off from the outside world, rummaged through his belongings, put him on a lorry and carried him off forever to rot in a camp and be thrown into a common grave. Since his last lines – so pure and so profound – have only reached us a quarter of a century later, Tsvetaeva's prophecy inspires a religious trepidation, almost horror:

> They will take you with bare hands – high-spirited! Stubborn!
> The countryside will be ringing all night with your cries!
> They will rumple your wings to all the four winds,
> O, Seraph! O, Eaglet!

The second of these poems is less concrete and less ominous, but the disaster theme is repeated.

> And if he falls asleep – eagles
> With screams and flapping wings fly towards him . . .
>
> (. . .)
> And he doesn't see a golden-eyed bird
> Sharpening its all-seeing beak.

It is significant that the hero of these poems perishes because of his verses.

I have no doubt that Tsvetaeva's premonition, or incantation, came to her spontaneously, that she did not know what she was doing, and never fully understood with what terrifying accuracy she had foretold Mandelstam's future. "I'm afraid of my verses." If she had realized what she was writing she would have thrown down her pen or hidden her exercise book in a bottomless desk drawer. She is much more of a sorceress and black magician here than where she so describes herself.

Was theirs a love affair in the ordinary sense? Yes — and the relationship meant more to Mandelstam than to Tsvetaeva. The "divine boy" and "beautiful brother" in Mandelstam were more important to her than the beloved, although her encounter with him brought about the definitive break with Parnok. Nadezhda Mandelstam wrote that it was Tsvetaeva who taught him how to love. I ventured to ask her whether Tsvetaeva was the first woman in his life. Not the first, but Nadezhda Mandelstam was nonetheless certain that the "wild and vivid Marina" had "unshackled his love of life and his ability to love freely and uninhibitedly". And also his ability to write love poems. Mandlestam's first true love lyrics are those addressed to Tsvetaeva. Anna Akhmatova says of his "Like a Black Angel in the Snow" (1910), which is addressed to her: "At that time Osip didn't yet (in his own words) 'know how to' write poems to and about a woman." Equally interesting is an entry in the diary of Sergey Kablukov, who was perturbed by the sudden appearance of "eroticism" in his young friend's verses. He spoke to Mandelstam about it on the last day of 1916: "The subject of our conversation was his most recent poems, which were frankly erotic, and which reflected his experiences during the past few months. Some woman had obviously entered his life. Religion and the erotic are somehow bound up together in his soul in a way that seems to me blasphemous . . . I reproached him bitterly for his disloyalty to the better tradition of *Stone*, that purest and most chaste treasure-house, every poem in which is a sublime spiritual achievement. Mandelstam was penitent, but could find no way out of "this situation". One surprising point is that Kablukov was upset by the "eroticism" of Mandelstam's last poem to Tsvetaeva "Not believing in the miracle of resurrection . . ." yet appears not to have noticed the presence of a woman in Mandelstam's first poem to Tsvetaeva, "In the polyphony of a maidens' choir", which he considered "excellent".

This first poem dated late February, is in fact profoundly imbued with the presence of Tsvetaeva. A comparison with Tsvetaeva's "You throw back your head" leaves no doubt that Mandelstam and Tsvetaeva are talking about the same thing:

> You throw back your head
> Because you are a proud man and a fibber.
> What a gay and cheerful companion
> This February has brought me!

> Pursued by ragamuffins
> And slowly emitting smoke,
> Like solemn-faced foreigners
> We walk through our native city . . .

Ragamuffins gaping at two strange poets, one of whom really is a foreigner, from Petersburg, looking at everything around him with wonder – this is almost a snapshot of Mandelstam and Tsvetaeva walking around Moscow. Tsvetaeva then pauses to say a few words about her companion:

> Whose careful hands have caressed
> Your eyelashes, beautiful boy . . .

(The length and thickness of Mandelstam's eyelashes was almost legendary. As Nadezhda Mandelstam said: "If there's a mention of eyelashes, then its about Osip.") The first line – especially through its repeated soft sounds – wonderfully conveys Tsvetaeva's tenderness towards Mandelstam . . . In another poem written on the same day she expresses bewilderment:

> Whence such tenderness?
> These are not the first curls
> I have smoothed, and I have known
> Lips darker than yours . . .

This degree of tenderness does not leave room for jealousy:

> Whose careful hands have caressed
> Your eyelashes, beautiful boy,
> And through what thorny paths
> The laurel-strewn road will take you –

The third and fourth lines are echoes of her previous anxiety on behalf of Mandelstam. She has a momentary premonition that the laurel-strewn road will lead Mandelstam to a crown of thorns. She then continues:

> – I am not asking. My thirsting spirit
> Has by now stifled its dream.
> What I am honouring in you
> Is a divine boy, ten years old.

Her "thirsting spirit" is lofty enough to accept the present for what it is. She does not begrudge the 'divine boy" his attachments either to other women or to the Muses:

> Let us linger by the river,
> Which rinses the coloured beads of lanterns,

> I shall lead you to the square,
> Which has been the witness of boy-tsars . . .
>
> Whistle away the boyish pain
> And squeeze your heart in your hand . . .
> My cold-blooded one, my frantic one,
> My slave set free — goodbye!

Where has this theme of "pain" come from? Why "squeeze your heart"? Why "goodbye"? . . . If Mandelstam is a "slave set free", it must be because she is letting him go, with gifts. Instead of herself she has given him Moscow — and Russia. It may be that she was the first person ever to show him the Kremlin:

> I shall lead you to the square
> Which has been the witness of boy-tsars . . .

"In the varied voices of a maidens' choir" is Mandelstam's response to the Kremlin Cathedral Square. In his mind the square itself has become confused with the woman who gave it to him:

> In the varied voices of a maidens' choir
> All the delicate churches sing in their own way,
> In the stone arches of the Cathedral of the Assumption
> I seem to see eyebrows, high and arched . . .

We all know how our perception of something is influenced by our feelings. In other circumstances Mandelstam might have seen the Cathedral of the Assumption as very masculine; he might have said that its cupolas were like the helmets of old Russian warriors . . . On this occasion, however, the Cathedral reminded him of girlhood. And this was not entirely fantasy on his part — the cupolas of the old cathedrals really do look like the traditional head-dresses of peasant women and girls . . . And their arches reminded him of Tsvetaeva's eyebrows. In another poem he sees these eyebrows as an expression of surprise:

> The Assumption Cathedral, wondrously rounded,
> All — a surprise of heavenly arches . . .

This is Mandelstam's own surprise in the face of a beauty he had never seen before. We next see Tsvetaeva and Mandelstam as they stand beside the Moscow river ("which rinses the coloured beads of lanterns"), climb up to the Kremlin and look across from Cathedral Square to the far side of the river. Behind them and to the left stands Archangel Cathedral:

And from the rampart fortified by archangels
I viewed the town from a marvellous height.
In the walls of the Acropolis I was consumed by sorrow
For a Russian name and Russian beauty.

Mandelstam still feels himself to be a foreigner in this city and on this square. A foreigner in many ways: as a Jew, as an inhabitant of St Petersburg and as a non-Orthodox (as a young man Mandelstam had been baptized a Lutheran). He is astonished at the beauty of Russia and regrets that it is still foreign to him. The poem's last two verses show that when Mandelstam feels "sorrow for a Russian name and Russian beauty", he is thinking not only of Russia, Moscow and the Kremlin but also of a particular woman. It is not for nothing that he uses the same archaic word for *garden* as is used in the Russian translation of the *Song of Songs*.

Is it not a miracle of miracles that we dream
Of a garden, where doves soar in a hot blue sky,
That a nun sings ancient Orthodox notes:
A tender Assumption – Florence in Moscow.

And the five-domed cathedrals of Moscow
With their Italian and Russian soul
Summon up for me the appearance of Aurora,
But with a Russian name and wearing a fur coat.

"A tender Assumption – Florence in Moscow" alludes to the fact that the builders of the Assumption Cathedral were Italian. But *Florence* – as a Mandelstam scholar has pointed out – is also an Italian equivalent of the word *Tsvetaeva* [both mean "flowering"]. And the Aurora with a Russian name and a fur coat is of course also Tsvetaeva – the fur coat is mentioned in Tsvetaeva's prose.

The last poems that Mandelstam and Tsvetaeva wrote to one another – Mandelstam's "Not believing in the miracle of resurrection" and Tsvetaeva's "Past the night-time towers" – are the most erotic in both their amorous and philosophical duet. Tsvetaeva in fact wrote three poems on 31 March – the first three poems of the cycle "Poems about Moscow". The first two are day-time poems: "Clouds", to her daughter, and "Receive from me this city not made by hand", addressed to Mandelstam. Perhaps she took them both for a walk around Moscow at about that time? From some high point – the Sparrow Hills or perhaps the Kremlin mount – she shows little

Alya Moscow and bequeaths this "wondrous" and "peaceful" city to her and her future children:

> Surrounded by clouds,
> Surrounded by domes,
> Over all of Moscow —
> As far as the eye can see! —
> I raise you up, best of burdens,
> Oh, my sapling
> As light as a feather!
>
> (. . .)
>
> Your turn will come,
> You too will hand over
> Moscow to your daughter
> With tender bitterness . . .

And at the same time, or a few hours later, she makes a present of Moscow to Mandelstam:

> Receive from me this city not made by hand
> My strange, my beautiful brother . . .

Together with him she surveys the whole city: through the chapel of the Iversky Virgin to Red Square, through the Spassky Gate into the Kremlin, to her beloved "Matchless circle of five cathedrals" — Cathedral Square.

The third poem written that day is a nocturne. It is difficult to know what actual event it refers to. Its opening lines take us out again into the streets of Moscow, which at that hour are for some reason frightening:

> Past the night-time towers
> The squares rush us away.
> Oh, how terrible is the roar
> Of young soldiers in the night!

It is possible that this moment is also reflected in a poem Mandelstam wrote around this time:

> Oh, this air, drunk with riot
> On the black Kremlin square!
> Trouble-makers shake the tottering "world",
> The poplars have a smell of fear.

Then comes the first and only outburst of passion in Tsvetaeva's "Mandelstam" poems.

> Thunder, thundering heart!
> Kiss with heat, O love!
> Oh, this brutal roar!
> Oh, the audacious blood!
>
> My mouth is burning,
> No good the holy look . . .

And yet for all their wild passion these verses speak of rejection, of breaking off the relationship:

> Put an end to your mischief
> And light a candle,
> So that what I wish on you
> Doesn't now happen.

The intimacy between Mandelstam and Tsvetaeva lasted until his visit to Aleksandrov in June. After his "retreat" to Koktebel Mandelstam sent her his farewell poem. This ["Not believing in the miracle of resurrection"] is indeed the most erotic poem that Mandelstam had yet written. (If that word can be applied to his poetry at all: in my view no love lyrics in the Russian language are more restrained than those of Mandelstam. Kablukov must have taken fright at the word "kiss", three times repeated, and, worse still, its proximity to the line "Not believing . . . .")

Was the attachment to Tsvetaeva Mandelstam's only reason for travelling backwards and forwards to Moscow in those months? When he met her his personality was already fully formed and he had very definite views not only about poetry ("knowledge of one's rightness") but on history and the cultural-historical process. Ancient Greece, Rome and medieval Europe were the cornerstones of his philosophy of history. He derived from Christianity his view of "man's place in the universe". He had already formulated his views in articles – "François Villon", "An Interlocutor", "Pyotr Chaadaev", "Pushkin and Skryabin". There is no doubt that in the ordinary business of living, Tsvetaeva was more mature and experienced than Mandelstam, but intellectually she was a child in comparison, and had never given a thought to the philosophical problems that interested him. They had in common their love for and understanding of Europe, their devotion to ancient Greece and to Germany. But in one thing Tsvetaeva the Muscovite was ahead of Mandelstam the Petersburger – her feeling for Russia. The two poets stood at opposite poles of Russia. Petersburg, new and stone-built, felt the pull of the West, ancient wood-built Moscow that of the East. Moscow was thought of as more Russian, more traditional, more Orthodox. Mandelstam was drawn to Rome and

Catholicism. Muscovite Russia and Orthodox Christianity had no place in his meditations on the history of European culture. Before his friendship with Tsvetaeva he had not been aware that his field of vision was limited in this way. Tsvetaeva revealed Moscow to Mandelstam – and a Russia he had never known before. She and Mandelstam clearly talked about all this, and this is why what she gave him was not concerts, not museums, but Moscow itself – which is what, at that moment, he needed more than anything. With the generosity of the true owner, Tsvetaeva bestows her own birthright on this "guest from a strange land".

> Receive from me this city not made by hand,
> My strange, my beautiful brother.
>
> Church by church – all forty times forty,
> And over them the young pigeons soaring.
>
> And the Saviour Gate with flowers,
> Where the Orthodox doff their hats.
>
> The star-studded chapel – a shelter from evils –
> Where the floor is worn down from kisses.
>
> The matchless circle of five cathedrals,
> Accept it, my inspired, my ancient friend.
>
> I shall take the guest from a foreign land
> To the garden with the church of Unexpected Joys.
>
> The golden cupolas will glitter,
> The sleepless pealing of bells will ring out,
>
> And from the purple clouds Our Lady
> Will let fall upon you a shroud,
>
> And you will rise up, imbued with wondrous strength . . .
> You will not repent that you once loved me.

These lines can perhaps be seen as a response to the religious and philosophical preoccupations which Mandelstam imparted to Tsvetaeva. They mark the beginning of another part of their poetic duet: four poems by Tsvetaeva and two by Mandelstam.

Inevitably, as they walked round old Moscow, the two poets spoke of the Moscow period of Russian history. Tsvetaeva's response was to write "Dimitry! Marina! In the world . . .", a poem about "The Time of Troubles". This poem, addressed to Tsarevich Dimitry, the False Dimitry and Marina Mniszek* (whose fate had always had a particular resonance for Tsvetaeva), ends with the lines:

---

* See note to p. 114.

> Marina! Dimitry! Peace be with you,
> Rioters, sleep on, my dears.
> Above the tender angelic sepulchre
> In the Cathedral of the Archangel
> A large candle burns for you.

Had Tsvetaeva and Mandelstam gone in together to the Archangel Cathedral and lit a candle at the tomb of Tsarevich Dimitry? The Archangel Cathedral also appears in one of Mandelstam's own poems:

> The Cathedrals of the Archangel and Resurrection
> Are translucent like the palm of a hand.

It is almost as though the light of the large candle mentioned by Tsvetaeva is shining through the walls of the cathedral . . .

The key poem of this group is Mandelstam's "On a country sleigh, laid out with straw". This exceptionally enigmatic poem constitutes Mandelstam's most profound response to the poems addressed to him by Tsvetaeva. He is no longer a stranger, he has taken the fate of Russia into himself and he has fused his own fate with that of his country. The poem begins with a "Moscow" verse: "we" – Mandelstam and Tsvetaeva perhaps? – are riding on a sleigh through Moscow. But the line "Ourselves barely covered by fateful bast-matting", however, makes one suspect that they are being taken against their will:

> On a country sleigh, laid out with straw,
> Ourselves barely covered by fateful bast-matting,
> We rode through immense Moscow
> From Sparrow Hills to a familiar little church.

In the second verse the scene abruptly shifts to Uglich [the town where the Tsarevich Dimitry met his mysterious death]. It becomes clear that the speaker – now *I* rather than *we* – is indeed being taken against his will. Where is he being taken and why? And why have three candles been lit – who is it that has died? A sense of doom – of some impending execution – hangs over the sleigh:

> And in Uglich children are playing at knucklebones,
> You can smell bread that's been left in the oven . . .
> I am borne through the streets without a cap,
> And three candles are glimmering in the chapel.

> Not three candles were burning, but three meetings:
> One of them was blessed by God himself,

A fourth is not to be, and Rome is far off —
And he never did love Rome.

This is not the place to attempt to decipher the third verse, though it does, of course, allude to the old claim: "Moscow is the third Rome, and there will not be a fourth". The most important point is clear enough: the poem's persona looks on Moscow as spiritually closer to him than Rome is. Not that Mandelstam is necessarily disavowing his love of Rome: the preceding lines are written in the first person — "I" or "we" — whereas here we have "*he* never did love Rome". Also, if this is indeed what is about to happen, we do not know why the hero is to be executed: because he never loved Rome, or because he has now renounced his love for Rome?

Mandelstam has now learnt to hear "the underground music of Russian history" to which he refers in his article "The Badger's Lair". The ecstatic surprise of a stranger has been replaced by the cool, sober perception of someone who feels at home. What he sees is simply everyday Russian life, a life that has continued like this for hundreds of years:

> The sleigh kept diving into black pot-holes,
> The people were returning from their revels.
> Skinny peasants and bad-tempered old women
> Were cracking seeds by the gates.
>
> The raw distance was growing black from flocks of birds,
> The bound hands had swollen up:
> They're bringing the Tsarevich, his body terribly numb,
> And the ginger straw has been set alight.

It has been suggested that the Tsarevich in the last lines is the son of Peter the Great, the Tsarevich Aleksey who was ordered by his father to be taken from Moscow to Petersburg and then executed. It is also, however, possible, that Mandelstam had in mind both the Tsarevich Dimitry — who died in Uglich — and the False Dimitry — who was executed in Moscow — and that he was consciously blurring the distinction between the false and the real. Tsvetaeva, after all, had done just this in her poem "Dimitry, Marina, in the world . . .".

But whether it is the true or the false Dimitry who is being taken somewhere by sleigh, it is also the poet himself. "On a country sleigh, laid out with straw" is Mandelstam's answer to Tsvetaeva, a resolution of the historical themes they had discussed, a catharsis. By accepting Moscow from her hands, Mandelstam accepted all of Russia — together with all its light and all its darkness. This is made very clear in the next poem, which begins "on the black square of the Kremlin" and finishes with a vision of inner light:

> The Cathedrals of the Archangel and the Resurrection
> Are translucent like the palm of a hand –
> Everywhere there is a secret burning,
> A fire concealed in pitchers.

This fire is now Mandelstam's own fire. Mandelstam was never to regret accepting Tsvetaeva's gift and he was never to renounce it. But as he took Russia into himself, as he began to see himself as a part of Russian history, he also foresaw his own doom. "On a country sleigh, laid out with straw" is Mandelstam's answer to Tsvetaeva's various prophecies; it is his first premonition – and acceptance – of his own fate.

At the time Tsvetaeva was twenty-three and Mandelstam twenty-five. It is doubtful whether either of them realized the importance of their time together. Mandelstam's widow, however, has spoken on his behalf in her *Hope Abandoned*:

His friendship with Tsvetaeva had in my view an enormously important influence on Mandelstam's life and work (and for him life and work were one and the same). This was the bridge by which he passed from one period to another . . . Tsvetaeva's gift of her friendship and of Moscow seemed to release him from a charmed sleep. It was a marvellous gift, because with Petersburg alone, without Moscow, there is no breathing freely, no real feel for Russia, no moral freedom . . .

On Tsvetaeva, too, their friendship left its mark. The seriousness and profundity of Mandelstam's meditations on the world, on history and culture, widened her horizons. She too began to "breathe freely". Her poetry became at once broader and deeper. Just as Mandelstam, in the verses to Tsvetaeva with which his *Tristia* begins, entered on a new stage in his poetic career, so for Tsvetaeva the "Mandelstam" poems mark a new departure. She reckoned that her work had never been influenced by literature, only by other people. This was certainly true of her love affair with Mandelstam. She was never influenced by his poetry, but ripened and discovered new possibilities in herself under the influence of his personality. The cycles addressed to Blok and to Akhmatova could not have been written before the verses to Mandelstam.

Seryozha left the hospital train that summer. He was drafted into the army, and sent to a school for junior officers. Before going he was able to spend a little time in his beloved Koktebel. "At least, he will get a bit of a rest before he goes on his course," Marina wrote to Lilya Efron. "Incidentally, I'm certain they'll discharge him soon – he feels horribly unwell." At Koktebel, Sergey had got to know Vladislav Khodasevich, a poet not given to extravagant praise, who mentioned him in a letter to his wife: "A charming boy (he's twenty-two). Going to Moscow to join the army. A student, been called up. Pity he's leaving." In another letter Seryozha is a "nice and clever boy". Everybody still thought of him as a boy, though he had been a "family man" for some time: little Ariadna was nearly four years old. (These letters, incidentally, refute his daughter's belief that he joined up voluntarily: he was in fact called up). He reported for training that autumn. The war had come closer to the whole family. There was a training ground at Aleksandrov, and Tsvetaeva could watch the recruits drilling. She and the children – Alya and her nephew Andrey – went down to the station to watch troop trains leaving for the front. "We waved handkerchiefs, and they waved their caps." "Loud singing mingled with train smoke buffeted our faces long after the last car had disappeared from view." She felt no more patriotic than she had at the beginning of the war, and had no dreams of victory. Her rejection of the war was reinforced by the absurdity of what was going on, the futility of all those millions of casualties. She saw the war through the eyes of a simple soldier's wife, without histrionics and high-flown words. Indeed she wrote very little about the war. One line from her "Poems to Blok" sums up her attitude: "And so much talk of the Germans you're sick and tired of it!"

All the same, her impressions of Aleksandrov were bound to find an outlet in verse:

A white sun and low, low-hanging storm-clouds
By the kitchen-gardens, behind a white wall, a church-yard.
And on the sand a row of dummies, made of straw,
Under cross-beams, the height of a man.

And bending over, across the pickets of a fence,
I can see: roads, and trees, and soldiers scattered.
An old peasant woman stands by a wicket-gate
And chews a hunk of black bread, sprinkled with coarse salt.

How have these grey huts roused your wrath,
Oh, Lord! and for what must so many have their chests shot through?
The train passed by with a scream, and the soldiers screamed,
And the receding track was covered in dust, covered in dust . . .

No, better to die! Better never to have been born,
Than this piteous, pitiful, wail of convicts
For black-browed beauties. – Oh, and how they sing now,
These soldiers! Oh, Lord God, my God!

She was soon to be a "soldier's wife" herself. In January 1917 Sergey
Efron was sent to a holding battalion for junior officers at Nizhny Novgorod.
This was, of course, better than the front line, but his family and friends
were full of anxiety for him. We can see this from a letter written by
Khodasevich to his friend the poet and critic Boris Sadovskoy – surely at the
request of Efron himself or of Tsvetaeva.

"Marina Tsvetaeva's husband, Sergey Efron, a nice and clever man
whom I know well, was posted yesterday to Nizhny, to some holding
battalion for ensigns. He is a sick man, not very good at looking after
himself, and he knows no one in Nizhny. I thought I would give him your
address. If he should come to you for help please don't refuse him . . . I repeat
– he's a sick man, like you and me . . . I apologize again, but I'm desperately
sorry for Efron. He was called up because of some monstrous misunderstanding." The misunderstanding was not corrected. Efron was cut off from
his pregnant wife and from little Alya. Marina was having a difficult
pregnancy, and had to cope with unaccustomed problems caused by the
war. Her difficulties were aggravated by her separation from her husband
and her anxiety for him. But even this did not arouse in her any hatred of
"the enemy". In the third year of the war she expressed her attitude to what
was going on around her in a formula which continued to serve her during
the Civil War:

This night I kiss the breast of all
This whole round world at war.

For Tsvetaeva the world was not divided into "our side" and "the
Germans". As she was to say, later: "If he bleeds, he is my son."

CHAPTER 4

REVOLUTION

There is no important contemporary Russian poet whose voice
did not falter, then grow firmer after the Revolution.

TSVETAEVA

TSVETAEVA WAS EXPECTING A CHILD, and determined, as her
mother had once been, that it should be a son. This hope made a difficult
pregnancy and her loneliness – there was no news from Seryozha – more
bearable. She spent her nights writing, trying to dispel her fears and
anxieties. She was not overwhelmed by a flood of verse as she had been the
spring and summer before, but still the verses came.

Moscow lived in anticipation of great events, but Tsvetaeva, absorbed
in her own hopes and forebodings, seems not to have noticed what was
happening. News of the coup in Petrograd reached Moscow on 27 February,
and that evening telephone lines between the two cities were cut. Next day
workers began to strike, trams stopped running, and there were no
newspapers. Excitement ran high in Moscow, but in spite of it all nothing
very frightening happened – there was no shooting, no street fighting.
Journalists remarked that "exemplary order reigned throughout". The
artist Yulia Obolenskaya wrote to a friend that "what was really strange
was getting your parcel with the dried fruit and coffee . . . on the first day of
the Revolution, while the street outside was wild with joy and gun carriages
with red flags were rolling by. You felt that outside there was a whirlwind, a
hurricane, but as far as your own little dog kennel was concerned it was like
being on an uninhabited island. Then suddenly – a ring and a parcel
containing blackcurrants! The 'island', of course, is hyperbole . . . in fact the
local telephone never stopped working, the supplies of candles and water
that some people laid in proved to be unnecessary, since everything was in
ideal order. All this added to the strangeness, the fairy-tale quality of what
was happening . . . ."

Many others felt the same exhilaration, the same wonder at the strange beauty of it all. When Nicholas II abdicated on 3 March and his brother refused the throne it seemed that a marvellous life and an era of general prosperity lay just ahead. A leading article in the *Historical Herald* said that "a bright sun has risen over the Russian land, on which its life-giving rays will shed warmth and light, bringing out the creative forces, so long repressed by the old regime . . .".

Aleksandr Blok, who had been in the army, returned to Petrograd in March and wrote to his mother that "a miracle has happened, and other miracles must follow. Not one of us could ever have expected to witness these simple miracles that are now daily occurrences. You might think that it would all be very frightening, but it isn't at all – this majestic freedom, these army vehicles with red flags, soldiers' greatcoats with red armbands, the red flag on the roof of the Winter Palace." And what was Tsvetaeva's reaction? It was hardly possible for her to go running round the city even if she had wanted to. But she too went out into the streets and saw the excited crowds, the soldiers, the red flags. She heard the whispers as well as the shouting. But her reaction was different from that of Blok.

> And they pass by – the colour of ash and sand –
> The troops of the revolution.
>
> (. . .)
>
> They have no faces, they have no names,
> They have no songs!

The Song was for Tsvetaeva the measure of truth. Her understanding of these events was determined not by the red flags but by the absence of singing. "Song" in this context is to be understood not only literally but also in an esoteric sense close to Blok's "world music".* Was it, perhaps, Tsvetaeva's shortsightedness that prevented her from seeing the Revolution, as Blok, Mayakovsky and many other contemporaries did, in a "miraculous light"?

> You have lost your way, Kremlin peals,
> In this windy forest of banners.
> Say a prayer, Moscow, lie down, Moscow to eternal sleep!

These lines are from a poem written on the day of Nicholas II's abdication. Chronologically it is the first of those included later in *The Camp of the Swans*. Tsvetaeva had never been a monarchist, and the abdication

---

* Blok gave the name "music" to the energy of the people which was suppressed in the age of bourgeois civilization and was reawakening in the years of revolution.

139

itself could not have inspired thoughts of doom. Rationalists may find the cause of her reaction trivial or irrational, but for Tsvetaeva the facelessness and songlessness of the revolutionary crowd boded ill. The image of the wind, previously connected with her own intimate experiences, is here externalized, and takes on an ambiguous and even sinister colouring. In the phrase "windy forest of banners" the adjective is to be understood in two senses – the wind plays noisily with the flags, but we are expected to think also of the common use of the adjective "windy", applied to a person, to mean empty, unreliable, frivolous, irresponsible. The tramping feet and loud voices of the revolutionary armies drown the ringing of the Kremlin bells – and Tsvetaeva sees in this a threat to Moscow. Such verses sounded a discordant note in the first heady days of revolution. A month later, on the first day of Easter, she addresses the dethroned monarch directly. Her attitude to the Revolution has not changed, but she has come to think that the Tsar shares the blame for what has happened:

> It fell without glory –
> The two-headed eagle.
> Tsar: – You were wrong.

She doesn't accuse, but merely states a fact: "You were wrong."

> Our descendants will mention
> Yet many times –
> The Byzantine perfidy
> Of your clear eyes . . .

We have here the beginnings of what would be a constant theme in Tsvetaeva's "civic" verse – what Pushkin called "kindness to the fallen" – compassion for the defeated. She feels pity for yesterday's Tsar, and wishes that he may:

> Sleep in peace
> In your Selo,
> Dream not of red banners
> In your sleep . . .

A day later, as though foreseeing the dreadful fate awaiting the Tsar and his family, she calls on Russia to pray, and not to punish but to "preserve" the former heir to the throne, the "lamb of Tsarskoe Selo, Aleksey". And in "First Light" "underground" Moscow secretly prays:

> For the life and the health
> Of Nicholas – servant of God . . .

So then, before October and the Civil War, Tsvetaeva had begun what was to be *The Camp of the Swans* on a note of pity.

If events in the outside world were serious, what was happening to Tsvetaeva and her family was even more so. On 13 April 1917 she gave birth to a second daughter, Irina. Her disappointment – she had longed for a son – perhaps explains why this event found no immediate reflection in her writing. She had not, however, begun to write about Alya until she was a year old. For some reason, she began writing her cycle on Stepan [or Stenka] Razin immediately after Irina's birth. She had not succeeded in "quitting these latitudes": the theme was in the air. Poets could use the great rebels Razin* and Pugachov† as personifications of the anticipated revolution – and of the two revolutions of 1917. Poets as different from each other as Velemir Khlebnikov, Sergey Esenin, Maksimilian Voloshin and Vasily Kamensky turned their attention to these two historical personages. Each poet saw them differently and used the theme as a vehicle for his own ideas on history and the present. Tsvetaeva, unlike the others, turns not to the historical Razin, leader of a Cossack rebellion who became a symbol of popular protest, but to the Razin of song whom Pushkin described as "the only poetic personage in Russian history". Like the author of the folksong she is not interested in Razin's reasons for rebelling, nor in the rebellion itself. She is attracted by that part of the Razin legend in which he falls in love with a Persian captive, then drowns her in the Volga, as a present to the great river which gave him refuge, and also "so that there should be no discord among free men", as the song puts it. This was Tsvetaeva's first work based on a theme from folklore and written in the style of Russian folksong. For the first time she introduces peasant speech into her verse. Of course, she finds a new meaning in the folksong – otherwise she would not have been interested in writing a "Stenka Razin" of her own. In her article "Pushkin and Pugachov", written twenty years later, Tsvetaeva reverts to the story of Razin and the Persian maiden. The folksong, she tells us, excuses Razin's villainous treatment of his captive. "Razin's comrades mock him, taunt him, because of this woman, wounding his pride as a man and a leader of men . . . Razin himself throws his beloved into the Volga, making a gift to the river of what is dearest to him, lifting her in his arms – embracing her, that is . . .". Comparing Razin with Pugachov, Tsvetaeva retells the story of Elizaveta Kharlova, to which Pushkin refers in his *History of the Pugachov Uprising*. After cruelly killing her parents and her husband, Pugachov spares Kharlova, and also her seven-year-old brother, because of

---

* See note to p. 49.

† Seventeenth-century brigand and leader of popular uprisings.

her beauty. "The young woman", writes Pushkin, "had the misfortune to win the pretender's affection." When, however, she "aroused the suspicions of jealous villains" Pugachov yielded to their demand and handed over his concubine to them. Kharlova and her seven-year-old brother were shot. Tsvetaeva stoutly defends Razin, contrasting him with Pugachov. "Razin's case is tragic, Pugachov's despicable. We feel pity for Razin because of his Persian girl, horror and contempt for Pugachov because of Kharlova." Nonetheless, in her "Stenka Razin" cycle she does not show her hero performing feats of bravery but introduces the motif of revenge for the Persian girl's refusal to love him:

> It wasn't to your taste, our bed –
> So, bitch, now come to terms with our font! . . .

which is in my view almost as despicable as Pugachov's behaviour. She sees in Razin (as Pushkin does) one of the "poetic personages" of Russian history, and speaks as though the song justifies his existence and all the evil deeds connected with him. "The people are the surest judge – they sing of Razin and his Persian, they are silent on Pugachov and his Kharlova. The fitness or unfitness of a thing for song is perhaps the only infallible measure of its value." The thought expressed here – that art is autonomous and unrelated to morality – was an extremely important one for Tsvetaeva.

Tsvetaeva introduces one other theme into the traditional treatment of Razin in song: the retribution which befalls him. He is not, as he is for Voloshin, Russia's punishment for her past – punishment awaits him for his cruel deed. In the last poem of the cycle the Persian girl appears to Razin in a dream and reproaches him for drowning her with only one shoe:

> Who would desire a beauty
> In only one shoe?
> I shall come to you, my friend,
> To fetch the other little shoe!

This dream – which will recur, for the Persian girl promises to come again – torments Razin, who realizes that with her he has drowned his happiness. There is in Tsvetaeva's lines that pity for Razin which she detected in the folksong, pity perhaps for an elemental force that knows not what it does. But the motifs which she introduced into this subject from folklore are connected with her first, spontaneous reaction to the Revolution. A year later, when there was a brief glimmer of hope for the Tsar's restoration, Tsvetaeva appealed to him and to God not to punish the people, who had been helplessly drawn into revolution. The people here are personified in Razin:

Tsar and God! For the sake of the feast
Let Stenka Razin go!

In "Free Transit", a sketch written in 1918, she describes her encounter with a "real live Razin" a soldier in a requisitioning party, who had served at the front in the Tsar's army, saved his regimental colours, won the St George Cross twice . . . She endowed him with the great-heartedness, the dash, the reckless bravery, denied to the hero of her poetic cycle. She recited her "White" verses and her "Stenka Razin" to this chance acquaintance.

The months of spring and summer were not easy for her. Her sister Asya's husband, Mavriky Aleksandrovich Mints, died suddenly in May. Asya, who had only just left for the Crimea with her two boys, rushed back but was too late for the funeral. She returned to Koktebel, to Pra and Max, with whom she could bear her grief more easily, but fresh sorrows were on her heels. Her younger son, the one-year-old Alyosha, died at Koktebel two months later. Tsvetaeva ached with pity for her sister, and was afraid for her, but could not go to her immediately and could only try to keep her spirits up by writing. "You *must* go on living," she told Asya.

She was beset with problems of her own. She had her own children, her husband and the future of her family to think about. In August we find Sergey Efron back in Moscow, serving as an instructor in the 56th Infantry Reserve Regiment. His health had not improved, and Tsvetaeva was trying, with Voloshin's help, to get him transferred to an easier (artillery) unit. "Please help with the artillery", Efron wrote to Voloshin, "the infantry is too much for me. Even now, in comparatively good conditions, just drilling soldiers makes me so tired that I feel sick and dizzy." Letters and postcards sped from Tsvetaeva to Voloshin all through August. Sergey wanted to get into the heavy artillery – the light artillery was "too safe". Marina's dream was that he would be posted to the South – she was worried about his lungs. At the very least she hoped that he would take some leave and spend it in Koktebel. He needed rest, warmth, sunshine, white bread. Food was getting short in Moscow, and people were saying that a really cold and hungry winter was on the way. The country was on the verge of collapse. Tsvetaeva wanted to leave for the Crimea herself, to wait in a quieter and safer place while the Moscow troubles ran their course.

That same August Tsvetaeva asked her sister to rent an apartment for her in Feodosia, saying that she hoped to be there in two weeks' time. But her journey was repeatedly postponed: efforts to arrange a transfer or obtain

leave for Sergey were unsuccessful. Tsvetaeva was afraid that the trains
might stop running. She badly needed a rest herself. For the first time she
spoke of her "terrible tiredness": "I've reached the point where I only write
postcards. I wake up feeling sick at heart, and the day looms like a
mountain." That she could only write postcards, not letters, is the most
powerful proof imaginable of her weariness. Not being able to write was, to
Tsvetaeva, something unnatural.

Nothing perhaps gave her greater happiness that summer than
Voloshin's article "Poets' Voices", in *Speech*. He put Tsvetaeva on a level
with her favourites, Akhmatova and Mandelstam, and spoke highly of her
latest poems – those which would have to wait five years before they were
published as *Mileposts: Part 1*.

She managed to get away to the Crimea in early October, alone. Life was
still livable there. Sugar and kerosene had been rationed for some time past,
but there was sunshine, the sea, white bread and grapes. There were people
she loved and needed – Asya, Max and Pra. The thought of returning to
them with her whole family was always with her, but she had made no
decision when she left for home on the last day of October, knowing nothing
about events in the capital. Her stay in the Crimea had taught her fresh
lessons about revolution and "freedom". In Feodosia she had witnessed the
sacking of the liquor stores by revolutionary soldiers. No longer a faceless
and silent crowd but a mob which had lost all semblance of humanity, raging
uncontrollably, seeing in freedom no more than the chance to commit
outrages with impunity.

> The wine store has been plundered. By the walls
> A precious stream flows along the canals,
> And in them dances a bloody moon.
>
> (. . .)
> The harbour drinks, the barracks drink. The world is ours!
> It's our wine in the cellars of the princes!
> The whole town is stamping like a bull,
> Bending down to a murky puddle, drinking.

Rewriting these lines twenty years afterwards Tsvetaeva remarked
that "the birds were drunk". The "bloody moon" is significant. Blood
flowing in Russia and dyeing the country red is a theme that will appear
again and again in Tsvetaeva's poems right up to the end of the Civil War.
In, for instance, "The Capture of the Crimea", written in November 1920,
after the final defeat of the White armies:

And terrible dreams I dream:
A crimson cart, behind
Bent double go the sons
Of my country.

Raising up a child with golden
Curly hair – the mothers
Howl. By the church porch
A cripple waves his fingerless hand
At a purple banner
And howls. A crimson rag burns
On the crutch of a legless man,
And red dust rises up to the sky.

Rusty wheels are squeaking.
The horse prances, maddened.
All the windows burn with flags.
Just one is curtained off.

Descriptive passages of this sort are rare in Tsvetaeva's work: she apprehends the world musically, not visually. But here visual images predominate, images unusually vivid for Tsvetaeva, perhaps because they are seen in a dream. It is an impressionist picture, in which various shades of red (red, purple, crimson), the colour of murder and destruction, are contrasted with the gold of a child's hair, the only pure colour left by wars and revolutions. (Tsvetaeva and both of her daughters were golden-haired.)

It was there in Feodosia that Tsvetaeva asked herself where she stood in the new situation and first defined herself as 'one amongst all'. Her pride, her contempt for possessions, her fearlessness and above all her poetic gift determined her place amongst people.

The strong and rich are suffering,
It's a yoke for a gentleman's back.
But I shall not lower my shining eyes
In front of the soldier there.

The town is in uproar and groaning.
The moon is clouded in wine.
But me no one will touch:
I am arrogant and poor.

On her journey home she learnt from the newspapers about the second revolution and the street fighting in Moscow. The details grew more terrifying from station to station, from newspaper to newspaper. The 56th – Seryozha's regiment – was defending the Kremlin. Casualties were counted in thousands, and every fresh report put the figure higher. The conversation in the carriage was excruciating. Tsvetaeva said nothing – she was simply horrified at the thought that she might not find her husband alive, and wrote in an exercise book a letter to him, dead or alive. It reads like the monologue of a delirious person. Despairing uncertainty struggles against hope, indeed against the unconscious certainty that all will be well, that her Sergey cannot come to grief. They had been together for more than six years, the first storms had already blown over, but Tsvetaeva looks up to him just as she did when they first met.

> How could you possibly stay at home? If everyone else had stayed away, you would have gone alone. Because you are beyond reproach. Because you cannot stand the thought of others being killed instead of you. Because you are a lion and you give up the lion's share – to all the others the hares and the foxes. Because you are unselfish and scorn self-preservation, because the "I" is unimportant to you, and because I knew this from the first!
>
> If God performs this miracle and leaves you alive, I will follow you like a dog.

This was an oath of loyalty which Tsvetaeva never broke. When she had lived much of her life, and was about to follow her husband to the Soviet Union, Tsvetaeva added this: "And go I shall – like a dog. M. Ts., Vanville, 17 June 1938 (21 years later)."

She got back from the Crimea on the day when fighting in Moscow ended. Her husband was alive and unhurt, all was well at home, if anything can be said to have been going well in Russia at that time. Tsvetaeva had not misjudged him, Seryozha had been in hell itself, in the Aleksandrov school. He had taken part in street battles and left the school only when the representative of the Provisional Government had signed the articles of surrender. The Bolsheviks had won. Carefully hiding his revolver, and muffling himself in a workman's sheepskin coat, he left the building surreptitiously, to avoid surrender.

The following day, 4 November, Tsvetaeva, her husband, and his friend Ensign Goltsev, set off again. The young officers were determined to make their way to the Don, where a volunteer army to carry on the fight against the Bolsheviks was to be mustered, while Tsvetaeva wanted to make sure for herself that Seryozha got to the Crimea. In the dark railway carriage, on the road to they knew not what, they recited poetry to each other: no war, no revolution could kill their love of poetry.

In Koktebel they found the Voloshins. Max exhibited "an enormous, almost burning joy to see Seryozha alive". All thoughts and conversations came back to one subject. The Revolution, and Russia's fate would, they knew, determine their own future. The Koktebel group heard details of the October events in Moscow from new arrivals. Conversation with them prompted Voloshin to write the most important section of his poetic work, "Russia's Paths". During Tsvetaeva's stay in the Crimea he wrote four poems – "Holy Russia", "Moscow", "Bonaparte" (subsequently included in the cycle "Two Steps", dedicated to Tsvetaeva), and "Peace". The second of these may have been an immediate response to Sergey's account of what he had seen in Moscow in October, not from the window of an apartment, but in battle, with a gun in his hands.

Unlike Voloshin, Tsvetaeva had no historiosophical theories, and she can hardly have shared his views on the past history and future of Russia. But they looked at certain historical and contemporary events in much the same way. Thus, at the height of the Civil War Tsvetaeva apostrophized Peter the Great:

> *You* – under this boiling cauldron
> Added the coals yourself!
> *You* are the father of the Soviets,
> The Assembly's prime supporter! . . .

And Voloshin unwittingly echoes these lines:

> "The Great Peter was the first Bolshevik . . ."

Common to their outlook was interest in and sympathy for the human being, the individual, irrespective of ideas or political parties. With Voloshin this was a firm principle to which he clung throughout the years of Civil War and rough justice, doing what he could to save Reds from Whites, and Whites from Reds. Having lived through the Red, the White, the German, the French and the English occupations, and the Tatar and Karaite governments, Voloshin still stuck to his principles: "even now political programmes and parties are less important to me than the human personality." Tsvetaeva's interest in people – not just in those close to her – shone out in those difficult years. Can it have been Voloshin who taught her to be interested above all in the individual character, not the group allegiance, of a person?

Max probably recited to his friends the lines he had just written:

> All is finished with Russia . . . In recent times
> We have bawled her out, lost her in idle chatter,
> Strewn husks upon her, drunk her to death, spat upon her,
> Besmirched her in dirty city squares,
> Sold her in the streets: would anyone like

147

> Some land, some republics or freedoms,
> Some citizens' rights? And the people themselves hauled
> Their land, like carrion, to the rubbish dump.

Tsvetaeva was at home with his way of looking at what was happening, but their feelings were different. Voloshin summed up and prophesied. Tsvetaeva noted his prophecies in her exercise book:

> And now, Seryozha, here is what is going to happen . . Remember. And in an insinuating, almost rejoicing, tone, like a good wizard talking to children, he shows us picture by picture how the Russian revolution will develop in the five years ahead: terror, civil war, shootings, barricades, the Vendée,* bestialization, loss of humanity, unleashing of elemental passions and blood, blood, blood.†

They knew that it was all true, that it would all happen: at that very time Tsvetaeva was writing about drunken, turbulent Feodosia. But she and Voloshin differed in their attitudes to all this. The words "almost rejoicing" were no slip of the pen: Voloshin welcomed the Revolution with all the horrors to come as an elemental force bringing just retribution and cleansing Russia of the foulness of centuries. He looked forward to the exaltation of Russia which would follow. Tsvetaeva simply rejected the Revolution.

She was ready to go home. It was decided that she would collect the children and return to Koktebel – "to live or die there, time will tell, but at any rate with Max and Pra, and close to Seryozha, who will have to leave Koktebel for the Don very shortly." Pra and Max urged her to come back quickly. She left the Crimea on 25 November 1917. This was the last she would ever see of them. Tsvetaeva was travelling on that route for the fourth time in two months. "The air in the carriage was thick with the words 'bourgeois', 'junkers' and 'bloodsuckers'", she wrote. "October in a railway carriage" was the title she gave to her published record of those months. She had plunged into the turbulent depths of a Russia in turmoil, seen and heard more of her country than in her whole life before. This was her first close contact with the people. People, people, people – of all classes, all ages, and conditions . . . Fear, hatred, stupidity, baseness . . . Kindness . . . Brutality . . . Foul-mouthedness . . . She had never before had such lessons from the school of life.

Getting out of Moscow was by now impossible. Voloshin's farewell prediction had come true: "remember that from now on there will be two

---

* Part of southern Brittany (where Tsvetaeva later lived), where in 1793, during the French Revolution, the legitimist peasantry rose against the Republic. See also p. ooo below.
† This was written in 1917.

countries, the North and the South." This situation dragged on for three years. Tsvetaeva found herself in the North, while Seryozha, Asya and the Voloshins were in the South.

Tsvetaeva's heart was split in two: one half remained in Moscow with her children, her everyday cares, her friendships and excitements. The other half wandered with her husband around the battlefields of the Civil War, loved, suffered, yearned, bled . . .

She had to begin again – to live a life quite different from that which had just been cut short. Until then Tsvetaeva had been one of fortune's favourites. Although she had lost her mother and begun to feel alone in the world at an early age, she had otherwise wanted for nothing: material independence, freedom, love, happiness, talent – all were hers. Talent? She was of course conscious of it, but her mother had drilled it into her that this was a divine gift which had to be paid for by work, that the gift implied a duty. It was at once a blessing and a burden. But the life of everyday had been in no way burdensome. There had been no worries about money, about housekeeping, there were servants, cooks, nurses for the children, yardmen . . . All this had suddenly vanished. Tsvetaeva was twenty-five. She was left alone with two small children in a city in which all the old certainties were crumbling and in which any semblance of ordered life would shortly disintegrate. Money in the bank was money lost, food and fuel had disappeared, clothes and shoes were wearing out. The pinch of hunger grew ever sharper. Life sometimes took on fantastic forms, but life had to go on – she had to rear her children, and to write. She would have to live through and withstand all the hardships of the Moscow years ahead. And she did withstand them.

We need not suppose that her life was all suffering. She was living, and working, more intensively than ever before. Voloshin's old joke had proved prophetic: at least four poets emerged under the name of Tsvetaeva.

A WHIRLING HEART

She had discovered the theatre. This was a by-product of her encounter with the poetry of Antokolsky, of whom she had first heard from Goltsev in a dark railway carriage on the way to the Crimea. Antokolsky was still wearing a student's jacket, still an apprentice playwright, poet and theatrical producer. Perhaps it was her memory of that last journey to the Crimea, with Seryozha and Goltsev, that made Tsvetaeva look up Pavlik

(Pavel Antokolsky) soon after her arrival in Moscow. They were friends immediately. He was only four years younger, but she thought of him from the first as much younger than herself, a mere boy. He was a drama student, a beginner. Whereas she . . .

> Yes, yes, I felt that they were all of them a little younger than myself, or that those of my age were my sons, because I had been married so long, had two children, published two volumes of verse – and had many more ready for publication – and so many abandoned countries behind me . . . I started remembering when I started living, and to remember is to grow old, so that I, in spite of my bursting youth, was as old as a rock with memory of its beginning . . .

"All of them" means the students of Evgeny Bagrationovich Vakhtangov, the theatrical reformer, who died young but influenced several generations in the Russian theatre. Antokolsky introduced Tsvetaeva to Vakhtangov's studio. But he began by introducing her to his friend Yury Zavadsky, later on a well-known actor and producer. At that time Zavadsky was an Adonis – tall, majestic, with angelically beautiful features, and curly golden hair with one grey lock. Was he a talented actor? Tsvetaeva wrote later that "Zavadsky knows how to impress but not to express," that he was "good in his own parts – where you don't have to *be* something, but only to appear, to be a presence, to parade, to pronounce".

Coming from her this is a lethal characterization, but at the time, in 1918–1919, it was for him that she wrote her romantic plays.

Pavel Antokolsky was "small and spry, curly-headed, with sideboards – even little boys at Pushkin* call him Pushkin". Tsvetaeva always remembered his "enormous heavy hot eyes" and the "enormous" voice in which he recited verse. On the first evening of her acquaintance with Zavadsky, Tsvetaeva was struck by the fact that he and Antokolsky were opposites as human beings, yet loving friends, and wrote for the two of them her poem "Brothers".

> They sleep with arms entwined,
> Brother with brother,
> Friend with friend,
>
> (. . .)
> Their arms I shall not loosen.
> Better I should,
> Better I should
> Burn in flames in Hell!

* A holiday resort near Moscow.

That was the beginning of a friendship which flared up into something warmer, went on for more than a year, and became a "theatrical romance", with sequels.

Tsvetaeva was infatuated with Zavadsky. As with most of her "romances" it is hard to say how real it was, and what the actual — as distinct from the literary — relationship between hero and heroine may have been. One thing is clear: Tsvetaeva was the active, loving and giving party. Zavadsky accepted her love, if at all, reluctantly. Tsvetaeva wrote later of "being under his spell — there is no other word for it". Her plays and a number of poems including the "Comedian" [or "Actor"] cycle, were the product of this enchantment. Long disenchanted, she wrote of him in "The Story of Sonechka". There she might appear to be revenging herself for an abortive love affair, debunking her hero in retrospect. But even in poems of hers written close to the event, love and hero-worship are interlaced with irony and self-mockery. This mouth-watering *jeune premier* brought much bitterness into her life. But Tsvetaeva was infatuated with the studio itself as well as with Zavadsky — with all its members at once, their youthful enthusiasm, their ardour, their merriment, with the whole atmosphere of theatre. Defying hunger, devastation and chaos they sought and found new paths in art. Tsvetaeva was infected with their adventurousness and discovered a new role for herself — that of playwright. Needless to say, she was not concerned in her plays to project reality. She plunged again into the world of "shadows" she had once loved so much. Passion for Zavadsky fused with her passion for the heroic figures whose parts he would act. Germany, Italy, France. The sixteenth century, the eighteenth (of which she was particularly fond), the beginning of the nineteenth . . . adventurers, lovers, high passions and mysterious happenings . . . Two of her plays are based on Casanova's memoirs, and the hero of the third is a lover no less indomitable, the Duc de Lauzun, a rebel who ended on the guillotine.

The genre was new to her, but she mastered it completely. Her plays are structurally and scenically quite simple. *Fortuna* begins with Lauzun's birth and ends with him mounting the scaffold. In between comes a series of amorous and political adventures. Tsvetaeva reveals her hero's inner world in soliloquies spoken before his execution. One major theme is the debunking of revolution. We can easily imagine the pleasure Tsvetaeva took in putting these words into his mouth:

> This you deserve for the threefold lie
> Of Liberty, Equality and Fraternity!

The action of *The Phoenix* takes place on New Year's Eve in the Bohemian castle of Dux, in which Casanova ended his tempestuous life as librarian. Tsvetaeva's Casanova is at odds not only with the mediocrities around him but with himself: "on the razor edge between greatness and the grotesque". His indomitable spirit is in contrast with his age and his "skeletal" appearance. The boldness and independence of his retorts belies his position as a petty servitor. In this old man who has outlived his time Tsvetaeva recreates Casanova's passionate and adventurous life.

The plays are written in limpid, easily spoken verse. She is not just indulging a caprice, trying her pen in a strange genre. The poet's voice has found new notes. She herself explained that her voice "had simply outgrown lyric verse". She was obviously attracted by the polyphony of a dramatic work, the opportunity to impersonate characters belonging to different social and cultural levels, speaking a variety of idioms. She could combine the romantic and the sublime with the colloquial and even the coarse. This device of mingling high and low styles, which in Russian poetry goes back to Derzhavin, became a regular feature of Tsvetaeva's work and gives it a peculiar expressiveness. In the plays it gave her wider scope for characterization through manner of speaking. But although the speech of Tsvetaeva's personages may be realistic, her plays are anything but that. They are essentially romantic in conception, in choice of subject and hero, and above all in the attitude to the world which they embody. She never realized her ambition of publishing the plays in a separate volume, nor did she ever see them staged. She has told us in "The Story of Sonechka" how well her *Snowstorm* was received by the Studio audience and by Vakhtangov himself, and how as soon as she had finished reading it to them they began distributing roles amongst themselves. But that was as far as it got. The reading must have taken place at the very beginning of 1919. In the spring of that year there was a schism in the Studio and nearly half of its members, including Antokolsky and Zavadsky, left. When Zavadsky returned a year later Tsvetaeva's liaison with him and the whole "theatrical romance" were already over.

I shall not pretend that the romantic plays are the summit of Tsvetaeva's creative achievement, although I am convinced that they are lively enough to be staged even today. The plays were important experimentally: she was trying to master the art of dialogue. Perhaps in an attempt to overcome that feeling of isolation from which she had suffered so acutely even as a child: the theatre was, after all, a collective endeavour. If so, Tsvetaeva failed in this too. Her encounter with the Vakhtangov group remained a unique episode, both on the creative and on the personal level.

No one can do violence to his own nature and his own character. Tsvetaeva returned to her own ways. Her work is one long tragic monologue. Her disillusionment in the theatre was greater than the creative pleasure it had given her. Two years later she wrote a prefatory note to "The End of Casanova" (the final scene of *The Phoenix*) with an epigraph from Heine: "The theatre is not propitious to the Poet, and the Poet is not propitious to the theatre." She renounced all ties with the stage: "I have always felt the theatre to be a violation. The theatre rudely breaks in when I want to be alone with my Hero, with the Poet, with the dream – it is the unwanted third person at a lover's tryst." Her own plays she referred to as "[narrative] poems",* she renounced all theatrical ambition, and no longer thought of staging them. Her later tragedies on themes from antiquity were not intended for the stage: they were merely long poems in dramatic form.

Her prefatory note, "Two Words on the Theatre" may also have been partly prompted by another unsuccessful attempt at collaboration – this time with the First RSFSR† Theatre, under Vsevolod Meyerhold. She was asked to translate Paul Claudel's *Tête d'or* and to work with Meyerhold himself, his assistant Valery Bebutov, and Mayakovsky, on an adaptation of *Hamlet*. She was very friendly with Bebutov at the time, and it was most probably he who introduced her to Meyerhold. For reasons which remain unclear, the proposal came to nothing, and indeed ended in a public brawl. After reading a report that she was one of those working on the adaptation of *Hamlet*, Tsvetaeva wrote to the journal (*Theatre Herald*) dissociating herself from Meyerhold's theatre. The same number contained an editorial note and letters from Meyerhold and Bebutov retorting in kind. Bebutov called her "a hothouse bard", and Meyerhold wrote: "You know how I shied away from this poetess after I had unfortunately told her about our planned 'Grigory and Dimitry'. You will remember the questions Marina Tsvetaeva asked us – questions which revealed a nature hostile to all that is sanctified by the idea of the Great October." This story vividly conveys the spirit and the language of those years, and tells us something about the character of Meyerhold himself. At a later date his assertions would have been enough to get Tsvetaeva arrested.

This passage of arms interests me more particularly as evidence that Tsvetaeva was already well known and established at the beginning of the twenties. Although she had not published a single book in the preceding seven years she had received an offer from a famous theatre to work side by

---

* *Poemy*. A *poema* is a long, usually narrative, poem.
† Russian Soviet Federation of Socialist Republics (now "Russia").

side with Mayakovsky. What is more, her share in the work was to have been the most important. Bebutov had written to Meyerhold: "I have, as you know, offered the verse parts to Tsvetaeva, as a sort of expert."

To come back to her poetry: the verse cycles "The Comedian" and "Poems to Sonechka", written at the same time as her romantic plays, are, interestingly, also an attempt on Tsvetaeva's part to speak in several voices. "The Comedian" which is addressed to Zavadsky, is one of her finest cycles of love poems. In it rapturous love and delight alternate, contend, and fuse with, contempt for the hero and for herself, irony at his expense, and mockery of her "enchanted" self. She loves and suffers, knowing that her love is unrequited, bruised and battered by her hero's insensitivity. But, while there is still life in her, she is, as lovers always are, impervious to reason:

> I shall not rest, until I see,
> I shal not rest, until I hear.
> Until your countenance I see,
> Until your words I hear.

> Something is not working out – a mere trifle!
> Who will correct the mistake in my task?
> Your very sweet, very sweet smile
> Came saltily, saltily hard to my heart!

> – Fool! – my grandchildren will write on my urn.
> And I repeat – persistently, weakly:
> I shall not rest until I see,
> I shall not rest until I hear.

In reality Tsvetaeva saw her hero more soberly and prosaically than in her verse. The irony of "The Comedian" is at once the product and the mask of this more sober and prosaic view. In rough drafts of an unwritten play, the antithetic heroes of which were to have been the Courtier and the Comedian, Tsvetaeva characterizes the latter as "a vain, heartless creature who loves only his mirror". The image of the Comedian came to life again twenty years later in "The Story of Sonechka". Tsvetaeva, long since cured of her "enchantment" with Zavadsky analyses realistically, unsentimentally, cruelly even, the phenomenon of "inanimate beauty". Her last play connected with Zavadsky she called *The Stone Angel*. She recalls her feelings for Zavadsky with something like bewilderment. It is difficult to believe that "The Story of Sonechka" and "The Comedian" were written by the same woman. When part of "The Story" was first published in the USSR (1976) it was said in Moscow that Zavadsky was upset by what he regarded as a defamatory portrait of himself. He was wrong. However ironically, however harshly at times Tsvetaeva treats her Comedian (meaning Yury), her feeling for him, and her portrayal of him in verse and prose, will live on. Surprisingly, in a long career as actor and producer Zavadsky never put on a single one of the plays which he inspired Tsvetaeva to write.

"The Comedian" ends with a discord – a poem not published in Tsvetaeva's lifetime and perhaps unfinished.

> The Devil himself paid me a favour!
> While I was tempted to redden
> My lips at the midnight hour –
> Red blood was flowing there.
>
> While a legion of giants was growing
> Small on the sands of the Don,
> I was making friends with a band
> Of Comedians in plague-ridden Moscow . . .

When she recovered from her theatrical infatuation Tsvetaeva began to feel that she had been lost in an alien world:

> Lest my Conscience burn under my shawl –
> The Devil himself rose up to help.
> Neither morning nor day – an unbroken
> Crazy, dissolute night . . .

Amazingly enough, the two following poems – "I remember a night in November's decline" and "Tsar and God! Forgive the small . . ." – were written within a few days of each other:

> I remember a night late in November.
> There was fog and rain. In the light of a lamp
> Your gentle face – strange and equivocal,
> Dickensian, a wan and misty face,
> Chilling the breast, like winter seas . . .
> Your gentle face in the light of a lamp.
>
> And the wind blew, and the staircase spiralled . . .
> Not tearing my eyes from your lips,
> Half in laughter, twisting my fingers in a knot,
> I stood there, like a miniature Muse,
> Quite innocent, like the most tardy hour . . .
> And the wind blew and the staircase spiralled . . .

And exactly three days later:

> Tsar and God! Forgive the small,
> The weak, the stupid, sinful, random,
> Those drawn into the terrible funnel,
> Those seduced and those deceived,
>
> Tsar and God! With cruel death
> Do not execute Stenka Razin!
>
> Tsar! The Lord will reward you!
> Enough from us of orphans' wails!
> Enough, enough from us of corpses!
> Royal Son, – forgive the Thief! . . .

How could the same person feel two such very different emotions, write two such different poems, at one and the same time? The poet is an unpredictable, unaccountable creature, unable to foresee what will demand utterance from one day, one hour indeed, to the next.

> . . . For the path of Comets –
> Is the path of poets. Scattered links
> Of causality – there's the connection! Head high –
> Despair! The eclipses of poets are not
> Foreseen by the calendar . . .

As Tsvetaeva saw it, the poet bore no moral responsibility for what was written. Two of her literary-philosophical essays – "The Poet and Time" and "Art in the Light of Conscience" – are devoted to problems of this kind.

A scene in "The Story of Sonechka" provides a commentary to the line "And the wind blew and the staircase spiralled". It describes the moment of farewell with Zavadsky: "I took him out by the back way, down the winding stairs, and stopped on the last step – he was still a whole head taller than I was". The winding back stairs, up which firewood and down which slop buckets are heaved, the wind blowing and the rain lashing through broken window panes, dirt and darkness, the only light from a distant street lamp – such is the "rubbish" in which the most romantic verse may originate.

"The crazed, feverish night" refers not only to the delirium of love but to the reality of Moscow in that "plague-stricken year nineteen", as she writes elsewhere. She had to make forays into the countryside to barter matches, soap and a roll of calico which had somehow survived, for food. She had to sell books, household goods, anything that could be sold, in flea-markets. She had to chop up for firewood the furniture lovingly chosen when she married. She had to feed stoves, make tea, cook, wash and mend clothes. Hands swollen with cold, she had to pick over poods of frozen potatoes and drag them home on Alya's toboggan. The same hands that wrote about Marie Antoinette, Byron, Casanova, The Comedian, and Russia's fate. "A thousand times I kiss your hands – meant only to be kissed, they shift cupboards and lift heavy weights – how immeasurably I love them for it." She treasured these words, written to her by Sonechka Gollidey. She didn't often hear such things.

She seems to have lived several lives at once: her own daily life in Moscow, the life of those fighting on the Don, which she followed with alternating hope and despair, and the "crazed" life in which the flesh-and-blood actors of the Studio merged with romantic heroes of the eighteenth century. Full of these contrasting thoughts and emotions the writer becomes a different Tsvetaeva every time she takes up her pen. Ever since she had first become conscious of the distinction between "daily living" and "Being" she had felt them to be antithetical to one another. "Daily living" was something to be got over, overcome. Tsvetaeva could exist only in the realm of Being. Casanova, the Comedian, Lauzun and the Don were her Being, frozen potatoes were "daily living". Her infatuation with the theatre helped Tsvetaeva to survive the first winters after the Revolution. Then Sonechka came on the scene.

SONECHKA

She appeared on a winter's day when Tsvetaeva was reading her *Snowstorm* in Vakhtangov's studio. Antokolsky introduced them: "Before me stood a little girl – Pavlik's Infanta, I thought! With two black plaits, two enormous black eyes, and burning cheeks. Before me stood a living fire. Everything was ablaze – she was all ablaze. And the eyes gazing from that conflagration – such rapture, such despair – said 'I'm so afraid! I'm so in love!' ("Pavlik's Infanta" because Antokolsky's play *The Infanta's Doll* was written for her and about her). Sofia Evgenievna Gollidey, at that time an actress in the Art Theatre's Second Studio, was just four years younger than Tsvetaeva, but her shortness, her big eyes and her plaits made her look like a girl of fourteen. Even in post-revolutionary Moscow, which was overfull with theatrical geniuses and theatrical happenings, she did not pass unnoticed. Gollidey became famous for her "monodrama" based on Dostoevsky's

"White Nights". (The genre itself was quite new at the time.) On an empty stage, "equipped" only with a kitchen chair (as Tsvetaeva recalls it) or a roomy armchair (according to others who saw the play), alone with this chair or armchair and with the auditorium, a tiny girl in a light spotted muslin dress, told the story of her life. For half an hour Sonechka became Dostoevsky's Nastenka. "It was the most remarkable display of talent I ever saw or heard in the Second Studio," wrote Vladimir Yakhontov, a fine actor who subsequently founded the first one-man theatre in Russia. "The whole city went to see Sonechka," Tsvetaeva wrote. "Have you seen her? Such a little thing, in a white dress, with plaits . . . Simply charming!"

They became friends – Sonechka was a frequent visitor in the spring and summer of 1919. She became fond of the house, its quaint rooms, its untidiness and confusion, and of the children – not only Alya, to whom she confided her intimate secrets, but Irina too. Sonechka was evidently one of the few who could play and converse with the sickly Irina. In that "time without presents", as Tsvetaeva's older daughter later called it, Sonechka would arrive with food for the children. Those were years in which a boiled potato and a lump of sugar were things of delight to a child – and Sonechka was in despair if she had nothing of the sort to offer when Irina begged for them.

Tsvetaeva's friendship with Sonechka was ardent and tense. What gave it a special piquancy to begin with was that both friends were attracted to Zavadsky. This somehow drew them together rather than setting them against each other. "Your Sonechka", Tsvetaeva's friends called her. And although the friendship lasted only a few months, it left its impression on Tsvetaeva's heart for years to come. Many people who came into contact with Tsvetaeva thought her hard and selfish, but her writings, which alone express her true nature, do not bear this out. It is a cause of continual astonishment to find how gratefully, how warmly she remembers those to whom she was close twenty or more years before. Her "myths" about her contemporaries were born of this warmth, which gave them the look and feel of reality: her myths about poets, for instance – Mandelstam, Voloshin, Bely, Kuzmin. I do not doubt that all her heroes were just as she recreated them: she had the ability to sense and preserve what was most important in a person, and what few others could see. And so it was with Sonechka. In this young actress, shabbily dressed and always hungry, but ready to share her last crust, inordinately brusque and difficult, forever unlucky in love, Tsvetaeva could see the "Woman-Actress-Flower-Heroine" to whom she dedicated her *Stone Angel*. Sonechka's selflessness made her beautiful and heroic in her friend's eyes. And – as always with Tsvetaeva – part of

Sonechka's attraction was her oddity, her unusual appearance and mentality. She was an actress, but there was nothing "actressy" in her attitude to life and to people, her presence, her dress. She had no affectations, though many found her awkward and off-putting. She was simply herself. Tsvetaeva lived by the same rules, and valued the fact that only with her was her friend at ease.

Enchanted by Sonechka's originality, and sharing her resentment that she was passed over by producers, Tsvetaeva wrote play after play in which the female roles were intended for her friend: Rosanetta in *Fortuna*, the girl in *The Adventure*, Aurora in *The Stone Angel*, and Francesca in *The Phoenix* all resemble Sonechka. Tsvetaeva deliberately gives each of them her friend's external characteristics. Yet they are all different, because she embodied in each of these young women a different trait of her friend's personality as she saw it. In the verse cycle "Poems to Sonechka", written at the same time as the romantic plays, there are several other hypostases of Sonechka. Surprisingly, reality finds no reflection in these verses. Only in the first poem do we catch some faint hint of the actual relationship: two young women are in love with the same unresponsive "boy". And in the poem – as in reality – there is no rivalry, no jealousy between Marina and Sonechka. While "The Friend" (the cycle of poems about Sofia Parnok) reproduces the experiences of the lyrical persona, in "Poems to Sonechka" Tsvetaeva effaces herself and simply registers various aspects of her heroine – the different roles she might have played on the stage, or the different sides of her character as they exhibited themselves to the poet's gaze. We have Sonechka the heroine – and Sonechka the performer of tear-jerking love-songs to the accompaniment of the hurdy-gurdy. Tsvetaeva tells us in "The Story of Sonechka" that her friend adored these "low" love songs. And she herself was not indifferent to them: in her early poems she had more than once described the music of the hurdy-gurdy in the yard, and the tears it provoked. Or else Sonechka was a Spanish street girl working in a cigar factory: "a geographic Spaniard, not an operatic one . . . wind her up like a top on a square in Seville and she will spin as though she belonged there". The lines about the "cigarrillo" are written in a rhythm which to Russian ears resembles a Spanish dance. But it is only fair to note that her Spanish girl is not so much "geographic" (where could Tsvetaeva have seen real Spanish girls?) as literary: her model is Mérimée's (if not Bizet's) Carmen . . . Then there is Sonechka, child of humble Russian town-dwellers (or in *Stone Angel* their sixteenth-century German counterparts): "A flowery curtain – and behind it, those enormous dark eyes . . . On the edge of town, in the backstreets". "All the later Turgenev", Tsvetaeva noted, "was smitten" with such black-eyed beauties. But perhaps Sonechka had fused in her memory with the Nastenka of Dostoevsky's "White Nights":

> Snow-white lily of the valley,
> Little crimson rose!
> Each said to her: tenderly
> "My little, little one."

There is something Dostoevskyan in the sub-text of "The Story of Sonechka": the strange friendships, the tension, the strained relationships "on the brink of the dark abyss" in the deadly plague year of 1919, the "extreme situation" of which Tsvetaeva is all the time conscious but in which she refuses to take a part. She never once mentions Dostoevsky's name, but she introduces two lengthy quotations from "White Nights" into her text. "The Story of Sonechka" was written in the summer of 1937, when Tsvetaeva learnt of Sonya Gollidey's death: a "reassessment" if you like, but one which shows a greater appreciation of Sonya's unusual character and of the importance of their friendship. A poem written in the "Sonechka" period, but included in the "Poems to Sonechka" cycle only in 1940, is interesting in this connection. It stands apart from the rest of the cycle and speaks with the poet's own voice.

> Two trees want to be with one another.
> Two trees, right opposite my home.
> The trees are old. The house is old.
> I am young, or it may well be
> I would not pity the trees of others.
> The smaller one stretches forth its arms,
> Like a woman, strains its very utmost –
> It is cruel to watch how it strains
> To that one, that other one which is
> Older, firmer and – who is to know? –
> Even more unhappy, it may well be.

In these lines the loneliness that Tsvetaeva tried to suppress, and to hide from others in those first five post-Revolutionary years, breaks through. It was this perhaps that plunged her in those years from one infatuation to another.

> Two trees: In the glow of sunset
> And in the rain, even under snow,
> Always, always: one to the other,
> Such is the law: one to the other,
> One law only: one to the other.

The two poplars outside her home in Borisoglebsky Lane had become a symbol of one person's need for another. For some months Sonechka was the "tree" that delivered Tsvetaeva from her loneliness. Then she vanished as abruptly as she had appeared. She fell in love with some Red Army officer, abandoned Moscow and the theatre and followed him to the depths of the countryside. "Sonechka left me, to fulfil her destiny as a woman," Tsvetaeva wrote. "Coming to me no more was simply obeying her mission as a woman – to love a man . . . My love for her, her love for me, the love we shared, had no place in any commandment."

Was this a lesbian relationship, like that with Sofia Parnok? The "Poems to Sonechka" cycle shows clearly enough that it wasn't. If we compare these poems with those addressed to Parnok we cannot help seeing how different the feelings behind the two cycles are. In "The Friend"* the I and the You, the two women in love with each other, are undisguisedly, almost defiantly, present: whereas the heroine of "Poems to Sonechka" is the conventional heroine of weepy romances, complete with certain characteristics of the real live actress Sofia Gollidey. "The Friend" throbs with passion, with jealousy, with erotic yearning, all of which are absent in the other cycle: there the emotions spring not from life itself but from tear-jerking traditional songs. In "The Story of Sonechka" Tsvetaeva describes her feelings most lovingly, tenderly, gratefully – and clearly stresses that there was no physical intimacy between them: "We never kissed – except on meeting or saying goodbye." And she adds in French: "Mais je l'embrassais souvent de mes bras, fraternellement, protectionellement, pour la cacher un peu à la vie, au froid, à la nuit. C'était la Révolution, donc pour la femme: vie, froid, nuit."†

This time Tsvetaeva was the older and she felt it her duty to protect her friend from the distress which she herself had experienced in her relationship with Parnok. ("It was," she wrote, "a dry fire, and no attempt was made to quench it . . . Suffering with no attempt to help.") As she finished "The Story of Sonechka" Tsvetaeva told Anna Tesková: "I've been writing my 'Sonechka' all summer – the story of a friend who died recently in Russia. It doesn't seem right to call her a 'friend' – it was quite simply love, love in feminine form. I never in my life loved anyone as I loved her." In any case, it was an enormously emotional experience for both of them. It brought Tsvetaeva the happiness of which there was so little in her life, and

---

* *Podruga*: a feminine noun, thus also translatable as "girlfriend" or "woman-friend".

† But I embraced her frequently, fraternally, protectively, to hide her a little from life, the cold, the night. That's what the Revolution was for a woman: life, cold, night.

she remained grateful to the end. Without mentioning Dostoevsky directly, Tsvetaeva ends her story with Nastenka's words of gratitude in "White Nights": "And now goodbye, Sonechka! Bless you for the minute of blissful happiness which you gave to another lonely and grateful heart! God in heaven! A whole minute of bliss! Is that not enough for a life-time?"

For Tsvetaeva it was infinitely much, especially when not only abstract "time bonds" but normal daily routine and natural ties with friends and family were collapsing.

Before the Revolution Tsvetaeva had lived in the rather narrow circle of the élite of university, of literature and theatre. Now want compelled her to hurry from queue to queue, from market to market, to jostle with the crowd on the Sukharevka and at the Smolensk market to buy and sell and haggle. She had to deal directly with "the people", "the crowd". She began writing down what she saw and heard and felt. She didn't keep formal diaries – her prose jottings crop up here and there in exercise books, in the margins of manuscripts, on the walls of her room, mixed up with rhymes and odd lines of verse. At that unlikely time her mind was, she noted, unusually sharp: "my whole being is full of passionate purposefulness, all the walls are scrawled over with lines of verse and NBs for my notebook." She can hardly have intended at the time to publish these jottings: the important thing was to seize, fix and give sense to the new experiences that had burst in on her life, and her own new feelings.

Once abroad, she would try to turn these notes into a book, to be called "Omens of the Earth". She explained that its title emphasized the antithesis between the "earthly" matters described in it and the life of the spirit, embodied in her verse.

Her journeys between Moscow and the Crimea in the autumn of 1917 had already given her some idea of what was happening to the country and its people. A year later she was plunged into the thick of events. She travelled to Tambov province in quest of food. In the struggle for existence townspeople were reduced to bartering, if they could, what was left of their possessions for such food as was left to the peasants. This need was catered for in Moscow by the markets (especially the famous Sukharevka!) and it would be hard to think of anything "former people"* did not offer for sale there. By the end of 1919 Tsvetaeva had sold everything she could. It was no easy business: her belongings were as odd as their owner, and the purchaser had to be a connoisseur. "Selling things is easier said than done," she wrote.

---

* *Byvshie lyudi*: people who lost their social status after the Revolution.

"My possessions were things I couldn't resist at the time I bought them – so now nobody else wants them." But in the country you could trade matches, soap and calico for food. Someone she knew was travelling to Usman in Tambov province with a friend and his mother-in-law. He invited Tsvetaeva to go with them. The mother-in-law had been there three times before, and promised them a "goldmine" – flour, wheat, even pork fat. Tsvetaeva, who could never tell a cook what she wanted for dinner, was now prepared to go from cottage to cottage haggling with peasant women. In September 1918 she obtained a semi-fictitious permit to travel in order to "study peasant needlework". Her travelling companions may have had some interest in this document because unauthorized persons were not allowed to travel, still less to transport goods, by rail: the new regime was doing battle with the new tribe of "bagmen" [speculators]. The entry in Tsvetaeva's pass read "free transit: may transport $1\frac{1}{2}$ poods".

This was at the very beginning of "war communism". The words "requisition", "requisition party", "cordon party", which crop up here and there in Tsvetaeva's "Free Transit", were not yet terrible symbols of the past but were grisly realities. The new state was making its first attempt to break the peasantry, with what Lenin called its "crusade for bread". Requisitioning parties were organized to deprive the peasants of their surplus, and cordons established to prevent either peasants, or townspeople who had somehow found their way into the country, like Tsvetaeva and her fellow-travellers, from transporting foodstuffs of any kind to the towns. A "bagman" might be relieved of all he had on the way back. Anything still left in the countryside was meant to fall into the government's hands, and no one else's.

Tsvetaeva learnt on the way that their destination was a requisitioning centre at which the mother-in-law's Red Army son was stationed. She acquired her first impression of "war communism" from this worldly-wise woman. "No wonder the peasants are furious. Anybody would be. Nobody hates his own property! They're robbed of everything they have. 'God will punish you', I tell my Kolya. Turning people into beggars – who ever heard the like? You've seized all the power – so all right, enjoy it, rule and welcome to it. You were born under a lucky star . . . Pay half what it's worth, then you'll have nothing to fret about and they won't be hurt. But what you're doing now is highway robbery."

The reality was worse than all the stories. Tsvetaeva and the mother-in-law spent the first night after their arrival in a village tea-house. The Red Army man, by way of entertainment for his mother, and to show her how far his power over the fate of others extended, arranged for the place to be searched. "There were shouts, weeping, the chink of gold, the old women (the owners) ran around dishevelled, there were bayonets, . . . featherbeds were gutted. They rampaged all over the house."

For a whole week Tsvetaeva played Cinderella – she was billeted with the wife of the commander or perhaps the commissar of the detachment, and became her unpaid maid-of-all-work. The members of the detachment went there for meals. She was able to observe the immediate executants of the Revolution at close quarters, and to listen every evening to stories about their "work". They robbed everyone around, they enjoyed it, they were exhilarated by it, taking everything they could lay their hands on – grain, pork fat, gold, fabrics. They shared out their booty on the spot. When the officer's wife leaned forward, a handful of gold coins slipped out of her bosom and rang on the floor. The nicest of the soldiers – Tsvetaeva's "Stenka Razin", to whom she recited poetry and presented a ring with a two-headed eagle and a book about Moscow – had four gold watches in his pockets. "Stenka" talked with equal enthusiasm about his policeman father, the Heir to the Throne, in whose regiment he had not so long ago been serving, and the bank he had robbed in Odessa.

Their shameless rapacity was terrifying . . . the "requisitioners", Russians, Jews, and Caucasians . . . the mother-in-law, flying at a "Levite" and threatening him with her Kolya ("as big a Bolshevik as anybody") . . . the lady of the house, with the gold coins in her bosom, her only thought money, her only reading Marx . . . The mother-in-law had previously been a seamstress, and had once done some work for Tsvetaeva's uncle's wife – and perhaps even for Tsvetaeva herself. The lady of the house had been the proprietress of a knitwear business in Petersburg. They were ordinary lower-middle-class townspeople from whom in other times Tsvetaeva could have expected nothing but polite and willing service. But now they were shameless: she was one of the "former people", they were the new people, the victors, and there was no need to pretend. Before the Revolution Tsvetaeva could never have imagined seeing them as they were at Usman. But perhaps they were not really like that? As, perhaps, her Stenka was not? He had been a model soldier, he had loyally served "Tsar and fatherland" – he hadn't been given two St George medals for nothing – in the past he hadn't robbed and killed like a bandit . . . She was witnessing the "bestialization" of which Voloshin had spoken when they last met.

She discovered, also, how senseless it all was. This was borne in on her during her six months or so in a newly established Soviet institution. Its offices were in a house which had belonged to the Counts Sologub (the Rostovs' house in *War and Peace*). This circumstance, quite as much as her need for a ration card and a wage, influenced Tsvetaeva's decision to take a job. The institution was impressively called "Information Department of the Commissariat for Affairs of the Nationalities". There was a large staff, with absolutely nothing to do. The work consisted in briefly summarizing in a "register of newspaper cuttings" articles relating to "your own" nationality and transferring these summaries to separate file cards. It soon became clear that there was no need to copy or summarize anything, that you could make up your summary without even glancing at the newspapers, because none of it was of the slightest use to anybody. The only good thing about it was that sitting in the office Tsvetaeva could write her romantic plays. She was, moreover, surrounded by people of different ethnic and social origins, and different attitudes, all trying to adapt to the new life and adapt it to themselves. She had one other office job from which she ran away on the first day: "I didn't leave the card index, my legs carried me away! The soul and the legs: the conscious mind could do nothing to stop them. That is what instinct means." She confessed to her sister that she had worked in an office for five and a half months in 1918 – then left. "I couldn't stand it, I'd sooner hang myself."

The realization that the Revolution had brought to the surface all that was bad and dark in people's souls, that the specious Bolshevik slogans concealed filth, lies and brutality, had as great an effect on Tsvetaeva as the physical sensations of hunger, cold and fear. Looting, beating and murders cloaked in revolutionary verbiage went unpunished – and that was what freedom had come to mean to the "liberators" and the "liberated people". The people, as they almost always do, remained silent, or at most expressed their discontent passively. Here is a scene recorded by Tsvetaeva as she left Usman for Moscow.

The platform was thronged. You couldn't move. And more people were arriving all the time: every man like the one before him, every woman like the one before her. They weren't people with sacks but sacks riding people. Heads turned to look at us suspiciously.

"The gentry!"

"They've eaten Moscow bare: now they've come to eat us out of house and home."

"Look how much of the peasant's property they've carried off."

"They got here last, but they'll be first on the train."

"Gentlefolk are first into Heaven, even!"

"Just you see – they'll be on the train and we'll be left behind."

"Sleeping out in the open more than a week now."

The crowd growls in impotent rage at the unarmed townsfolk, and not of course at the Red Army men.

There it was – Russian folk: the artisans, labourers, peasants with whom Tsvetaeva had never come into close contact before. In earlier days wherever she had travelled – abroad, to country villas, to the Crimea – she had always been "young lady" or "madam". Now she was "citizeness", like everyone else. This was the first time she had found herself in a Russian village, associating with the people on equal terms – or on rather less than equal terms, because country people made it clear that they distrusted her, and tried to cheat her in every way possible. But for Tsvetaeva it was an invaluable encounter: she feasted her eyes and ears on Russia.

> I look around (in a peasant hut). Everything is brown, as though bronzed: ceilings, floors, benches, pots, tables. There is nothing inessential, nothing that is not age-old. The benches seem to have grown into the walls – or rather grown out of them. And the women's faces are brown to match. And the amber beads round their necks! And the necks themselves! And on all this brownness – the last blue of late Indian summer.

She is hurt and irritated by their distrust, their sullen dislike, their efforts to cheat her when they barter. But she can rise above all that and delight in their speech, their candour, their beauty. She can sense their essential kindness, although they show none to her. She is drawn to these peasant women by a common misfortune – almost all of them, like Tsvetaeva herself, are husbandless: their men are away, some in the Red Army, some with the Whites. Only women are to be seen in the village market. "The market. Skirts – piglets – pumpkins – cockerels. The soothing and enchanting beauty of the women's faces. They are all black-eyed, and all wear necklaces." Tsvetaeva would not have been Tsvetaeva if she had described the village differently – the dirt, the poverty, the work-calloused hands, the prematurely old faces.

The Russian village enriched Tsvetaeva's emotions, her language and attitude to life. It was not just that she began writing on "Russian themes", but that she became conscious of her own Russianness, conscious that she belonged with the Russian people and shared their destiny. Before the Revolution she could never have written:

> I bless the labour of each day,
> I bless the sleep of every night.
>
> (. . .)
>
> I also bless, oh Lord, the peace
> In an alien home, bread in an alien stove.

Not so very long ago no one and nothing outside her own world could claim her attention. Now people had become closer; she had learnt that they suffered just as she did from hunger and cold and separation from their loved ones. She formulated the rule by which she lived in these lines:

> If a soul has been born with wings –
> What need has it of palaces, what need of huts!
> What to it is Genghis Khan and what the Golden Horde!
> Two enemies I have in the world,
> Two twins, inseparably entwined:
> The hunger of the hungry and the satiety of the sated!

This poem, written in August 1918, is the first in which Tsvetaeva likens the Bolshevik Revolution to the Tatar invasion of ancient Russia.

And – most important for a poet – Tsvetaeva's ear was opened to, ravished by, another variety of Russian: not the bookish, literary, poetic Russian she had known from her earliest days but the Russian spoken by the common people in flea-markets, on trains, in church, in the village. This encounter awakened her interest in Russian folklore, and prompted her to write "Russian" poems of her own. The new linguistic element transformed Tsvetaeva's diction and her metre, and remained with her to the last.

The epigraph to this chapter is taken from the article "The Poet and Time", written in 1932, in which Tsvetaeva muses on the Poet's relationship with the times he lives in and with Time in general. She was thinking particularly of changes in herself and in her writing. And what she said of Voloshin in a memorial essay – "he became and would remain a Russian poet – for this we have the Russian Revolution to thank" – can with some qualification be said of herself.

Nonetheless Tsvetaeva refused to accept the Revolution. It is certainly possible to quote passages out of context and show her speaking positively of the revolutionary spirit in poetry, contrasting the émigré reader with his counterpart in Russia, and complaining bitterly of the émigré world and her position in it. She was full of enthusiasm for Mayakovsky, the "poet of the Revolution", and wrote an approving article on Soviet children's books published in 1931, in the émigré journal *The Will of Russia* [*Volya Rossii*]. And of course she did go back to the Soviet Union. These facts can be manipulated, as they were by Soviet scholars, in an attempt to annex Tsvetaeva to Soviet literature. But it is quite impossible to prove that she ever embraced or even reconciled herself to the Soviet system. They try to get round this with the formula "she didn't accept the Revolution because she didn't understand it". It grieves me to confess that I myself wrote – and what is worse thought – that way at one time. But if you read Tsvetaeva carefully, and make an effort to penetrate the logic of her thoughts, her feelings, her behaviour, you will be convinced that the opposite is true: Tsvetaeva understood the true nature of the Revolution immediately, and therefore could not accept it.

The testimony of Ariadna Efron (Alya) on this point is interesting. Tsvetaeva's younger daughter Irina starved to death in revolutionary Moscow. Her sister Ariadna wrote to Pavel Antokolsky in 1966:

> Irina's death played an enormous part in Mama's decision to emigrate –
> quite as large a part as the fact that Papa was abroad already. Mama could
> never put it out of her mind that children can die of hunger here. That's
> why I see red when I read the usual cliché – that Tsvetaeva "didn't
> understand" and so "didn't accept". *Nothing was easier for her to understand,
> or more impossible for her to accept.*

We can assume that there, in a letter to a very old friend of her mother, Ariadna Efron is saying exactly what she thinks: that Tsvetaeva saw the cruel senselessness of the Revolution, and so refused to accept it. This is particularly important because in her published utterances Tsvetaeva's daughter has stuck to the official version and in general has always been ready to "straighten out" her family's tragic history in order to get her mother's works published. She has written about the "*infinitude*" of her father's "mistake" in 1917, which had as its consequence another "fatal mistake", Tsvetaeva's emigration (in print Ariadna has never mentioned the part which Irina's death played), and has said that but for these mistakes Tsvetaeva's life would have worked out much better.

The reality was not quite as she thought it was, and not at all as she said it was. Ilya Erenburg, as I have pointed out before, held that it was not her husband's departure for the Volunteer Army that made Tsvetaeva the bard of the Whites, but that on the contrary *her* reaction to events impelled *him* to take that course. We can surely see indirect confirmation of this in the fact that she "carried Sergey off" to the South at a time when movement by rail or road was extremely difficult. Besides, her first verses of "rejection" were written before Efron went away. She knew as early as May 1917, "between the two revolutions", what revolutionary freedom would shortly mean:

> From a severe and graceful temple
> You emerged to the screech of squares . . .
> Freedom! The Beautiful Lady
> Of Russian Princes and Marquises.
>
> A frightening choir practice is taking place,
> The celebration of mass still lies ahead!

> Freedom! A street-walking wench leans
> On a wanton soldier's breast!

If we didn't know their date we could read these lines as an answer to Aleksandr Blok's presentiments and dreams of the Revolution, and to the revelation he experienced in "The Twelve". The first stanza identifies the long-awaited Freedom with the "Beautiful Lady", who is at once Russia and the Revolution. Tsvetaeva's "street girl" is an anticipation (by several months) of Blok's Katka, the "liberated" prostitute of "The Twelve."

> And Vanka and Katka are in a pub . . .
> She's got banknotes stuffed in her stocking!

She is a personification of that freedom which Russia actually received. And, to continue the comparison with "The Twelve", it is the "liberators" themselves who kill freedom, just as the Red Guard kill Katka. Why was Tsvetaeva so much more far-sighted than so many of her contemporaries, of her own age or older? Why did she never succumb to illusions? Nadezhda Mandelstam writes in her memoirs of the way in which the Revolution split the inner world of the Russian intellectual.

> Many of my contemporaries who accepted the Revolution experienced a serious psychological conflict. They were caught between a reality which deserved condemnation, and a principle which demanded justification of things as they were. At one moment they would shut their eyes to reality so that they could assemble excuses for it, at the next they would open their eyes and see how things were. Many of them had been looking for revolution all their lives, but when it became the reality of every day they took fright and averted their eyes from it. Then there were others who were frightened by their own fear – afraid that if they blinked they would miss something, that they wouldn't see the wood for the trees . . . One of these was Osip Mandelstam.

Tsvetaeva did not belong to this category. The "revolutionary" enthusiasms of her adolescence had long ago been superseded by other preoccupations. But those of whom Nadezhda Mandelstam speaks included not only her husband, Aleksandr Blok and Andrey Bely, but a very large number of writers, artists and academics, to whom "Revolution with a capital R, the faith in its power to save and to renew", and the idea of "social justice" had been dear long before these events. When they invoked revolution they had no idea what shape it would assume in Russia, and how it would affect them.

Ilya Erenburg, a Bolshevik at fifteen and a political émigré at seventeen, rushed back from France as soon as he heard about the February

Revolution. The reality of revolution horrified him, and in 1918 he published a volume of verse called *Prayer for Russia*, consisting entirely of apocalyptic visions and prophecies of doom.

> You will tell your children: "We lived before and after.
> While it still lived we saw it
> At the place of execution."
> You will say: "In the autumn
> Of the year one thousand nine hundred and seventeen
> We crucified it."

Russia is murdered: her crazed children crucify their motherland. Voloshin welcomed *Prayer for Russia* enthusiastically – its author shared his own way of thinking: "The poet has succeeded in finding words as crude and terrible as the sights he has seen, and fusing them in the fire of a single all-conquering emotion." He went further, and wrote that: "The book is the first transmutation into literature of the terrifying devastation of Russia, a book which the bloody year 1918 can cite as its only justification." To find any justification for 1918 you had to start like Voloshin from the hope that Russia would be cleansed in the fire of revolution. Voloshin put *Prayer for Russia* on the same level as Blok's "The Twelve" – his article was in fact entitled "Poetry and Revolution: Aleksandr Blok and Ilya Erenburg".

Prayer for Russia was read with different eyes by Mayakovsky, who stood "on the other side of the Red barricades". From its first day he had made himself the bard of "the great battles of the Russian Revolution" and was already living by the rule he formulated later:

> He
>   who today
>   sings out of tune with us,
> he
>   is against us.

He was brusquely contemptuous of Erenburg's book: "Dull prose printed to look like verse . . . The myopic eyes of a petty clerk overburdened with family cares and worn out by pen-pushing peer at us from these grey pages . . . one of the frightened intellectuals".

Note that "intellectual" is for Mayakovsky abusive, or at any rate an expression of contempt – and it passed into ordinary Soviet usage with those overtones. In the same review article, headed "Fraternal Grave" and printed in the *Futurists' Gazette*, Mayakovsky aimed a blow at Tsvetaeva too. He seems not to have read the books which he was shovelling into a "fraternal grave" at all thoroughly – he simply picks out a few quotations to suit his purpose. Thus, he could spare only three lines for the collection *Thirteen Poets*. Making fun of the book's subtitle, "In response to War and Revolution" he wrote: "Amongst other lines there is one by Tsvetaeva – 'Pray for the life and the health of God's servant Nicholas!' Surely you could find something else to 'respond to', ladies and gentlemen."

And that is all he has to say about a volume in which at least four fine poets were represented – Akhmatova, Tsvetaeva, Mandelstam and Mikhail Kuzmin.

But even Mandelstam, who was closer to Tsvetaeva, and might have been thought capable of understanding her, rejected outright the poems she was then writing. In 1922 he published a survey of literary Moscow in the journal *Rossia*. Worst of all, he declares, in "Literary Moscow", is its women's poetry. Of Tsvetaeva he says:

> The saddest sign of all for Moscow is the holy-virginal petit-point of Marina Tsvetaeva, who echoes and is echoed by the dubious grandiosity of the Petersburg poetess Anna Radlova . . . Adalis and Marina Tsvetaeva are prophetesses, and Sofia Parnok is another of them. Prophecy is for them what needlework on the domestic hearth is for others. At a time when in men's poetry the high-falutin', insufferably bombastic has given way to a normal use of verbal resources, women's poetry continues to vibrate on the very highest notes, insulting our ears and our feelings for history and for poetry. The bad taste and historical falsity of Marina Tsvetaeva's folksy and pseudo-Muscovite poems about Russia makes them immeasurably inferior to the verses of Adalis, whose voice occasionally achieves a masculine strength and truthfulness.

What can have provoked such a harsh and hostile reaction to the poems of a woman once close to him, and certainly not in the enemy camp as a poet? The "vibration on the very highest notes" which is characteristic of Tsvetaeva was indeed uncongenial to Mandelstam, who many years after this, called himself an "anti-Tsvetaevist". We can safely assume that he was irritated by Tsvetaeva's voice when it became shrill:

> Yes, hurrah! – For the Tsar! – Hurrah!
> The enchanting mornings
> Of all grand entrances, since the universe began! . . .

But neither the shouting nor the "bad taste" he finds in her deserved such harsh language. The explanation probably lies in the words "historical falsity", "a folksy and pseudo-Muscovite", and in the contrast he draws between Tsvetaeva's poems and those of Adalis, in which he detects the ring of "truth".

Mandelstam himself was still seeking a philosophical explanation and justification of what was happening, trying hard to peer through the murk of Russia's troubles and discern a bright spot at the end of them. He could not accept that what had happened was senseless – he had to try and make sense of it, and to hope. In spring 1918 he wrote some lines entitled, when they were first published, "Hymn".

> Brothers, let us glorify the twilight of freedom,
> The great year of the twilight.
> Into the seething, nocturnal waters
> A weighty mass of snares is lowered.
> You rise up in the sombre years,
> O sun, o judge, o people . . .

Twilight, of course, occurs twice a day – before dawn breaks and before night falls . . . Mandelstam appears to be speaking of the dawn ("You rise up . . ., O sun"). But the word *"sumerki"* (twilight) and its adjective *"sumerechny"* have connotations of darkness, gloom and despair. The intimation that the world and time are caught in the soils of "twilight" is quite distinctly audible in these lines. We can see why Mandelstam renamed them "Twilight of Freedom". Nonetheless he appeals to hope:

> Well then, let us try: an enormous, clumsy,
> Creaking turn upon the tiller.
> The earth's afloat. Take courage, men . . .

Perhaps the experiment which Russia was undergoing would yet succeed? It was at roughly the same time that Mandelstam, writing about Blok, spoke of "the highest satisfaction" to be found in "serving Russian culture and the revolution".

Many years were to pass before Mandelstam clarified his attitude to the Revolution, and his relationship with the time. To say goodbye to one's hopes is no easy matter. Echoes of his poem "Twilight of Freedom" can still be heard in "Humanism and the Present Age", an article written in 1922.

> Everyone senses the monumentality of the forms of the approaching social architecture . . . It casts its shadow on us . . . We move in that shadow full of fear and bewilderment, uncertain whether it is cast by the wing of approaching night or is the shadow of the city which we must enter as our own.

The poet with his prophetic insight senses that the "twilight of freedom" will be followed by night, but the man needs to hope that all will be well, that what he sees is the darkness before the dawn . . . He naturally calls the poet who leaves no hope at all a false prophetess. Mandelstam's "Hymn" was written at the same time as Tsvetaeva's requiem for Russia.

> Over the meadows resounds a requiem.
> The secret book of the genesis of
> Russia — where the fates of the world are concealed —
> Has been read to the end and shut up for ever.
>
> And the wind blusters, and scours through the steppe:
> Russia! — Martyr! — Sleep in peace!

In contrast to Mandelstam Tsvetaeva, who stood aloof from politics and had no interest in it, shows a remarkable historical sense. Perhaps a detached viewpoint of this sort can assess things more soberly? And how accurately she foretold Russia's future significance ("where the fates of the world are concealed"). This "domestic needlework", as Mandelstam called it in his irritation, foretells what we now see before our own eyes.

Erenburg in his memoirs speaks condescendingly of Tsvetaeva's "White" poems: "No one persecuted her for this. It was merely bookish fantasy, absurd romanticism, and a wrecked and wretched life was the price Marina paid for it." She did indeed pay the heaviest of prices. But what Erenburg calls absurd and romantic was not for Tsvetaeva a pose. She prized individuality, the uniqueness of human beings above all else, and this, in my view, is the basic reason for her total rejection of the Russian Revolution. In the facelessness of the revolutionary mass, which so shocked her in March 1917, she caught a glimpse of the future and made up her mind once and for all. "The main thing is to realize, from the very first second of the Revolution, that all is lost! After that all else is easy."

If you read the reminiscences of her contemporaries and reflect on the course their lives took you see that such an uncompromising attitude was exceptional. Most of them needed time to make up their minds about what was going on, to rid themselves of illusions about the "purifying force", and define their own position in the new world. Even a clever and unromantic person like Vladislav Khodasevich did not think at the beginning of 1920 that what had happened was a catastrophe. He wrote to Boris Sadovskoy: "There is nothing bad or shameful about being a Bolshevik. Frankly, there is much in Bolshevism that I find congenial". He did not, of course, become a Bolshevik himself, but he still believed that the Bolsheviks would assist in the revival of Russian culture. A year later in a talk on Pushkin he would be speaking of "the gathering gloom". And a year after that he would realize that in that gloom it was impossible to preserve one's individuality. Khodasevich emigrated at about the same time as Tsvetaeva.

It is impossible to speak summarily about those of their contemporaries whose lot it was to live their lives in the Soviet Union – it is a different horror story for almost every one of them. I shall speak instead of the most fortunate possible case. Erenburg has described in his memoirs his own troubled evolution from *Prayer for Russia* to acceptance of and collaboration with the new regime. His explanations sound almost like a polemic with Tsvetaeva:

> The most important thing was to understand people's passions and sufferings in what we call "history", and to realize that what was happening was not just a dreadful bloody rebellion, not another Pugachov Rising on a gigantic scale, but the birth of a new world with different conceptions of human values.

According to his own account it was because he came to understand and accept these new ideas of human values that Erenburg became a Soviet writer. This was the path followed by many intellectuals: you had to live and "co-exist" with the victors. Erenburg did not disclose what attracted him in these new conceptions. They were, of course, the ideas of communism, which even in theory imply levelling and the depersonalization of the individual, and which in practice led to the destruction of individuality and the physical extermination of all who tried to preserve it. This was something Tsvetaeva could not accept.

Tsvetaeva interpreted the October "Overturn" as a catastrophe threatening to destroy Russia, Ariadna Efron told Antokolsky in the letter previously mentioned. Irina's death, Stakhovich's suicide, the execution of Nikolay Gumilyov, the death of Aleksandr Blok from starvation were simply confirmations of her worst forebodings. Blok's death, perhaps, above all, because she ranked him with the immortals.

ALEKSANDR BLOK

The news of Blok's death was a heavy blow to her. She wrote immediately, in August 1921, four poems about his end which might be entitled "Ascension". The key word in the cycle is "wing". It occurs six times. The "wing" is a symbol of the poetic gift, of an otherworldly seraphic nature. The last thing to die in a poet is:

> Not a rib broken in half –
> But a wing broken in twain.

Not a breast shot right through
By executioners. This bullet

May not be removed, nor wings mended.
He walked quite mutilated.

Clinging, clinging is the crown of thorns!
What care the dead for the murmur of the mob,

The swan's down of a woman's flattery . . .
He passed by, deaf and solitary,

Freezing the sunsets with the
Emptiness of eyeless statues.

Only one thing still lived in him:
The wing broken in twain.

The wing is what weighs down the poet ("Bent shoulders bowed by the weight of wings"), the wing is what is most vulnerable in the poet ("Torn raiment, a wing all blood"). And yet it is the wing that bears him aloft. These poems soar into the empyrean, their subject is a soul which has finally broken free of the "accursed" earth and soared to the heavens.

The just man has torn out his soul – hosanna!

In this cycle there is no lament for the dead man – only joy at his emancipation. Tsvetaeva wrote to Akhmatova at the time that she felt Blok's death to be an "Ascension", the ascent into heaven of a soul that had greatly suffered, and was also divine. Tsvetaeva did not hesitate to use words spoken by Christ himself in her description of Blok.

On his face it was written so clearly:
My kingdom is not of this world . . .

All the same, if Tsvetaeva had not seen Blok a year before his death she would not have felt that his death was a release from earthly trammels. She had heard two of his readings in Moscow 1920 – on 9 May in the Polytechnic Museum and on 14 May in the Palace of Art. Alya, who went with her to the second, recorded her impressions of Blok and his poems in her diary.

It was early evening and still light when we left the house. Marina told me that Blok was as great a poet as Pushkin. My excitement and anticipation of something beautiful grew with every word she spoke.

Marina sat in a corner, looking stern, her lips pressed tightly together as if she was angry. From time to time her hand took the flowers which I was holding, and her beautiful aquiline nose breathed in the odourless smell of the leaves. There was no trace of joy on her face, but there was rapture.

There could be no trace of joy: she saw before her a tired and sick man, who was hardly there at all:

> And along his temple he'd run, he'd run,
> An absent-minded finger . . .
>
> (. . .)
>
> Thus, like a prisoner alone with himself
> (Or is it a child talking in its sleep?) . . .

What she saw before her was hardly a human creature, and certainly not a man declaiming to an audience, but a sort of spirit, a seraph who had appeared to deliver a message and would soon fly away. "The stern face" and "tightly pressed lips" tell us how intensely she listened to Blok. And of the awe which seized her, as if she had encountered something sublime and beyond human understanding. That Alya at seven could distinguish between "happiness" and "holy awe" shows how sensitive a creature she was, and helps to explain the extraordinary friendship which bound mother and daughter together.

Alya presented Blok with her mother's poem inspired by his previous recital – the last poem she addressed to him before he died. In a footnote Tsvetaeva has told us that on the day of Blok's first recital "the powder vaults on the Khodynka* blew up, breaking windows in the Polytechnic Museum" – hence the "roar of bursting shells".

> Like a faint ray through the black gloom of hells,
> Such is your voice in the roar of bursting shells.
>
> And thus in peals of thunder, like some seraph,
> In a dead-sounding voice he lets us know
>
> – From somewhere out of ancient misty mornings –
> How he loved us, blind and nameless as we were,
>
> For the blue cloak, for the sin of perfidy . . .
> And how – more truly than all – he loved the one,
>
> Who plunged deeper than all into night – for evil deeds!
> And how he did *not* cease to love you, Russia!
>
> And along his temple he'd run, he'd run
> An absent-minded finger . . . And of what
>
> Days await us, how God would be deceitful,
> How you would start to call the sun – and it would *not* rise . . .

* A square in Moscow.

Thus, like a prisoner alone with himself
(Or is it a child talking in its sleep?)

Over the wide square before us there appeared
The sacred heart of Aleksandr Blok!

She means the words "sacred heart" quite literally – they distinguish Blok from mere humans, distance him from earth. Amongst mere mortals there is no place for a sacred heart. Because she already knew this, a year before his death, there would be no grief in the poems written a year later, only a serene feeling of justice done. But she had begun singing her "hosannas" to Blok back in the spring of 1916 . . . In the first cycle of her "Poems to Blok" she had spoken of their inevitability.

Mine is to glorify
Your name.

And she exalts Blok in humble prayer, shutting her eyes to his earthly, human aspect. For Pasternak in his later work the image conjured up by Blok's poetry was the wind, for Tsvetaeva it was snow: he was "the snowy bard", the "snow-white swan". Something bright, unearthly, half-real, something that at any moment might melt, disappear. In her representation of Blok the only reality is suffering. She is attempting to paint an icon in verse, to portray the "holy countenance" of the Poet: "Into that hand so pale from kisses I shall not drive my nail", "To the waxen, sacred countenance I make my reverence from afar". There is a religious solemnity about the poem "You pass by towards the Setting of the Sun":

You pass by towards the Setting of the Sun,
You will behold the light of the evening,
You pass by towards the setting of the sun,
And the snowstorm covers over the track.

By my windows, quite impassive,
You will pass in the silence of the snow.
My fine just man of God,
Gentle light of my soul.

(. . .)

And standing under the slow-falling flakes,
I shall go down on my knees in the snow,
And for the sake of your sacred name,
I shall kiss the evening snow.

There, where with majestic tread
You passed by in grave-like silence,

> Gentle light of sacred glory,
> All powerful ruler of my soul.

Holiness, suffering and light are the ideas associated with Blok in Tsvetaeva's mind.

It was then, in 1916, that Tsvetaeva wrote her first lines about Blok's death. She tactfully omitted certain lines when she wrote out a copy of the cycle for the sick poet:

> You thought he was a man!
> And you made him die.
> Now he is dead forever.
> – Weep for the dead angel!

These lines are evidence that Tsvetaeva associated the theme of death – violent death – with Blok from the beginning.

In November 1921 came a new eruption of poems to Blok. In less than three weeks she wrote ten poems about him. In the first of them the word "cradle" makes a surprising appearance.

> No call, no word –
> As a thatcher falls from the roof.
> But perhaps again
> You have come – and lie in a cradle? . . .

At the end of the poem the cradle becomes a grave, but the word was not lightly chosen. Only three of the ten are addressed to Blok directly; the others formed two small cycles, "The Friend"* and "Bethlehem". Tsvetaeva had recently made the acquaintance of Nadezhda Aleksandrovna Nolle-Kogan and her eighteen-month-old son, Sasha. Nadezhda was the Friend, and Bethlehem was dedicated to "Blok's son, Sasha". The legend that Blok was the father of Nadezhda Nolle's son lingered on in literary circles, and has perhaps not been finally laid to rest even now. The truth of the story need not concern us; what matters is that Tsvetaeva at first believed it, though she changed her mind some years later. She learnt from Nolle herself about her relationship with Blok, read Blok's letters to her and saw the presents he had sent for the newborn child. Nolle and her husband P. S. Kogan, a senior official concerned with cultural matters, gave Blok material assistance in the last years of his life, sending food parcels to him in Petrograd, and pleading his cause in Moscow. Blok stayed in their apartment on his visits to Moscow in 1920 and 1921. Nolle's stories were

---

* *Podruga*, but not to be confused with the cycle of the same title addressed to Sofia Parnok.

enough to give rise in Tsvetaeva's imagination to the myth of the beloved female friend whose mission it was to love and support and save the Poet:

> Seize him! Firmer!
> Only love him and love him!
> (. . .)
> Tug at him! Higher!
> Hold him! Only don't give him up! . . .

Perhaps only the devotion of his "last friend" could keep him here on earth? Or if not that, ease his last torments? Even after the Poet's death she remains the Mother of his Son. Losing all sense of proportion, Tsvetaeva glorifies Blok's "last friend" as the Mother of God and her son as the Son of God. What did Blok mean to Tsvetaeva? She looked up to no other poet, past or present, with such absolute devotion. Every other poet, whether she was drawn to him or repelled by him, and irrespective of the age in which he lived, was a being of flesh and blood, with his own passions, joys and faults. Even Andrey Bely, whom she called the Captive Spirit, lives in her reminiscences as a human being: "old-fashioned, elegant, exquisite, birdlike – half great master, half mountebank", alone (and incomprehensible) amongst his numerous entourage. Tsvetaeva always writes of other poets as though she had known them intimately. When you read her on Pushkin and Goethe you feel that she could have walked the streets of Moscow and Weimar in conversation with them. Of Pushkin she wrote:

> To an ancestor – a workmate:
> In the same workshop!
> Every mark of a pencil –
> As though by his hand . . .

There is no poet whom she could not approach, with whom she could not find common ground. Except Blok. At his recitals she stands beside him, shoulder to shoulder in the crowd – and cannot reach out to give him her verses. The first time Vera Zvyagintseva is her intermediary, the second time it is Alya. Why? Why is it only Blok who passes through her verse like an insubstantial shadow, not a man but a deified being who inspires her to prayer? He belongs to no circle, not even that of the poets.

In Tsvetaeva's literary criticism references to Blok are virtually non-existent. A lecture she gave in Paris in 1935 (its text has unfortunately not survived) was entitled "My meeting with Blok", although in the ordinary sense of the word there was no meeting. They "met" in another dimension, outside the physical world. She considers Blok's "case" in greater detail only once, in her article "Poets with History and Poets without History".

Briefly, poets with a history are always in motion, always developing, discovering themselves in the world. Poets without a history – pure lyric poets – do not move, do not develop, they discover the *world in themselves*. She realizes with surprise that Blok alone does not fit into this classification. In her eyes he is indeed a "pure lyric poet", but he also "develops, has a history, a path". Development, however, so Tsvetaeva tells us, implies harmony. "Can there be such a thing as catastrophic development?" she asks with Blok in mind. Blok's path is within him, a path that leads nowhere; he is "running away from himself in circles". Blok ended where he began: "we should not forget that 'Christ', the last word of 'The Twelve' was one of Blok's first words." She defines the specific character of this "pure lyric poet" in these words: "throughout his poetic career Blok was not developing but tearing himself to pieces." Tsvetaeva's theorizing about the two types of poet is of course debatable, but this is not the place for theoretical argument. We may, however, note in passing one characteristic of Tsvetaeva's writing on literary and philosophical subjects. The movement of her prose is so swift and sure, she is so rapid and resourceful in argument that the reader has no time to think. She overwhelms us with her certainty, hypnotizes us with her word play, compels belief as long as we are actually reading. Only afterwards, when we emerge from under the spell, do we begin to reflect on the validity of her arguments and venture to contradict her.

Wild enthusiasm, rapture, exaltation, often hyperbolical, are the constants of Tsvetaeva's lyrical verse. But the worshipful awe with which she approaches Blok is unique. Trying to discover its source, to decide what Blok personified for her, I unexpectedly found the answer in a letter written by her little daughter Alya to Elena Ottobaldovna Voloshina on 8 November 1921: "Marina and I are reading mythology . . . Orpheus is like Blok: pitiful, but he can move stones." That was what Blok was for Tsvetaeva: a modern Orpheus, the idea of the Bard made flesh. Orpheus himself was not a mere human, but the son of a god and a muse, yet mortal. This was what she meant (subconsciously, perhaps?) when she wrote in 1916:

> You thought he was a man!
> And you made him die . . .

Now, in 1921, as she wrote about Blok's death, a poem about the tragic end of Orpheus was born – untitled to begin with, because the images of the two poets merged in Tsvetaeva's mind. The heading "Orpheus" appeared only in 1940.

> Thus they swam: only head and lyre,
> Down, into the retreating distance.
> And the lyre was affirming: peace!
> But the lips kept repeating: pity!
>
> Pouring along the swooning Hebrus
> The double traces of silvery
> Blood and blood-red silver!
> My gentle brother! My sister!

These lines are Tsvetaeva's answer to the hesitant question in the "Blok" poem written a few days earlier:

> Was it you
> That did not bring her rustling gown
> On your return
> Through the gorge of Hades?
>
> Was it not
> This head that swam
> Along the sleepy Hebrus,
> Filled with silvery sounds?

In times immemorial were you not Orpheus? Yes, it is his head floating throughout eternity down the Hebrus. It was he, Blok-Orpheus, who had tried to lead his beloved out of the kingdom of the dead, he whose voice had sundered the darkness of hell:

> Like a faint ray through the black murk of hells –
> Such is your voice . . .

The images of "Orpheus" and those of "Poems to Blok" are identical. "Orpheus" could very well be included in the "Blok" cycle, so naturally does it fit in to that memorial wreath for the poet.

As for Eurydice, it was, so Tsvetaeva once said, her fault that Orpheus looked back. If she, Tsvetaeva, had been in Eurydice's place she would have willed Orpheus not to look back, and they would both have been saved. And that is surely how we should understand what she says about her "non-meeting" with Blok: "If we had met he would not have died". In the poem "No call, no word" and in the cycle "The Friend" she sings of an ideal Eurydice who would have known how to save Orpheus. But Tsvetaeva's ideal Poet replicates himself to infinity: Orpheus returns to earth. In our age he had returned in the guise of Aleksandr Blok. And that is not the end of it.

> But perhaps again
> You have come – and lie in a cradle?

181

Blok's cradle is his own grave – but also the cradle of his new-born son. In "Bethlehem" Tsvetaeva glorifies not so much the real Sasha, Nadezhda Nolle's son, as the heir to the bard, the next incarnation of Orpheus – Blok.

I must emphasize once more that Blok, according to Tsvetaeva, was a *modern* Orpheus. An Orpheus without Orphean harmony, but instead with a hypertrophied modern sense of catastrophe in his soul. Orpheus was torn to pieces by Bacchantes at the end of his journey. Blok was tearing himself apart all his life. "The surprising thing," Tsvetaeva said in a letter to Akhmatova, "is not that he has died but that he ever lived . . . He was so much a creation of the spirit, so much a spirit made visible, that we must wonder how life could permit him to exist at all."

In one of her casual jottings Tsvetaeva, speaking of Communists, confesses that "it isn't them I hate, it's communism . . . For two years now," she adds in brackets, "people all around me have been saying 'communism is fine, but the Communists are horrible.' My ears ring with it." Once again, she is in opposition to the majority, but not, we can be sure, out of bravado or a desire to shock. The same thought recurs, in different words, on a number of occasions. She could not accept communism as an idea which made it possible to trample on people. She judged people, Communists included, as individuals. During the Civil War what she felt above all for other people was pity.

She needed sympathy and help herself. Life took on more and more fantastic forms, and Tsvetaeva's home was one of the first to collapse. Her older daughter said later that the house looked as if it had suffered shipwreck. Their rooms no longer looked lived-in, their belongings no longer had any meaning or function. The rooms gradually found their way to other people, and the belongings to the Sukharevka flea-market. All that Tsvetaeva had left of a large comfortable one-and-a-half storey apartment was her own small room, the kitchen, the nursery, and, upstairs, the "attic" which had been Seryozha's, and was greatly loved for that reason.

> My loft-like palace, my palace loft!
> Go up and see. A mountain of manuscripts . . .
> There . . . Your hand! Keep to the right,
> Here is a puddle from a leaky roof . . .

Prince Sergey Volkonsky, grandson of the Decembrist and former director of the Imperial Theatre, dedicating a volume of memoirs to Tsvetaeva, recalled what her life had been like in Borisoglebsky Lane: "an unheated house, sometimes without light, a bare apartment . . . your little

Alya sleeping behind a screen surrounded by her drawings (white swans, and St George Bringer of Victory) . . . no fuel for the wretched stove, the electric light dim . . . The stairs were dark and cold, the banister did not go all the way down, and there were three treacherous steps at the bottom. The dark and the cold came in from the street as though they owned the place." The bell didn't work, the street door could not be locked, and anybody could walk in as freely as the dark and cold . . . A thief did in fact walk in one day and "was horror-struck by the poverty he found . . . You asked him to sit down," Volkonsky wrote, "and talked to him – and when he left he offered you money."

Her appearance changed a great deal in those years. Hunger and worry are not good for anyone's looks. The high colour which had distressed her so much in early life had vanished, and for the rest of her days her complexion was dull and clayey. Her first wrinkles appeared. All that was left of the former Marina was her golden hair, her green eyes, and her fleet-footedness. Vera Zvyagintseva remembers how Tsvetaeva looked in 1919–1920: "corn-coloured hair, which Marina was always washing in the bathroom when she visited us. Her hair was luxuriant and beautiful. Her face was pale and puffy, because she lived mainly on frosted potatoes, her eyes green – 'pickled, peasant's eyes', as she once wrote . . . She was always tightly belted, and I nicknamed her 'dzhigit' [a Caucasian rough-rider]. She wore a corset for support." Tsvetaeva dressed as her poverty, her contempt for fashion and her sense of duty dictated. It was this last that made her wear a belt – "not an officer's belt, but the sort worn by cadets at the First Peterhof School for Ensigns. And a knapsack – this time an officer's knapsack – over my shoulder . . . which I should have considered it treason to take off." She wore felt boots in winter and low shoes, often without laces, at other seasons. She wore her old frocks as long as she could, and made up others from door curtains, ex-overcoats, anything she could find. The results, Zvyagintseva says, were "bizarre". It would never have entered her head to dress up in the "original and enchanting" frocks she had once worn. She had no more use for them, and two which escaped the flea-market went to Sonechka Gollidey together with a remarkable coral bracelet. Tsvetaeva was not yet thirty, but she had said goodbye for ever to her youth.

> Not for nothing do I touch your hand,
> I'm saying goodbye to you as to a lover.
> O my youth, snatched out of the depth
> Of my breast! Go to others!

She wrote these lines with no special regret, but without irony or bravado either. She realized that her life, and her poetry, were undergoing a qualitative change.

Tsvetaeva, and Alya later on, called their home a slum. Casual visitors may have taken the signs of "shipwreck" for "poetic disorder". Tsvetaeva herself tried to ignore this side of life. She was brave and long-suffering, and the life of the spirit was more important to her than bread and butter. All the same, she must at times have been reduced to despair by the cold, the shortage of water and light, and the impossibility of feeding her children adequately. She did not feel at all humiliated by charitable gifts. Two women neighbours with large families of their own, and the milk-woman Dunya, helped her because they could not bear to see her daughters hungry and neglected, and sometimes she took bread home from someone else's table. She herself was always taking people under her wing: letting them live in her "slum", giving away her belongings, sharing her last bowl of soup, last potato, last scrap of tobacco. With her natural pride and dignity she could view her situation only with cheerful contempt. And those around her took this at face value, and considered her relatively well off. It was easier for them that way. She wrote in 1919:

> It is indecent to be hungry when others have full stomachs. My sense of decorum has more power over me than hunger – even my children's hunger.
> "So how are things? Got all you need?"
> "So far, thank God."
> What sort of person would one have to be to disappoint, embarrass, annihilate someone else with a negative response?
> "Just a mother."

A little further on we read an appeal to "friends":

> My hard-hearted friends! If only instead of treating me to pastries at your tea-table you would just give me a little slice of bread for tomorrow morning. But it's my own fault. I laugh too much when I'm in company. And anyway, when you leave the room I'll steal your bread.

This last statement appears to be the literal truth. Tsvetaeva had her own peculiar ideas of right and wrong, of what was and what was not permissible. She found it impossible to beg, to make another person feel the depth of her poverty and despair. That was immoral, because it put the other person in the intolerable position of an almsgiver. In her view, riches and plenty must be a crushing burden at such a moment. Whereas if you simply took without asking you were under no obligation to show gratitude. I have written down something that Vera Zvyagintseva told me: "she was apt to lay hands on books and things." I confess that I deliberately let this go without comment: I felt it would be improper to ask what exactly the words "apt to lay hands on" implied. Writing about this period Anastasia Tsvetaeva mentions in her memoirs "a vague rumour – but remembering Marina's contempt for the letter of the law it may be true – that she sold some furniture temporarily stored with her" and belonging to acquaintances of her brother Andrey. An entry in Alya's diary, recollected by Zvyagintseva, is interesting in this connection: "my main vices as a child were lying and stealing."

Outwardly, Tsvetaeva was calm, cheerful and self-assured. Perhaps only Alya saw – though we can hardly suppose that a child not yet ten years old would fully understand – her mother's real state of mind. In an unpublished chapter of her memoirs Ariadna (Alya) quotes a note she made as a child, in March 1921, on a visit to the "Writers' Shop" to sell some books. This bookshop was one of the sources of existence. Tsvetaeva sold through it not only books from her library but collections of her own verse in manuscript, as did many other writers ("overcoming Gutenberg", it was called). Some of Tsvetaeva's handwritten booklets have survived.

The plentiful supply of books for sale was one of the remarkable features of Moscow at that ruinous time. The American journalist Julius Hecker wrote in the Berlin magazine, *New Russian Book* (*Novaya russkaya kniga*), as follows: "Yes, there are bookshops in Moscow, and their number grows every day . . . Those selling the books are no less interesting than their wares. They are mostly writers themselves . . . Berdyaev, Osorgin, Zaytsev, Yakovlev, Dzhivelegov and Griftsov, all well-known names in the literary world, are amongst those doing a lively trade. Need has forced them out of their studious reclusion, forced them to take up a practical occupation – and they are not at all bad at it, their turnover is counted in millions (millions of Soviet roubles, of course)." This was the place Tsvetaeva and her daughter frequented, laden with books:

> We are near the Writers' Shop. Marina crosses herself, although there is no church in sight.
> "Why, Marina?"
> "Alya, d'you think I'm bringing too many books?"
> "No, of course not. The more the better!"
> "You think so?"
> "I don't think, I'm sure!"
> "Alya, I'm afraid they'll take them out of charity!"
> "Marina! They're honest people, they'll always tell you the truth . . ."
> Marina brightens up, but still goes in rather apprehensively. She greets those inside with elaborate but distant politeness.

That was all for the benefit of outsiders. Only Alya was allowed an occasional glimpse of her fears, her uncertainty, at times her despair. Alya became her mother's comforter and her consolation, the "genius of the hearth". She helped in the house – washed dishes, warmed food, carried out the slops. She helped as best as she could, unenthusiastically perhaps: she says that her slowness irritated her mother. She was, after all, only a child – and deprived of her childhood. But in Alya Marina had a friend, a true kindred spirit. To some extent she took the place of the absent – and for all Marina knew, dead – Seryozha. She looked like Seryozha, and, like him, she loved and accepted Marina without reservation. They prayed for him together, and dreamt of his return. Tsvetaeva shared her thoughts and feelings with, and read her verse to, Alya. Alya knew many of Marina's poems by heart. She wrote verse herself, and they wrote poems to each other. This is one of Alya's, called "Your Room".

> It smells of a Rose and Homeland,
> Perpetual smoke and poetry.
> Out of the mist the grey-eyed genius
> Sadly glances into the room . . .

Tsvetaeva added a note to the third line: "Portrait of her Father". She published twenty of Alya's poems as the last section of her "Psyche", entitled "Verses by my Daughter". We know of a poem written jointly by mother and daughter. And there is another, written by Alya but included by Tsvetaeva in her "Quatrains" as her own. It is interesting for its unchildlike, unromantic irony.

> Be not ashamed, land of Russia!
> Angels always go barefoot . . .
>
> The devil himself took away the boots.
> The shod are the frightening ones today!

Alya was intelligent, gifted, an unusual child. She was also beautiful. A child to be proud of.

IRINA'S DEATH

Irina was more of a burden than a joy to her mother. From birth she had been a rather sickly child. And constant under-nourishment, cold, and lack of proper care prevented her from developing normally. She walked with difficulty and could hardly talk. It was impossible to "pump" anything into her. She was not an interesting companion, as Alya was, and as Mur was later on. You couldn't boast to friends about her. Irina's name is hardly ever mentioned in the recollections of people who met Tsvetaeva in those days. Maria Grinyova has a lot to say about Alya, but spares Irina only a few lines: "I looked into the first room . . . There was a little bed, and Marina's younger daughter, two-year-old Irina, was all alone in it, rocking herself. Rocking herself and humming. No words, just humming, but it was surprisingly tuneful and coherent." She adds in a footnote: "Irina Efron, who was weak and sickly from birth, died of starvation in winter 1920."

Vera Zvyagintseva, who made friends with Tsvetaeva in summer 1919 and met her frequently, first heard of Irina when she once stayed the night at Borisoglebsky Lane. "We chatted all night, and Marina recited poetry . . . When it was beginning to get light I saw an armchair heaped with rags, and a wobbly head sticking out of them. It was Irina, the youngest daughter, of whose existence I was unaware till then. Marina put her in some orphanage, and she died there." Zvyagintseva also remembers Irina's amazing little voice.

Tsvetaeva was a bad mother, not only to Irina, but to all three of her children. Perhaps her poetic gift, her self-absorption, were incompatible with the unruffled patience and level-headedness so essential in those who deal with children day in and day out. She ruined her children by her hysterical, crushing love and her efforts to remake them as she wanted them (Alya and Mur), or else by indifference (Irina). But for the Revolution she might have been able to bring up her children in the old-fashioned way, and their lives would have been more normal and happier. As it was, she was compelled to feed and look after and train her children all by herself, and she was incapable of being "just a mother". Anastasia Tsvetaeva recalls how shocked she was, when she got back to Moscow in Spring 1921 after four years of absence, by the dirt and disorder of her sister's neglected home. She took advantage of Marina's absence to start tidying up: washing, scrubbing, ironing . . . Instead of thanks, what she heard from Marina on her return was: "As far as I'm concerned that's *completely unnecessary* . . . *Don't waste your strength!*" Anastasia felt that Marina had been offended by her desire to help. And she took offence herself. "One question wouldn't go away: what was the different between us? Had I really suffered any less in the fires of Civil War, from famine and disease, from the loss of those dearest to me?"

There was a difference – Marina was a poet. Her soul had room for the whole world – but could find none for sweeping floors, washing dishes, ironing. She did all those things – but only insofar as they were absolutely essential. It was the same with her children: where their minds and hearts were concerned Tsvetaeva was always ready to give, to "pump in", but in more prosaic matters she was capable of less than any ordinary mother. Irina needed care and attention, like any sick person, and especially any sick child, and might have tied her mother down. She could take Alya anywhere: to the studios, to see friends, to literary soirées – whether or not that was what a seven to nine-year-old really needed ... When they went out Marina and Alya often tied Irina to a chair, so that she wouldn't fall. Tsvetaeva probably loved her younger daughter after a fashion, but Irina sometimes irritated her sister and her mother, and was a nuisance to them. This may be one reason why people close to her urged Tsvetaeva to put her daughters into an orphanage – temporarily, of course. But the main thing was that there was warmth and food there: the Kuntsevo orphanage was considered exemplary, and was supplied with American foodstuffs by ARA.* They had to get through the coming winter (of 1919–1920), and Tsvetaeva was obviously *incapable* of keeping her children warm and well fed. She knew this better than anyone, and sent them at the end of November to Kuntsevo. She missed them very much. At least, she missed Alya. Read a poem she wrote at the time, and you will not realize that Tsvetaeva had two children:

> Tiny homespun spirit,
> Genius of my home!
> Here it is, the parting of
> Two related inspirations!
>
> What a pity, when in the stove
> Are embers which you cannot see!
> Through the door, star of my night,
> You will not rise, nor yet depart!
>
> (. . .)
>
> On the window doves are tapping,
> With the doves there is no fun!
> The winds cry to me a greeting,
> What good are they to me, the winds!
>
> Nor the grey winds,
> Nor the flocks of doves
> Will be able to call
> In your miraculous voice: Marina!

Logically, it is easy enough to explain why Alya lavished on her mother

* American Relief Administration, which functioned in Russia 1920–23.

188

a tremendous love that sustained her and helped her to live. But it is difficult to understand and accept the indifference (if that is all it was) shown to her own sick child by someone so rarely indifferent to anything.

Kuntsevo in those days was a distant suburb. There was no transport, and visits to the children were few and far between. When Tsvetaeva turned up, roughly a month later, to see her daughters, she found Alya ill, almost at death's door. She snatched her up, got a lift on somebody's sledge, took her home, and fought for her life. The illness dragged on for two months or more, the doctors could not agree on a diagnosis, and the child's temperature was always more or less critical. Tsvetaeva's hopes and fears fluctuated with every rise or fall of a tenth of a degree in the thermometer. Verse would not come to her, and this dumbness was oppressive. Khodasevich told her that manuscripts could be sold in LITO — Soviet institutions with strange names like this were springing up by the dozen; this one meant "Literary Division".* She needed money more than ever before. And although the head of LITO was her old ill-wisher, Valery Bryusov, she decided to try her luck. It was more than six years since she had published anything, and she began collecting poems written between 1913 and 1915. The new volume was naturally called "Youthful Poems". She lost herself in her work. Memories of that incredibly happy time took her out of herself and gave her strength. Everyday realities receded; she was back amongst those who had once fascinated her, and who, so she thought, had long been dead to her. This work took her mind off the prowling presence of death.

She was afraid for Alya. Afraid for Irina too and reluctant to think of her. Her friends talked about taking the child out of the orphanage — but how and where to? Who would look after two sick children? The morning temperature in Tsvetaeva's room was 4–5 °C. There is some inconclusive evidence that Seryozha's sisters wanted to take Irina over — on condition that it was for good. But there was friction between them and Tsvetaeva, and she would not agree. Lilya Efron was ready to take Irina to the village where she worked in a "People's House". But it is difficult to see how someone as helpless as she was could have coped with a sick child.

Tsvetaeva greeted the new year, 1920, in company with A. S. Erofeev, husband of the actress and poet Vera Zvyagintseva. Zvyagintseva had gone to a New Year's Eve party, at her theatre, leaving her husband with her friend and a bottle of wine — nothing out of the ordinary in their circle.

---

* From "*Literaturny ótdel*": this was a division of Narkompros, the (State) Department of Public Enlightenment.

Three days later Tsvetaeva presented Erofeev with a poem commemorating their New Year's Eve.

> I kissed him on the head,
> Didn't think to – on the lips!
> But still, remembering times past,
> You, Love, are beautiful!
>
> It would have been nice to drink some
> Cheerful wine and doff one's coat,
> Oh how, remembering times past,
> The blood would have hummed!

One can imagine this young man and woman seeing the New Year in in a house so cold that you dared not take off your fur coat, and finding it ironically amusing. In the lines that follow Tsvetaeva describes Venus, axe in hand, "wrecking" the basement for firewood, and "Cupid who had exchanged his wings for a pair of felt boots. She begs Cupid not to leave her for ever – the "hell of ice and plague" will pass away, and life will go on!

> Oh, lovely creature!
> Weave to me a little rope,
> And sit, remembering times past,
> At the bedside of the girl.
>
> – Until we meet again! –
> Till once more we learn
> That it is better to kiss the boys
> Not only on their heads.

These light and elegant verses, in complete contrast to the situation in which Tsvetaeva found herself, are an example of her ability to take refuge from reality in poetry. She herself spoke of her "light-hearted attitude to difficulties". From the poem it might be thought that "the most pestilent, the blackest, the deadliest of all those Moscow years" was indeed over. But it dragged on, and ended tragically. On 2 or 3 February (Tsvetaeva gives both dates, in different places) Irina died.

Tsvetaeva lacked the spiritual strength to see her daughter buried. She was stunned and crushed by her death. She had sometimes thought that it would end that way. She concealed Irina's death from her sister for a long time. She knew that those around her blamed her for it. I found echoes of their censure in the correspondence of Magda Nakhman with Yulia Obolenskaya. "Have you heard that Seryozha's daughter Irina has died in an orphanage? . . . Lilya wanted to take Irina over, and now blames herself for her death. I feel terribly sad for the child – nothing but hunger, cold and beatings in her two years of life on this earth."

It is horrifying to read that Irina was beaten, but we have no grounds for accusing Nakhman of prejudice. Rumours originating with a family close to Tsvetaeva's allege that Alya's attitude to Irina was ironically contemptuous. Perhaps her remark that "Marina does not like small children" reflects her own as well as her mother's attitude to Irina? What other "small children" had Alya ever seen with Marina? Nadezhda Mandelstam told me how shocked she and her husband were when Tsvetaeva showed them how she used to tie Irina "to one leg of a bed in a dark room". Tsvetaeva's attitude to her younger daughter was no secret. Obolenskaya answered Nakhman's letter in the same vein: "I can understand Lilya's distress about Irina, but saving her from death would not necessarily have been an act of charity. What did that unhappy child have to live for? She wouldn't have been left with Lilya for ever. Lilya would have been wearing herself out just to prolong the child's sufferings. No, it's better this way. When I think of Seryozha I understand how Lilya feels. But she is not in the least to blame."

It seems monstrous that the mother's name is not even mentioned in connection with her child's death. This studied avoidance of her name ("Seryozha's daughter is dead"), these expressions of sympathy for the father alone, the casual mentions of beatings, that "what did she have to live for?", the very restraint they show amount to a harsh condemnation of Tsvetaeva. She herself felt guilty, and now realized that she had not done all she could to save Irina.

> I understand many things now: my fatalism, my ability to make light of difficulties, and also my good health, my monstrous toughness, are to blame for it all. If you find life easy, you can't believe that others are having a hard time.

This confession was made in a letter to Zvyagintseva and Erofeev. She wrote to them twice shortly after Irina's death, and her letters are cries for help, for pity, for compassion. She knew that these new friends were deeply sympathetic. The letters have survived. The first thing that strikes you is that Tsvetaeva seems to show little pity for her dead child. Indeed, she refuses to accept that her daughter was dead, and not having seen her dead made this all the easier. She rejoiced that (in her dreams) Irina was alive. But there are no live memories of her daughter, of her prettiness, of things she did and said, of Irina happy or Irina crying. Panic – fear for Alya, and pity for herself – those are the feelings that cry out from the pages of these letters: "And then – I was so alone! Everybody has somebody: a husband, a father, a brother. I had only Alya, and Alya was ill, and I had no thought for anything but her illness, so God punished me . . .".

Most painful of all was the thought of Seryozha's reaction to Irina's death. Would he blame her, Marina, as others did? This, and not knowing whether he was dead or alive, drove her to contemplate suicide: "the most dreadful thing is when I start imagining that with Irina gone Seryozha doesn't need me, that it would have been better – more fitting! – for me to die. I'm ashamed to be alive. How am I going to tell him?" What could anyone say in reply to such letters? Zvyagintseva and Erofeev went to see her, took her things to eat. Erofeev sawed up attic beams for firewood. They often invited Marina and Alya to their home. Alya, her nearness and the need to save her, kept Tsvetaeva from utter despair. All her life she had to have someone who needed her: for the present there was such a person – Alya.

This complex of emotions was not directly reflected in her poetry. She remained numb and silent for some time, and even when this was over she did not write about Irina's death. Though there is, I think, an allusion to it in her cycle "Parting"* written eighteen months later.

> Tiny hands, tiny hands!
> In vain you call,
> Lethe's sinuous staircase lies between us.

The only time that Tsvetaeva wrote directly about her daughter was three months after her death – to excuse herself. Had she not been able to do so it would have been difficult for her to go on living, in expectation of her husband's return. The version given in her poem is truthful as far as it goes. Only one essential detail is concealed – her indifference to Irina. Ariadna Efron subsequently adhered to this version.

> Two hands lightly lowered
> Onto an infant's head!
> Two little heads were given me –
> One hand to be lowered on each.
> But with both hands, tight clenched,
> Fiercely, as best I could!
> Seizing the elder from out of the dark,
> I failed to save the younger.
>
> Two hands – to smooth and to caress
> Two fluffy, tender little heads.

* A cycle included in the book *Craft* (she also published a book of poems entitled *Parting*).

Two hands – yet one of them
Proved superfluous over night.

Fair-haired – on a slender little neck –
A dandelion on a stem!
I haven't completely grasped
That my child is in the earth.

Tsvetaeva returned to the theme of a mother made to choose between two daughters in "A Mother's Tale" (1934). Here the mother, asked to choose which of her daughters shall die and which live, prefers to die with her children rather than make the choice. Like most "fairy tales" this one ends happily: awed by the mother's resolve the robber-murderer withdraws, and all three heroines are unharmed.

Before long Tsvetaeva had found others to blame for Irina's death – her husband's sisters. She wrote to Asya, in the Crimea: "Irina died in February of starvation, in an orphanage outside Moscow . . . Lilya and Vera behaved worse than animals. In fact everybody deserted us . . . If you track Seryozha down write to him and say it was pleurisy." Why didn't she want her husband to know the truth? Was she sparing him, or did she assume that he would not believe that his sisters had been cruel to his daughter? A few months later, writing to the Voloshins, she went into greater detail: "Lilya and Vera are in Moscow. They are well, and have jobs. I broke with them some time ago because of their inhuman treatment of children. They let Irina die of starvation in an orphanage, because they hate me. That is the simple truth." The "simple truth", however, contradicts what she says in her letters to Zvyagintseva and Erofeev in the first throes of despair: that Vera Efron, not knowing that Irina had died, wanted to remove her from the orphanage, and that Seryozha's relatives would have helped her with food for Alya. She adopted, perhaps unconsciously, the version most convenient for herself, with no thought for the Efron sisters' good name.

After Irina's death friends procured a ration card for Tsvetaeva. The event had obviously distressed other writers, and alerted them to Tsvetaeva's situation. Help came too late for Irina, but Alya recovered – with Tsvetaeva feeding her as a hen-bird feeds its chicks.

As time went by Tsvetaeva's thoughts turned more and more to her husband. The hope of moving to the Crimea, frustrated in 1917, never left her. She would be closer to him there, or so she imagined. She had thought of leaving in the summer of 1919, fearing the terrible winter ahead. But how could she have travelled with children across a country in the grip of civil war? Afterwards she had lost track of Efron completely, and given up the idea of leaving Moscow, assuming that if he were still alive it was only there that he would be able to find her.

The children were part of Seryozha, and Irina's death and fear for Alya heightened her feeling that she was bound to him by an unbreakable bond, and responsible to him. She was afraid that losing her children would mean losing all claim to her husband. Tsvetaeva took it for granted that life would be meaningless without Seryozha and Alya. "I am contemplating death again," she wrote, reporting a deterioration in Alya's health, ". . . If Seryozha is no longer alive life will be impossible for me anyway." Her Civil War poems are instinct with anguish and dismay in the face of life and death. Only a small number of her "White" poems were published, in various almanacs and anthologies, at the time. But she often gave readings, before very mixed audiences, at literary soirées. Sometimes the listeners were Red cadets. She had to earn a little money any way she could, and young people in those days thirsted for poetry. Poetry was the most important literary genre. By reciting "White Guard" verse to Red Army men she was, in her own mind, fulfilling her duty as the wife of a White officer. Her readings were always well received. Tsvetaeva asserted later that "the contemporary relevance (which in Russia's case means the revolutionary character) of a piece is not confined to its content . . . It is sometimes there in spite of the content . . . There is something more important in poetry than its meaning – and that is its sound." That was how she explained the success of her "White" verses with the Red cadets. Her lines conveyed the music, "the noise" of the time, its tempo.

They were "not *about* revolution, they *were* revolution itself: its onward march". This is close to something Mayakovsky wrote at the beginning of the First World War: "We don't have to write *about* war, but what we write must *be* war". The very sound of Tsvetaeva's verse was revolution in poetry. Everyone could hear it in his own way: the Reds as the music of revolution, the Whites as the music of counter-revolution. These poems later made up the volume called *The Camp of the Swans*.

The book was evidently put together in summer 1923, which is when Tsvetaeva first mentions it in her correspondence. It was not published then, but some of the poems appeared over the years in Russian émigré publications. Before she went back to Russia she made a copy of the collection and left it with part of her archives in Basel. *The Camp of the Swans* did not see the light of day until 1957.

The first poem in the volume – out of chronological order – is "On your dagger is 'Marina' ", a declaration of loyalty to her husband and to the

White cause. There follow sketches of the scene around her reactions to newspaper reports, fragments of her own day-to-day experience, thoughts and feelings about current events. The theme of "Moscow desecrated" emerges, then that of the White Guard, and the White Don – and here the refrain from the very first poem is that the White cause, though just, is hopeless. Her other theme is the Poet's place in the revolution. She invokes André Chénier, who fought the Jacobin dictatorship in verse, and perished on the guillotine. She draws a contrast between him and herself.

> André Chénier ascended the scaffold.
> But I'm alive – and that's an awful sin.
> There are times – of iron – for everyone.
> When powder is about, one should not sing.
>
> And it's no father who, trembling by the gate,
> Tears from his son his soldier's armour.
> There are times when sunshine is a mortal sin.
> Whoever in our days can *live* is not a man.

The subject matter becomes more and more dramatic. The detached onlooker vanishes. The poet is caught up in and carried away by events. Tsvetaeva becomes a participant in all that is happening to her native land. Gradually the White Army is personified, and becomes a white swan, "my" white swan. The Angel, The Warrior, Seryozha, the beloved – her anxious longing and her fear for him are intertwined with anxiety and fear for all the others, for the White cause. This is at once a history and a love letter, written in the hope that some day it will, by some unforeseeable path, reach the ears, the eyes, the heart of the beloved. With every month that passes it becomes less likely. Tsvetaeva tells us in her notes how she and Alya ran down to the front door whenever they heard, or thought they heard, a knock, hoping against hope for some news. *The Camp of the Swans* begins to look more and more like a letter in a bottle. The climactic poem in the collection, born in the terrible "dumb days" of February 1920, is "This book I am entrusting to the wind".

> This book I am entrusting to the wind
> And to the cranes I chance to meet.
> Long, long ago I destroyed my voice
> In shouting down our parting . . .

As the heroines of Greek tragedy addressed space – the gods, the chorus – so Tsvetaeva too addresses space – nature, the winds, the birds . . . The role of fate in Greek tragedy has passed to a power no less inexorable:

Parting. Parting – estrangement – non-meeting is a theme that runs through all of Tsvetaeva's subsequent work. This is no longer merely a personal tragedy. It expresses the tragedy of Russia. I have said that Tsvetaeva had no philosophy of history, but the clearly heard theme of *The Camp of the Swans* is that Russia has diverged from her historical path. Tsvetaeva blames Peter the Great. She is, of course, not the first to do that. All Russian literature after Pushkin remembers the threatening "Just you wait!" uttered by Evgeny to Peter in "The Bronze Horseman". But in Tsvetaeva's poem "To Peter" the burden of the charge is different from that in Pushkin. Peter is guilty of diverting Russia onto an alien path, imposing on her a destiny not her own – which has now become her doom. The whole complex of historical associations in *The Camp of the Swans* becomes an irreversible process, destined to end in disaster as we watch: "Martyred Russia! Rest in Peace!" Yaroslavna, the twelfth-century Kievan princess in *The Lay of the Host of Igor**, plays a special part here. The lyrical "I" of *The Camp of the Swans* is transformed: Marina Tsvetaeva, grief-striken and tormented by uncertainty about her husband, becomes Yaroslavna grieving for Russia and her warriors, and becomes Russia mourning her sons. But, unlike Yaroslavna, Tsvetaeva means not merely to weep for Russia and all her dead but to be the chronicler of this tragedy.

She sees it as her duty to lament for *all*. In the early days of the Revolution she had been with those who were then the defeated, and against the triumphant victor, but gradually the conviction takes shape in her verse that there will be no victors in the Civil War. The Poet mourns for the just and the guilty alike, for all who have perished in the fratricidal war. The tragic liturgy takes the form of a traditional Russian lament for the dead.

> O mushroom mine, little mushroom, mushroom white!
> That's Russia, reeling and lamenting in the field.
> Help me, I am not firm on my feet!
> My blood's ore has enshrouded me in mist!
>
> To the left and to the right
> Are jaws, blood-dripping,
> And every wound says:
> Mother!
>
> And only this is
> Clear to me, in my drunken state,
> Out of the womb and into the womb:
> Mother!

* See notes to p. 123.

All lie side by side,
No boundary can be drawn.
If one looks: it's a soldier.
Where is ours, where is theirs?

He was white – and became red:
Blood crimsoned him.
He was red – and became white:
Death whitened him.

Who are you? – a White? – Can't hear! – stand up!
Or did you spend time with the Reds?

Not only in the face of death but in the eyes of Russia, all who have died are equal and are right, for each of them died for Russia, for her happiness as he understood it. But to end the book with a keening would have seemed unnatural to Tsvetaeva. In the most tragic situation she sought the light. She ended *The Camp of the Swans* with a poem written as the New Year 1921 approached. The Civil War was over, the Bolsheviks had won. A sizable part of the White Army was evacuated via Turkey to Europe. The rest were scattered all over Russia. Tsvetaeva still had no news of her husband – another six months would go by before his whereabouts were known. The country's future seemed to have been determined, but Tsvetaeva's own future and that of her family was hazy. Her New Year poem was addressed to her husband's comrades, and entitled when first published "To those at Gallipoli" – and so to Seryozha, if he was alive and amongst them.

Happy New Year, Camp of Swans!
Glorious fragments!
Happy New Year, warriors with knapsacks,
Far from home!

The Reds can't catch you up, they dance,
Foam at the mouth!
Happy New Year, beaten – fleeing –
Motherland, beckoning!

Bow to the earth and the whole earth rings
In a drinking song.
Igor, it's Russia weeping across seas
Like Yaroslavna.

Wearied with sadness, anguished, groaning:
My Brother! Prince! Son!
Happy New Year, young Russia beyond
The dark blue sea!

This is catharsis: Fate has conquered, but duty has been done in full. *The Camp of the Swans* ends on a high note. Hope has for the moment triumphed over despair in Tsvetaeva's soul. Few could have guessed that she was so desperate. On the contrary – she was censured for her frequent amours. It is easy to imagine the female gossip: husband away at the war, nobody knows where, may even be dead, and *she* . . . She did in fact have a number of affairs, some ephemeral, some quite serious, in those years. She wrote poems to many men. The "comedian" Zavadsky, Alekseev and Antokolsky at the "Studio", Meyerhold's assistant the producer V. M. Bebutov, the playwright V. M. Volkenshtein, the fledgling poets E. L. Lann and E. L. Mindlin, Prince Sergey Volkonsky, the artist N. N. Vysheslavtsev (a whole large cycle of poems is addressed to him), the man I have called "The Travelling Companion", the Red soldier ("Stenka Razin") described in "Free Transit", Boris Bessarabov (another Red soldier, dedicatee of "The Bolshevik"), Aleksey Aleksandrovich Stakhovich . . . And we don't know how many others there may have been. She was a seeker. A seeker for adventure, she says in her poems, but that is untrue. What she was in search of was a kindred soul. She hungered and thirsted, she soared to ecstasy and was plunged into disenchantment, as she went from one infatuation to another. It was not just sex. Perhaps it wasn't sex at all, or was sex of a sort unknown to ordinary mortals. Tsvetaeva used to say at the time that her "great passion was for somebody to talk to. Physical love affairs are necessary because that is the only way to penetrate someone's soul." The body was only the integument of the soul with which she longed to fuse.

> . . . Without touching lips
> We cannot assuage our souls!

If it helped at all it was not for long. Tsvetaeva was soon left with her loneliness again. There was no escape and she knew it. Loneliness was the beginning and the end of all that happened in her life. And poetry was her only means of rising above it.

Some decades later Salomeya Andronikova, a friend of Tsvetaeva's during her émigré years, said something to me that may come as a surprise to many people: "Marina didn't go in much for love affairs." So what were all those infatuations that made her fling herself upon people like a hungry man upon a crust of bread? Perhaps the hidden explanation is one of the secrets of the poetic process – perhaps the infatuations fed her poetry. There is indirect confirmation of this in the fact that Tsvetaeva was just as passionately enamoured of certain people with whom an "affair" in the ordinary sense was impossible: with Aleksey Stakhovich, for instance, whom she hardly knew and for whom she wrote poems after his death, or with Sergey Volkonsky, who was known not to be interested in women. Tsvetaeva dedicated amazing poems, with no trace of the erotic, to both of them. Perhaps there is in poets a sort of spiritual vampirism, crudely mistaken for a sexual manifestation? Tsetaeva's infatuations came in rapid succession: it may be that she sometimes liberated herself from one of them through poetry, and then went on to the next. Interestingly, nothing written in connection with these "encounters" has anything erotic about it. You get the feeling that every loved one –

> (How I wished that each should flower
> In the centuries with me! . . .)

– not only set the stream of poetry flowing but confirmed for her the reality of her own existence. Without them it might perhaps have seemed still more ephemeral to her. Once the flow of verse was spent, whoever had released it was of no further use. Tsvetaeva didn't just lose interest; she abused those to whom her verses were addressed, or simply forgot them. This accounts for her not infrequent changes of dedication.

Nadezhda Mandelstam, who saw at close quarters how poems are "made", has tried to fathom the secret of the connection between poetry and sex. It is, she writes, "so deep that it is almost impossible to speak about it. The peculiar tension of poetry, its character, at once sensuous and prophetic, changes a person much more than any other art or than science does". Mandelstam himself felt "betrayal" of his poetry to be more serious than any betrayal in the ordinary sense of the word. "His verses to Natasha Shtempel also caused him suffering, and he implored me not to break with her, but I could see nothing in the lines to occasion a break with a real friend. He concealed the second poem from me altogether, and if there had been a chance to publish it he would probably have refused it. What he said was 'these treacherous verses will never be printed while I live', and 'we are not troubadours'."* This last is particularly interesting, because Mandelstam's verses to Shtempel, like Tsvetaeva's to Volkonsky, show not the slightest tinge of eroticism.

Whatever Tsvetaeva may have thought about her own "treacherous" verses, she did not publish them. Here is a dialogue between her and the eight-year-old Alya, used as an epigraph to a letter to E. Lann.

---

* *Author's Note*: I am quoting here a passage from the first draft of the manuscript of N.Ya. Mandelstam's *Second Book* [translated as *Hope Abandoned* (see Bibliography)] which I copied out long ago and kept amongst my papers. Subsequently N.Ya. evidently altered this passage; I have found only echoes of it there.

"Marina! Which would you like best – a letter from Lann, or Lann himself?"

"A letter, of course!"

"What a strange answer! Here's another one, then: do you want a letter from Papa or Papa himself?"

"Oh! Papa!"

"I knew you would!"

"Because that's love, and the other's just romance!"

This casual phrase defines Tsvetaeva's attitude to her husband and to all the others. Neither the poems, not yet the emotions which prompted them, affected the most important thing – her relationship with Seryozha. He was unique: the rest was just "romance". In a letter to her sister in December 1920, Tsvetaeva confessed: "I'm very lonely, although Moscow is full of people I know. All these years I've had somebody at my side but I'm still alone."

This may have been unfair to those who were "at her side", but it was how she felt. She and Seryozha were a world to themselves, bound by oaths and obligations of their own. Tsvetaeva may well have kept her most intimate feelings to herself in the years of revolution, when fear, pain, and longing for her husband were her constant companions. She concealed her feelings from outsiders, although as the years went by her uncertainty became more and more unbearable, her fear for him and her longing more and more acute. When the Civil War ended and she still had no news of her husband, she was on the brink of despair. Letters from the Crimea told her that he was still alive in autumn 1920 – and there the flow of information abruptly ended. Tsvetaeva would not allow herself to think that he could be dead. She must wait and search. She asked Erenburg to make enquiries when he left for Berlin in spring 1921 and sent after him a poem full of hope, conjuring fate to bring back her "one and only". She learnt that her sister Asya, Andryusha (Asya's son), the Voloshins, the Gertsyks and Parnok were alive and in the Crimea. They had survived all the horrors of the Civil War – the rapid and unpredictable changes of régime, the murders, the executions, the famine, the epidemics . . . Asya and Andryusha had also had to live with the knowledge of Andryusha's father's death. The Crimea was still hungry and unsafe, the victorious régime was suspicious and swift to punish. Tsvetaeva was eager to help the "Crimeans". Quite incapable of providing for herself, she could do a great deal for friends: she appealed to public sympathy, went from one government office to another, helped to "wangle" ration cards and "immunity certificates" for their houses. In her letters she tried to persuade Asya to make her way to Moscow: they yearned for each other, and Marina was sure that they would be all the closer for their years of separation. "I think of him (her husband – V.S.) day and night. You and he are the only ones I love."

In any case, she thought, it would be much easier for them living together. She even found work for Asya in Moscow, and got Boris Bessarabov to take her flour for the journey, money and an official invitation – without which it was impossible to get to Moscow. Tsvetaeva's response to other people's hardships and disasters was instant and generous. When times were hardest for her she would share a crust, a cigarette, the warmth of her little stove. When the young poet Mindlin moved in with her for a while she washed his shirts ("Why wash *his* shirts?" a woman friend expostulated. "He's a terrible poet".) She copied Prince Volkonsky's manuscripts – she had met him at Vera Zvyagintseva's place, and immediately felt drawn to him. Zvyagintseva told me that Tsvetaeva occasionally stayed with her overnight at this time and in the middle of the night would say: "Vera dear, wake up. I want to talk about Volkonsky." She was attracted by his ancestry – princes, and one of them a Decembrist – his "breeding", his theatrical past, his cast of mind, and the things he wrote. Few people interested her as much as he did. Talking to him, or even copying his prose, gave her intense pleasure. He was, perhaps, the first of his generation (the "fathers") with whom she was on such intimate terms: as a boy Volkonsky had seen and heard the great Tyutchev in his mother's drawing room! It was thanks to Volkonsky that poetry "came back" to her – or so she thought. It would not be true to say that she had not been writing in the immediate past, although it seemed to her that her silence had lasted a long time. But it is a fact that from summer 1920 only a few poems had come to her, and that this depressed her. After meeting Volkonsky she was swept off her feet again by a torrent of new poems, still in full flow when she left Russia. Once again, as in the days of her "Youthful Poems" or the first *Mileposts*, her verses were a lyrical journal and quite naturally formed themselves into a book, which she later called *Craft*. She had reached the stage of poetic maturity:

> Oh, this hour, when like a ripened ear
> We bend beneath our weight.

She saw Volkonsky as her teacher, and *Craft* begins with a cycle called "The Pupil." In Volkonsky's "school" she completed her apprenticeship. From adolescence on she had felt the need of a Teacher. The young Tsvetaeva and her sister had fallen under Ellis's spell: he was older than they were, was already a "real" poet, and introduced them to a literary circle. In fact Ellis turned out to be not a Teacher, but merely a Magician, and Tsvetaeva's verses addressed to him have an ironic ring. It may have been this need of a Teacher that made her look briefly towards Valery Bryusov; but then they soon went their different ways, because their philosophies, their poetic aims, and their temperaments were incompatible. A year before she met Volkonsky Tsvetaeva had fancied that Vyacheslav Ivanov might become her Teacher. We know hardly anything about their association, but in spring 1920 she dedicated to him a group of poems in which she calls him "Rabbi". This was how Christ was addressed by his disciples. But Tsvetaeva had nothing to learn from him either. Unlike Bryusov as he was, he too belonged to a "different breed". These lines, addressed to him, almost say so in so many words:

> You write with your finger in the sand.
> And I come up and read . . .
>
> (. . .)
>
> O Master, O Master, I fear
> I read not that which you write! . . .

This tells us that she is eager to be taught, but not that she has found a Teacher.

In the "Pupil" poems the word "Teacher" is deliberately never used. We can if we wish identify the Pupil with Tsvetaeva herself, and the Teacher with Volkonsky. But the poems do not admit of a literal interpretation. The Teacher is not Volkonsky the descendant of the Decembrist, the prince, writer and philosopher, but a figure embodying all the characteristics of that generation which Tsvetaeva came to think of as not merely "the fathers" but her "kin". If in her lines to Ivanov she sees herself "at his feet" (incidentally, the heroine has here the characteristics of a boy pupil: she speaks of her "boyish breast"), in "The Pupil" Pupil and Teacher are together, side by side.

> Quietly they went up onto the hill
> The eternal two.
>
> Closely, shoulder to shoulder,
> They stood in silence.
> Two breaths rise together
> Under one cloak . . .

Tsvetaeva conceives of her apprenticeship as a novitiate and as service to a master. The Pupil longs to share the Teacher's past:

> Father, take me back
> Into your life, father! . . .

and his future:

> Father, take me into the sunset,
> Into your night, father!

In the present they are side by side and the Pupil is ready to serve the Teacher, sharing the cloak that protects him from rain and wind, shielding him in battle, mounting before he does the pyre on which he is to be burnt. "Being the Pupil means surrendering yourself without expectation of return, ie. surrendering yourself completely," she explained to one of her critics. And the Teacher acknowledges his Pupil, addresses him as "My Son!". There is one troubling line in the cycle – the last. The Pupil follows the Teacher, or rather his cloak, over hills, over desert sands, over waves . . . and, suddenly:

> Following the cloak that lies and lies . . .

What does it mean? Is the Teacher false because he accepts the Pupil's service without deserving it? Does the Pupil suddenly doubt the truth which he sought to serve? Does the wind, playing with the cloak, awaken the thought that all things are deceptive? Or has that blessed "supreme hour of loneliness", foretold in the second poem of the cycle, now arrived? For the "hour of pupillage" cannot last forever.

Strangely, "The Pupil" is followed by the cycle "Marina", dedicated to the memory of the Polish beauty Marina Mniszek, the "Tsarina" crowned together with her husband, the False Dimitry (the Pretender Grishka Otrepiev), at the beginning of the seventeenth century. Tsvetaeva felt mystically tied to Marina Mniszek by her noble Polish origin and her name:

> To your glory I sin
> The sin of the tsar – pride.
> Your glorious name
> Gloriously I bear . . .

She wrote that in 1916. Her attitude to her namesake was by now more ambiguous. There are four poems in the "Marina" cycle, obviously written for two different voices. In the first and third the lyric heroine, Tsvetaeva, is reincarnated as Mniszek; in the second and fourth she looks at and judges Mniszek from her own perspective and that of her own time. The first voice is like that of the Pupil: intimate, womanly, loving . . . Has the hero of the earlier cycle changed sex: is the boy pupil now Marina the beloved? No – the first voice in "Marina" develops its theme without reference to sex. Only the first two and last three lines in the first poem of the "Marina" poems are written in the feminine gender; everything else in the masculine. The third poem is written in such a way that gender and sex are absent altogether:

> – Heart, treachery!
> – But not separation!
> And the thieving, swarthy hand
> To white lips.

This turns the reader's thoughts to the theme of fidelity in the general human, rather than the specifically sexual, sense. "The Pupil" and "Marina" begin similarly:

> To be your fair-haired boy . . . ("The Pupil")

> To be his eagle-like beloved dove! ("Marina")

To belong to, to serve someone to whom you are indispensable – that is Tsvetaeva's eternal theme: "I yearn for people." In both cycles Tsvetaeva's understanding of "service" is heavily emphasized:

> From all offences, from all earth's wounds
> To be a cloak for you . . . ("The Pupil")

> As a seraph and guard dog
> To watch over troubled sleep . . . ("Marina")

> And at the first stone cast by the rabble
> To be a shield and not a cloak! ("The Pupil")

> She threw open the shawl on her breast.
> Arms wide open! – That on your judgment day
> You should not rise up in Basmanov* blood . . . ("Marina")

To protect, to defend, to follow Him everywhere . . . Over hills, over desert sands, over seas . . . Pupil following Teacher.

> On horseback, or crawling, or swimming!
> Through reed, through osiers, through marsh,
> Or flying – where no horse can go . . .

Marina following her Beloved . . . Even death with Him is a blessing, the best of all possible ends.

> And with a smile of inspiration be
> The first to ascend your funeral pyre. ("The Pupil")

> And – with a second jump –
> On to the spears! ("Marina")

* Military commander who perished defending the False Dimitry.

Her Marina is an idealized, a romanticized reincarnation of a real historical personage as her own poetic self. An entry in one of her notebooks written much later tells us: "If I were writing her history, I should write about myself – not, that is, about the adventuress consumed by ambition, not about the Pretender's mistress, but about myself as a loving woman, myself as a mother. Or most probably myself as a poet."

This is exactly what she did in the first and third poems of the "Marina" cycle, putting herself – poet, loving woman, "more than mother" – in Marina Mniszek's place. The second voice in the cycle, passing judgment on the historical Marina Mniszek, is that of Tsvetaeva, woman and poet, made wise by her experience of revolution, of partings and of deaths. The author and her heroine are brought closer by the similarity of the historical periods in which they lived. Tsvetaeva was not the only one to find a resemblance between the Civil War and the seventeenth century Time of Troubles. The second voice conjures up the ambitious adventuress, the traitress, who is not even Dimitry's lover: in Tsvetaeva's eyes that would have gone some way towards justifying Mniszek. There is a stark contrast between the first and second poems. The first announces what she, Marina, should and could have been to her beloved; the second recounts all that she failed to be, all that she did not do. Every stanza, except the last, ends with a negation: *you* who "bore him no son", "did not wave after him", "did not shield him with your body", "did not wipe away his sweat". The final stanza upbraids Marina Mniszek unmercifully:

> Self-seeking blood!
> Accursed, accursed be you,
> Who were able to be False Marina to False Dimitry!

Both "The Pupil" and "Marina" are, I think, intimately connected with her thoughts about her husband, and her need to be with him. In "The Pupil" the note of epic self-abnegation is stronger; in "Marina" that of dramatic passion. "To be more than a mother – to be Marina!" is to be just what Tsvetaeva was to Sergey Efron, and what Marina Mniszek never became to the False Dimitry. Reading between the lines we hear her saying "if I had been in Mniszek's place", "if I had been given the chance, as she was, to share my beloved's lot", "if I had been at his side I would not have let him die or would have died with him". But perhaps, deeper in her subconscious, there lurked self-condemnation: I was *not* beside him. Perhaps that is why there are echoes of the Mniszek story in the first poem of the "Parting" cycle: the Kremlin square again, the booming bells, the Pretender's body flung out onto the cobbles.

Cast off into the night,
As if by a hand —
Fight . . .

Tsvetaeva projects their situation onto her own, equating Mniszek's betrayal and her own parting with Seryozha. These poems are an attempt to escape from the misery of uncertainty. "Parting" is a tragic cycle, in which the theme of parting (perhaps for ever) with the beloved is bound up with the theme of parting from a child (memories of Irina's death) and with thoughts of suicide. This last was not just poetic licence. She really did see it as the one way out. In a letter to Zvyagintseva she says:

> I have no future, no will to go on, I'm afraid of everything. It seems to me that it would be better to die. If S. is not alive I shan't be able to go on living anyway. Think of it — a long, long life — an enormous life — and everything strange — strange towns, strange people — and Alya and I — abandoned by everybody — just the two of us. Why prolong the agony if you can put an end to it?

Relieving her suffering in verse was not so easy. As she came to the end of "Parting" she said in a letter to Lann that these poems were: "difficult to write and impossible to read. (For me to read to others.) I am writing them because I jealously keep my pain to myself, I talk to nobody about S., and anyway have nobody to talk to. (Asya has enough to bear, she too has been without S.) I mean that poems are an attempt to break through to the surface. It works for half an hour at a time."

In spite of this last statement the theme of overcoming earthly suffering through poetry appeared for the first time in "Parting". This cycle was the beginning of a new stage in Tsvetaeva's poetic procedures. Her spiritual malaise no longer found expression in the strict classical form of, for instance, "The Pupil". The association of ideas becomes more intricate; thoughts remain half-expressed; sentences are put together with some major component missing. Thus "The Leader's Homecoming" is written without a single verb. The reader is present at the birth of the verse; he is made to share the poet's experience to the full. In "Parting" the new still exists side by side with the old, explicit Tsvetaeva, but gradually her verse becomes more and more complicated and cryptic, and towards the end of *Craft* threatens to plunge the reader into chaos.

Asya and Andryusha arrived on 21 May. Loneliness, it seemed, was at an end; two kindred souls were re-united, and life would be only half as difficult. They moved in with Marina. Asya had to begin life all over again.

In the years of the war and revolution she had lost everything: money, home, possessions. Marina was ready to share whatever she had. But it was evident from the first few days that the old intimacy was no more. "Asya irritates me," Marina told Zvyagintseva, to her astonishment – she knew how impatiently, how passionately Marina had looked forward to her sister's coming. Their sufferings seem to have intensified in each of them whatever it was that divided them in early childhood. Tsvetaeva began trying to find a separate, even if only temporary, refuge for her sister.

Suddenly – the happy news that had seemed so improbable! Erenburg had located Seryozha! Alive and well in Constantinople. On 1 July 1921, after three and a half years of separation and nearly two without news of him, Tsvetaeva received her first letter from her husband. She was working on her "Georgy", where Seryozha was portrayed as the knightly St George Bringer of Victories. The verses break off in mid-sentence, and Tsvetaeva's note reads "unfinished because of the letter". In her manuscript, beside the abandoned "Georgy", she has written: "From today – life begins. I am alive for the first time." Their first letters to each other have been preserved in Tsvetaeva's archive, and were published in part in their daughter's memoirs. Seryozha wrote:

> . . . My dear friend, Marinochka, I got a letter from Ilya Grigorievich [Erenburg] today telling me that you are alive and well. When I had read it I wandered round the city all day, crazy with joy. What can I tell you? Where shall I begin? There's so much I need to say, but I've got out of the habit of talking, let alone writing. I am living to be with you again. There will be no life for me without you – stay alive! I shall make no demands on you – all I want is for you to be alive . . .
>
> Through all the years we have been apart – every day, every hour – you have been with me, inside me. But you must know that yourself . . .

He adds the following note for Alya: "Thank you, my joy. All my love and all my thoughts are with you and your mama. I believe that we shall see each other soon, to start a new life together, and never part again . . ." Tsvetaeva wrote in reply:

> My Seryozhenka! If people don't die of happiness they can be paralysed by it. I have just received your letter, and I feel paralysed. The last news I had of you was your letter to Max. Then – a void. I don't know where to begin – so I'll begin where I shall end – with my love for you . . .

Her husband's letter arrived in time to give a new twist to a poem about him. Tsvetaeva interrupts her requiem to sing a hosanna.

Alive and well!
Louder than thunder –
Just like an axe –
Joy!

(. . .)

So, you're alive?
Closing your lids,
You breathe, they call –
Can you hear?

(. . .)

Dead, and alive again?!
Breath just enough,
Like a stone from the sky,
Like a crow-bar

On the head, –
No, up to the hilt,
Like a sword in the breast – Joy!

The news turned her life upside down. She did not doubt for a moment that she must go to her husband. It wouldn't be easy. Even their letters had to go via Erenburg to begin with – correspondence with Constantinople was probably rather dangerous. She would have to go through the tedious business of getting permission, and raising the money. Almost a year went by before she could leave. We know very little about the life of Sergey Efron, and so I was very glad to discover that letters of his to White Army friends – Olga Nikolaevna and Vsevolod Aleksandrovich Bogengardt – had survived. They had in common not only their comradeship at the front, and the fact that they were refugees, but also anxiety for their loved ones: some of the Bogengardt family were also back there in Russia. The Bogengardts were still living in Constantinople when Efron's first letter from Prague, dated 11 November 1921, arrived.

Dear friends,
    I am writing from Prague, where we arrived just two days ago. The Czechs have given us a remarkably warm welcome – I hadn't expected anything like it. Love for Russia and Russia's is a centuries-old tradition here. All the best people here speak Russian . . . It's how French was to us in times gone by. At the university, in the streets, in shops, everywhere any Russian is surrounded by kindness and courtesy . . . We are living in a worker's house hired specially for us. We each have a little room of our own, very clean and light, like a ship's cabin. The furniture consists of a

bed and a small stool. I think we're also going to be given a little table.

The day after I arrived in Prague I got a letter from Marina. She writes that her plans to leave Russia have failed twice. But she isn't giving up hope, and is sure that she will manage to leave by next spring. She is having a very difficult time of it.

Correspondence between Prague and Russia is very easy. The mails are working normally – a letter to Moscow gets there in two weeks. Erenburg has written to say that letters can be sent to the capitals without the least danger.

I trust him, and posted a letter to Marina yesterday. You can even send parcels from here. I shall enquire about it immediately . . .

It was only four months since Sergey and Marina had found each other, and already she had twice had to abandon plans to leave Russia. But she was losing no time in looking for a third way out. In Sergey's life, meanwhile, there had been a major change: he had not only moved to Prague but had recommenced his education. He informed friends that he had settled on the Faculty of Literature – he had remained as impractical as ever through the years of war and wandering. What good would studying literature do him? How would he support his family? The most practical of the former White Volunteers became engineers. We do not know how Sergey had lived in the year between evacuation from the Crimea and his letter to the Bogengardts. But we can imagine what a gruelling time he must have had if he considered a cramped lodging provided by public funds, without food, first-rate accommodation. And back home, in Moscow? Life was difficult, and the food parcel which Sergey shortly sent could not have been more welcome. Now that he was in Prague he felt able at last to write home directly, and not via Erenburg. The writer of a letter from Constantinople would have been identified immediately as a White Guard. This is probably why the memoirs of Erenburg, Anastasia Tsvetaeva and Ariadna Efron are all silent about Sergey Efron's stay in Constantinople: they write as if he had landed in Prague miraculously. The only reference is in Tsvetaeva's poem "Glad Tidings", in which the Volunteers fleeing from the Crimea approach the Turkish shore and safety.

> And there – far off –
> Saint Sofia's dome . . .
> O my wings,
> My ships, my cranes!

A few months later Sergey Efron writes to the Bogengardts, who had by then moved to Czechoslovakia and were living in Moravia, giving them, for the benefit of Vsevolod's mother, precise details of the steps she would take to leave Russia and join them. Tsvetaeva and Efron were now able to correspond regularly. She tried to conceal from him how great her difficulties were, but probably with little success. She writes more frankly to Erenburg than to her husband:

> I learnt today from Yu. K. [Baltrushaitis] that to get to Riga and pick up a visa there costs 10 million. They might as well say "take the Cathedral of Christ the Saviour with you". If I sell Seryozha's old fur coat (mine is worth nothing), the antique chandelier, the mahogany furniture, and two books (the *Mileposts* collection and *Phoenix*) I could just about scrape together 4 million – but even that's pretty doubtful; in my hands gold turns to tin and flour to sawdust . . . But I shall go just the same, even if I have only just enough for the ticket.

The letter is headed "Moscow. 21 (r) October 1921": "r" means "Russia" – Tsvetaeva would continue living by the Old Style (Russian) calendar for a long time yet, though the New Style (Gregorian) calendar had been introduced more than three years previously. She ends her letter to Erenburg with a request "not to let S. know just how difficult things are for me" and to "reassure him that we shall be coming. I write to you because I have nobody to tell all this to, and because I know that for you it's just an illustration of what life is like in revolutionary Moscow, 1921."

GOODBYE

As soon as she heard that Seryozha was alive she knew that she must leave. There were never any doubts: they had to be together, and he could not come back, so she must go to him. Ariadna Sergeevna Efron said to me many years later: "Mama wrecked her life twice because of Father. The first time when she left Russia to be with him, the second when she returned to be with him." I thought that her words contained, to say the least, some daughterly exaggeration. Now, however, I agree with her that Marina did leave her native land for her husband's sake. Or rather, the need to be with him provided the decisive impulse to leave. But gradually emigration acquired an additional psychological motive.

In the first shock of happiness she had written (to Akhmatova) that she was "yearning to go, now that I know he's alive . . ." but gradually the yearning to be with him became in her mind an urge to flee: she was not just "yearning towards . . .", she was, more and more eagerly as time went on, "running away from . . .". This theme emerges in the cycle "Prisoner of the

Khan", which she began in September 1921 and continued until she left Russia. Once again, themes and images from *The Lay of the Host of Igor* make their appearance. To Tsvetaeva the Bolshevik victory is exactly comparable with the Polovtsian, or the Tatar, invasion. Events separated by two centuries – the Polovtsian incursions of the twelfth century and those of the Tatars in the fourteenth – have fused in her poems. "Captivity with the [Polovtsian] Khan" and "the rabble Tatars" are images of enslavement with deep roots in Russian history. "Russia, My Land" is seen as a wild horse. And "Mamay" [a Tatar Khan] is the rider who succeeded in bridling and taming it.

> Slant-eyed vileness,
> A thieving palm . . .

Was she perhaps thinking of Lenin? Everybody would recognize those "slant eyes". We recognize, once again, Tsvetaeva's remarkable feel for history. Mamay is not in the saddle by mistake; he is the only one whom Russia cannot throw.

> If you mount, you must jump!
> Once up – don't grumble!
> Only one horseman
> To your taste – Mamay!

Mamay is the rider to suit Russia, and the implication is perhaps that the Bolshevik Mamay is there to stay. This fits in with Tsvetaeva's conviction that the White movement was finished. Its end is seen as a tragedy for all Russians, and perhaps even for the whole world. Russians in emigration went on for many long years planning the defeat of the Soviet régime, organizations were set up and desperate attempts were made to resurrect the White movement. But Tsvetaeva knew for sure in 1921 that "the ball is over!" All that remains is to lament what has happened and say farewell to her hopes. Tsvetaeva writes two poems with the same title, "A New Year's", which is unclear – a New Year's *what*? Eve? party? song? or, maybe, death?* – and in them she allows the White Volunteers to make their own farewells to the past. What remains, after all their heroism? Brotherhood, loyalty, "deeds and hearts pure as crystal". I offer no judgement on the realities of life in the White Army – as with every army it had its cruel and sordid aspects – nor on the historical significance of the Volunteers. I am

---

* *Novogodnyaya*: the title of the poem is a feminine adjective without a noun; not to be confused with her 1927 poem entitled *Novogodnee* (a neuter adjective without a noun), translated here as "New Year's Greeting". The author suggests possible feminine nouns to accord with the feminine form of the adjective "New Year's".

concerned here only with Tsvetaeva's attitude. Her poems are an exalted requiem for the movement. When *The Camp of the Swans* was first published in 1957 reviewers noted that no one had hymned and mourned the Volunteer movement more eloquently. The book, and those reviews, appeared of course in the West. The Soviet Union preferred to say nothing.

Tsvetaeva's attempts in those last months to interpret what had happened are fraught with a tragic sense of finality. Before all else she had a personal question to answer: Why can I not go on living here? She had survived two revolutions, the Civil War, and War Communism.* She had lived to see the Bolsheviks introduce NEP,† and by now she was certain that this régime "didn't suit" her. NEP disgusted her even more than War Communism. She wrote to the hungry Voloshin about Moscow:

> It is grotesque. A malignant growth. A festering sore. There are 54 food shops on the Arbat: the buildings vomit groceries. The people are as bad as the shops: they'll give you nothing except for money. Ruthlessness is the general rule. Nobody cares about anybody. Believe me, dear Max, I'm not saying this out of envy; if I had millions I still wouldn't buy their bacon. All these things smell too strongly of blood. There are many hungry people, but they're tucked away in holes and slums, and what you can see is all splendid.

Marina and Asya tried to collect money from Moscow writers for hungry writers in the Crimea, but purses were opened reluctantly. She sent the Voloshins 100,000 roubles of her own, "to shame our rich colleagues" . . . She had to flee, because she could not live in a country where the smell of blood was too strong.

> Having tasted my fill
> Of the Khan's captivity,
> I raise my wing
> To the god of flight . . .

It was not just escape, but an act of protest – she would sooner die than submit to an alien, unjust and cruel régime.

> Death, seize me by my plaits!
> Scythe away my red-coloured cheeks!
> I shall not bow down at the feet
> Of my slant-eyed Tatars!

Knowing that her decision was correct and inevitable she still suffered

---

* The period from the 1917 Revolution to the end of the Civil War, characterized by a State trade monopoly, grain requisitioning and hunger.
† The New Economic Policy: Partial restoration of private trade during 1921–1924.

agonies. At such moments she was more keenly aware than ever of her unbreakable ties with what she was about to leave for ever. For Tsvetaeva parting with Russia was a sort of death, the separation of the soul from the body. The theme of death recurs insistently in her farewell poems. She no longer coquets with the word "death", as she had done in "Youthful Poems". Here life and death are treated seriously. We are shown a new Tsvetaeva, whose courage and wisdom declare her maturity. Tragedy is becoming her natural element. Tsvetaeva's farewells to her past extended over many months. She was able to look around herself, to look back and take stock. Before all else she looked into herself, looked at herself – and realized that her youth was over.

After all she had experienced and felt and suffered she could not go on living as before. She felt like Jairus's daughter, raised by Christ from the dead, needlessly, and against her own will. She was, so to speak, condemned to compulsory life after death. Past sufferings had given the Poet glimpses of death and Eternity. Now they are the veil through which she sees the present. Taking leave of one's youth is a tragic event, demanding a conscious effort of will:

> My youth, torn from the depths of my breast,
> So to others!

As she renounces her youth Tsvetaeva tries to look at herself with her husband's eyes. They will soon be meeting – how will she look to him?

> I have not grown more fair in the years of separation!
> You will not get angry at my hands grown coarse,
> Reaching out for salt and bread?
> All horny from the labour of comradeship! . . .

She wrote in a notebook that "at 29 . . . I have taken leave of my youth once and for all". Renouncing femininity, she also takes leave of her "Muse". If not altogether identical her "youth" and her "Muse" somehow merge in Tsvetaeva's mind. Parting with her Muse causes her no pain. The mature Tsvetaeva chooses herself a new patron, her "Genius". The ancients supposed that only a male person could have such a patron. In commiting herself and her poetry to her "Genius" Tsvetaeva affirms that she sees herself not as a "poetess" but as a poet.

As she surveys the past her thoughts constantly turn to those who have perished. She knows her "White Swan" is alive, but cannot and does not want to forget the horrors of fratricidal war. Her attitude to the "Reds v. Whites" dilemma is unique. In a world divided into two camps which hate each other she reaffirms what is for her the only acceptable position:

One amongst all – for all – against all!

From the "White" camp Zinaida Gippius issued her call:

One should not turn to
Calls for vengeance
And cries of exultation:
After preparing the rope –
In silence let us hang them . . .

And from the "Red" camp Aleksandr Bezymensky shook his menacing fist:

But know that toiling hands
By the throat will seize you all and . . . strangle you . . .

Not once during the war did Tsvetaeva call on anyone to fight or to hate. And now that it was all over she was still less likely to do so. She did not doubt the rightness of the White cause. But she showed her pity for all who had fought and died. She went to the communal graves on Red Square, in which the Red Guards who fell in Moscow in October 1917 were buried. She knew, I imagine, that there had been a proposal to bury all the fallen – Red Guards and officer cadets – together, but that the victorious Bolsheviks had not agreed to this. Tsvetaeva stood before the communal graves and bowed her head in farewell, acknowledging the Red Guards, her supposed enemies, as "just", because they had sincerely believed that their "wrong" was "right", had given their lives for an unjust cause they thought just. This reminds us of the lines she wrote at the beginning of the Revolution, in which she begs indulgence for simple people –

The weak, the stupid, sinful, random,
Those drawn into the terrible funnel,
Those seduced and those deceived . . .

because "they know not what they do". Tsvetaeva is ready to say goodbye to Moscow with words of forgiveness. But the thought of those who had perished, the thought that their blood had been shed in vain, arouses her anger. After all the terrible events she had witnessed she cannot reconcile herself to the idea that all is forgotten so quickly, that the blood of brothers has been betrayed. As is well known, many "on the other side of the Red barricades" were bewildered, troubled, horrified by the NEP. A howl went up all over the country – "what were we fighting for?". There were several suicides amongst people who saw the NEP as a betrayal of the Revolution.

Tsvetaeva's assessment from the opposite side, is exactly the same.

> All the old past, onto the scrap-heap!
> This day, welcome!
> And on blood, on fresh blood —
> There is food and dance.
>
> So for those, for all, for brothers
> — I shall not do penance! —
> Forgive me, Iversky Mother*!
> I recant.

She renounces her "bloody", her "ferocious" motherland, where "the smell of blood is too strong", renounces the "wondrous" city, which she has loved and sung, the city which is flesh of her flesh. She renounces it, fully realizing what the future may hold. That this sobriety of judgement was compatible with her romantic ideas about the world and the poet's place in it remains a mystery to me. But it is a fact which should never be overlooked.

Leave-taking meant looking into the future as well as into the past. Tsvetaeva's farewell to Moscow began with a poignant anticipation of orphanhood. She was about to exchange her native city, in which her birthright was undisputed, for an alien land where she was nobody, and belonged to nobody. She was ready for orphanhood, ready to share it, with those already in the alien land. But her thoughts of the future were tinged with apprehension. She wrote to Erenburg:

> You mustn't misunderstand me . . . what I'm afraid of isn't hunger or cold . . . but dependence. My heart tells me that people there, in the West, are *harder*. Here a broken shoe is unfortunate or heroic, there it is a disgrace. People will take me for a beggar and chase me back where I came from. If that happens I'll hang myself.

This seems to contradict flatly her feelings about Moscow in the letter to Voloshin quoted above, but we all experience contradictory moods.

> As migrants —
> Into what New York?
> Universal hostility
> Piled on one's back . . .

Tsvetaeva now views the destruction of the Volunteer movement, and the

---

* The chapel containing the especially revered icon of the Iversky Mother of God was situated near the entrance to Red Square.

mass emigration from Russia as a tragedy not only for all Russians but possibly, at some future time, for the whole world. Her poem "The Migrants" echoes Blok's "Scythians".* Blok's "swarms of us, swarms of us" becomes in Tsvetaeva's:

> But there, from the swarms –
> Are throngs and hordes
> Of such as we . . .

Blok's Scythians have "slanting, greedy eyes", and Tsvetaeva writes of a "half-slanting steel slit"; Blok's "Yes, we are Scythians! Yes, Asiatics!" echoes in Tsvetaeva's

> But then we are bears!
> But then we are Tatars!

In spite, however, of the similarities Tsvetaeva's interpretation of the theme is in complete contrast with that of Blok. In her poem there is nothing resembling a call to peace and brotherhood – the time for that was past, the Russian horde had already burst in on the West. What threatens the world is not "Panmongolism", not Russia's "historic mission", but the elemental hatred unleashed in Russia. A hatred capable of resurrecting the dead, a hatred in which the executioner is at one with his victim. Tsvetaeva feels for the "migrants", but dreads the uncontrollable flight from Russia, which will spread hatred throughout the world.

> "White tablecloth world!
> Just you wait!"

We are reminded of Pushkin's "Just you wait!" [in "The Bronze Horseman"], in which the threat to the world might be taken as a prophetic anticipation of communism.

Her practical problems were just as serious. She had to go through her archives, decide what to leave behind and with whom, and what manuscripts to take with her. A great deal was distributed amongst friends. Then she had to raise the money for her departure. The formalities proved to be less easy than Sergey had thought, though Tsvetaeva's lack of push may have played a part here. Whatever the reason, their departure was repeatedly postponed. In a letter to Erenburg dated 11 (24) February 1922

---

* In this poem, which Blok wrote in January 1918, immediately after "The Twelve", his famous poem about the Revolution, Russians – conscious of being half-barbarian – beg the West to respond to an invitation to peace and friendship, warning that otherwise they will cease to be a barrier between East and West and Mongols will destroy Western civilization.

she writes: "my passport expires on (your) March 7th. It is now (your) 24 of February; Yu. K. [Baltrushaitis] arrives on (your) March 2nd, and if they give me an extended Lithuanian visa on the 3rd, and a diplomatic carriage is ready before the 7th – we've won. But if Yu. K. is held up, or the diplomatic carriage doesn't leave between the 3rd and the 7th, I shall have to get my Cheka visa renewed, and that could mean a month's wait."

We do not know what exactly happened, but Tsvetaeva did not leave on 7 March, nor on 7 April, nor even on 7 May. In the month before Tsvetaeva's departure Tatyana Fyodorovna Skryabina, the composer's widow, died. Tsvetaeva had been friends with her for two years past, and had written the poem "Sleeplessness" for her. At Skryabina's funeral she met, for the last time in Russia, and by chance as on all previous occasions, Boris Pasternak, with no presentiment of the enormous place he would shortly occupy in her life.

Her sister was going away for the summer, and could not stay behind to see her off. Saying goodbye was difficult for both of them, with no hope that they would see each other again. Marina longed to help Asya, to *give* her something – but what? Anastasia Tsvetaeva remembered receiving in Zvenigorod, when Marina was already out of the country, an envelope with some money: "To Asya and Andryusha – for milk."

The day of departure arrived – 11 May 1922. They had done all their packing. Most important were the case containing her manuscripts, and a few things of sentimental value – like the rug which her father had given her a week before he died. Nothing substantial had survived: it had all been worn out or sold or broken in the years of revolution. They travelled light. And their departure was almost unobserved. No one came to see them off except A. A. Chabrov-Podgaetsky – musician, actor, and theatrical producer, remembered by Tsetaeva's daughter because "in that time of no presents he once gave her (Marina) a rose". They travelled in two cabs – Marina and Alya in one, Chabrov in the other. Tsvetaeva was worried, afraid that they might be late. They had to go right across Moscow – from the Arbat to the Riga station. What were Tsvetaeva's thoughts and feelings? Had she any hope of seeing her native city again? Was she saying goodbye to it for ever? Did she try to add to her store of memories as she left? Or was she too absorbed in last-minute chores? She and Alya crossed themselves whenever they passed a church as they rode across the city. And that is all we know about it.

The journey was a long one, with a wait and a change of trains in Riga. Ariadna Efron remembered that her mother was preoccupied and uncommunicative throughout, as though stricken by an inner chill. She did not sleep until they were on the train from Riga to Berlin. They arrived in Berlin on 17 May. No one met them at the station. Sergey was in Prague. They sent him a telegram. A note of his to the Bogengardts, dated 17 May, has survived: "Dear friends, hurrah, Marina and Alya are in Berlin. Warmest greetings. S. Efron. Details follow." Details, however, did not follow. There were too many other things to think about. They had a new life to begin.

CHAPTER 5

AFTER RUSSIA

WHEN A FRIEND OF TSVETAEVA'S, Vera Zaytseva, arrived in Berlin, she wrote: "I still can't believe that we are *outside* Soviet life. For the time being I am enjoying everything: the air, the people, the flowers, the cleanliness, – and above all there is no mist of blood." There is no direct record of Tsvetaeva's first impressions of "abroad", but I would imagine that other émigrés, Tsvetaeva included, gave a similar sigh of relief on reaching Berlin. The poem "To Berlin" gives us some idea of her state of mind at the time:

> On the most magical of orphanhoods
> You took pity, you barracks!

She too must have felt, at least momentarily, a sense of peace, a sense of life being more merciful.

Berlin was merely a "staging post" for Tsvetaeva and Alya, a city where they were to live for just two and a half months. In intensity, however, the intensity of literary activities, friendships and romances, these weeks were the equivalent of years elsewhere. Only three days after her arrival Tsvetaeva was reading poetry – both her own and Mayakovsky's – in the Russian House of Arts, and after only another ten days she was engaged in a fierce polemic with Aleksey Tolstoy.

Tsvetaeva's first friends in Berlin were the Erenburgs. She and Alya went to them straight from the station, and Erenburg gave up his room to them. Earlier in the year he had overseen the Berlin publication of "Poems to Blok" and *Parting* and he continued to play the role of Tsvetaeva's protector in literary matters. His wife Lyubov looked after Tsvetaeva with regard to more everyday affairs, taking her to shops to buy clothes for herself and Alya and generally showing her round. After a while, however, the Erenburgs left for a seaside vacation and Tsvetaeva moved to a small hotel where she remained for the rest of her stay in Berlin. Here they had two rooms and a balcony that was to stay in Alya's mind as part of an almost idyllic picture:

As a house-warming present Seryozha gave me a pot of pink begonias which I watered generously every morning, attempting not to sprinkle the passers-by – the Germans don't appreciate practical jokes! My clearest memory of our time in the Trautenau-Haus is of something quite unimportant: of looking out every morning, first down and then around, at a clean, faceless, sunny little street with its first unhurried pedestrains – a sense of something ephemeral that had been momentarily frozen.

The nine-year-old Alya fortunately had no idea of her mother's feelings at the time. Tsvetaeva herself was prompted by the sight of this same balcony to think of suicide:

> Ah, to crash from the sheer perpendicular
> Down into dust and tar!
> To salt with a tear – for how long? –
> The short weight of earthly love.

"Short weight" takes the reader away from the balcony and back to starving Moscow; at the same time it calls to mind the line "hands grown coarse, reaching out for salt and bread". "The short weight of earthly love", sprinkled with the salt of her own tears, marks a step in Tsvetaeva's spiritual growth. Never before would she have defined love with such a coarse and simple image. For the first time she had recognized that no earthly relationship could ever satisfy her "hunger for love", that an earthly relationship could only be a surrogate, enough to prevent her from dying of hunger but never enough to live on. In real life, of course, she would continue to pursue the mirage, but then poetry is wiser than poets. The trinity of love, poetry and death had now taken root in her consciousness:

> A balcony. Through salty showers
> Comes the tar of spiteful kisses.
> And a sigh of ineluctable
> Hatred: To breathe oneself out in poetry!
>
> Squeezed in one's hand into a ball
> What: the heart or a rag
> Of cambric? To these lotions
> There is a name – Jordan.
>
> Yes, for this struggle with love
> Is savage and merciless.
> In order, soaring from granite brows,
> To breathe oneself out in death!

For Tsvetaeva sex was always of secondary importance, merely an accompaniment to her search for Soul, her search for emotional and spiritual closeness. This was the reason for her disillusion with the "short weight" of earthly love. To breathe herself out into death would be to put an end to the unequal battle with love, to her wanderings through a kingdom of alien souls. The presence of death, however, always gave birth to poems and as a result death itself – at least temporarily – would recede.

"Balcony", together with several other poems written in Berlin, is dedicated to Abram Grigorievich Vishnyak, the owner of the publishing house Helicon and someone with whom Tsvetaeva had a brief and tempestuous affair. On this occasion Alya appears to have been quicker than her mother to sense that the search for love and Soul would end in disappointment, writing in her diary: "Everyday life is the weight that holds him down to earth and without which he thinks he might suddenly shoot off upwards like Andrey Bely. In actual fact he might not shoot off. He has very little soul; he needs peace, rest, sleep and comfort, everything that soul never allows. When Marina enters his office, she is herself like the Soul that raises a man up and returns him to himself, alarming him and taking away his peace." It is interesting to note that, many years later, when she was compiling her last collection of poems, Tsvetaeva gave the title "Omens of the Earth" to the poem-cycle addressed to Vishnyak. The passing of time had made him seem further than ever removed from the soul.

Tsvetaeva's relationship with Andrey Bely, however, even though it lasted only six weeks, was a true meeting with a Soul. Her attitude towards him was in some ways similar to her attitude to Volkonsky; even though she did not look on him as a Teacher, she was willing to "serve" him. Her relationship with Bely was entirely free of all pride, jealousy and pretension. This relationship was neither with Boris Nikolaevich Bugaev [Bely's real name], a middle-aged eccentric whom normal people looked on with bewilderment; nor was it with the renowned writer, Andrey Bely. What she loved was the Spirit of a Poet. Her essay in memory of him – entitled "Captive Spirit", was written at a time when Tsvetaeva was considering the nature of the poet's place in the world and in time. Bely, a captive spirit equally unable either to merge with the world around him or to break free of it, embodied her concept of the Poet better than anyone.

> They put a tiara upon you – a jester's cap,
> Turquoise teacher, tormentor, potentate, fool!
>
> The fop would create chaos, like snowflakes on Moscow,
> Obscure, not obscure, inarticulate, easy, confused . . .

These lines are from a poem of Osip Mandelstam's, written on the day of Bely's funeral. Mandelstam knew Bely longer than Tsvetaeva – her own relationship with him came to an end in autumn 1923, with the last letter he wrote before his return to the Soviet Union. Mandelstam's views on poetry were very different from Tsvetaeva's, but the image of Bely that emerges from his poems is similar to that in Tsvetaeva's essay. In the following lines of Mandelstam we see the same captive spirit, timid, ready to escape beyond the limits of earthly life and yet penetrating into its depths:

> When suddenly the profundity of events
> Appears to the soul, so hasty, so shy,
> By a winding pathway it runs away . . .

The summer of 1922 was a critical and tragic time in Bely's life and Tsvetaeva was glad to be in a position to help him. "It may be that I have never in all my life, with all, all my love, given so much to anyone as to him, simply through the presence of friendship," she wrote. She even accepted the fact that he appeared to take little notice of her as a person in her own right. "Beside him," she wrote, "I always felt that I was preserving complete anonymity." In this, however, she was somewhat mistaken. It may be that Bely failed to understand the essence of her personality ("you're so simple," he would say to her happily), but this did not prevent him from understanding and valuing her poetry. "As regards the *melody* of verse, so important after the slovenliness of the Muscovites and the lifelessness of the Acmeists, your book is *supreme* (with no reservations)," he wrote after his first reading of *Parting*. More important still was Bely's declaration that it was through reading this book that he returned, after a long interval, to writing poetry himself. The resulting collection of poems, published that same year in Berlin, was entitled *After Parting*, and the final poem was dedicated to Tsvetaeva. Tsvetaeva, in contrast, merely wrote that she had no understanding either of Bely's rhythms or of his views on poetry.

On 27 June Tsvetaeva received a letter from Boris Pasternak – a letter that marked the beginning of a relationship that was to light up her life for many years. Pasternak's voice seemed the voice of a brother, if not of a twin; it was hard to imagine that they had met a number of times over the years, made polite conversation, even heard one another's poems – and yet remained entirely indifferent to one another. Erenburg had tried more than once to interest her in Pasternak, but his attempts had been counterproductive: Tsvetaeva didn't want to love what somebody else already loved. Pasternak, for his part, as he wrote in his first letter, had "blundered" with her poetry and "passed it by without ever seeing it". He was deeply shaken, however, by the second edition of *Mileposts* and some poems reduced him to tears. Towards the end of his life Pasternak was to reminisce:

> I was immediately captivated by the lyric power of Tsvetaeva's form, intimately felt, anything but weak-chested, fiercely compressed and concentrated, not just flaring up for the odd line but embracing whole sequences of stanzas in the development of its periods – and without the least break in the rhythm. Something close to me lay behind these qualities, perhaps something similar in the influences we had undergone or the experiences that had formed our characters, a similarity in the role played by music and by our families, a uniformity in our points of departure, aims and preferences.

In this first letter Pasternak placed Tsvetaeva on the same level as "the unsullied talents" of Mayakovsky and Akhmatova, addressing her as "My dear, golden, incomparable poet". She replied two days later – after leaving his letter "to cool off" – enclosing copies of "Poems to Blok" and "Parting". At this point she had still not glimpsed Pasternak's volume *My Sister – Life*. A week later, however, she was offering a review of it to the Berlin journal, *The New Russian Book*: "Let me say in advance that *I cannot shorten this*. Please be kind and give me an answer soon, it's my first article ever and it's a combative one. I don't want it to lie around." It was indeed a combative article, an energetic attempt, full of quotations, to convince the reader of Pasternak's power. She referred to him as "the only poet", and to his poetry as "a downpour of light".

At the same time she wrote her first poem to Pasternak:

> Life tells lies inimitably:
> Beyond expectation, beyond lies . . .
>
> But from the trembling of one's veins
> You can recognize it: life!

Continuing the conversation begun by her letter and her review, she tried to convey her innermost feelings on reading *My Sister – Life*. She felt as though she had met a twin soul, a soul which had entered into her own and enchanted it:

> And do not reproach me, my friend,
> Our souls are so easily charmed
> In our bodies . . .

A letter she wrote to Pasternak in November serves as a commentary: "It was Summer and in Berlin I had my own balcony. Stone, heat, and your green book on my knees. (I was sitting on the floor.) I had been living on your book for ten days, as though on the crest of a high wave. I yielded (obeyed) and I didn't swallow water . . ."

The most important thing in all this is that not only did Pasternak make the first move, but also that he wasn't frightened by Tsvetaeva's intensity, by the exalted pitch to which she immediately elevated their relationship. Pasternak's letter had changed her life; she now had a companion, an equal. Vishnyak, Bely, Pasternak, Erenburg . . . A meeting with Vladislav Khodasevich, who arrived soon after Tsvetaeva . . . A friendship with Mark Slonim that was to continue for many years in Prague . . . A young artist called Lyudmila Chirikova who designed the Berlin edition of *The Tsar-Maiden* . . . Poets, prose-writers, artists and publishers . . . Countless literary enterprises sprang up and collapsed, countless friendships, affairs and families came and went . . . Full of people with the most disparate aspirations, "Russian Berlin" led its feverish life. Political émigrés who could never return to Russia lived side by side with half-émigrés attempting to earn themselves the right to return. And there were more Soviet citizens living in Berlin than at any time since – permitted to travel there for their work or for reasons of health. Tsvetaeva herself had left Moscow on a Soviet passport. This was the time of "the changing of landmarks";* *On the Eve*, a Change of Landmarks journal, had first come out not long before Tsvetaeva's arrival, its literary supplement open to both Soviet citizens and émigrés and edited by Aleksey Tolstoy.

On 4 June a letter from Petrograd was published in this literary supplement, addressed to Aleksey Tolstoy by Korney Chukovsky. Chukovsky had written extremely critically of several of his fellow Petrograd writers, mentioning that they had "disparaged the Soviet régime". At the same time as praising Aleksey Tolstoy in the most extravagant terms and begging him to return to the Soviet Union, Chukovsky abused such "inner émigrés" as the "cissy" Evgeny Zamyatin and referred to the Petrograd House of Arts† as a "cesspit". This letter evoked a storm of indignation, directed against both Tolstoy and Chukovsky himself. An open letter from Marina Tsvetaeva to Aleksey Tolstoy was published on 7 June by *The Voice of Russia*. What enraged Tsvetaeva were the aspersions cast on the political reliability of writers still living in the Soviet Union, the fact that the letter was to all intents and purposes a denunciation:

---

* A movement associated with the volume of essays *Smena vekh* (Change of Landmarks), published by six Russian émigré writers in Prague, 1921, urging people to give up their hostility to Soviet Russia, return there and collaborate with the Soviet authorities.

† Set up by Gorky in 1919 to improve living and working conditions for writers, artists and musicians, the "House of Arts" published a literary almanac and offered a place to meet, work and sleep; it was closed down in 1922. Chukovsky's letter was an attack on members of the "House of Arts" who were not true Communists.

Or you are really just a three-year-old child, with no suspicion either of the existence in Russia of the GPU (yesterday's Cheka), or of the fact that all Soviet citizens live in a state of dependence on this GPU, or of the shutting down of "Chronicles of the House of Men of Letters", or of many, many other things . . . Imagine that after $4\frac{1}{2}$ years of "doing nothing" (which is what Blok, incidentally, died of) one of the persons you name should wish to make his way to freedom – what will be the effect of your letter on the question of his departure? The New Economic Policy which you evidently look on as the promised land, is concerned least of all with ethical matters: justice towards the enemy, mercy towards the enemy, nobility towards the enemy. [. . .] Five minutes before my departure from Russia (11 May this year) a man came up to me – a Communist, a nodding acquaintance who knew me only from my poetry – and said: "A Chekist will be travelling with you. Don't say anything superfluous." I shake his hand, but not yours. Marina Tsvetaeva.

Tsvetaeva is often referred to as apolitical. Mark Slonim writes that she said to him, possibly during their very first meeting: "I'm not interested in politics, I don't understand it." She did, however, have a strong sense of morality, and it is this that either determined her political sympathies or else substituted for the lack of them.

Tsvetaeva had left Russia for the sake of her husband. He himself, however, arrived in Berlin only during the first half of June, when his wife's affair with Vishnyak was at its most passionate. We know little of their feelings on meeting – after nearly five years of separation – but a poem Tsvetaeva wrote on 25 June is almost certainly dedicated to her husband:

> Greetings! Neither arrow, nor stone:
> I – the most alive of wives,
> Life itself – flying with two arms
> Into your unfinished dream.

> Mine! and what can Heaven hold
> When in my arms and at my mouth
> Is life: the wide-open joy of greeting
> Each other in the morning!

Beneath all this, however, lurks the image of the snake, fork-tongued, changing his skin. Here we glimpse the bitterness that poisoned the joy of their meeting. Nevertheless, "the main thing is that they were alive and that they had found each other," writes Ariadna Efron. She remembers that on the day of his arrival they for some reason arrived late at the station and met him only when he had already left the platform: "Seryozha ran all the way up to us, his face contorted with happiness, and embraced Marina – who opened her arms to him very slowly, as though they had gone numb. They stood there for a long, long time, in a tight embrace, and only then did they slowly move their palms down one another's cheeks – which were wet with tears . . ." This happiness, however, was soon poisoned. It was probably because of Vishnyak and not – as their daughter suggests – "in order to prepare diligently for the beginning of the academic year", that Efron was so quick to leave Berlin.

It had been agreed that they should live together in Prague. Sergey Efron received a grant to study at the Charles University, and they hoped that Marina would receive one of the grants offered by the Czech government to Russian scholars and writers. All this was more than they could count on in Germany, ravaged as it was by war and the threat of inflation. Tsvetaeva had published several poems in Berlin, including the volume, *Craft*, but such earnings were far from reliable: Russian-language publishing in Berlin might come to an end any day. Nor did Tsvetaeva have any personal reasons to remain in Berlin. Bely had left. Her affair with Vishnyak had exhausted itself – to such a degree that she no longer had any time even for the poems she had written to him: "it is nauseating! . . my revulsion to poems relates to the people who evoked them – never to the feelings themselves, since the feelings are me!" She and Erenburg were no longer friends, supposedly because he didn't approve of her "Russian" poems. In his memoirs he writes, somewhat inaccurately, that they had quarrelled as a result of *The Camp of the Swans*, which he hadn't wanted her to print; the poems, however, did not yet exist as a collection and it was not until a year later that Tsvetaeva first tried to have the book published. Whatever the truth of all this, there were also more personal reasons for the breakdown of their friendship. Above all, Tsvetaeva felt confused and out of place in the complex web of relationships being woven between herself, the two Erenburgs and the two Vishnyaks: "many people, everything in silence, everything in public, a crossfire of romances (none of them genuine), all in the Prager Diele [a café] everything in joke." Finding all this intolerable, Tsvetaeva – in her own words – "escaped from Berlin as though from an oppressive dream". Not even a proposed visit to Berlin by Pasternak was enough to hold her back: for her, in any case, a non-meeting always bore more creative fruit than a meeting.

The Tsvetaeva who left Berlin was no longer the person who had arrived there six weeks earlier. Mark Slonim has left us the following description of her at this time:

She spoke quietly, quickly but clearly, casting down her large grey-green eyes and not looking at the person she was speaking to. Now and again she would throw back her head and her light, golden hair, cut in a fringe, would fly about in the air. With each movement she made, bracelets would jingle on her strong arms; her somewhat plump fingers, also covered in silver rings, clutched a long wooden cigarette case – she smoked continually. Her large head on a long neck, her broad shoulders, the neatness of her slim, delicate body and her general carriage combined to create an impression of strength and lightness, impetuosity and reserve. Her handshake was strong and masculine.

PRAGUE

Tsvetaeva and her daughter arrived in Prague on 1 August. A few days later, in order to save money, they moved to Mokropsy, one of several villages near Prague that were then "occupied" by Russian émigrés.

If Paris was the capital of émigré political life, if Berlin was at that time the capital of Russian émigré literature, then Prague was the capital of émigré scholarship and student life. The recently constituted Czechoslovakian Democratic Republic not only granted émigrés right of asylum, but also offered them financial support. Anyone whose education had been interrupted by the Revolution and the Civil War was invited to continue it in Czechoslovakia. Russian scholars and writers were allowed a monthly grant; Tsvetaeva herself received 1000 crowns – a sum which for many years constituted the main part of her income. The students also received a grant, together with hostel accommodation if they were single. (A former Prague student informed me that her grant was 300 crowns and that a meal in a student canteen cost three and half crowns.) Sergey Efron found lodgings for his family in a village, but at the same time kept on his "cabin" – now at last furnished with a table – in the hostel. It would have been difficult to commute to Prague every day and so he chose to live in the hostel and spend just two or three days a week with his family.

The passions of Berlin had burnt themselves out and had been replaced in Tsvetaeva by a sense of irony, a sense that Berlin had ravaged her, destroyed her as a woman, perhaps even as a human being, and left her only the gift of song. In her first "Czech" poems, the cycle "Sibyl", she writes:

> Like a lump of grey stone,
> Severing kinship with the age.
> Your body is the cave
> Of your voice.

Rather than merely comparing herself with the Sibyl – as she had done in a Moscow poem "Like the ancient Sibyl" – Tsvetaeva has now been transformed into her:

> The Sibyl: burned out. The Sibyl: a stump.
> All the birds have died off, but the god has come.
>
> The Sibyl: drained dry. The Sibyl: all dry.
> All her veins have dried out: Husband is jealous!
>
> The Sibyl: has gone. The Sibyl: jaws
> Of fate and death! – a tree amongst maidens . . .
>
> . . . Thus into the greyness of grasses
> Goes transient virginity, becoming a cave
>
> To the magical voice . . .
> – thus into the stars' whirl
> Goes the Sibyl, no longer amongst the living.

As for Vishnyak, he was now remembered only with hostility – as a "black velvet non-entity". Eventually, after repeated requests from Tsvetaeva, her letters and manuscripts were returned and she was free of him. Ten years later these letters were to form the basis of a story she wrote in French, "Florentine Nights", but what she wrote then was a final liberation:

> That in me you should not flower
> Too much: in thickets – in books –
> I shall mislay you alive:
>
> I shall girdle you with fantasies,
> I shall powder you with imaginings.

A period of calm lasting almost a year now began for Tsvetaeva. From her poems – and from the cycle "Trees" in particular – it appears that the Czech countryside did much to help her shake off the delusions of Berlin and so return to herself:

> When my angered soul has become
> Besotted with resentment,
> When full seven times I have refused
> To battle with the demons –

> Not with those like torrents of fire
> Hurled downwards into the abyss:
> But with earth's daily vileness,
> With the inertness of people –
>
> Trees! I come to you! To save myself
> From the roar of the market-place!
> How much the heart is eased
> With the swaying upwards of the trees!

The trees represent the opposite of human life, free both of tragedy and of "earth's vileness". They lift Tsvetaeva up into the only worlds where she feels at home: the Elysium of the Greeks, the Palestine of the Bible, the clear heights of Goethe. The poems are filled with the same restless movement that is present in *Mileposts*. The wind is never named, but its presence is felt constantly – in the sound of leaves and the thrashing movements of branches. This physical restlessness, however, is somehow able to remove emotional anxieties and restore Tsvetaeva's balance of mind:

> Prophetic tidings of a tree!
> The forest speaks: here,
> Above the mass of lies
> Is the perfect life . . .

The autumn trees evoke a variety of visual associations that is unusual in Tsvetaeva's poetry. Seeing the trees as people, she paints pictures in a wide range of emotional hues. The second poem, for example, reminds me of the Last Judgment, while the tone of the third poem is almost idyllic.

The orientation of the cycle is upwards, away from the earth. Tsvetaeva does not want to sense the earth, she would rather see it from a distance, from above:

> That once again, as once the earth
> *seemed* to us . . .

She wanted to see it as a star, as the Rilke she evokes in her poem "New Year's Greeting" was later to see the earth. In these poems the thrust to escape from the earth is paralleled by a pull towards light, by the way in which the transparent and diffused light of other worlds overcomes the bright colours of autumn. To Tsvetaeva this represents a delivery from suffering. Rather than attempting to paraphrase or explain the mysterious "Sibylline" speech of the trees, Tsvetaeva is satisfied to know that

> . . . you heal
> The offence of Time –
> With cool Eternity.

This is how she herself was healed, and this is the way of healing she suggests to Pasternak: "Go to the gods, to the trees! This isn't lyricism; this is medical advice." Her friendship with Pasternak, however, also played a part in healing the wounds of Berlin.

This first year in Prague was a time of peace and happiness for the family as a whole. Soon after the arrival of Marina and Alya, Efron wrote to the Bogengardts:

> I was spinning around like a squirrel in a wheel, travelling to Germany, applying for visas, looking for rooms, taking exams and so on and so on. Don't be angry – I was beside myself.
>
> Now everything has been more or less sorted out – Marina and Alya are in Czechoslovakia, in a dacha – and I can stop to breathe . . .
>
> Marina has changed little, but Alya has changed into a huge hippopotamus whom I am unable to lift in my arms . . .

For Alya this was the beginning of her only real childhood; it was a great joy for her to be her parents' child rather than her mother's most intimate friend. She was with her parents, whom she adored, and taking part in their life. She herself has described this period very well in *Pages from the Past*:* Evenings when Seryozha read to them by the light of a kerosene lamp and Marina darned socks and stockings or mended clothes; meeting Seryozha as he came back from Prague and then seeing him off again at the little village station. Innocent little joking letters they wrote to one another; decorating the Christmas tree – and then Christmas itself with its presents and parties; lessons with her mother, who continued determinedly teaching her both French and Russian; and arithmetic lessons with her father.

Russian émigré life in Prague was very different from that of Berlin or Paris. There was nothing of the frenzied pursuit of ephemeral pleasures that had so repelled Tsvetaeva in Berlin. Nor was there the sharp division between rich and poor that was later to upset her in Paris. Everyone was more or less equally badly off, they were mostly young and they were ready to help one another. Tsvetaeva and her husband gathered round them a circle of friends. They all visited one another, went on picnics together and celebrated special occasions together. One especially important friendship was with the Lebedev family. Vladimir Ivanovich Lebedev had been a well-known revolutionary and a member of the Provisional Government, his wife Margarita was a doctor and a former Socialist Revolutionary, and their daughter Irusya became Alya's friend for life. Margarita Lebedeva gave

---

* A. Efron's memoirs have not been translated into English.

Tsvetaeva the key to her house and was always ready to be of help to her. Before her final return to the Soviet Union, Tsvetaeva left the Lebedevs a large part of her archive.

Daily life in the villages around Prague was simple and far from easy. Everything had to be done by hand – that is by Marina's hands or sometimes by Alya's: water had to be carried from the well, firewood had to be fetched from the forest, and then of course there was all the normal housework – lighting fires, cooking, ironing, mending clothes and scrubbing floors. After revolutionary life in Moscow, however, it was not difficult to adapt to life in a village. Everyday life was demanding, but she had time to write and so these demands did not plunge her into the same despair as in later years. Tsvetaeva herself described her life at this time as follows:

> A tiny village in the hills, we live in the last house, a simple village hut. The main actors are: a chapel with a well where I go for water, usually at night or in the early morning – with a dog on a chain and a squeaking gate; a forest that starts just beyond; a high cliff to the right; a village full of streams; two shops just like the shops in a small town in Russia; a Roman Catholic church with a cemetery full of flowers; a school; two "restaurations" – as the Czechs refer to restaurants; and a band on Sundays. It's a bourgeois village rather than a peasant village. The old women wear shawls, while the young ones wear hats. By the age of 40 they are witches.
>
> At night, in each little house, you can always see a light: a Russian student. They are all more or less half-starving, the prices here are unbelievable and nothing can ever teach Russians to take care of money. The day they get their grants is all feasts and picnics, a week later they are all very serious. The students are mostly former officers, "young veterans" as I call them. They study as in the old days in Russia – to be the first in everything, even in sport! With rare exceptions they live for Russia, for their dream of service to her. We have a wonderful choir here [. . .]
>
> Life is not communal (everyone is very busy), but it is friendly; people help someone when they are down, there is no gossip or scandal, and there is a real feeling of cleanliness.
>
> It's like a colony, that's how I think of it, a colony that increases the weight of each member a thousandfold. A kind of agreement to *live*. (To live long enough!) – A collective guarantee.

Efron was one of the "young veterans". He too studied diligently. When he was at home, Marina tried to feed him as best she could, and to make him rest; she never forgot his weak health. In Prague, after a break of over ten years, he once again began to write – at his wife's instigation. She herself admitted: "The main channel I am directing him down is, of course, writing." She considered him talented and was sure he could become a critic – either of films or of literature. It was at this time that he began work on "Notes of a Volunteer", based on his diaries from the time of the Revolution and Civil War. These memoirs were never in fact published in book form, and may not even ever have been completed. Some associated writings, however, "October 1917", "The Rear" and "Typhus" were published in periodicals. Efron also became an editor of the student journal, *Our Own Paths*, in which he published a series of articles on politics – his chief interest in life.

Tsvetaeva for her part worked as though she were possessed. In the course of a year she wrote ninety short poems, finished "The Swain" – a folk tale in verse of which she was very fond –, planned a trilogy of plays to be called "The Rage of Aphrodite",* and finished going through her Moscow papers with the aim of compiling a book, "Omens of the Earth". She was working hard on this last book in early 1923, with the aim of taking a completed manuscript to Berlin. When, however, she learned that she would be unable to meet Pasternak there, she lost interest in compiling the book. "There will be a book," she wrote to Pasternak, "but no you. I need you, not the book." In the end the book was never published.

Their year of village life finished peacefully – apart from the fact that their landlord took them to court for failing to take adequate care of their room. Tsvetaeva's own indignant explanation was that the dacha season was beginning and he wanted to be rid of them in order to re-let the room for a higher price. The affair ended with them triumphant: the court and the entire village took their side. They were very glad, however, to move to Prague and find a room without a landlord on the premises. Alya went to the high school in Moravská Třebová, and Tsvetaeva and her husband had the prospect of spending months together, living and working in a city. "I am now," wrote Tsvetaeva, "at an inner (and outer!) crossroads, my year of life in the forest – with poetry, trees and no people – is over. I am on the eve of a great new city (perhaps a great new grief?!) and a great new life there, I am on the eve of a new self. I'm dreaming of doing something big, I've been drawn to that for a long time." As she wrote this, Tsvetaeva was drafting "Theseus" and spending long hours collecting material in the library, in charge of her own time for the first occasion in years.

*

* She later referred to the planned trilogy as "Theseus"; she wrote two of the plays – *Theseus*, later called *Ariadne*, and *Phaedra*. (The third would have been "Helen".)

Tsvetaeva was also at this time engaged in a correspondence with a young critic whom she had never met, Aleksandr Bakhrakh. She had been struck by the depth of understanding with which he reviewed *Craft*, had sent him a grateful letter and had become carried away by the ensuing correspondence and by thoughts of a possible meeting in Berlin. The poems she wrote between July and mid-September 1923 are all linked to this friendship.

When Bakhrakh eventually published the letters and poems Tsvetaeva had sent him, he wrote of her letters in general:

> The man to whom her feelings were directed at a particular moment is less important than the pouring out of these feelings on paper. . . . The people with whom Tsvetaeva maintained contact at a deeper level were all "invented" by her; she created them in accord with her fantasy, making them up at whim, barely taking their true nature into account at all.

Tsvetaeva did indeed "create" the heroes of both her physical and her epistolary romances. Nevertheless, Bakhrakh is at least partly mistaken: Tsvetaeva's fantasies were always founded on some quality that was an essential part of the man in question, something particular to him alone. It is this that makes all her cycles of love poems so different from one another. Her poems to Bakhrakh, for example, are all centered on the theme of his youth – he was twenty years old – and his purity.

> Through your virginal script
> You seem to me a red shoot,
> Whose innocence is woven round
> With breeding, as with a liana.
>
> Prolong your saintliness! Preserve
> The sacred vessels of your eyes and mouth! . . .

In these poems Tsvetaeva gives free rein to her unsatisfied dreams of a son, creating an image of a spiritual son, a "fosterling" whom she would finish creating and then send out into the world: "I won't do you any harm, I want you to grow up big and wonderful, to forget me but never to part with that – other – world, *my* world!" She wanted to create a son from this youth she had never met, just as she had made Alya into *her own* daughter.

> A mother's ear, that hears through sleep.
> I bend my ear towards you . . .

Her poems to Bakhrakh, however, are by no means purely maternal, either in a spiritual or a more natural sense of the word. Her maternal feelings are at the same time erotic, especially in the poem "Shell". Here a shell is seen as an image of a woman's hands, cherishing, preserving and cultivating the pearl that is her son:

> From the lazar-house of lies and evil
> I summoned you and took you
>
> Into the dawns! from the deathly sleep of epitaphs
> Into my hands, into both these very palms,
>
> Shell-shaped – grow, be at peace:
> You will become a pearl in these palms!

The shell is both home and cradle, and at the same time an abyss – the womb where the fruit ripens; all this lends an extraordinary closeness to the relationship between shell and pearl:

> . . . No haughtiness of any beauties,
> Which touch upon your mysteriousness,
> Will appropriate you, as does
> That mysterious shell-shaped vault of
> Non-appropriating hands . . .

During a month of "silence" from Bakhrakh – apparently the fault of the post – Tsvetaeva kept a diary in the form of a letter, entitled "Bulletin of an Illness". Near the beginning she wrote: "What lies behind this silence? Lack of time? Carelessness? Calculation? A habit? An over-scrupulously fulfilled request? I'm lost . . .". Two days later she wrote: "Illness? Love? Hurt? A sense of guilt? Disillusion? Fear? Leaving aside illness, then probably love: but how can your love for someone else interfere with your *friendship* towards me?" She went on to analyse her relationships with other people and with Bakhrakh in particular: "Soul and Youth. A kind of meeting of two absolutes. (Did I really look on you as human?) I thought of you as Youth, as an element able to contain me – and everything mine!" Shortly before this she had written: "A request. Don't treat me as a person. But as a tree rustling its leaves to greet you." This sense of their meeting as something elemental appears still more strongly in the poems she wrote at the same time. These echo passages from the letters and the "bulletin", but in them she gives herself away still more completely:

> Between us is a double-edged blade,
> I've sworn – to lay it there even in thought . . .
> But sometimes there are passionate sisters!
> But sometimes there is brotherly passion!

These lines, written three weeks after she began "Bulletin of an Illness", no longer show even the least trace of maternal feeling. Instead they register a cry of passion that no boundaries can contain:

> The double-edged blade – it separates?
> It brings together! So tear through the cloak
> And bring us together, ferocious guard –
> Wound into wound and gristle into gristle!
> (. . .)
> The double-edged blade that was tempered in blue,
> Will turn red . . . A double-bladed
> Sword we shall plunge into ourselves.
> That will be the best way to lie down!

When their correspondence was renewed – after "Blade", which Tsvetaeva never sent to him – she repeated that her passion was neither literary nor physical, but something different from either – a passion of the soul. Now, however, she wanted a meeting. Both letters and poems appear to be merely a prelude to something else that was on the point of beginning, to some furious passion that was about to find an outlet. And this passion did indeed find an outlet – but not through Bakhrakh. Her Hour of the Soul with him was never consummated. When the time came, he proved too ethereal.

Why was Tsvetaeva drawn to Konstantin Boleslavovich Rodzevich? All those who remembered him from that time found him generally unremarkable. One of the other émigrés writes: "Rodzevich was a short man with strikingly pink cheeks. He was friendly, but in social intercourse he didn't stand out in any way." A fellow-student of Rodzevich's writes more harshly: "Marina paid bitterly for trusting someone who was crafty and deceitful by nature." Mark Slonim, whose shoulder Tsvetaeva cried on during the agony of separating from Rodzevich, writes: "I saw him twice, he seemed self-centred, a bit shy, not without a sense of humour, somewhat gloomy and generally mediocre." Ariadna Efron is alone in portraying him as a charming and chivalrous young man rather like the heroes of Tsvetaeva's own romantic plays. Soviet commentators, of course, have followed her line, emphasizing his heroism as a Red Guard during the Civil War (who *happened* later on to side with the Whites), as a battalion commander in the International Brigade in Spain, and as a member of the French Resistance. Despite being a Party member, however, he never returned to the Soviet Union, not even after being liberated from a German concentration camp by the Red Army. Tsvetaeva's hero was evidently not as clear and straightforward as she imagined. (The fact that he was freed from a German camp by the Red Army is in itself suspicious. It is common knowledge that the "liberators" not only never released the men and women they "liberated" from German camps, but that they also tracked down former prisoners of war and émigrés throughout the whole of Europe. Everyone they laid hands on was returned to the Soviet Union, many of them to labour camps. So it seems likely that Rodzevich was a Soviet agent.) We must be grateful to him, though, for two very important long poems by Tsvetaeva – "Poem of the Mountain" and "Poem of the End".

Once again – what drew Tsvetaeva to this man? Rodzevich himself, whom I met in summer 1982, said: "It was elemental. I never courted her. She was writing letters to her distant friend and lover, but was looking for greater affection. And that is how it happened – we were living not far from one another." The Hour of the Soul, in short, gave way to the Hour of Eros – who now frenziedly demanded his rights:

> . . . As though the soul were pulled out
> With its skin! Like steam through a hole
> The notorious, nonsensical heresy
> Has vanished, that is called the soul.
>
> Pallid feebleness of christianity!
> Steam! Apply fomentations!
> Of course it never existed!
> There was the body, it wanted to live . . .

Bakhrakh was in Berlin, Rodzevich was close by. "We had a similar tendency," Rodzevich told me, "to give ourselves away completely. There was a lot of sincerity in our relationship, we were happy." This happiness, however, lasted three months at the most.

"Poem of the Mountain" is a poem of doomed love, of a love that foresees its inevitable end at the very moment of greatest happiness. The mountain represents spiritual heights, emotions, the triumph of *being* – the lovers' being – over everyday life. "Poem of the End" shows us what form this doom took. Tsvetaeva was indeed happy with Rodzevich – and this is evident above all from the pain with which she eventually tore herself away from him. She had great hopes of this love. Knowing that she was more Poet, more Soul, than she was woman, she shared with Rodzevich her hope that "maybe this present moment will bring about a miracle for me; maybe – God willing! – I really will become a human being, *fully incarnate*" (my emphasis – V.S.). She did indeed become fully incarnate, and was able to embody this sense of her womanliness in the two poems. Only a woman who had truly experienced these emotions could write with such passion, tenderness, pain, longing and self-renunciation. After reading "Poem of the

End", Boris Pasternak wrote to her: "Four evenings running I have stuffed into my coat a piece of darkly slushy, smokily misty, night-time Prague, with a bridge now far in the distance now suddenly right in front of your eyes . . . and with shaking voice I initiate them (his listeners – V.S.) into that abyss of wounding lyric with Michelangelesque scope and Tolstoyan deafness that is called 'Poem of the End'."

In these poems Tsvetaeva renounces love for the sake of love, so as not to allow love to become debased, so as not to allow the mountain to be transformed into a suburb. Even as she tore herself away from Rodzevich, however, she still longed to bear him a son. In a letter to Bakhrakh, now her involuntary confidant, she wrote: "Dear friend, I am very unhappy. I have parted with *him*, still loving and still beloved, at the height of love; no, I haven't parted from him, I've torn myself away from him! . . . With him I would have been *happy* . . . I should have liked a son from him . . . I desired that son passionately (though fearfully!) and, if God didn't send him to me, it must be because he knows better. That's what I wanted until the final hour." In the poem itself she wrote:

> The mountain yet grieved: if at least
> He would let Hagar go with the child!

Tsvetaeva was never able to separate sexual and maternal love. She always wanted either to bear her lover's child – as in the cases of both Pasternak, whom she seldom met and appeared not to wish to meet, and Rodzevich; or to make her lover into her child – as she did with Efron when they were both young, and with Nikolay Gronsky and Anatoly Shteiger at a later date. Her maternal impulse – at least at a spiritual level – was more powerful than her sexuality. "Poem of the Mountain" and "Poem of the End" are an exception to all this: in these poems she is a woman, a loved woman, overwhelmed by her own feelings. This may be what Pasternak had in mind when he wrote of the "Tolstoyan deafness" of "Poem of the End" – that the heroine is able to hear only herself, her own love and her own grief. Even the hero of the poem is a misty figure, visible only through a film of rain or tears. And Prague itself, a city Tsvetaeva was to remember for the rest of her life with tenderness and love, appears "Lethean", half real, like something out of a dream.

The two narrative poems (*poemy*) are at the same time pure lyrics – their story is told, as Pasternak pointed out, in the first person. Nevertheless, a reality outside the speaker's thoughts and feelings does sometimes burst in, does sometimes thrust itself upon the "dwellers in the heaven of love". This external reality is seen as something irredeemably bourgeois and hostile. In passages that prefigure "The Rat-catcher", the epic she later wrote about the Pied Piper of Hamelin, she curses the triumphant bourgeoisie:

> There will be no place for frivolity,
> You bodies, on my blood!

The conflict in these poems is not just that between *him* and *her*; it is also the conflict, inescapable for Tsvetaeva, between the poet and the world. As she began work on the poems, she wrote: "He asks for a home, but she can *only* give him her soul." This is the central theme of the poems. In real life, of course, the conflict was between Rodzevich – an ordinary man who just wanted a comfortable home, and Tsvetaeva – the Poet, the "naked Soul". "I was weak," Rodzevich admitted to me in words that form an exact counterpart to Tsvetaeva's note quoted above. "There was too little I could do for her. I was unable to offer her a home, I was an émigré and I lived on my grant . . ."

In due course the affair came to its disastrous end. Some of the onlookers pitied Tsvetaeva, others gloated. From Tsvetaeva's own words Mark Slonim got the impression that Rodzevich "was stunned and frightened by the tidal wave of Marina's passion and that he ran away from the storm and thunder to the quiet haven of bourgeois life and a safe marriage." Elsewhere he wrote less circumspectly: "They decided to separate so that he could marry someone else. This of course shattered her. She suffered terribly." Reading the poems carefully, you sense Tsvetaeva alternately accepting and then rejecting this interpretation. It was difficult for her to admit the full truth even to herself. And so, probably unconsciously, she created a legend. The actual basis of this legend is that she would indeed never have left her husband – she was devoted to him and she had too strong a sense of duty. The fantasy with which this truth is adorned is that this was the only reason for the breakdown of their relationship. Her pride and her wounded feelings gave rise to the conviction that Rodzevich loved her as passionately as she loved him, that he wanted to be united with her for ever. This legend helped her to survive. Not long before she "crashed" against Rodzevich, Tsvetaeva sent "Bulletin of an Illness" to Bakhrakh with the words: "Keep these pages! . . . Keep them for the hour when you crash against every wall and suddenly find yourself doubting the existence of the Soul. (Love.) Keep them so that you can know that someone once – once in your life – truly loved you." It was with similar feelings that Tsvetaeva cherished her own memories of Rodzevich. Ten years later, when her marriage was again in crisis, she wrote to Vera Bunina:

> I never left *them* – never in all my life, even though, sometimes, I wanted to
> SO badly! I wanted another life, myself, freedom, my full stature, myself at

large; I simply wanted a blessed morning free of all obligations. In 1923, no, 1924! The call of mad love, the fiercest in all my life. I strained at the leash but, *of course*, I stayed since S., and Alya, my family – what would they do without me?! My last word at the time was "I can't be happy on other peoples' bones." Vera, I have no regrets. That was – me. I simply couldn't have done anything else. (I loved him – madly.)

Meanwhile – what of Tsvetaeva's family? Alya for her part appears to have known nothing. The entire drama took place in her absence. She was eleven years old and going to school for the first time, boarding at the Russian high school in Moravská Třebová. The school was funded by the government and each pupil received a grant. The Bogengardts taught there – which may be why Tsvetaeva chose the school. Tsvetaeva had no doubt that her daughter would queen it over the other children. She wrote proudly from Morvaská Třebová that Alya, "questioned by the other children (five hundred of them!) as to who she was and where she was from, immediately replied: 'A star – from the heavens!' She is very beautiful and very unconstrained, not embarrassed for a moment, spontaneity itself – she will be loved, because she doesn't need anyone." The reality of Alya's first days at school was, of course, very different. Accustomed to being a *Wunderkind* in the society of adults, Alya didn't know how to behave with other children. The children, for their part, were simply irritated by the little sayings which Tsvetaeva found so delightful. And so a "dungeon" was constructed for her: a blanket was thrown over her head and she was beaten up – the only such incident in the history of the school and something Tsvetaeva may never have found out about. In spite of all this, however, Alya soon found her footing and began to make friends; she wrote poems for special occasions and even plays that were produced in the school theatre. She and her mother wrote to one another frequently. "I often receive letters from Alya – she says that everything is going well and she has a new girlfriend with each letter. She isn't notable for her constancy." As is clear from the last sentence, Tsvetaeva – who had "pumped" so much of her own soul into her daughter – was upset that Alya "was becoming an ordinary little girl", escaping into the freedom of an ordinary childhood. What weighed on her still more, however, were her fears about Alya's health. Not even the romance with Rodzevich was enough to distract her and banish her worries about imaginary illnesses. On one occasion she wrote to the Bogengardts: "We're desperately worried about Alya. It's a whole week now since we had a letter. I'm afraid she's ill and that you're keeping it secret on purpose, waiting for the course of the illness to become clearer. In general, I'm afraid of everything. For the love of God, don't torment me – if she's ill, say what it is! I'm beside myself with fear, Seryozha and I have been lying in wait for the postman all morning."

A week or so later she wrote again, thanking Antonina Bogengardt for a telegram and letter, and explaining her anxiety:

> I was in agony over Alya at the time. If you only knew how frightened I am of separation! In this regard I am of course quite abnormal: not by nature, but because life has made me that way. At the time of the Revolution, in 1920, a *month* before I got rations, my youngest daughter died in an orphanage and I was only just able to save Alya. I didn't want to surrender them to an orphanage, they were *torn away* from me: I was accused of maternal egotism, I was promised that the children would be looked after and taken care of in every way – and then, after ten days – one of them falls ill; and after two months – the other one dies. Ever since then I have felt desperately afraid of separation [. . .] I am certain that Třebová is good for Alya. It is so long since she was a child, she has so seldom been able to enjoy the simple joys of childhood, and now, all of a sudden – friends, a proper daily routine, games and study. If she had continued to live with me, she would have grown up unhappy, I was never really a child myself and so I don't understand too much from my own (my one).

Not long after this, shortly before her parents' Christmas visit, Alya really did fall ill. And when she came home for the summer, patches were discovered on both her lungs. Deeply afraid of tuberculosis as she was, Tsvetaeva immediately began trying to raise money to take her daughter to Italy. After a while, however, she decided to postpone the journey till the autumn; for the time being they just moved to another village outside Prague.

During the summer Alya recovered her health and the trip to Italy was forgotten. She did not, however, go back to school. Instead she just stayed at home, studying with her mother and helping with the housework.

Alya may not have known about Rodzevich; "all Prague", however, did know – including Efron himself. Tsvetaeva would in any case have been unable to keep it a secret. For Sergey Efron this was a terrible blow, a blow from which he may never have fully recovered. According to Rodzevich, "Seryozha gave her her freedom and then withdrew." The reality was more dramatic and more painful. Sergey had of course known from the very beginning that Marina was not "like everyone else", that she never could be and never would be. He had long ago endured her affair with Sofia Parnok and had left Berlin on finding out about Vishnyak. He had tried to adapt to her and may have had at least some sympathy for her. The affair with Rodzevich, however, was more than he could bear. In his despair he wrote Voloshin a letter which allows us a rare glimpse of his true feelings:

My Dear Max,

I received your splendid, affectionate letter long ago and have been unable to reply all this time. You are of course the only person to whom I could say all this, but it's not easy to say it even to you – for me, in matters like this, saying something seems to make it happen. Not that I have any hope, I was just held back by human weakness. Once I have said something, this needs to be followed by definite action – and I am quite lost. My weakness and complete helplessness, Marina's blindness, my pity for her, my feeling that she's got herself stuck in a hopeless dead end, my inability to help her clearly and decisively, the impossibility of finding any satisfactory way out – it's all moving towards a standstill. Things have reached the stage where every exit from a crossroads could lead to disaster.

Marina is a woman of passions. Considerably more than in the past – before I left. Plunging headfirst into her hurricanes has become essential for her, the breath of life. It no longer matters who it is that arouses these hurricanes. Nearly always (now as before) – or rather always – everything is based on self-deception. A man is invented and the hurricane begins. If the insignificance and narrowness of the arouser of the hurricane is soon revealed, then Marina gives way to a hurricane of despair. A state which facilitates the appearance of a new arouser. The important thing is not *what* but *how*. Not the essence or the source but the rhythm, the insane rhythm. Today – despair; tomorrow – ecstasy, love, complete self-abandon; and the following day – despair once again. And all this with a penetrating, cold (maybe even cynically Voltairian) mind. Yesterday's arousers are wittily and cruelly ridiculed (nearly always justly). Everything is entered in the book. Everything is coolly and mathematically cast into a formula. A huge stove, whose fires need wood, wood and more wood. Unwanted ashes are thrown out, and the quality of the wood is not so important. For the time being the stove draws well – everything is converted to flame. Poor wood is burnt up more quickly, good wood takes longer.

It goes without saying that it's a long time since I've been any use for the fire.

When I travelled to Berlin to join Marina, I immediately felt that I had nothing to give her. A few days before I arrived the stove had been lit by someone else. For a while. Then everything whirled round again and again. The final stage – the most difficult for both of us – was her meeting with a friend of mine from both Constantinople and Prague, someone quite alien to her and whom she had always ridiculed. My unexpected departure served as a pretext for the beginning of a new hurricane.

I found out about it myself by chance, though her friends had been informed by letter. It became necessary to put an end to our absurd life together, nourished as it was by lies, clumsy conspiracies and other poisons. That was my decision. I would have done it before, but I kept thinking that I might be exaggerating the facts, that Marina couldn't lie to me, and so on.

This last affair brought out into the open a whole string of previous meetings. I told Marina about my decision that we should separate. For two weeks she was in a state of madness. She rushed from one person to another (she had moved in with friends for a while), she didn't sleep at night and she became very thin – it was the first time I had ever seen her in such despair. Finally she informed me that she was unable to leave me since she was unable to enjoy a moment of peace – let alone happiness – with the thought of me being somewhere or other on my own. (That – alas! – is what I knew would happen.) If Marina had ended up with someone I trusted, then I would have been firm. But I knew that the other man (a little Casanova) would abandon her in a week, and with Marina in her present state that would have meant death.

Marina longs for death. The ground long ago disappeared from beneath her feet. She talks about this incessantly. And even if she didn't, it would be obvious enough to me. She has come back. All her thoughts are with *him*. His absence inflames her feelings. Now it's her poems to him that she lives on. With regard to me – total blindness. An inability to come near me, very frequent irritation, almost malice. I am at one and the same time both a lifebelt and a millstone round her neck. It is impossible to free her from the millstone without tearing away the only straw she still has to clutch. My life is utter torment. I am in a fog. I don't know what action to take. Each succeeding day is worse than the one before. Solitude à deux is a burden.

My immediate sense of life is destroyed by pity and a sense of responsibility. Maybe it is just my own weakness? I'm too old to be cruel and too young to be both present and absent at once. But today my *today* is just putrefaction. I'm so completely defeated that I feel a revulsion towards everything in life, as though I had typhoid. It's a kind of slow suicide. What can I do? If only, from a distance, you could direct me back onto the true path! I haven't written anything about Marina's life in Moscow. I don't want to write about that. I can only say that on the day of my departure (and you know what I left for), at the end of a brief stay in Moscow during which I looked at everything "for the last time" Marina shared her time between me and someone else whom she now laughingly calls a fool and a rascal.

She blamed the death of Irina (Alya's sister) on my own sisters (something she sincerely believes) and I only recently found out the truth and re-established contact with L. and V. (Lilya and Vera – V.S.) But that's enough. Enough of today. What can I do? This cohabitation cannot go on for long. Or it will be the end of me. M. is deeper than Asya. In personal life it's a sheer destructive impulse. All this time I have been attempting to avoid being harsh and yet to prepare both Marina and myself for the coming separation. But how can I do that when Marina is trying with all her might to do the opposite? She is convinced that she has now sacrificed her own happiness in order to forge mine. She expects to be able to satisfy me by attempting to preserve the outward appearance of living together. If you only knew how difficult and confused it all is. This sense of burdensome weight doesn't leave me for one second. Everything around me is poisoned. I don't feel one strong desire, just complete and utter pain. The loss that has hit me is all the more terrible because during recent years – as you have witnessed – it has been mainly the thought of Marina that has kept me alive.

I loved her so strongly, and straightforwardly, and unshakeably, that I was afraid of nothing except her death. M. has become so inseparable a part of me that now, as I try to separate our paths, I feel a sense of such devastation, such inner laceration, that I try to live with my eyes half-closed. The complexity of the position is still further exaggerated by one of my most fundamental characteristics. With me, ever since childhood, the feeling "I can't do otherwise" has always been stronger than the feeling "This is what I want". The static prevailing over the dynamic. Now all my sense of the static has gone to hell. And it was my only strength. As a result – complete helplessness.

I await the coming days and months with horror. "The pull of the earth"* is pulling me down. I am trying with all my strength to scramble out. But how and where?

If you were here, I know you would be able to help M. a great deal. I hardly ever talk with her about the main thing. She has grown blind to me and to what I say. Or maybe it's something to do with me, nothing to do with blindness at all. But that can wait for another time.

I'm writing this letter to you alone. No one yet knows anything. (Or perhaps everyone knows.)

The letter is undated, but a postscript is dated 22 Jan 1924. This includes the passage: "I have been carrying this letter around for a month. Today I've made up my mind. Marina and I are continuing to live together. She has calmed down. And I have postponed any radical solution to our question. When there is no way out, time is the best teacher. Isn't that so?"

---

* Reference to the old epic poem in which the hero is dragged to destruction in the earth through applying his own strength.

His wife's affair with Rodzevich destroyed Efron. "I am trying with all my strength to scramble out. But how and where?" He now understood that Tsvetaeva's "destructive power" was destroying his own personality, that he needed some other fulcrum in his life, something independent of his family, some possibility for *him* to apply *his own* strength. Might this not have been the time when he first conceived the idea of returning to Russia? "Recently, for some reason, I keep dreaming of returning soon to Russia," he wrote to Voloshin a month later. "Perhaps because a wounded animal crawls back into its lair." It may be that with his unconditional faith in his wife now shattered, he felt he had to turn to something he considered truly unshakeable; it may have been for this reason that he now began to reassess his past and slowly to change his political views.

Astonishingly, on the same day that Efron finally sent off his tragic confession to Voloshin, he also wrote a very different kind of letter to the Bogengardts. In this letter, after telling them about an exam he had just taken in Egyptology and reminiscing about their Christmas visit to Moravská Třebová, he paints a picture of the quietest of family idylls:

> Here we have a thaw. Mountains of snow have melted overnight. The sky, the warmth and the wind are all like Spring. The mud is quite Homeric.
>
> It's evening now. Marina is copying out poems for a journal. A damaged primus-stove is hissing and wheezing on top of the wash-basin, sending out clouds of fragrant steam. The saucepan containing our dinner is on the boil. A mixture of every kind of both earthly and unearthly fruit – that is the secret of Marina's cooking.

Life continued, with both storms and periods of calm. Efron and Tsvetaeva appear to have recognized that they were joined together inseparably. In his unpublished memoirs, "How Life was Lived", Valentin Bulgakov quotes a sentence from one of Efron's letters to Tsvetaeva: "A day I haven't seen you, a day I haven't spent together with you, I look on as wasted." As for Tsvetaeva and her romances – was there anyone else apart from Efron who had known her father and sister, with whom she had shared her youth and had common friends, who knew both Koktebel and Tryokhprudny Lane, Max and Pra? Was there anyone else who could have endured her "hurricanes"? Was there anyone other than Seryozha to whom she could have turned in thought after Irina's death? During her calmer moments Tsvetaeva understood all this. Each of them knew that they were essential to the other. And so it was impossible for there to be any kind of "final" decision:

> The most supersenseless word:
> Par-ting. Am I just one of a hundred?
> Simply a word of two syllables,
> Beyond which lies emptiness.
>
> Stop! in Serbian, in Croatian – ?
> Or the Czech in us is playing tricks?
> Par-ting. That we should part . . .
> Is the most supernatural nonsense!

In "Poem of the End" this monologue is addressed to Rodzevich. In reality the only man to whom Tsvetaeva could have said this is her husband:

> The verb "to part" means: separately,
> But we're – fused.

Tsvetaeva was, of course, an exceptionally difficult person and she does, at least sometimes, appear to have been aware of this. In a letter to a friend she once admitted:

> I am afraid that the trouble with me (my fate) is that I don't really love anything, am not able to love anything, to the very end, i.e. without end, except for my own soul . . . I feel cramped everywhere – with every person and every feeling – just as I feel cramped in every room, whether it's a hole or a palace. I am unable to live, i.e. to continue; I don't know how to live in days, day after day – I always live *outside* myself. This illness is incurable and it's name is: soul.

She felt certain that communion with the soul was far more important than ordinary relationships; as a result she always either upset people and pushed them away or else felt destroyed by them. Her poem "An Attempt at Jealousy" begins with a confession in the form of a question:

> How is it living with another, –
> Simpler, yes? . . .

These lines contain not only irony, but also pain. For all her exuberant mockery of her rival, she is upset that the man she addresses should find life simpler – and therefore better – with this other woman. The man's answer, in the fifth stanza, exemplifies Tsvetaeva's awareness that she was an unusually difficult person:

> "Enough of spasms and missing heart-beats –
> I shall rent a house for myself" . . .

This awareness, however, does not in any way induce Tsvetaeva to be prepared to lower herself to a level she considers unacceptable. "What people need is different from what I give them," she wrote in a letter to her friend Tesková. This in turn was a cause of suffering. The day she wrote "An Attempt at Jealousy" – with all its furious self-assertion – she wrote another poem in a very different tone:

> The blizzard sweeps into the floors.
> All is rupture and dissent!
>
> Tears of strong brine,
> Pearls coarsely ground,
> Mark the gay and coloured scarf.

"An Attempt at Jealousy" is without any overt dedication and it is debatable whether it is addressed to Rodzevich or to Mark Slonim – or even to both of them. In my view, though the poem does indeed draw on feelings relating both to her separation from Rodzevich and to her unconsummated relationship with Slonim, it is in fact addressed to all her past and future lovers, perhaps to the "collective mediocrity" she speaks of in another poem she wrote at this time: "Sleep".

Of all her numerous objects of infatuation, Mark Slonim is the only one with whom she went on to form a lasting friendship. As she wept over Rodzevich on his "friendly shoulder", she fell in love with him, wove fantasies about him and then felt hurt and disillusioned when she realized that these fantasies had no connection with reality. Slonim himself writes: "She felt hurt that I felt neither passion towards her nor demented love, that I could only offer her the affection and devotion of a comrade and dear friend." Initially indignant at this "refusal' and unwilling to pardon such a "betrayal", Tsvetaeva finally had to accept Slonim's terms; she came to value his friendship, his understanding of poetry and his constant readiness to help. "Of many people – over many years – he is the closest to me: for his cast of mind that is neither masculine nor feminine, but of some third kingdom . . . And if it wasn't for the triteness and *terribleness* of this word (not the feeling itself!), I would simply say that I love him."

In summer 1924 Efron and Tsvetaeva left Prague and moved to the suburbs; they lived for a while in Jíloviště and then settled – for the rest of their time in Czechoslovakia – in Všenory. Tsvetaeva finished "Poem of the End" and returned to "Theseus", a tragedy of unconsummated love that now had a new resonance for her and which inevitably contains echoes of "Poem of the End":

> You think they love? No, they chop it down
> Like that! No, they kill it! No, they tear the veins.

Oh, how little and how badly do they love!
Love, chop down – the sound is similar,

Deathlike! And this you honour
With the name of love? Play of muscles –
And no more! . . .

Life slowly returned to its usual course, Alya was with them once again, once again Tsvetaeva had to fetch water and firewood and carry out all the various tasks of village life . . . And very soon Tsvetaeva realized that she could expect a son. Yes, she didn't for one second doubt that she would have a son, that she could "conjure" herself a son by her passionate longing. In expectation of a son her life had taken on a new meaning.

MUR

She seemed to have been dreaming of him all her life. She had barely recovered from Irina's death before she was trying to convince herself:

Thus, stepping out from the sleepless blackness
Of the Kremlin's lofty towers,
There appeared to me in the pre-dawn gathering,
He, who was yet to come – *my son.*

And she had promised her husband, in an attempt to console him for Irina's death: "We shall without fail have a son." Maria Grinyova remembered a conversation with Tsvetaeva the day before she left Russia: " 'If I really do leave, then in a year's time I shall have a son,' said Marina with conviction. 'And I shall call him Georgy.' "

There is, of course, something odd about the strength of Tsvetaeva's longing for a son. "My son", "like me", "for me": it may be that she needed a son – a living incarnation of herself, a reaffirmation of both her soul and her body – in order to feel more fully alive, more anchored to the physical world.

It was in summer 1924 that Tsvetaeva first realized she was pregnant. This is almost certainly when she wrote the poem "Island":

There is an island. Seized from the Nereids
By some subterranean shock.
A virgin. Not yet discovered or
Explored by anyone . . .

This unknown island, forming in her own depths, would be her son:

I only know: he figures nowhere
Save in the latitude

Of the future . . .

A few months later, Tsvetaeva would write with pride:

– Woman, what's that under your shawl?
– The future!

For the time being, however, there were few changes in her life. Tsvetaeva remained as slim as always and for some time it was not even noticeable that she was pregnant. She continued to write, to do all the housework herself and to go for long walks in the surrounding hills and forests. . . . And in November Tsvetaeva was elected a member of the editorial committee of a literary anthology to be published by the Union of Russian Writers and Journalists; Efron for his part was elected treasurer of the Union.

Confident of her own health, and perhaps partly out of fatalism, Tsvetaeva didn't so much as attempt to find a doctor until almost the last month. Even after she had found a hospital, she didn't have the least intention of giving birth there – good hospitals were beyond her means and she was put off the cheaper ones by their huge wards, their no smoking policy and their similarity to hospitals in Soviet Russia. Doctor Altschuller, then a young doctor working in the Prague University Clinic, has described how Tsvetaeva visited him a few weeks before she was due to give birth and announced: "You're going to deliver my child!" He protested that he wasn't an obstetrician and didn't know how to deliver a baby, but she just repeated: "You're going to deliver my child!" This scenario was repeated several times and so it was no surprise to Doctor Altschuller when a village boy came round on the evening of a snowstorm to announce that Tsvetaeva was in labour. He immediately set off, taking a short-cut down a forest path where the snow was up to his knees. There was no other doctor or midwife, but he was helped by the wife of Evgeny Chirikov. It was a difficult birth, the baby was half-strangled by the umbilical cord and it took Altschuller twenty minutes to fully resuscitate him. He was astonished at Tsvetaeva's calm: "All this time Marina just smoked in silence, looking at the child, at me and at Mrs Chirikova." Everything, however, ended happily: a son had been born to Tsvetaeva, two weeks early, on 1 February 1925. Tsvetaeva, superstitious as ever, saw everything as a sign of how remarkable a man her son would become. In a letter to Tesková the following day, she wrote: "My son was born on Sunday, at noon. In German that makes him a *Sonntagskind*, someone who understands the language of birds and animals, who discovers stores of treasure. The stone for February is an amethyst. He was born during a snowstorm."

The boy immediately became her idol. He had in fact been her idol ever since she first knew she was pregnant. A week after the birth she wrote in a letter: "It's eight days since the boy was born. The general opinion is that his face is just like mine: a long, straight nose . . . narrow eyes (his eyebrows and eyelashes are still white), and a mouth that's very obviously my own – a Tsvetaev in short. Do you remember, you prophesied that my son would be like me? You were right. A daughter would have looked like Seryozha."

Life now became more difficult for the family, largely because of their constant lack of money. They were in debt to the nearby shop, they often lacked even the barest essentials and Tsvetaeva needed outside help – after such a difficult birth she had to spend nearly two weeks in bed. Alya, of course, was only too glad to help, but she was still a child herself. It is clear from Tsvetaeva's letters, however, that the baby did gradually "accumulate" the necessary belongings: someone gave him a little bath, someone lent him some baby-weighing scales, both friends and strangers gave him huge quantities of childrens' clothes, bonnets, swaddling clothes and blankets. The editorial board of *The Will of Russia* presented him – "as one of their future collaborators" – with the gift of a pram. Neither Alya nor Irina ever had such a dowry. "It's the dowry of a prince," announced Tsvetaeva. She loved everything about the baby: the way he slept in his basket ("like Moses"), the way he ate, how well he behaved, even the way he "wailed" at night . . . She was truly happy: this is the only time in her letters that she uses the word "happiness" in the present tense, even if not entirely without reservations: "But in general, obviously, I'm happy."

It was difficult to decide on a name for him. Instead of Georgy [George], Tsvetaeva now wanted him to be Boris – in honour of Pasternak. However . . . "he was Boris for nine months inside me and ten days outside," she wrote in a letter to Pasternak, "but Seryozha's wish (but not demand!) was for him to be called Georgy – and I yielded. Since then things have been easier." And so her prediction of three years earlier had now come true – she was the mother of a son called Georgy. At home, however, he was called "Mur" – a nickname invented by his mother that stuck.

The christening didn't take place until the summer – on 8 June, "Whit Monday and Pushkin's birthday", as Tsvetaeva pointed out in a letter to the absent godmother, Olga Chernova. The service was conducted by Father Sergy Bulgakov, and Tsvetaeva went on to describe it in detail:

The ceremony is a long one, all exorcism of devils, you can feel their terrifying force, a real struggle for power. And the church pushing with all its might against a dense mass, a living wall, of sorcery and devilry (was she thinking of her own poem "The Swain"? – V.S.): "I forbid you! – Go away! – Depart!" It's a real battle. Quite remarkable. In one place, where they were banishing more fiercely than ever, *eternally* banishing (such as "I renounce his ancient charm . . ."), two huge tears – not crocodile tears! – suddenly rolled down my cheek; it was as though *I* had been barred access to Mur. And Alya said something splendid the evening before: "Mama, what about when he says, 'blow and spit'* – will you suddenly vanish?" She asked in a timid voice, as though she were begging me not to vanish. I then told Father Sergy. He listened anxiously – maybe he was afraid of the same thing. (Or secretly hoping for it?)

Mur was quite charming during the whole ceremony . . . He looked handsome, the appearance and size of a baby of seven months. He wasn't totally immersed – not one of the vast Czech laundry tubs in the neighbourhood was big enough. A boy like him could only have been totally immersed in the sea.

Tsvetaeva admired everything about Mur: his size, his weight, his large head, his beauty, his face – which she thought similar to Napoleon's – his mind, and his general precocity. In her eyes he was unusual, in the eyes of some of her friends he seemed strange, even unpleasant. One woman has written of her introduction to a ten or eleven-month-old Mur: "we went in . . . there was a cradle in the corner. I really love little children and I went straight there, smiling tenderly in advance. I bent down – and was dumbfounded: a sleek, handsome, rosy-faced, forty-year-old peasant was looking up at me through eyes that were cold, blue and malicious. I can honestly remember it to this day – I felt frightened." Although there is indeed one photograph of Mur – at six months – that answers this description, there are others where he looks very beautiful: golden curls, a straight nose, beautifully outlined lips and "eyes like lakes". Even in these photographs, however, his eyes look sullen, joyless, lacking in candour. Vera Traill has written: "During the twelve years I knew him, I never once saw him smile." Mur was not a straightforward child; in her letters even Tsvetaeva herself occasionally lets slip the word: "difficult".

Mur was indeed difficult – and it was his mother who was to blame. She was ready to sacrifice everything for his sake – even her own work. In 1928 she was still able to write that Mur was her only concern apart from her poetry, but a year later she had come to put this somewhat differently: "*He* must not suffer from the fact that I write poems – it's better that the poems should suffer!" For Tsvetaeva this was a renunciation of her own self. And

* During the Orthodox christening ceremony the godparents are required to "blow and spit" at the devil.

she renounced not only her own life but Alya's as well, expecting Alya too to live entirely for Mur. Some of those who knew Tsvetaeva consider that she turned Alya into a housemaid.

As a result of all this, Mur grew up with the sense that he was the centre of the universe. On one occasion, when they were on the beach together, Vera Traill asked Mur to move because he was blocking the sun. And – "profoundly indignant, not in the least jokingly, Marina shouted out: 'How can you say that to such a sun-like creature? . . .'". Tsvetaeva admired everything about him, even what other people found most repellent. She relates with pride that she had to buy him clothes intended for twelve-year-old French boys when he was five, that she couldn't find a single hat that would fit his large head. Salomeya Andronikova, on the other hand, has written to me that once, when Tsvetaeva and Mur came to visit, "the chamber-maid came running in and called out: 'Madame Zvétaéva avec un *monstre.*' He was monstrous then and he probably never changed." In fact, Mur did change. He grew up tall, slim and handsome, with a proud carriage of the head and a fine manly face. A woman who knew the Efrons after their return to the Soviet Union has written: "Do you remember these lines from Kuzmin's 'Alexandrian Songs'?

> The third, ah, the third, was so handsome,
> That his own sister strangled herself with her plait
> From fear of falling in love with him . . .

Well, that's how handsome Mur was. I tried not to look at him, so he wouldn't be able to read my face – after all, he was just a boy, about fifteen." By then Tsvetaeva really did have something to be proud about: Mur was not only handsome but also intelligent, and unusually well-educated. He had an equally fine command of both Russian and French, together with a splendid knowledge of both literatures. She had taught him to read and write in Russian by the age of six and had sent him – at considerable cost – to a good private school in Paris. Determined that he should not suffer as a result of her writing poetry, she had taken him to and from school twice a day herself.

For all his education, however, it is clear that Mur was indeed an extremely difficult child. Like Alya at his age, he spent most of his time with adults and behaved as though he were their equal, interrupting everyone including his mother. Other people found him intolerable, though Tsvetaeva herself appears to have refused to admit this. In 1936, on a visit to Brussels, Tsvetaeva appears to have suddenly realized how boorish and badly behaved he was, but she was convinced that this was superficial and would pass soon enough. Even the fact that, in her own words, "the part of him that is least developed of all is his soul", appears not to have alarmed her.

Mur had barely been born before his mother was feeling jealous of future nannies and wives, worrying about how one day he would grow up and begin to separate from her. And she had begun to worry about the military call-up for the year 1946 before he had even been born. She was afraid both of the actresses with whom he would fall in love and of the fact that he might "engage in revolution – or counter-revolution, which to me is much the same – and serve time in jail, with me bringing him parcels. In a word – he's *terra incognita*. And here I am holding this *terra incognita* in my hands."

Her years in Prague were the only time Tsvetaeva lived *inside* "literature": she was in close contact with editors, she played an active part in the life of the Writers' Union and she gave readings at evenings held by the Czech-Russian cultural society. In this respect her years in Paris were only superficially similar: the editors who published her there looked on her just as an "author", an outsider; she only contacted the Paris Union of Writers and Journalists when she needed financial assistance; and she organized and publicized her own literary evenings – with the aim of paying the rent, paying for Mur's school or perhaps a summer holiday.

In Prague, on the other hand, there were several places where Tsvetaeva could feel at home. Slonim introduced her to *The Will of Russia*, one of the best Russian émigré journals. He was himself the editor of the literary section. When he offered her work, he warned her that the journal was edited by Socialist Revolutionaries. "She immediately answered: 'I'm not interested in politics, I don't understand it and anyway Mozart tips the scales'": Slonim had mentioned that the office was in the house where Mozart was reputed to have written *Don Juan*. He goes on to say: "I am convinced to this day that Mozart really did influence her decision." *The Will of Russia* had in fact, at Slonim's instigation, published her poems when she was still in Berlin. The office was somewhere she could drop in freely, where people listened to her with interest and respect. She went to their "literary teas" on Tuesdays. And – most importantly of all – the editors published everything Tsvetaeva offered them from 1922 until the journal closed down in 1931; they never edited or abridged her work and they published a number of her longest and most complex poems. All this seems still more remarkable when one remembers that Tsvetaeva's "White" poems, extremely well known at the time, expressed a viewpoint that was entirely unacceptable to the journal's Socialist Revolutionary editors.

The Will of Russia not only defended Tsvetaeva from such critics as Georgy Adamovich, who accused her of writing wilfully extravagant and undisciplined nonsense; it was also the only journal which consistently followed the evolution of Tsvetaeva's work and discussed it as an important phenomenon in the history of Russian literature as a whole. Slonim himself, Svyatopolk-Mirsky and others all championed her as one of the finest and most original poets of the day.

The journal *Our Own Paths* was also sympathetic to Tsvetaeva. Efron himself was one of the editors and Tsvetaeva was on friendly terms with his colleagues. It was in the pages of this journal that she published what can be considered her poetic credo. This took the form of a letter to Balmont, who had then been writing poetry for thirty-five years:

Dear Balmont!

Why am I greeting you in the pages of the journal *Our Own Paths*? Because I am captivated by the word, and consequently by meaning. What are our own paths? Paths that grow up beneath our feet and become overgrown in our wake; neither the highway of luxury nor the rumbling track of labour, but our own paths, pathless paths. Pathless!* There – I've reached my favourite word. You, Balmont, are pathless, I am pathless myself, all poets are pathless – they follow their own paths.

I am equally captivated by each of the words that form the title of this journal. What can the poet call his own apart from his path? What would he want to call his own apart from his path? Everything else belongs to others; everything else is "yours" or "theirs", but my path is my own. A path is the only property of the "pathless"! It is their only possibility of property – and, more generally, it is the only instance of any kind of property being sacred: the solitary paths of creative work. . .

I am also captivated by the fact that the title is not *Our Own Path*, but *Our Own Paths*,† that there are many, many paths – just as there are many different people and many different passions!

As a postscript to this important declaration, made halfway through her literary career, it is interesting to note Tsvetaeva's ecstatic response, seven years later, to Adamovich's mention of her in an article about the lost paths of poetry. "No," wrote Adamovich, "that is no way to write, that cannot possibly be considered a path. . . ." "He is absolutely correct," responded Tsvetaeva, "only I take it not as a reproach but as the highest praise, that is – as the truth about me, for I have said that '*the truth of poets is a path that*

---

* *Besputny* more often means "dissipated", but here Tsvetaeva puns on its surface meaning of "without a path" (*bez puti*).

† *Svoimi putyami.*

becomes overgrown in their wake'." The sad thing is that Adamovich himself had clearly forgotten Tsvetaeva's letter to Balmont (he had dismissed it at the time as "very bad").

Tsvetaeva's third literary "home" was *The Ark*, the name of the anthology that was eventually published by the Union of Russian Writers and Journalists in Czechoslovakia. The editorial board consisted of Professor Sergey Zavadsky, Valentin Bulgakov and herself. The anthology had been planned for a long time and was intended to comprise two volumes; the second, however, was never published.

The three editors worked harmoniously together, coming to a joint decision on the fate of each manuscript. The time of most intense work coincided with the last months of Tsvetaeva's pregnancy and the first months after Mur's birth; she was seldom able to visit Prague and her husband acted as courier. Efron also submitted a short story, "Typhus", "anonymously . . . so as not to lay the editorial board open to accusations of nepotism." Bulgakov and Zavadsky gave the story their approval without guessing the name of the author.

Tsvetaeva's letters to Bulgakov give an extraordinarily interesting insight into her abilities as a reader and editor of works by other people. She comes over as efficient, serious, dedicated and flexible. Her approach is humane and down to earth. She is well aware that it is out of the question to offend "the old men" – Vasily Nemirovich-Danchenko, who had been an important literary figure for over sixty years, and [the novelist and playwright] Evgeny Chirikov. She wrote to Bulgakov with regard to Nemirovich-Danchenko: "The two and a bit – perhaps three?! – pages of Nemirovich are our fated tribute to age and fame." Another writer, Iosif Kalinnikov, won her heart through the tenacity with which he stood up for his work. He had submitted a story that Bulgakov described as "absolutely unprintable", a vividly written account of life in a wild god-forsaken village, under the title "The Devil's Fumes". "Efron and I read it," Bulgakov continues, "and attempted to keep it hidden from Marina Tsvetaeva. She and Zavadsky trusted our taste and judgment." Kalinnikov was asked to send another story, but he repeatedly refused. When he finally agreed, Tsvetaeva thanked her fellow-editors as though Kalinnikov's success was a matter of personal concern to her: "I am infinitely grateful to you and Sergey Vladislavovich with regard to Kalinnikov. Do you know what I found so attractive about him? His authentic pride as a writer – something the very opposite of vanity: he would rather not have been included at all than submit something he looked on as weak. Remember his poverty, remember his craftiness (I call him the snake-woman). For someone like him renunciation is a real achievement. If he had just whined and kept on insisting, I wouldn't have intervened."

For all this, Tsvetaeva was not afraid to offend people – even such a friend as Balmont. She decided against a long poem of his dedicated to D. Krachkovsky – in spite of the fact that Krachkovsky himself was insisting on its publication. The entire poetry section was, of course, entrusted to Tsvetaeva. In spite of the fact that she is usually seen as someone unworldly and arrogant, she carried out a number of difficult tasks with great tact and diplomacy. Her professionalism is evident from her letters to Bulgakov, with such passages as the following:

> I am sending you Nechitailov – I've done all I can. One song ("Moscow Tsaritsa") I would myself leave out altogether – nothing can be done about it, it's all over the place. I don't know the metre of the original. (I've noted this in the margins.)
>
> I've read and commented on Turintsev's poems. The best, in my view, is "Locomotive". "Parting" is weaker, especially the end. I definitely wouldn't take any of the others. What do you and Sergey Vladislavovich think?

Work on the anthology dragged on for a long time. Tsvetaeva joked that Mur would grow up and be able to write something for it. Eventually, however, it was published. Bulgakov writes: "The anthology ended up quite impressive in size, varied in content, and reasonable in quality. Marina Tsvetaeva thought up the title: *The Ark*. S. V. Zavadsky wrote a rather witty and ingenious preface on behalf of the editors. And so the anthology remains as a small notch in the history of Russian cultural life in Prague."

Reading *The Ark*, together with the related memoirs and correspondence, made me think of Pushkin's journal, *The Contemporary*.* *The Contemporary* is, of course, infinitely more important than *The Ark*, but what the two journals have in common is a similarity in the atmosphere around them, the atmosphere of literary life, of life lived *inside* literature. I realized that if Tsvetaeva had lived in a more normal time, she too would have been a part of a similar world, the centre of a defined literary circle and someone with influence on the poetry of her time. As it is, however, most of her life was lived outside literature; her years in Prague were the exception.

These years stand out in many other respects as well, not the least important of which was that she had a regular income: her "maintenance" and Efron's grant, supplemented by royalties and money for her editorial

---

* In 1836 Pushkin founded the literary quarterly *Sovremennik*, which continued publishing until its suppression in 1866.

work. In general Tsvetaeva and her husband led a very full life in Prague. In addition to his studies and his involvement with the Writers' Union, Efron took on a considerable amount of voluntary work. He also helped to set up a dramatic studio and in spring 1925 was asked to play the part of Boris in Ostrovsky's *The Storm*. In Tsvetaeva's words, "he acted *very* well, nobly, gently, true to himself. It's a hopeless role – the hero's a slobberer and a clown – but he made it quite charming."

In the end, however, as a result of his generally weak health, a poor diet and overwork, Efron fell ill. His tuberculosis recurred and he had to spend part of the summer in a Russian sanatorium, seventy kilometres from Prague, where he could be treated free of charge. He was due anyway to finish his studies at the end of the year. Inevitably the question arose as to what he and his wife would do next.

Tsvetaeva herself had wanted to leave Czechoslovakia for some time. She had never quite settled there and had never felt at home with Czech culture or the Czech language: "How harsh and savage the Czech language seems to my ears and lips," she wrote to the Bogengardts. She didn't want her children to have to learn Czech. On the other hand, she had a wide circle of friends and fellow-writers, she had her "maintenance", she was able to get her work published, and she had time to write. The most understandable of her reasons for wishing to leave is the desire to escape the demands and burdens of everyday life, to escape the inevitable autumn mud that came up to her knees, to escape having to fetch firewood and water and having to light stoves. She could have escaped all this, however, merely by going to Prague.

"I think of Paris," Efron wrote to Olga Chernova, "as the source of the miracle-working balsams that must heal all of the (wounds? – V.S.) which Marina has acquired in Czechoslovakia, from living the life of a camel and so on, and so on, and so on." Both he and Tsvetaeva thought that Paris would open up more possibilities of publication and so of earning money through her writing; that it would bring her to the attention of a wider public. Paris had by then taken over from Berlin as the centre of Russian literary life and Tsvetaeva already had contact with several of the journals and newspapers that were published there. Her name appeared regularly in critical articles and reviews; she was in fact a well-known poet – irrespective of the personal likes or dislikes of particular critics. A more particular temptation held out by Olga Chernova and her husband was their promise to organize a literary evening for her. The Chernovs had also offered to share their apartment with Tsvetaeva and her family. Wary as she was of the possible difficulties of life in a shared flat, Tsvetaeva accepted the offer before the end of August.

At the time she still believed she was just going on a temporary visit. She sorted out her affairs in Prague, obtained visas with the assistance of Mark Slonim – together with money for the journey – and made arrangements for her husband, who was to remain in Prague. She also obtained a guarantee that her Czech "maintenance" would be continued for the next three months.

It is impossible to say what would have happened to Tsvetaeva if she had stayed in Prague, whether or not she made a mistake in leaving. While I was pondering these questions, however, I kept thinking that there must have been some other, hidden reason for her decision to leave. I now believe the answer is contained in "The Rat-catcher", the long poem which Tsvetaeva was working on in Všenory and which she completed in Prague:

> – Removal! –
> Don't regret a long warmed seat!
> Over the bridge!
> Don't regret a long warmed nest!
> Thus the piper – perish frugality!
> – Changes! –
> Thus the peacock
> Does not count its opalescent colours . . .

As the rat-catcher's flute lured away the children of Hamlin, so Tsvetaeva's own flute called her to the open road:

> Ti-ri-li –
> Through the seedlings of the German land,
> Ti-ri-li –
> Through all its cities
> – Not one lags in beauty –
> I pass by,
> My mistress, Music, I glorify . . .

Ariadna Efron believes that Tsvetaeva first conceived the poem in Moravská Třebová: the quiet, comfortable, medieval little Germanic town in the centre of Moravia suddenly made her think of the equally quiet and comfortable little town of Hamelin with its famous legend of the Pied Piper. Tsvetaeva visited Moravská Třebová twice: in early autumn 1923 and during Christmas 1924. After her first visit she wrote to Olga Bogengardt: "I often return to Třebová in my thoughts; I see a little square with quite huge cobblestones, with crests on the gates and dancing saints. I remember our walks together – do you remember the mushrooms? And some kind of tall, fluffy grass, rather like feather-grass . . ." The grass ended up in the poem, associated with the silence of Hindustan:

> As a bowman
> After thickets and alarms
> Goes into the grass –
> Into your quietness, Hindustan . . .

The poem was first conceived in Třebová, but work was not begun on it for over a year. In the end "The Rat-catcher" became Tsvetaeva's most important long poem, a complex and many-layered epic containing elements of both satire and lyricism. The well-ordered and self-sufficient life of a small town – twentieth-century Moravská Třebová or thirteenth-century Hamelin? – is described with vivid and mocking wit, from a number of viewpoints. Who, though, are the hungry rats who descend on this well-fed town, almost overwhelming it with their voracity? In the Middle Ages, of course, plagues of rats were just a common natural disaster and ratcatchers were members of a recognized profession; but in Tsvetaeva's poem the rats are somehow linked to the threat to peace posed by the Russians. Now, though, it is no longer the "White" émigrés who pose this threat – as in the earlier short poem, "Migrants" – but it is the "Reds" themselves. The word "Bolsheviks" is never used, but it is implied in one passage by some insistent and unambiguous rhymes:

> – There is such a road – a bolshoi road . . .
> – In that country, where strides are broad,
> So we were called . . .

These lines, significantly, are omitted from the Soviet edition. The identification of the rats with the Bolsheviks is also confirmed by every detail of the language the rats use in the poem. Tsvetaeva's rats are in fact an amalgam of the Communists she was thrown up against in Usman, during the early days of the Revolution, and the various "well-fed" people who had so appalled her during the first days of the New Economic Policy. The rats are on the point of being transformed into the burghers and aldermen whom they had previously struggled against and were now devouring. Both the rats and the burghers are equally ready to crush anything living that doesn't serve their lust for possessions. Tsvetaeva hates both parties alike and disposes of each of them with equal venom. All this, however represents, merely the satirical side of her "lyrical satire": her central, most personal and most lyrical theme is art itself. Art in relation to everyday life, art and the artist, art and time, art and morality – all the themes which Tsvetaeva was later to explore in her theoretical prose, are present in "The Rat-catcher" – some fully developed, others merely hinted at.

In summer 1984, on the seven hundredth anniversary of the dis-appearance of the children, I saw a representation of the Pied Piper legend in the town square of Hamelin. There were many similarities between this production and Tsvetaeva's own interpretation of the legend; the mayor and the aldermen, in particular, were portrayed with similar mockery. What was entirely absent, however, was the romanticism with which Tsvetaeva portrays the figure of the Pied Piper. The hero of Tsvetaeva's poem is, in fact, neither the town of Hamelin nor even the Piper, but his Flute – the Flute which lures away the rats, the children, and the Piper himself. It is not for nothing that Tsvetaeva's stage directions emphasize the voice of the Flute itself rather than that of the Piper:

> The Pipe, *insistently:*
> Changing places!
> Don't regret a long warmed place!
> Changes!
> Don't regret walls warmed by breath!
> Fallen stars – don't regret even those! . . .

Tsvetaeva's own inner flute was demanding a change; she felt cramped in hill-encircled Všenory, in the little country of Czechoslovakia. She felt that a period of her life had come to an end and that her flute was calling her elsewhere. All this is confirmed by her choice of poems for the collection, *After Russia.* Although it was published more than two years after she left Czechoslovakia, she did not include a single one of the many poems she had written during that period. The book concludes with the last poem she wrote in Prague: "My greetings to the Russian rye . . ." In saying goodbye to Slavonic Prague, Tsvetaeva may well have been saying goodbye once more to Russia itself.

She always continued to love Prague, from a distance, and it is possible that this love was a sublimation of her homesickness for Russia – a homesickness she could never name and which even in her poetry she could write about only indirectly. Nevertheless it is about Prague that she repeated year after year, in letter after letter: "Oh, how I long for Prague and why did I ever leave! I thought it was for two weeks and it turns out to have been for 13 years."

PARIS

On 1 November 1925 Marina Tsvetaeva and her two children arrived in Paris. She moved in with the Chernovs in their apartment in the twelfth arrondissement. Efron – who arrived after Christmas – described the area as follows: "I'm sitting in Marina's room on the rue Rouvet . . . Down below you can hear Paris. Trains thunder past every minute along the Eastern railway which passes, not far away, at the level of the third floor. Outside the window is a forest of smoking factory chimneys that hoot twice a day . . ." The building, however, was new and the spacious three-room flat had central heating, a gas cooker and a bathroom. It was a long time since Tsvetaeva had lived in such comfort. A woman known as "Crocodile" came twice a week to clean and to help with Mur's nappies. All this "civilization" made Tsvetaeva's life easier and gave her more time for writing. The apartment was, of course, crowded – Olga Chernova had three daughters – but Tsvetaeva and her children were given a room of their own. And one of the daughters married soon after Tsvetaeva's arrival and moved out of the house.

The atmosphere on the rue Rouvet was harmonious. The two families did what they could to help one another, often taking it in turns to prepare meals which they would eat together. The Chernovs and all their friends were obsessed with literature. The youngest daughter – Ariadna – and the husbands of all three daughters were published authors. Each of them went on to write at least one article about Tsvetaeva; the family looked on her as an established master. Natasha Reznikova (née Chernova) writes of their life together:

> Tsvetaeva used to get up early (Mur was a baby) and feed him with "jíška": this was the Czech and German system. . . . Then Marina would sit down at her writing table. She was spirited, even merry, very polite and smart. She "prided herself" on her cooking; she used to say that she felt more proud if someone praised her cooking (since that wasn't "her thing") than if they praised a poem of hers. She often made jokes. There were no rows. To tell the truth, everyone loved, respected and admired her. The only person with whom she was irritable was Alya. Alya was lazy, but she always ended up helping . . . Marina was very equable with Seryozha, and talked to him like a friend (they used the polite form of "you" to one another. Alya also used it to her mother). She did in general ask a lot of Alya, but it was clear she valued her [. . .] There was something old-fashioned about Alya, in what she read and the way she had been brought up.

During her stay in this over-populated apartment Tsvetaeva worked extremely hard. According to Efron: "It was difficult to work with him [Mur] around, but Marina managed to write even in his noisy presence." She finished "The Rat-catcher" and prepared a whole series of poems and articles for various periodicals; by the end of February she had finished her article, "The Poet on the Critic", together with the appended "Flower Garden".

Neither Tsvetaeva nor her husband had any idea how long they would stay in Paris and what they intended to do there. The mentions of Tsvetaeva's arrival in the newspaper, *Latest News*, were more than a little contradictory: "she has arrived to take up permanent residence", "has now moved to Paris", "only for a short period", "now visiting Paris". As for Efron, although he continued to edit *Our Own Paths* and was still treasurer of the Prague Union of Writers and Journalists, he was immediately swept up by Paris life – much more so than Tsvetaeva herself. In early March he wrote an "exultant" letter to Bulgakov in Prague: "I'm telling you *in secret*. A new bi-monthly is being started up in Paris (literature, art, and a little science), quite outside politics. I am one of the three editors [together with Prince D. Svyatopolk-Mirsky and P. Suvchinsky]. It's the first émigré journal that is entirely free of any political allegiances. We have managed to raise the money and the first issue is now being printed. The tone of the journal is very dynamic; in Paris it will create the effect of an exploding bomb." Efron was right as regards the impression created by the journal, but it ended up as an annual rather than a bi-monthly; only three issues were published – in 1926, 1927 and 1928. Efron was himself responsible for seeing the journal through the press and Tsvetaeva published work in each issue. Like *The Ark*, it was "their own" journal: even its title, *Mileposts*, was borrowed from her earlier collection of poems.

Even before the appearance of *Mileposts*, however, Tsvetaeva and Efron had become closely involved with another journal, *The Loyal*, published from Brussels by the young poet, Prince D. Shakhovskoy. Tsvetaeva had been invited to contribute when she was still in Všenory; she had sent off a poem and an excerpt from her Moscow diary, "On Gratitude". Between the first and second issues of the journal, Tsvetaeva met and became friends with both Shakhovskoy and Svyatopolk-Mirsky. They both visited her apartment and discussed not only future issues of their journals but also contemporary literature in general. Their shared idea of what was contemporary – including, as it did, work that was then being published in Soviet Russia – went far beyond the boundaries of what was then acceptable in the émigré world. This view of literature – that it was something of value in its own right, something both outside and above politics – was characteristic of all three journals in which Tsvetaeva and her husband were both involved: *Our Own Paths*, *The Loyal* and *Mileposts*. It was also the view held by Mark Slonim.

The Loyal, unfortunately, folded after three issues: unexpectedly for his colleagues the twenty-three-year-old Prince Shakhovskoy decided to turn away from literature and the world and begin a new life as a monk. In the second issue Tsvetaeva had published "The Poet on the Critic" and "Flower Garden". She had read these works to Svyatopolk-Mirsky while they were still unfinished and he had praised them warmly. He had only fully discovered her poetry after meeting her and it was her most recent poetry that he read first. Unlike some critics he was free of any tendency to hark back to the greater simplicity of her early poetry. "Bear in mind," he wrote to Shakhovskoy, "that at present we have no poet who is *better* than she is . . ." Svyatopolk-Mirsky thus became both Tsvetaeva's friend and one of her few serious critics. "The Poet on the Critic" and "Flower Garden" were both begun at his suggestion. And – like his own articles – these pieces did indeed create the effect of an exploding bomb; that, however, was somewhat later – after Tsvetaeva had left the rue Rouvet.

Tsvetaeva's central reasons for coming to Paris had been to give a poetry reading and to publish a volume of her poems. Both these projects were to hang fire for a long time. On 19 November *Latest News* wrote that "Marina Tsvetaeva, now visiting Paris, is arranging an evening of her poems in the near future. The poetess has prepared for publication her volume 'Intentions' – poems from 1922 to 1925." A publisher was not found until more than a year later, and the evening – her first since Moscow – took place only in February. She and her friends had to organize everything themselves, from finding the hall to selling the tickets. Several people whom she approached refused to be of any help, probably offended by her abrupt manner. "The most difficult thing of all," Tsvetaeva complained to Shakhovskoy, "is to ask for something on my own behalf. It would be all right if it was for someone else." Eventually, however, the arrangements were completed and the date and programme were announced: "During Marina Tsvetaeva's evening on Saturday 6 February, at 79, rue Denfert-Rochereau, the following musicians will be taking part in the concert section: Madame Cunelli – old Italian songs; Professor Mogilevsky – violin; V. E. Byutsov – piano". This newspaper announcement quite astonished me: used as I was to poetry evenings in Moscow in the late fifties and early sixties, I could hardly believe that Tsvetaeva (!) should need a "concert section" to bring in the public. In the event, however, it is clear that there had been no need for her to "insure herself" with music – the success of the evening exceeded everyone's expectations. Soon after the evening Efron wrote to Bulgakov:

9 ii 1926
Dear Valentin Fyodorovich,
    Marina's evening took place on the sixth. It was extraordinarily successful – in spite of the fierce ill will shown to Marina by nearly all the Russian and Jewish ladies who could most have helped with the distribution of tickets. All these ladies, offended by Marina's reluctance to grovel and beg, refused to help us in any way. But to their great surprise (they had predicted a complete disaster) by two hours before the beginning of the evening a crowd was besieging the unfortunate cashier; it was as though they wanted tickets for Shalyapin. Not only was every seat taken – even the entrances, exits and gangways were all jammed solid with people. Around 300 people were unable to get tickets. Some of them gathered in the yard, listening and looking in through the windows. It wasn't a success, it was a triumph. M. read about forty poems. The public wanted more and more. The verse carried extremely well and was considerably better understood by the listeners than by some of M.'s editors [. . .] Since the evening the number of Marina's ill-wishers has expanded considerably. Other poets and prose-writers, both venerable and not-so-venerable, are full of indignation. You are the first person I have written to about Marina's success. I know you will be very pleased. The newspapers aren't saying anything for the time being (Khodasevich, Adamovich and Co.). It's impossible to get hold of Marina's books in Paris – they've all gone. Marina has finally got right through to her reader. I'm very glad for her, I hope that we'll soon be able to sort out the practical side of our lives too. At present it is still a burden.

Tsvetaeva may very well have shared her husband's enthusiasm. All we know for sure, however, is that she earned some money – enough to take the children to the seaside in the near future. "All I want from 'fame'," she wrote, "are as high royalties as possible, so I can go on writing. Also – some quiet . . ."

Before the seaside, however, came a trip to London – something worth mentioning, if only because it was the first time for years that she had been alone for two whole weeks in a foreign city, without children and without domestic responsibilities. Tsvetaeva read at an evening of contemporary Russian poetry. "I'm going to philosophize, and Marina Ivanovna is going to read poetry, both her own and other peoples'," wrote Svyatopolk-Mirsky, the organizer of the trip. While she was in London, Tsvetaeva managed to proof-read "The Poet on the Critic" – she corrected proofs with painstaking care and was always deeply upset by misprints. She also had time for walks around London (a city which delighted her, though she was surprised by its lack of similarity with the London of Dickens) and for an affair with Svyatopolk-Mirsky – after which they returned to their former friendship.

In London she read Mandelstam's first book of prose: *The Noise of Time*. It was probably given her by Svyatopolk-Mirsky, who had just written ecstatic reviews of it. But the book filled Tsvetaeva with indignation; she wrote from London: "I'm sitting here tearing to pieces Mandelstam's vile book, *The Noise of Time*." Why did she say this, why did she consider the book vile? In an attempt to answer this question, I once asked Ariadna Efron if she would allow me to look in her archive at Tsvetaeva's unfinished review of *The Noise of Time*. I recorded her answer almost word for word:

> There is no article about Mandelstam. It is not even a draft, merely her very first fragmentary jottings. Even I [. . .] find it very hard to make out her writing. Some words are just designated by their first letter. [. . .] I still haven't deciphered it all. It is not an expression of Tsvetaeva's general attitude towards Mandelstam. Her complaint about *The Noise of Time* is along the lines of: "He's sold out to the Bolsheviks", this is what angered her. Mandelstam allowed himself to laugh at some people he knew – not even friends, just distant acquaintances. And Tsvetaeva got very indignant. I think it was something to do with some cavalry captain and the sick sister he was nursing. Tsvetaeva was furious that Mandelstam could allow himself to – not even mock, but just poke a little fun at them. They've done this and this for you – she wanted to say to Mandelstam – and look what you say . . .

Now Tsvetaeva did indeed tend to leap to the defence of anyone who had been unjustly treated, even if the injustice was merely imaginary. And if it really were just a matter of Mandelstam's portrayal of Colonel Tsygalsky in the chapter "The Royal Mantle of the Law", it would appear that she had read *The Noise of Time* in a hurry. Mandelstam draws a portrait, veiled in the gentlest of irony, of a man of unusual purity and goodness of heart, a man who felt the pain of Russia and who was isolated among the subhuman rifraff around him – inspired as they were by "the possibility of unpunished murder". What struck me most in Ariadna Efron's reply, however – especially considering her extreme caution and the fact that we were talking on the telephone – were the words: "sold out to the Bolsheviks". They allow only one possible interpretation: that Tsvetaeva was enraged by Mandelstam's extremely negative attitude towards the White Army. The difference between their attitudes is, of course, a reflection of their very different personal experiences: for Tsvetaeva the White cause was an ideal that had been made incarnate in her husband; Mandelstam, on the other hand, had spent time inside a White jail – it was, incidentally, Colonel Tsygalsky who rescued him – and had seen the White movement from inside. His view of it emerges only too clearly from such passages as this: "Colonel Tsygalsky nursed (. . .) a sick eagle, a pitiful, blind eagle with broken talons – the eagle of the volunteer army". It is hardly surprising that Tsvetaeva was infuriated. In the end, however, Tsvetaeva never completed her outburst against Mandelstam. It is very likely that her reasons for not doing so were primarily ethical: Mandelstam lived "there", and for that reason alone it was impermissible to enter into a political argument with him.

Instead of replying to Mandelstam directly, Tsvetaeva began work on a poem about the White Army, "Who are *we*? The land's drowned in tears . . .":

> All Russia with trained muzzles
> They bore on their hunched shoulders.
>
> They couldn't make it! Flight on foot –
> At night, hawked up by the people! . . .

Years before when she was still in Moscow, Tsvetaeva had dreamed of being the historian of the White movement. She never abandoned this idea. In 1928–29 she wrote a poem, "Perekop", based on her husband's Civil War diaries. Like *The Camp of the Swans*, it is less a piece of history than a hymn. The poem is centered on one – victorious! – episode in the war in the Crimea: the Whites' rout of the Reds at Perekop, and the long and difficult siege that preceded this victory. In "Perekop" Tsvetaeva attempts to recreate every aspect of the siege – the inevitable hunger and despair, the doubts of some Volunteers and the inflexibility of others. In a number of short chapters the reader sees everyone from private soldiers to both the previous Commander-in-Chief, Brusilov, who had gone over to the Bolsheviks, and the present Commander-in-Chief, General Vrangel:

> Here he is, avenger
> Of torture-chambers, sculptor
> Of battles, in a black Chechen cloak
> With hand on hilt
>
> Of the wh-ite, r-ight
> Cause: hur-ra-a-h!

Tsvetaeva conveys the life and feelings of the men of Perekop very faithfully. She is not afraid to write about soldiers and officers who were deserters or turncoats. The heroic pathos of the poem is based not so much on a rejection of reality as on the heroism of the Volunteers in overcoming reality. "Perekop" concludes with a resounding victory – Tsvetaeva's ability to convey the joy and power of that victory, even though she had lived through the Whites' eventual final defeat, can only be described as astonishing.

Another poem written in 1928–29, "The Red Steer", is about the early death of one of the "young veterans". In an attempt to make sense of this death, Tsvetaeva thinks back to the Civil War as a whole:

> Long, long, long, long
> The road – three years on foot!
> Clay, clay, clay, clay
> Clinging to soldiers' boots.
>
> "Home", "home", "home", "home",
> When we take Moscow . . .
> The Don, the Don, the Don, the Don:
> Jelly and savoury black earth . . .

The dying man dreams of a red steer surrounded by green grass. Tsvetaeva sees this steer as an image of "red" death:

> I am the eldest,
> A Bolshevik,
> I paint the fields with blood.
> Red is the poppy,
> Red is the bull,
> Red is our age!

Both "Perekop" and "The Red Steer", however, were written considerably later. Tsvetaeva's immediate "response" to Mandelstam was the poem, "Who are *we*? The land's drowned in tears . . .", a poem about the generation of White Volunteers as a whole. From the first words – which only appear to be a question – Tsvetaeva leaps immediately into the attack:

> Those who've dealt with six men, as with a woman,
> – Could it be us, the gilded youths,
> Princes from the Mokhovaya and from the Bronnaya,
> Us, with the gold epaulettes?

I should mention that Moscow University was situated on Mokhovaya Street and that nearby Bronnaya Street was mainly inhabited by poor students:

Paris

> We put up barricades in the year Five,
> When we were children.
> – History . . .

This is a curious point of view; that the men of the White Army are the same men who took part in the 1905 revolution. But what disturbs Tsvetaeva most of all, is not the history of the former Volunteers so much as their present fate – scattered around the world in search of work ("Who are *we?* We're in every station! Who are *we?* We're in every factory!" . . . "Grave-diggers, bedbug-catchers". . ., Dish-washers, rat-catchers . . ."). She sees them as a lost generation, a generation with no firm ground to stand on, going mad with longing for Russia and for a past where their lives had meaning. One of these former Volunteers, of course, is her own husband:

> Barricades, but nowadays thrones.
> Yet still the same horny shine.
> And now not even the Charentons*
> Have enough room for Russian despair.
>
> We die of it. Under the torn trenchcoat
> We die pointing our guns at the madness . . .
> Reorganize the houses of Bedlam:
> They're too small for Russia's ills!
>
> The crutch in delirium dreams of being a spur –
> You're joking! – The empty cuff sees a machine gun.
> In the heart, that's distinct after autopsy,
> There's the sign of an icy campaign.
>
> All their tortures haven't expelled it!
> And let this be known – *there*:
> Doctors will recognize us in the morgue
> By our hearts' unusual largeness.

True to her principles, Tsvetaeva praises the defeated. No Russian poet has written of the White Volunteers with such love and pride, such delight and pain.

In late April 1926 Tsvetaeva and her children moved to the little fishing village of St Gilles-sur-Vie in the Vendée. She wanted to live by the sea and Vendée may have appealed to her through having been the last stronghold of

---

* A mental hospital near Paris.

the French "Volunteers" at the time of the French Revolution. It was here that she finished the poem quoted above.

Tsvetaeva had wanted to leave the apartment on the rue Rouvet for a long time. She had begun complaining about it in her letters almost as soon as she arrived in Paris. She was oppressed by the constant noise and by not having a separate room in which she could write:

> At least a hide-away –
> Only without others!
>
> (. . .)
>
> For quietness –
> Four walls.

It would be easy to put Tsvetaeva's obviously unjust complaints down to simple ingratitude; I think myself, however, that they are of a different order. When she was still in Czechoslovakia, Tsvetaeva had in fact written to Olga Chernova: "The right to indignation – isn't that something I have secretly attained in life?" Tsvetaeva's complaints about life in the rue Rouvet should not be taken at face value; they are not so much a reflection of her – relatively fortunate – circumstances at the time, but rather an inner protest against life itself, against any form of mundane, worldly existence. This protest formed part of her inner world and helped to nourish her high romanticism.

What she genuinely did miss on the rue Rouvet was the natural world. Wherever she lived Tsvetaeva was used to finding some tree, some hill or stream that she could take to her heart – like the juniper bush on the hill at Mokropsy that she wrote about to Pasternak in 1923 and remembered for many years and recalled again in a letter to Tesková just before returning to the Soviet Union. Her move to the Vendée was a return to nature. To begin with she enjoyed everything: the old-fashioned way of life, the stern landscape, the empty spaces. She rented a small cottage with two rooms and a kitchen. She had to fetch water from a kitchen but there was gas and she had a tiny garden where Mur, who was now learning to walk, could "graze". "Life is simple and eventless – and I'm glad of it. Anyway, I'm not capable of anything else. The main roles are played by the well, the milkmaid and the wind," she wrote to Olga Chernova.

It was while she was in the Vendée that Tsvetaeva was caught by the storm of indignation that greeted her article, "The Poet on the Critic". No other work of hers appears to have attracted so much attention. A surprising number of people felt personally offended – not only those whom she mentioned by name. "The Poet on the Critic" might not deserve special attention in this book (her later articles, "The Poet and Time", "Art in the Light of Conscience" and "Pushkin and Pugachov", are more profound and also more artistically whole) if it were not for the fact that this was her first attempt at thinking aloud about the concept of poetry in the light of her own experience. The article arose out of her desire to make sense of the principles and the approaches of contemporary criticism. By this time she already had some experience of writing criticism herself; she had published "Downpour of Light" (about Pasternak), "Cedar" (about Sergey Volkonsky's book *Motherland*), and "Hero of Labour (Notes on Valery Bryusov)". Reading other critics, Tsvetaeva had noticed that literature as an art was nearly always only of secondary interest to them – and often not even that. "Flower Garden" is an anthology of examples of inaccurate, contradictory and irresponsible criticism, culled from articles by Georgy Adamovich and accompanied by her own extremely biting comments. Its role was to illustrate the main points in her article "The Poet on the Critic". It offended not only Adamovich, but also many other critics whom she referred to merely by such sobriquets as "the dilettante critic" and "the mob critic". The tone of the article and its accompanying "Flower Garden" is snappy and often mischievous, but the content was essentially justified. It is clear that in her attack on a politicized approach to art, Tsvetaeva is not in any way taking a political stand herself. Many critics, most notably Zinaida Gippius – probably because she was unable herself to conceive of an apolitical approach to art – entirely failed to understand this; Gippius even accused Tsvetaeva of veiled Bolshevik sympathies. Answering the question, "Who am I writing for?", Tsvetaeva had claimed: "Not for the millions, not for one person alone, and not for myself. I write for the sake of the thing itself. The thing writes itself through me." This attitude, equally abhorrent to both Marxists and émigrés, attracted only abuse – often of an extremely personal nature. Aleksandr Yablonovsky published a pamphlet (hardly an article) called "In a Dressing Gown" which accused Tsvetaeva of over-familiarity and of lacking a sense of "what is permissible and what is impermissible", and went on to portray her as a "lady", holding "a little dog under her arm" and screaming at the cook. He also spoke of her "coming to literature in her curling papers and her swimming costume, as though going into the bathroom". Zinaida Gippius, for her part, affected to feel sorry for Tsvetaeva: "I have no doubt of M. Tsvetaeva's sincerity. She is one of those who have been deceived (by the Bolshevik sympathizers – V.S.); but she has been created in such a way as to be always deceived, even doubly deceived: both by those in whose interest it is to deceive her and by her own hysterical impetuousness."

Even a well-disposed critic, M. Osorgin, saw "The Poet on the Critic" as a "literary escapade", something marred by "provincial over-intimacy". Nobody bothered to notice that Tsvetaeva had conceived a new form of relationship with the reader, that her apparent lack of discipline was in fact a literary innovation comparable to Vasily Rozanov's once controversial "domesticity". In all her subsequent prose – both her memoirs and her critical writing – Tsvetaeva was to address the reader directly, in the first person. She leads the reader into her own inner world, into "the secret of secrets", where the creative process begins and (in her essays on childhood) self-awareness arises. It was natural for her to support her arguments with evidence from her own experience both as poet and as reader of the poetry of others. Tsvetaeva was not alone in writing like this – Mandelstam's prose, Pasternak's "A Safe Conduct" and Mayakovsky's "How to Make Poems" are all written in a similar manner – but she did take this manner further than other writers. Tsvetaeva's critics, however, were appalled at the degree of self-exposure in her prose. Like Mayakovsky, she was accused of egotism and self-advertisement. It is interesting, incidentally, to notice to what degree Tsvetaeva's and Mayakovsky's testimonies about the conception of poetry coincide.

It is not for nothing, however, that Zinaida Gippius refers to Tsvetaeva's impetuousness. Tsvetaeva did indeed live in a state of perpetual motion, casting off poetic "skins" one after the other, thus proving how far-sighted Voloshin had been when he said that there were ten different poets within her. People who had grown used to today's Tsvetaeva were confronted the following day with a new face, once again elusive and incomprehensible. In his article, "The Poet Marina Tsvetaeva", Osorgin confesses his love for her, calls her "the best Russian poet today" writes that "simple-minded readers are a little afraid of her", and then goes on to admit: "Nevertheless I shall always prefer her ancient book in the leather binding (*The Magic Lantern*, 1912, – V.S.) to the extremely musical nonsense of 'The Rat-catcher' ". If a writer and professional critic could see in "The Rat-catcher" only "musical nonsense", then what could be expected from the "uninitiated?" Tsvetaeva, in short, was a poet who lived not only outside politics and outside literature, but also outside time – any time:

> For I was born
> *Outside* time! . . .

Rather than looking in general at contemporary critical assessments of Tsvetaeva, I shall focus on Georgy Adamovich's attitude towards her. For several decades Adamovich was the mouthpiece of the accepted literary

Marina Tsvetaeva, Sergey Efron
and their daughter Ariadna (Alya), 1916

Sergey Efron in an ensign's
uniform, 1917

Sofia Evgenievna Gollidey as
Nastenka in an adaptation of
Dostoevsky's *White Nights*, 1920s

Yury Aleksandrovich Zavadsky, 1919

Sergey Efron, Prague 1923   Marina Tsvetaeva, Paris, 1925

On the outskirts of Prague, summer 1923. Seated: Marina Tsvetaeva, E.I.Elenevna,
K.B.Rodzevich and Lelik Turzhansky. Standing: Sergey Efron and N.A.Elenev

Aleksandr Blok, 1920s

Andrey Bely, 1916

Boris Pasternak, 1920s

Rainer Maria Rilke, Paris 1925

Tsvetaeva's children: Alya and
Mur (Georgy)

Right: Sergey Efron, K.B.Rodzevich
and Mur

Mur, Versailles, 1929

Marina Tsvetaeva and Mur,
Favières, summer 1935

Alya Efron, 1935

Seeing off V.I.Lebedev at a Paris railway station, September 1936. From left to right: V.I.Lebedev, Irina Lebedeva, Mur, Marina Tsvetaeva, M.N.Lebedeva

Marina Tsvetaeva, Moscow, 1939

Right: Anna Akhmatova, 1940

Top: The house in Elabuga where Marina Tsvetaeva hanged herself on 31 August 1941

Above: Mikhail Ivanovich and Anastasia Ivanovna Brodelschchikov, the owners of the house in Elabuga

Left: Mur, 1943[?]

The last photograph of Marina Tsvetaeva, Kuntsevo, 18 June 1941. *Standing:* Marina Tsvetaeva, L.B.Libedinskaya. *Seated:* A.E.Kruchenykh and Mur

A petition from Marina Tsvetaeva to the writer's organization Litfond

To the commission of Litfond:
I request that you employ me in the capacity of a dishw...
in the cafeteria which is opening up at Litfond
M.I.Tsvetaeva
26 August 1941

On this side of the cemetery lies buried
MARINA IVANOVNA
TSVETAEVA
Born 26 September 1892
in Moscow
† 31 August 1941
at Elabuga

The exact site of Tsvetaeva's grave is not known

wisdom of the time, someone who was listened to attentively both by the general reading public and by the younger generation of writers. Although Adamovich has often been called "capricious" and "inconsistent", he was remarkably consistent at least in his rejection of Tsvetaeva. His tone when writing of her is always contemptuously ironical. He refers to her as "a young lady from Moscow", finds her prose "hysterical", and considers the passion, energy and resonance of her verse to be a kind of artificial intoxication. He is irritated by Tsvetaeva's language, by Tsvetaeva's syntax, by her excessive use of dashes, question marks and exclamation marks – by everything, in short, that went beyond the accepted conventions of the time. "One must love Tsvetaeva's poetry very much indeed in order to pardon her prose. I have to admit: I do very much love her poetry. At least half of her poems are no good at all, they are just bad works. Tsvetaeva has no restraint: she writes a great deal, she doesn't carry anything inside her for any length of time, doesn't think anything over, doesn't throw out anything. Nevertheless (Adamovich is surprised! – V.S.), she has been endowed – as have very few! – with 'the miraculous gift of song', and a rare, nightingale-like voice. Some of her lines, and sometimes entire poems, are quite irresistible and are filled with deep charm . . .", "Tsvetaeva has never been discriminating or demanding, she writes on the wing . . .", "Marina Tsvetaeva, had she wished to develop a genuine style, had she not been content with whatever phrase first comes to mind . . .". Still more surprising than Adamovich's deafness in regard to Tsvetaeva is his claim that she didn't work at her poetry. How could he say this of a poet whose notebooks contain sometimes dozens of variations of a single line? . . .

Following this example, younger writers adopted a similar tone of mockery in regard to Tsvetaeva – a tendency that is exemplified by the first issue of a literary journal, *The New House*, that was edited by Nina Berberova together with other members of the younger "unnoticed" generation. Tsvetaeva is discussed in two articles – in V. Zlobin's review of the first issue of [the journal] *Mileposts*, and in V. Fokht's review of the current issue of *The Will of Russia*. After dealing with the supposed connection between *Mileposts* and the Bolsheviks, Zlobin goes on to discuss the problem of "the new temperament". Without beating about the bush, he consigns Tsvetaeva to a brothel: ". . . the red flag flying over the journal should be replaced by a red lamp. Then a number of things would immediately make sense . . . There is nothing to say about Marina Tsvetaeva. She has, in any case, found her place . . .". Zlobin backs up his argument by alternately quoting lines from "Poem of the Mountain" and passages from the Soviet press. Fokht, for his part, accuses Tsvetaeva of "dissipation and morbid eroticism". In fairness I should note that not all the young generation joined in this attack on Tsvetaeva. *The New House* was in fact the subject of considerable controversy at a meeting of the Society of Young Writers and Poets. Vadim Andreev and Vladimir Sosinsky attempted to organize an official protest against the journal's abusive tone, but the chairman refused to allow either of them to speak. The newspaper *Days* wrote that "in the end Mr Sosinsky gave a short nervous speech [. . .] He claimed that *The New House* was giving space to vicious attacks and insults masquerading as criticism: We stigmatize the editors of this journal, we consider their conduct disgraceful . . . We would like the editorial board of *The New House* to look on these words as a public slap in the face . . .' At this point there were cries from the public: 'In the person of Marina Tsvetaeva all women have been insulted!' " But Tsvetaeva had very few supporters among the young, and less young, Russian writers in Paris.

After living through so many cataclysms and upheavals, other writers appear to have wanted nothing more than peace, silence and comfort. This is probably precisely what they found in the work of Georgy Adamovich, a proponent of a gentle, undemanding asceticism. He spoke of "the vanity of all poetic activity since the time of Pushkin" and attacked "all verbal 'mannerisms', all kinds of play on sounds and images". The group of young writers round this "quietest of poets" became known as "the Parisian note". Everything about Tsvetaeva was alien to them – her elevated tone, her unusual rhythms, her complex metaphors, her heroic romanticism. All this was too excessive, too disruptive of the peace and comfort they so longed for. "You may not like her too loud voice," wrote Konstantin Mochulsky, "but you can't not hear it." No one appears to have noticed that Tsvetaeva also wrote "quiet" poems herself. To many people she was a laughing stock, known as the "Tsar-Fool", a parody of her poem "Tsar-Maiden".

If the "Parisians" were repelled by Tsvetaeva's lofty romanticism, her pull away from the earth, she for her part was repelled by the limitations of their earth-bound world. And she was too much of an individualist, of course, to have time for any "schools" or "notes". Unlike her enemies, however, she did not stoop to personal insults.

From the vantage point of the present these issues may seem unimportant: Tsvetaeva lives, while her enemies are consigned to a small place in the margin of literary history. I do, however, have one lasting regret – that Tsvetaeva's enemies controlled most of the literary journals and publishing houses. If Tsvetaeva had had a weekly column, like Georgy Adamovich, Georgy Ivanov or Vladislav Khodasevich, she would no doubt have complained bitterly about the demands on her time, but her life would have been considerably easier and more secure. It is an extraordinary fact that during fourteen years in Paris she managed to publish only one book . . .

Why did Tsvetaeva not reply to the attacks on *The Loyal* and *Mileposts*? It seems unlikely that she was unconcerned about the opinion of her fellow writers. She was in fact deeply pained by their incomprehension of her work. In any difficult situation, however, her motto was "Ne daigne" – Don't let me sink to your level. She would say what was necessary and no more. And in any case she now had an ally, a friend, a brother who understood and accepted every syllable of her verse – Boris Pasternak.

PASTERNAK

> When I write, I don't think of anything except the thing itself. Later, when it's finished, I think of you. And when it's published, then I think of everyone. TSVETAEVA TO PASTERNAK

> Throughout several years I was kept in a state of constant happy elation by everything your mother wrote, by the strong, delightful resonance of her precipitate, uncircumspect spirituality.
> PASTERNAK TO ARIADNA EFRON

Tsvetaeva's relationship with Boris Pasternak was unlike any other of her relationships. In the first place, its nature is extremely hard to define. Was it love or friendship, an epistolary romance or a correspondence between two fellow poets? Secondly, the nature and importance of the relationship was constantly changing: sometimes it was a sea that spread to the horizon and filled the whole of their lives, sometimes it was a barely trickling spring – a spring, however, that never, until the end of Tsvetaeva's life, entirely dried up. One thing one can say for sure is that it was the most important relationship in Tsvetaeva's life; it is also clear that the relationship was more important to her than it was to Pasternak.

At a mundane level, however, their relationship appears almost nothing – simply a flight of fantasy. A few chance meetings in Moscow. A shared euphoric enthusiasm for one another's poetry, giving rise to an extraordinary sense of closeness. Two non-meetings in Berlin – once because Tsvetaeva left for Prague without waiting for Pasternak, once because she was unable to travel to Berlin before he left for the Soviet Union. Further unfulfilled plans – for a meeting in 1925 in Weimar, birthplace of Goethe whom they both worshipped, and for a joint visit in 1927 to Rainer Maria Rilke, who, in the modern age, personified Poetry for both of them. Rilke died at the very end of 1926; but Tsvetaeva had already decided to put Pasternak off so that she could have Rilke all to herself. After Rilke's death, she dreamed of going to London with Pasternak; again, nothing came of her plans.

Nevertheless, this "unreal" relationship was one of the most real parts of Tsvetaeva's life. Borrowing Efron's expression, one could say that Pasternak "kindled the fire" and brought it to a higher temperature than anyone else. The "hurricane" begun by Pasternak raged all the more powerfully in the absence of actual meetings or physical intimacy. His "spiritual" flame burnt longer and more brightly than those "kindled" by Rodzevich and others. Tsvetaeva herself spoke of fire in this connection. After Pasternak had sent her his volume, *Themes and Variations*, she wrote: "Your book is a scald . . . Well, I've been scalded, I've got burnt, I've *caught fire*, – and there is no sleep and no day. Only You, You Alone." (My italics – V.S.) This fire gave birth to short poems, long poems, letters – and mad dreams of living together . . . As though they didn't each have their own family! As though they were not separated by a frontier that was growing increasingly insurmountable:

> Patiently, as stone is crushed,
> Patiently, as one waits for death,
> Patiently, as news ripens,
> Patiently, as revenge is cherished –
>
> I shall wait for you . . .

Tsvetaeva promises to wait for Pasternak in the same way as she had once waited for her White Officer husband. In "Wires", the poem-cycle addressed to Pasternak, there even appears an image of the "far places of the Don", that seems to have leapt across into it from *The Camp of the Swans*.

The "blaze" begun by her friendship with Pasternak lasted for many years, from "Life tells lies, inimitably . . .", written in Berlin, to "Nostalgia for the Motherland", written in 1934. There are around forty poems altogether, a huge monologue that allows one only now and again to guess at Pasternak's replies. This monologue touches on everything that was important to Tsvetaeva, including all the "unreal" things that constituted the meaning of her life: love, poetry, the soul, parting, and, of course, Russia itself. Tsvetaeva was sure that all these things were as important to

Pasternak as they were to her. She looked on him as her double and was convinced that he read her poems exactly as she had written them, that he was her ideal reader. What is not clear is whether her Boris Pasternak was the same Boris Pasternak that other people knew, the Pasternak whom we ourselves know from his published correspondence and from memoirs about him. It is very probable that her treatment of the living but distant Pasternak was similar to her treatment of poets of the past in her various essays – that she released his essence from the shell of the everyday, and cast aside everything trivial or in any way alien to that essence. What mattered about Pasternak was that he was a Poet and that he was her comrade, ready to respond to any sound she made. And so her monologue to him expands, changes direction, becomes alternately ecstatic and solemn, turns into a passionate confession and appeal, and then modulates to a sob. The highest pitch of passion is reached in one of her most dramatic cycles, "Wires". The lyric voice swings between hope and despair, alternating between a scream and a whisper; the broken rhythm conveys the fractured speech of someone desperate to say the most important thing of all and choking from the finality of her own words, from the spasms clutching at her throat:

> To tell you all . . . but no, it has all been squeezed
> Into rows and rhythms . . . The heart is broader!
> I fear that for such misfortune the whole of
> Racine and the whole of Shakespeare is not enough! . . .
>
> (. . .)
>
> Torments! Neither shores, nor milestones!
> Yes, for I affirm, mistaken in the number,
> That I lose them all in you, all those who,
> Anywhere or anytime, *did not exist*!
>
> (. . .)
>
> Vanity! It is within me! Everywhere!
> Closing my eyes: bottomless! Without daylight!
> And the calendar date lies . . . Like you – Severance,
> I am no Ariadne and no . . . – Loss!
>
> Over what seas, through what towns
> Should I seek you? (Invisible – to me, the sightless!)
> I entrust the task of seeing you off to wires,
> And, leaning against a telegraph pole, I weep.

A meeting with a twin soul, with a Poet, was an incomparable joy, a joy Tsvetaeva was afraid of frightening away and losing. Tsvetaeva longed to merge with this twin soul, to give all of herself. Giving, as always, was more important to her than acquiring. And she could do this only through poetry – prose and letters were too limited to convey the intensity of her emotions. "What I have to say to you is immense: something to make havoc of one's chest!" she wrote in one letter, promising to "make herself into a major poet". Elsewhere she wrote: "Learn, in the end, to be someone who *needs* to hear this, to be a bottomless vat that withholds nothing (*Read carefully*!!!) so that – through you, as through God! – it FLOODS!" Pasternak, for his part, received as generously as Tsvetaeva gave. His delight in her poetry, his response to everything she sent him, compensated a hundred times over for the lack of recognition from others.

The climax of their relationship came in spring and summer 1926 when, quite unexpectedly, they both began to correspond with Rilke. His participation in their correspondence endowed their feelings with a still greater intensity. Pasternak asked Tsvetaeva to decide for him whether he should come to join her then or whether he should wait for a year in order to sort out his affairs in Moscow. It was at this time, May 1926, that he wrote his first acrostic-poem addressed to her: "A glimpse of hands and feet, and after it . . .". Pasternak was considerably less free than Tsvetaeva in expressing his feelings in poetry: between 1926 and 1929 he wrote only three poems to her; less free and more restrained. While Tsvetaeva addressed Pasternak as though he were her ideal love, separated from her by the will of fate:

> Di-stance: the versts, spaces . . .
> We have been unpasted, unsoldered,
> Crucified, we were divorced by force,
> And they didn't know that this was fusion
> Of inspirations and of sinews . . .

"Fusion of inspirations and of sinews" denotes an ideal, unrealizable intimacy. Tsvetaeva looks back to the "sundered couples" of antiquity for other examples of such closeness. These poems of hers are full of passion and longing, the pain of separation alternating with hopes of meeting:

> Wherever you might be, I shall reach you,
> I shall reach you through suffering and bring you back . . .

If not here in an earthly dimension, then in dreams:

> Spring brings on sleep. Let us fall asleep.
> Although apart, yet it seems, sleep

Brings together all that is asunder.
Perchance in dream we'll see each other.

She repeatedly assures him — and herself — that they will be happy together: "Boris, Boris, how happy we would be together — in Moscow, in Weimar, in Prague, anywhere in this world and even more so in that other world that already exists *in its entirety inside us*." Most likely, indeed, their meeting would be in another life:

Give me your hand — for all that other world!
Here, both my hands are full.

She repeats these sentiments more than once. When she sent Pasternak her poem-cycle "The Two", she addressed it to: "My brother in the fifth season of the year, the sixth sense and the fourth dimension — Boris Pasternak."

Brother, but with such a strange
Admixture of
Disturbance . . .

(. . .)

Up to the funeral pyre —
A brother, but on condition:
Into paradise and hell together!

Tsvetaeva saw her relationship with Pasternak as a mystical marriage; she believed that inspiration bound them together more closely than any other possible bonds:

Not in down, but in
Swan's feathers marriage lies!
Marriages differ, marriages diverge!

The conviction that Pasternak belonged to her helped Tsvetaeva to withstand the everyday world. It also appears that this "fire", unlike the fire kindled by Rodzevich, did not interfere with her marriage.

In *Spektorsky* Pasternak describes the relationship between the hero and Maria Ilina as follows:

And both would fly off into the Empyrean,
Inspiring each other to fly — apart . . .

Researchers have rightly suggested that there are elements of Tsvetaeva in the figure of Maria Ilina; this is confirmed by these two lines: Pasternak and Tsvetaeva did indeed "inspire each other to fly" in their poems and letters and their contact was indeed always in the Empyrean.

> By the chain of singing piles
> On which the Empyrean is resting,
> I am sending you my share
> Of earthly ashes . . .

The plot of *Spektorsky*, bears, of course, little relationship to the story of the meeting that took place between Pasternak and Tsvetaeva; the feelings of the hero and heroine, however, their spiritual intimacy and mutual absorption, correspond very closely to what both Pasternak and Tsvetaeva felt at the time. *Spektorsky* is the most intimate and lyrical of all Pasternak's poems concerning Tsvetaeva.

The three short poems Pasternak wrote to Tsvetaeva in the twenties, on the other hand, are anything but love lyrics. Unless one already knows, one would hardly even guess that they are addressed to a woman. Only in the very last line of the poem, "A glimpse of hands and feet, and after it . . .", does this become clear:

> Reply with leaves, with tree trunks, with sleep of
> Branches, with wind and with grass to me and *her*.

Both this poem and "Momentary snow, when the cobble is seen" are in fact acrostics, the first letters of the first word in each line spelling "Marina". The third of the poems is dedicated "To M.Ts.". It might appear at first glance that the impersonal – or transpersonal – quality of these poems is inconsistent with the passionate intensity of Pasternak's letters to Tsvetaeva; in fact, however, the poems relate to their most passionate shared concern: the question of what it is to be a poet. The most important part of their unusual closeness was the fact that they were both poets. Everything else emerged from or led to that. It is not surprising that questions about the nature of poetry are raised again and again both in their poems to one another and in their most intimate letters. It is equally unsurprising that Tsvetaeva frequently cites Pasternak in her theoretical work and that she devoted no less than three articles to his poetry: "Downpour of Light", "Epic and Lyric of Contemporary Russia (Vladimir Mayakovsky and Boris Pasternak)" and "Poets with History and Poets without History". After finishing "The Poet and Time" in January 1932, Tsvetaeva added an "Afterword" in which she cited some recent remarks of Pasternak's in support of her views:

The sensation of the discussions* was Pasternak's speech. Pasternak said first of all that

"Some things have not been destroyed by the Revolution . . ."

He then added that

"Time exists for man, and not man for time."

In spite of all the prohibitions and distances between us, both internal and external (Boris Pasternak is for the Revolution while I am not for anything), in spite of his being *over there* and my being *here*, Pasternak and I, without prior arrangement, are constantly thinking about the same thing, saying the same thing.

This is what it is to be contemporary.

To say that he is "for the Revolution" is of course an over-simplification of Pasternak's constantly changing views. A writer's attitude towards "Revolution" is not necessarily the same as his attitude towards what happened during the actual Revolution. In theory Tsvetaeva and Pasternak came to a similar resolution of the question of the Poet and his Time:

> Don't sleep, don't sleep, O artist,
> Do not give way to sleep.
> You are a hostage of eternity,
> A prisoner of time.†

What is not clear, however, is to what extent Tsvetaeva understood how much Pasternak's views were complicated by his being "over there", within the Soviet system. Was she able to imagine the double pressure to which he was exposed: that of Time in general and that of his own time in particular? For Tsvetaeva there was just the problem of everyday life, something whose demands were difficult and at times unbearable, but from which she could shut herself off. It was only after her return to the Soviet Union that she came to know time in the Soviet sense, that feeling of dependence on something elusive and terrible, something whose tentacles penetrate everything around you and attempt to enter your soul. Time in this sense is something that you cannot shut out; every day you go to bed thinking about it and every morning you wake up thinking about it. Tsvetaeva may refuse to accept Time, but her sense of it is free of the sinister qualities so characteristic of time as portrayed by Pasternak:

> Seize him, through the darkness of the ages!
> Livelier blow the horns! Tally ho! . . .

* Tsvetaeva had read in a newspaper about a public debate on poetry held in Moscow.
† From "Night" (1956) by Boris Pasternak.

(. . .)

He should glide away in verse into the darkness of the ages;
Such treasures lie in tree-hollows and the mouth.
But he has to carry it from lair to lair: Tally ho!

And turning to his age, setting himself and Tsvetaeva against it, Pasternak asks:

Century, why no desire to hunt?
Reply with leaves, with tree trunks, with sleep of
Branches, with wind and with grass to me and her.

What Tsvetaeva noticed in these lines was not the "Tally-ho!", not the hunt, but the naturalness of Pasternak's deer. Pasternak's poet is indeed a manifestation of nature, something always unexpected, an "immortal suddenness", breaking into everyday reality like "wild snow in summer" (from the poem "Momentary snow, when the cobble is seen . . ."). Nevertheless the relation of the poet to his time is coloured not only by a sense of high tragedy, but by a sense of profound horror that is considerably closer to Mandelstam's "wolf-hound century" than to Tsvetaeva's "world of heavy weights", "world of measures", "where weeping is called having a cold". In the poem "To steal through . . ." Tsvetaeva suggests:

But it may be that the best victory
Over time and gravitation is
To pass by so as not to leave a trace,
To pass by so as not to leave a shadow
On the walls . . .
                    Perhaps to win by
Refusal?
                    . . . Perhaps to win by
Deception? To quit the latitudes?

These questions are all posed in the form of romantic rhetoric. To her fellow poets in Soviet Russia, however, the question of one's relationship to one's time was a matter of life or death. It wasn't a matter of

Falling apart, leaving no ashes
For the urn . . .

but of whether one should preserve oneself as a poet in spite of the threat of violent death, or betray one's poetry in an attempt to survive. The most profound treatment of these questions is in Nadezhda Mandelstam's remarkable volumes of memoirs.* The life of Tsvetaeva's contemporaries in Soviet Russia may have been no more tragic than her own, but it was more terrible. Tsvetaeva did not know the terror described by Mandelstam in the lines:

> And instead of the source of Hippocrene,
> A stream of long-standing fear
> Will burst into the jerry-built walls
> Of the evil dwellings of Moscow.

We do not know whether she understood the literal meaning of these words addressed to her by Pasternak:

> He thought: "Where is she – at this moment, today?
> Happier than I am and freer,
> Or more enslaved and more dead?"

She may not have realized that it was not so much a matter of being enslaved by Eternity as by daily life, nor have understood how literally Pasternak meant such phrases as "our tailor age has cut us to the blood" and "fates crushed into a flat wafer". In some sense Tsvetaeva and Pasternak lived in different worlds and it is possible that this may have been part of the reason for their eventual estrangement.

Pasternak's letters to Tsvetaeva are another matter. In them he is able to leave the world of time and soar, together with Tsvetaeva, into the Empyrean. In their correspondence they are both extraordinarily intimate, perhaps considerably more so than they could have been if they had met. Not all their letters have survived, and not all of those that have survived have been published. In spite of – or thanks to – the ever decreasing likelihood of their ever meeting again, what they felt for one another was indeed love – with all its flights and sudden falls, all its quarrels and reconciliations. At times the tone of their correspondence becomes quite feverish – as they jump from subject to subject, from an analysis of "The Rat-catcher" or "Lieutenant Shmidt" to discussions of their feelings and plans for the future, to descriptions of nature or thoughts about other people. The lines of Hölderlin chosen by Tsvetaeva as an epigraph to "Poem of the Mountain" could well be used as an epigraph to their correspondence: "Oh my beloved! Are you surprised by these words? All those who are separating speak as if drunk and love solemnity." Tsvetaeva and Pasternak

---

* *Hope Against Hope*, New York, 1970, and London, 1971, and *Hope Abandoned*, New York, 1972, and London, 1974.

were always separating – from the very first moment of their correspondence and in spite of all the subsequent torrent of letters, hopes and feelings. Unconsciously each of them knew that fate had decreed they should be a "sundered couple".

To know this unconsciously, however, is very different from hearing it from a third party. When Boris Pilnyak visited Paris in February 1931 and Tsvetaeva happened to hear from him that Pasternak and his wife had separated, it was like a bolt from the blue. She immediately recorded the conversation in a letter to her friend Raisa Lomonosova:

An evening at the house of Boris's friend, the French poet [Charles] Vildrac. He had asked me to meet Pilnyak, who had just arrived from Moscow. We were introduced, we sat down.

> Me: And Boris? Is he well?
> P: Very well.
> Me: Thank God!
> P. He's now living with me, on Yamskaya.
> Me: Have they had to leave the flat?
> P. No, he and his wife Zhenya have separated.
> Me: And the boy?
> P. He's with her.

. . . For eight years (1923–31) Boris and I have had a secret agreement: to keep on until we can be together. But the CATASTROPHE of a meeting kept being postponed, like a storm somewhere the other side of the mountains. Occasional peals of thunder, and then nothing – life just goes on.

Although Tsvetaeva attempts to console herself by saying that there wouldn't be a new wife if she were there beside him, the word "catastrophe", singled out in capitals, is far more eloquent. She goes on to say: "A real meeting between us would have been first and foremost a great grief (me and my family, he and his family, my *pity*, his *conscience*). Now it will never happen. Boris is not with Zhenya, whom he met before me, Boris without Zhenya and not with me but with *another woman who is not me*, this is no longer *my* Boris, but merely the finest Russian poet. I immediately let go." For Tsvetaeva all this truly was a catastrophe: she had lost not only a potential husband, but the only person who was her equal, with whom she could be herself: Ariadne, Eurydice, Phaedra, Psyche, the Sibyl . . . But she had always known that in the real world men prefer Eve – and she had no desire or pretentions to play that role. "How can one live with a *soul* in an *apartment*?" she had once asked. And eight years previously she had written:

Orpheus should not go down to Eurydice,
Nor should brothers trouble their sisters.

Still, however well she understood the impossibility of her ever living with Pasternak, his new marriage felt like a betrayal. "Even just five years ago," she wrote, "my soul would have been torn apart, but five years is a lot of days and every one of them has taught me the same thing . . ." She knew she had to go on living and she knew that she would. Their "catastrophe of a meeting" was yet to come.

In late June 1935 Pasternak came to Paris for ten days, for the International Congress of Writers in the Defence of Culture. He had been depressed for some time and had at first refused to go to the Congress but had been forced to do so on the direct orders of Stalin. At some point, either in a corridor of the Congress building or in his hotel Pasternak "saw" Tsvetaeva and her family; this is the verb he himself used of their meeting in a letter to Titsian Tabidze. Tsvetaeva referred to it as a "non-meeting". And a week before Pasternak left Paris, she went on holiday with Mur to the seaside. It may indeed be true that Mur had just had his appendix removed, that she needed to take him somewhere to convalesce, that she had bought cheap train tickets long before she knew Pasternak would be coming . . . Nevertheless, in the past she had said that, for the sake of a meeting with Pasternak, she would travel – at the drop of a hat – to the furthest corner of Europe.

Their previous mutual understanding had clearly evaporated. It may well be that Pasternak was no longer so enamoured of Tsvetaeva's poetry; his own creative evolution was leading him in a very different direction. This is partly confirmed by his first letter to her after his return to Moscow: listing the symptoms of a depression that had lasted several months, he includes the fact that, "although I had your offprints, I didn't read them". In the past something written by Tsvetaeva could have cured him from any illness whatsoever. And when Pasternak finally did read these offprints, his response was uncharacteristically restrained.

Whatever the reasons for the barrier that had arisen between them, neither of them was able to overcome it. There were probably many contributing factors. Pasternak was not only depressed – he was also terrified, and he was acutely aware of the falsity of his position at the Congress. And Tsvetaeva was shy, proud, quick to take offence, and suffering from an increasing sense of isolation as her marriage deteriorated. According to her daughter, she was unable to understand that such a thing as depression could even exist. Rather than attempting to understand the full horror of Pasternak's position, she just expressed haughty surprise: "Boris Pasternak – whom for years on end, in spite of the hundreds of miles between us, I had looked on as a second self – whispered to me at the Writers' Congress: 'I didn't dare not to come, S(talin)'s secretary called on me, I was frightened'." Did Pasternak really not make any further attempt to explain? And could she not hear the shout in his whispered words: "Marina, don't go back to Russia, it's cold there, there's a constant draught"? He was, after all, shouting a line of her own poetry:

> That the Russian draught should blow away my soul!

She didn't hear. It may be that he muffled this shout with other, contradictory remarks. In a letter to Nikolay Tikhonov she writes:

> I get a confused feeling from Boris. I find him difficult because everything that is right for me is for him a vice or an illness.
> How he spoke to me, then: "Why are you crying?" "I'm not crying, it's my eyes crying." "If I'm not crying now, it's because I've decided to restrain myself from all hysterical or neurotic behaviour . . ." (I was so surprised that I straightaway stopped crying.) ". . . You will come to love the collective farms."

> > In reply to my tears – "Collective farms"!
> > In reply to my feelings – "Chelyuskin"!*

All we can say for sure is that they never had a real conversation. Tsvetaeva never told him about the conflict that was tearing her family apart, and he never told her about his own life or about what was happening in the Soviet Union. In his memoirs Ilya Erenburg paints an idyllic picture: "During the debates Marina Tsvetaeva read poetry to Pasternak in the corridor". Needless to say, it would have been impossible to talk about anything in a corridor!

A few days later Pasternak met Lomonosova. In a letter to her husband, dated 6 July 1935, she describes their meeting: "Pasternak and a group of other people arrived the day before yesterday. He is in a terrible moral and physical state. The whole situation is sadistically absurd. It's impossible to write about it all. I'll tell you . . . To live in eternal fear! No, it would be better to be cleaning out lavatories." Lomonosova clearly relates

---

* The icebreaker *Chelyuskin*, built in 1933 and named after Semyon Chelyuskin, the eighteenth-century Russian polar explorer, set out to voyage from Murmansk to Vladivostok in a single navigation, but was crushed by artic ice and sank, in February 1934. Tsvetaeva wrote a poem about the heroic crew of the *Chelyuskin* in October 1934.

Pasternak's depression to the general "situation" in Russia. Unable to do this, Tsvetaeva herself left Paris with a heavy sense of perhaps irrevocable loss. She and Pasternak were to meet once more – several years later, in Moscow.

Tsvetaeva's six months in the Vendée are coloured by Pasternak – and also by Rilke, whom Pasternak "gave" to her. Pasternak had idolized Rilke since his youth; when he heard from his father that Rilke knew of him and thought well of his poetry, Pasternak wrote to him. In this first – and only – letter he told Rilke about Tsvetaeva, gave him her address in Paris and asked him to send her some of his books. Rilke did as Pasternak asked. For Tsvetaeva this was as great a miracle as her friendship with Pasternak himself – or a greater one: Pasternak was her equal, but Rilke was one of the gods, the most recent incarnation of Orpheus: "a German Orpheus, that is to say Orpheus who *this time* has appeared in Germany. Not *Dichter – Geist der Dichtung* [Not a poet – but the spirit of poetry]". It was for this reason that she had never approached Rilke herself – just as she had been reluctant to approach Aleksandr Blok. To correspond with him, to receive copies of his books with dedicatory inscriptions, to send him copies of her books and know that they were lying on his writing desk and that he was trying to read them (Rilke had known Russian well in his youth, but had forgotten most of it) – all this was more than enough.

The essence of Tsvetaeva's life now became poetry and her intense correspondence with Rilke and Pasternak. Everyday life – taking Mur for walks, sitting with him and Alya on the beach, shopping, washing and cleaning, cooking meals – all this went on but appears to have been less of a burden than usual. The family were in good health, Mur was learning to walk, Alya was growing up, Efron was resting and recovering his health. Life flowed smoothly on – although not entirely without unpleasant incidents.

In the middle of the summer of 1926 Tsvetaeva received a letter from Bulgakov to the effect that her Czech grant would be cut off unless she returned to Czechoslovakia. Efron replied to it:

> Your letter was a bolt from the blue. Our position is as follows. Counting on the Czech (Zavazal's)* half-promise, we have squandered all the money earned in Paris on the rental of rooms in the Vendée. We have paid up till the middle of October. We were intending to live on Marina's literary grant. My salary from *Mileposts* doesn't count, since I am paid by

---

* Dr Zavazal was in charge of Russian emigration matters in the Czechoslovak Ministry of Foreign Affairs.

the issue, rather than monthly – and only kopecks at that (which have been spent long ago). And now, without warning, this terrible (I do not exaggerate) material blow – which, of course, is also a blow of several other kinds . . .

For the first time in ten years we have had the chance to take a holiday by the sea – and then comes this blow. It is as though we are being mocked by Fate.

All of the writers in Paris are comfortable except us. In order to get oneself fixed up comfortably one needs to grovel. You know Marina.

Tsvetaeva and Efron saw the refusal of a grant – perhaps with justification – as the result of the intrigues of her Russian "friends". Letters and requests were immediately sent to Prague. Tsvetaeva's main intercessor was Bulgakov himself. A month later it was decided that her grant – reduced from 1000 to 500 crowns – should be continued for another two months, until she returned to Czechoslovakia. After subsequent discussion it was agreed that this reduced grant should be continued indefinitely.

Time-consuming as they were, none of these anxieties appears to have seriously upset Tsvetaeva. After telling Pasternak, in a letter, that she might be losing her only constant source of income, she told him how a scornful comment made by Mayakovsky had been passed on to her. She then added: "*Between ourselves* – such an attack from Mayakovsky grieves me much more than the Czech grant . . .". This was not bravado on Tsvetaeva's part – nothing merely material could ever wound her deeply.

During the summer Tsvetaeva wrote three *poemy** concerning her relationships with Pasternak and with Rilke: "From the Sea", "Attempt at a Room" and "Staircase". They are all extremely complex. She described "From the Sea" as being "instead of a letter". It is both like a letter and like a dream. In the poem she is carried by the sea wind from St-Gilles to Moscow, where she appears to Pasternak in a dream. The poem fulfils the promise she had made to Pasternak in "Wires":

> . . . sleep
> Brings together all that is asunder.
> Perchance in dream we'll see each other.

In this "shared" dream, she gives Pasternak a present of some "splinters" thrown up by the sea: crab-shells, cockle-shells, the skin of a snake . . . In the dream these objects seem linked to the relationship between the dreamers – and to human relationships in general:

* Long narrative poems.

This? – is some left-over of love . . .

(. . .)

This is a nibbled piece – not of love, but
Of conscience. What should one shed
A tear for – I gnaw it . . .

(. . .)

This – and tomorrow's fragment
Of our game . . .

(. . .)

Stop: the sloughed off skin of the rattle-snake:
Jealousy! Renewing itself,
It was called pride.

As happens in dreams, all this is interwoven with apparently quite irrelevant themes: censorship, the origin of the earth, the birth of life, Russia. Everything is linked together by the image of the sea. The sea is alien and incomprehensible, it knows nothing of human joy or sorrow; nevertheless, Tsvetaeva still hopes to find something human in it.

The sea was playing. To play is to be good . . .

(. . .)

The sea was playing, to play is to be stupid . . .

(. . .)

The sea grew tired, to be tired is to be good . . .

At the same time the sea represents a separation that can be overcome only in dreams:

The sea relates one to Moscow . . .

This may have been Tsvetaeva's last impossible hope . . . In the poem, however, the sea is embodied in something quite concrete: what links "Soviet Russia to the Ocean" is a starfish. The five-pointed star of Soviet Russia, the country that has renounced the Star of Bethlehem, is seen as the most ancient star of all – the starfish:

That on the poop of the ship, Russia,
Lies all its failure:
A thing of five points . . .

These lines express a veiled hope that Soviet Russia may be doomed, may be wrecked under the sign of the "sea-star" or star-fish. There is also a considerably more overt pun, running through the entire poem, on the name "Marina" – woman of the sea. What she has brought as a present to Pasternak is herself – together with all the sea's little splinters and fragments, together with everything inside her, whether dark or light.

Tsvetaeva's name is also used to explain a remarkable coincidence. In the dedicatory inscription on his last book of poems, written in French and entitled *Vergers*, which he sent her that same summer, Rilke had presented Tsvetaeva with "gifts of the sea":

> Please accept the sand and seashells from the bottom
> Of the French waters of my soul –
> Which is so strange . . .

Long ago Mandelstam too had given her sand – sand from Koktebel – as a keepsake:

> Please accept from me the sand
> Which I pour from palm to palm . . .

Surely the sand she is now playing with, on the shores of the Ocean, is the same sand?

> Only sand, which flows between the fingers . . .
>
> (. . .)
>
> Only sand, which splashes between the fingers . . .

Mandelstam and Rilke give presents of sand to Tsvetaeva, she then gives sand and seashells to Pasternak. Why such strange presents? The answer may be in some lines of Mandelstam:

> All steal from eternity,
> But eternity is like the sand of the sea . . .

Through giving each other "splinters" of sea, they become part of Eternity themselves. As Tsvetaeva writes in "From the Sea":

> Eternity, flourish an oar!
> Draw us in . . .

The poem "Attempt at a Room" is equally dreamlike. It began, according to Tsvetaeva herself, as an answer to a question of Rilke's: "What will the room be like where we meet?" Attempting to imagine this room, Tsvetaeva discovers – probably unexpectedly – that this meeting can never take place in the real world, that a meeting of souls is possible only in "the other world", in the "palace of Psyche" . . . The walls, the floor, the furniture, the house itself are transformed before her eyes into something intangible, into a vacuum between the sky's "eye" of light and the earth's green "breach". In this emptiness Rilke and Tsvetaeva also became incorporeal:

> . . . Above the *nothingness* of two bodies
> The ceiling truly sang –
> With all the angels' voices.

In retrospect, "Attempt at a Room" turned out to be not only a renunciation of the possibility of ever meeting Rilke but also an anticipation of his imminent death.

In August 1926 Rilke suddenly stopped answering Tsvetaeva's letters. At the end of the summer Tsvetaeva and her family moved to Bellevue, a Paris suburb. They were never again, after the rue Rouvet, to live in Paris itself; during the next twelve years they lived in four different flats in three different suburbs. In early November Tsvetaeva sent Rilke a postcard with her new address and no message except the words "Do you still love me?" She received no answer. She knew he was unwell, but could not conceive that he might be mortally ill. On 29 December 1926 Rilke died. And on December 31 Tsvetaeva learnt of his death.

> On the twenty-ninth, on Wednesday, into the mist?
> Into the clear? There is no information! –
> Not only you and I are orphaned
> On this penultimate
> Morning . . .

This first response to the news was naturally addressed to Pasternak: the two of them had been orphaned together. For both of them this death turned out to be simultaneously a wound that was slow to heal and a creative stimulus. Tsvetaeva wrote "New Year's Greeting",* her one and only requiem.

To call it her only requiem may seem surprising. Tsvetaeva did indeed go on to write poems on the death of three other poets: Vladimir Mayakovsky (1930), Maksimilian Voloshin (1932) and Nikolay Gronsky (1935). She knew all three of these poets personally. She had met Mayakovsky in Moscow and she followed everything he wrote; unlike most

---

* *Novogodnee.* See note on p. 40. A translation of this poem by Walter Arndt can be found on pp. 222–28 of *Letters, Summer 1926: Boris Pasternak, Marina Tsvetayeva, Rainer Maria Rilke* (see Bibliography).

émigrés, she considered him a real and talented poet. In autumn 1928 she wrote an open letter* to him which caused her to be branded as "pro-Soviet". Some émigré circles began to ostracize her and the important daily newspaper, *Latest News*, stopped publishing poems from *The Camp of the Swans*. It was five years before the newspaper published any of her work again – a serious financial blow. There was, of course, nothing pro-Soviet in Tsvetaeva's letter to Mayakovsky; it was simply that in many circles the least mention of Mayakovsky was like a red rag to a bull. To Tsvetaeva he was a poet – something far more important than any ephemeral, political beliefs he might happen to hold.

Mayakovsky's suicide in April 1930 was the occasion for hypocritical "excuses" from the Soviets and torrents of abuse from the émigrés. Amidst all this, Tsvetaeva's cycle "To Mayakovsky", composed in August-September, struck a jarring note:

> The departed – once each century –
> Comes back . . .

It is possible that these lines are an answer to Khodasevich, who had asserted, both before and after Mayakovsky's death: "He has trampled over Russian literature with the gait of a horse – and I think he is now at the end of his path. A horse's life is fifteen years." Perhaps the phrase, "the gait of a horse" led Tsvetaeva to focus on the "rough, strong boots, tipped with iron" that Mayakovsky wore in his coffin. These words from a newspaper serve as an epigraph to the third poem in the cycle:

> In heavy boots, which were tipped with iron,
> In boots, in which he took the hill . . .
>
> (. . .)
>
> In heavy boots, in which, with knitted brow,
> He bore the hill and took it and cursed it and sang.

(no one appears to have noticed the word "cursed")

---

* *Author's Note*: The following is the text of Tsvetaeva's article about Mayakovsky as published in *Eurasia* on 24 November 1928:

TO MAYAKOVSKY

On 28 April 1922, on the eve of my departure from Russia, I met Mayakovsky early in the morning on Kuznetsky Bridge [in Moscow], which was entirely deserted.
  "Well, Mayakovsky, and what do you have to say to Europe?"
  "That the truth is here."
On 7 November 1928, as I left the Café Voltaire [in Paris] late in the evening, I was asked:
  "What would you say about Russia after Mayakovsky's reading?"
  "That strength is over there."

(. . .)

In heavy boots, almost like a diver's:
A foot-soldier's, or in clearer speech:

In heavy boots of a grandiose campaign . . .

Where other émigrés saw Mayakovsky as fawning on the Bolsheviks, Tsvetaeva saw him as serving the Revolution. Mayakovsky was still the "leading soldier" of contemporary revolutionary poetry, its "ringleader". "Without him the Russian Revolution would have suffered a grave loss, just as Mayakovsky would have been the poorer without the Revolution," Tsvetaeva was to write two and a half years later, as she began to look more deeply into the reasons for his suicide. In 1930, however, she was still content to accept the official explanation. While she was in the middle of writing the poem-cycle, she asked Salomeya Andronikova: "how do you see Mayakovsky's end? Do you think it has to do with the woman he was in love with during his last visit? Is is true that she got married?" Tsvetaeva, of course, could understand this story only too easily; in Prague she might well have committed suicide herself but for "Poem of the Mountain" and "Poem of the End". The theme of these two poems is, after all, perfectly summarized by the famous line from Mayakovsky's last poem: "The boat of love has smashed against everyday life." In her pity for Mayakovsky there is pity both for herself and for anyone else in a similar position:

> – My beloved enemy!
> There are no new love-boats
> Under the moon.

Tsvetaeva reproaches Mayakovsky – who had himself not so long ago condemned Esenin's suicide – for being untrue to himself:

> Like the Junker, who, at the opera,
> Fired a shot – from dejection!
> Fellow! Not like Mayakovsky
> Do you act, but à la Shakhovskoy*.

There is no mockery in this irony, however, only a sense of tragedy.

The complex structure of the cycle is similar to that of Mayakovsky's early poem "Man". The sixth and central poem corresponds to the chapter "Mayakovsky in the Sky". But while Mayakovsky hides the element of tragedy under a clown's mask, Tsvetaeva brings it out into the foreground. The meeting in the other world between the newly arrived Mayakovsky

* *Author's note:* Tsvetaeva is referring to the princely family Shakhovsky as representatives of the aristocracy for whom suicide would have been a more natural mode of behaviour than for the proletarian poet Mayakovsky.

and the "old-timer" Esenin takes place in the unseen presence of the bloodstained shades of three Russian poets who had died in the last decade: Blok, Sologub and Gumilyov. It is as though Tsvetaeva had almost understood the reasons for Mayakovsky's suicide, but not quite pursued her thoughts to their conclusion. Her main concern is to defend Mayakovsky's honour, to protect him from slander, to proclaim for him "Eternal Memory".

"Ici-haut", the cycle addressed to Voloshin, is in this respect very similar. But in "New Year's Greeting" her main concern is with the problem of immortality. And whereas "New Year's Greeting" is suffused with a sense of piercing loss, in the two later poems any sense of loss is muffled by the fiercely combative tone.

Rilke had never been a reality in Tsvetaeva's life, and it is perhaps for this reason that she needed to feel it was still possible to communicate with his soul. His absence left an emptiness in the world that could only be filled by the knowledge of his presence in the heavens – or rather of his omnipresence. In order to be sure of this, Tsvetaeva goes as far as denying the concepts of life and death:

> Life and death I long since put in quotes,
> Like rumours already known to be empty.

She could survive without others, but separation from Rilke was unthinkable. Unlike the poems in memory of Mayakovsky, Voloshin and Gronsky, "New Year's Greeting" is a true requiem – imbued as it is with the lacerating pain of separation, the solemnity of saying farewell and, most important of all, with Tsvetaeva's joy in resurrection.

Evidently Tsvetaeva's religious sense changed over the years. "To Mayakovsky", "Ici-haut" and "Epitaph" (her poem in memory of Nikolay Gronsky) were written respectively three and a half, five and a half, and eight years after "New Year's Greeting". The irony with which she treats the belief in immortality in the last of these poems is surprising:

> Only in fairytales and paintings
> Do people go to heaven! . . .

Tsvetaeva had been friends with Gronsky when he was still almost a boy. He had become enamoured of Tsvetaeva and her poetry and had written poems to her himself. She was delighted by his enthusiasm and wanted to make him her pupil. Their friendship had been at its most intense during the summer of 1928 and they had then gradually stopped seeing one another. In late 1934, after his accidental death – he fell under a train in the Paris metro – his parents had asked her to go through his papers. As she

looked through his almost unread poems, Tsvetaeva began a cycle of poems
in his memory:

> In vain by eye – as though with nail,
> I pierce through the black soil:
> Acknowledging – more truly than the nail:
> That you are not here, that you are not.

While she was grieving over Rilke, Tsvetaeva had asserted that the
only place where he could not be found was the tomb. His presence was
everywhere. Gronsky, however, was neither in the sky, not was he
anywhere else:

> In vain I turn my gaze
> And scour the vault of heaven:
> – Rain! Nothing but a tub of water.
> You are not there, and you are not.

For Tsvetaeva, Gronsky has departed, entirely and irrevocably, and the
only place where he remains is in the memory of those who love him:

> And if somewhere you *are*,
> It's in us. For you, departed,
> The highest honour is to disdain
> The split: You've gone. You've altogether gone.

It would be wrong, however, to conclude with any certainty that Tsvetaeva
had lost her belief in immortality. It may simply be that Rilke was the only
one of these poets whom she saw as an "immortal" genius.

It is significant that the four poem-cycles discussed above are all works of
some length, almost short *poemy*. Ever since her years in Prague, Tsvetaeva
had been moving away from the purely lyrical. In 1923 Tsvetaeva had
retorted to Bakhrakh – who had written in a review of *Craft* that her future
path would lead to "pure music": "No! From the Lyric (which is almost
Music) to the Epic. The flute, having given all that it can, must fall
silent . . .". It is not that her lyric impulse had dried up, simply that her
poems were no longer a "lyrical diary", an essential reflection of each day.
This shift had begun while she was working on "Poem of the Mountain" and
"Poem of the End", and had been completed with "The Rat-catcher". By
sub-titling this poem "a lyrical satire", Tsvetaeva clearly emphasized that,
whatever the genre, she still considered her writing to be lyrical. This
emphasis is entirely justified: Tsvetaeva's tragedies, her long poems and

even her prose are indeed lyrical. And she did, of course, continue to write short lyrics — around ninety in the last thirteen years of her life, including such fine poems as "Homesickness . . .", "To the Fathers" and "Desk".

During the late twenties and early thirties Tsvetaeva wrote a considerable number of "lyrical epics": "Phaedra" (1927), "Poem of the Air" (1927), "The Red Steer" (1928), "Perekop" (1928–9), an unfinished poem "The Singer" (1935), and her last long poem, "The Bus" (1934–6). And throughout this period, from 1929 to 1936, she was also working on an epic about the end of the last Tsar and his family. As always, she was "one against all". If by 1929 even "people who had fought there had lost interest in Perekop", then who – in the middle of the thirties – needed a poem about the Tsar's Family? Tsvetaeva was not a monarchist and had never been linked to the far right. In her own words: "I was never – because of their profound philistinism – published by the right." By the time she was working on her epic, she and Efron were more often suspected of Bolshevism than of sympathy for the overthrown House of Romanov. What made her take up this theme, conscious as she was that "the thing I am writing now will lie around unpublished for longer than anything else"? She herself answered the question as follows: "No one needs it . . . Posterity? No. It's just so I can have a clear conscience. And because I have a sense of strength: of love and, if you like, talent. Among those who love them only I can do it. And so I must." If Tsvetaeva loved the Tsar's Family, it was of course because of their tragic fate. She would never have written odes to a ruling dynasty. When an editor refused to print her "Opening of the Museum" because of its "sympathy towards certain members of the Tsarist Dynasty", she said indignantly: "That's exactly it – to him they're a "Dynasty", to me they're a *family!*"

Mark Slonim was told by Tsvetaeva "that she had first conceived the poem long before, as an answer to Mayakovsky's 'The Emperor'." She saw Mayakovsky's poem as an attempt to justify a terrible execution on the grounds that it was the "verdict of history"; believing as she did that it was the duty of poetry to take the part of the defeated, Tsvetaeva felt morally bound to reply. Her first mention of "something big" was in the summer of 1929 when she turned to Salomeya Andronikova for help in finding materials. In late August she told her: "I've read everything available on the Tsaritsa, and I've got hold of one very interesting unpublished account – by an officer who was a patient in her field hospital . . .". Tsvetaeva was now working in a new genre, and she was full of enthusiasm: "A huge amount of work: a mountain, I'm Glad."

Tsvetaeva understood how to work with the raw historical data that she was transforming into poetry. She had written in "The Poet on the Critic" that "for me any contribution from the outside world is a gift . . . One cannot write weightlessly about weightless things" and that she listened with especial attention "to the voice of all workmen and artisans". At the time most critics had treated these words with scepticism, but Tsvetaeva's sincerity is confirmed by her work on "Perekop", "Poems to Bohemia" and "Poem on the Royal Family". And what I find most striking of all is a story I once heard from the poet and translator, Semyon Lipkin.

Lipkin, the translator of the Kalmyk epic, "Dzhangar", once happened to tell Tsvetaeva that in the first version of "The Monument" Pushkin had written: "the Kalmyk, the *son* of the steppes". N. Bichurin, a well-known Orientalist, however, had remarked to Pushkin that the Kalmyks, far from being indigenous inhabitants of the steppes, had only migrated there from the mountains in the seventeenth century. Pushkin had then immediately altered the line to "the Kalmyk, the *friend* of the steppes". This story had filled Tsvetaeva with delight: "That's the way one must work! All lyricism must be based on knowledge."

Tsvetaeva worked slowly and painstakingly for many years on both the poem itself and the associated historical research. She never had any hope of seeing the poem in print; and there were very few people, even among her close friends, whom she could expect to be sympathetic towards it. There are occasional, somewhat brief, mentions of the poem in her correspondence. She included an early outline in a letter to Lomonosova: "I am now writing a long poem on the Tsar's Family (their end). I have written: The Journey by River to Tobolsk – Tobolsk of the Governors (Ermak, the Tatars, Tobolsk *before* it became Tobolsk, when it was still called 'Isker' or 'Sibir' – the origin of the word 'Siberia'). Still to come are: The Royal Family in Tobolsk, the road to Ekaterinburg, Ekaterinburg – the road to The Mine of the Four Brothers (there the burning was done) . . .". Unfortunately, all we now have left of the poem is the short chapter, "Sibir" – or, as Tsvetaeva originally referred to it, "Tobolsk of the Governors" – which was published in Tsvetaeva's lifetime; both the rough drafts and the completed manuscripts of the rest of the poem were lost during the war. We do, however, know – from Mark Slonim's memoirs – that the poem was eventually completed. He heard Tsvetaeva read it – it took her over an hour – in early 1936. He writes that "some chapters deeply stirred" him, that "they had a tragic resonance and were successful as literature", and that this reading, which took place at the Lebedevs', was followed by heated argument as to the poem's political implications. Unfortunately the Socialist Revolutionaries no longer had their own journal. *The Will of Russia* had folded several years before – and there was no one else who would publish the poem. This may be one of the reasons why it took so long to write and why Tsvetaeva had sometimes felt she would never be able to complete it.

Another reason why it took so long may well be that Tsvetaeva changed her mind about which historical events to include. In the outline sent to Lomonosova, the poem begins with the Tsar and his family being sent off to Siberia. But it is clear from her letters to Salomeya Andronikova that Tsvetaeva became interested in preceding events: the coronation, Khodynka,* the Russo-Japanese War, and Rasputin. She may well also have included other events that were not mentioned in the original plan.

There is no doubt that Tsvetaeva studied the history of this period with the utmost thoroughness. The real task was the transformation of history into poetry. "The historian and the poet in me are locked in eternal and passionate combat", Tsvetaeva wrote in regard to some of her prose. "I know this from my enormous (unfinished) work on the Tsar's Family, where the historian drove out the poet." I am not sure whether we should take this statement at face value. The importance of Tsvetaeva's historical researches goes beyond this one important poem. As one link of a chain draws the next link behind it, so this poem led to "Grandfather Ilovaysky" and to the short essays about Tsvetaeva's father, Ivan Vladimirovich Tsvetaev, and the museum he created: "The Museum of Alexander III", "The Laurel Wreath" and "The Opening of the Museum". Tsvetaeva's train of thought is very natural: Ilovaysky was not only her "grandfather" but also a convinced monarchist, one of the most conservative of Russian historians. Tsvetaeva wrote that her sense of Russian history came from "grandfather's" textbooks – books that had been banned from her numerous, always liberal, schools, but which were written with true artistry: "we see *living* people, living tsars and tsaritsas – even living monks, living scoundrels, living villains!" Tsvetaeva had heard from her brother Andrey that Ilovaysky had dreamed of continuing his portrait of Russian history "right up to the present day". This is precisely what Tsvetaeva attempted in her Poem on the Tsar's Family.

It was inevitable, however, that while she was collecting materials for it, Tsvetaeva should remember both her own meeting with the Tsar's Family at the opening of the museum and her father's account of a separate visit made to the museum by the Tsaritsa. One link in the chain of memories led to another. What Tsvetaeva eventually wrote was a living history of Russian culture, linked to the history of her own family. Insignificant as

* Festivities in Khodynka square, the day after Nicholas II's coronation in 1896, led to hundreds of deaths when spectators' stands collapsed.

some episodes of the "family chronicle" (as Tsvetaeva once called her essays) might appear at first glance, they all helped to complete the picture of an almost vanished world that she considered it her duty – as a daughter, a human being and a writer – to engrave for posterity. It is possible that, if she had had more time, Tsvetaeva might have gathered all her various memoirs into one whole. I have already said that her autobiographical prose brings together impressions remembered from childhood, philosophical and psychological meditations, and her own unique form of literary criticism. At the same time she succeeds in representing the intellectual and spiritual climate of the time, in portraying the generation of the "fathers" in whose honour she wrote the cycle "To the Fathers" (1935).

> In the world, which roars:
> – Glory to those who are to come!
> Something whispers in me:
> – Glory to those who have been!

These lines are a challenge. "Fathers and Sons" was one of the most burning issues of the day in émigré circles during the thirties. Tsvetaeva's answer, needless to say, was the opposite to that put forward by the majority. The thirties were a time when the elder generation was being blamed for all the woes of Russia. A number of neo-Bolshevik and Fascist organizations held sway over émigré youth, and the very concepts of democracy and the freedom of the individual were violently denied. All that mattered to members of these organizations was the collective.

As an individualist, Tsvetaeva naturally found all this extremely alien. "To the Fathers", however, arose not just from contrariness, but from a desire to determine her own genealogy, to find her roots. The world of the "fathers" entered her prose and poetry legitimately – it had attracted her since her youth. In 1913–14 she had written poems to the young generals of the year 1812 and to Sergey Efron. Her romantic ideal, an embodiment of which she had found in her husband, was one of fearlessness, loyalty and contempt for death. She had found other embodiments of this ideal in the generals who had first defended Russia against Napoleon and then taken part in the Decembrist revolt.

During her last years in Moscow she had found this same ideal embodied in the figures of Stakhovich and Volkonsky. If one is to generalize, one can probably best define the qualities which drew Tsvetaeva to these real people and imaginary heroes as: spiritual freedom, independence, inner dignity and truth to oneself. They could be summed up more simply as: "personality".

> To the generation with lilac
> And with Easter in the Kremlin,
> My greetings to the generation
> Up to their knees in the ground,
>
> To the greybeards in the stars!
> To you, more audible than rushes,
> – The air will give a ripple –
> You, who are saying: soul!

Tsvetaeva never dedicated any poems to her father, but I consider this cycle to be at least partly addressed to him. I say this not only because the poems were written at the same time as she was working on her autobiographical prose, but also because of the cast of mind she portrays in the poem:

> Generation that soared!
> That was drawn – *away from*
>
> The earth, *above* the earth, away
> From the worm and the seed!

Her father's devoted service to *his* dream – the museum – shows that he was certainly someone who "soared", someone who was contemptuous of "the flesh" and of material comfort:

> Generation! I am yours!
> Continuation of mirrors.
>
> Yours – in essence and being,
> And with respect for the mind
> And contempt for the temporary
> Clothes of our flesh!

Tsvetaeva saw the generation of "the fathers" as people like herself, people who chose their "own paths", even if they led to the scaffold, people who lived in the world of Being:

> To you, who have contrived *to be*
> Solely in the unprecedented . . .

Her profound sense of her own incompatibility with the contemporary world made it all the more crucial for her to seek moral support from a generation to whom she felt she belonged and to whom she felt deeply grateful:

> To those who turned towards a star
> Till the very last hour,
> Departing race,
> Thanks be to you!

It was not for nothing that Tsvetaeva turned to the past at this time. As well as being out of step with the outside world as a whole, Tsvetaeva was now losing a number of the people who were most precious to her. Rilke had died. Pasternak had remarried. Her relationship with members of her own family was deteriorating – as can be seen from the gradually changing tone of her letters. In a letter to Anna Tesková written in 1929 she placed herself in opposition to her husband for what was probably the first time: "S. Ya. ... lives ... through his love for Russia. But Mur, like me, lives through his love of life." In another letter to Tesková, written in 1932, she speaks of Alya with a certain bitterness: "during the seven years of my France, Alya has grown up and turned away from me." Her isolation grew increasingly intense over the years; in the end she had almost no escape from it apart from her epistolary romances. Her only inner support was from the past and from art.

The thirties were a time when Tsvetaeva had to reappraise all her values. To do this it was necessary to turn to prose. It is worth noting, incidentally, that Tsvetaeva never wrote to commission – only from inner necessity. The lasting values that she eventually found and which she examined in her prose were those of the world of her childhood and those of Poetry.

"MY PUSHKIN"

The years incline towards stern prose,
The years chase away playful rhymes . . .
ALEKSANDR PUSHKIN

A number of Tsvetaeva's contemporaries misunderstood the "my" in "My Pushkin" – the title of one of her essays – as a claim to personal possession, a claim that she alone could truly understand Pushkin. In fact, Tsvetaeva was using the word as a demonstrative rather than a possessive adjective; she meant that she was speaking of the Pushkin whom she had known and loved since before she could read – when all she had known of him was the statue on the Tverskoy Boulevard – to the present day. She wasn't trying to take Pushkin away from other people; she just wanted them to be able to read him through her eyes. I have said earlier – in connection with "The Poet on the Critic" – that this strictly personal approach was something very new, but that it was also adopted by Mayakovsky. Mayakovsky was himself frequently reproached for his constant use of the word "I", and he once answered half-jokingly: "If you want to declare your love for a girl, you don't say: 'We love you' . . .". Tsvetaeva would have appreciated this remark: everything she ever wrote about poets and poetry was first and foremost an expression of love and of gratitude.

In one of Tsvetaeva's early diaries there is a fine definition of gratitude: "*Reconnaissance* – recognition. To recognize – in spite of all the masks and wrinkles – the true face, once seen, at some particular time. (Gratitude)." She needed a French word because its scope is broader than that of the Russian [or English] equivalent. For Tsvetaeva to see truly – to recognize – is to feel grateful. And the task of anyone who writes about poetry is to express this gratitude.

The centre of Tsvetaeva's existence was poetry and the greatest of all poets was Pushkin. She turned to him repeatedly throughout her entire life. What is more remarkable of all is the lack of constraint in her relationship with Pushkin. In her early poem, "A Meeting with Pushkin" (1913) she talks to him just as though she were a little girl with a friend:

> We would have laughed and run
> Down the mountain, hand in hand.

Although her attitude towards Pushkin naturally changed as she grew older, this sense of a friendly, brotherly hand was never to leave her.

> All his wisdom
> Is power. It's bright – I look:
> I squeeze Pushkin's hand
> But do not lick it.

Tsvetaeva's first works about Pushkin were on the subject of his marriage and his subsequent death in a duel. The poems, "Happiness or Sorrow" (1916) and "Psyche" (1920) are unequivocal condemnations of Pushkin's wife and what is seen as her "emptiness": "To keep flourishing without a wrinkle on one's forehead", "The empty froth of a ballroom gown . . .". It was very like Tsvetaeva to refuse to accept Pushkin's wife and – as with Akhmatova, who also detested Natalya Goncharova – there was certainly an element of sexual jealousy in her attitude. That the whole story had been played out more than fifty years before either Akhmatova or Tsvetaeva had ever been born was entirely irrelevant to them. In her portrait (1929) of the other Natalya Goncharova, the modernist artist, Tsvetaeva took her thoughts about Pushkin's marriage to their logical conclusion. It was probably only because of their family relationship and the coincidence of name that she first became interested in the second Natalya Goncharova –

Tsvetaeva was an aural rather than a visual person and she was indifferent to the visual arts. The two women were introduced by Mark Slonim and they appear to have liked one another. First Tsvetaeva and then Alya would visit Goncharova's studio, and Alya studied with her for some time. Tsvetaeva had a brief friendship with Goncharova and studied her work. The friendship did not last – each was too deeply immersed in her own world – but it did bear fruit. Tsvetaeva wrote her fine sketch entitled "Natalya Goncharova" and Goncharova was inspired by Tsvetaeva's *poema* "The Swain" to do illustrations for it. This in turn inspired Tsvetaeva to translate "The Swain" into French – an experience that was to be of great help in her later attempts to translate Pushkin's poetry.

The main reason why Tsvetaeva hated Pushkin's wife – or "that woman" was that she felt her to be entirely soulless. "There was only one thing about her: she was a beauty. Just a beauty, nothing but a beauty – without the correction of mind, soul, heart or talent. Naked beauty that struck like a sword." The disparity between this "empty place" and the man she considered "more alive and livelier than all" hurt Tsvetaeva the more because of her deep conviction that genius needed understanding, needed "the participation of sympathy". Nonetheless she saw Pushkin's marriage not as an unfortunate coincidence but as a decree of fate: "Goncharova was not the reason but the occasion for Pushkin's death – something that had been predestined since the cradle"; "He took Goncharova, who did not love him, *in dem Kauf* (as part of the bargain) along with D'Anthès, that is along with his own death." In Tsvetaeva's ruthlessness towards Natalya Goncharova I believe one can hear the claim she made more directly in regard to Blok: if *I* had been there beside him, he would never have died.

It is not surprising, given Tsvetaeva's views on Pushkin's wife, that she was so delighted by *The Duel and Death of Pushkin*, a book by P. Shchogolev that she first read in summer 1931. Without being so extreme as Tsvetaeva, he puts forward a well-argued view which she recognized as very similar to her own. In one letter she wrote: "that was when I was reading Shchogolev and choking with indignation." She was full of indignation against all "hypocrites both then and now", against everyone who contrived to transform the living, passionate, contradictory and unpredictable figure of Pushkin into the tedium of anthologies and "scholarship" – everyone who tore him apart into quotations as though they were trying to kill him again.

Pushkin – measured by a Pushkinist?

This passionate indignation was the driving impulse behind "Poems to

Pushkin", a cycle that was published in part in 1937, the centenary of his death.

In a review of this cycle Khodasevich remarked that the poem, "Scourge of the gendarmes, god of the students", perhaps contained too much argument with Pushkin's admirers and too little about Pushkin himself – "although what 'narration' it does contain is excellent". This reproach is not entirely justified: in her dispute with the "Pushkinists" Tsvetaeva does also describe Pushkin as he appears to her:

> Ruddier and *swarthier* than all
> In the whole wide world till now,
> More alive and livelier than all!
> Pushkin in the role of mausoleum?
>
> (. . .)
>
> What are you up to, pygmies,
> Bluer than olive-trees is this
> Most free, most extreme
> Brow – which you've branded
>
> For ever with the double baseness
> Of gold and a golden mean?

The scope of the cycle is broad. Pushkin as someone with the muscles of an athlete, as an inexhaustible walker, as a lover of cards, as a hard worker. Many of the details are drawn from Veresaev's book, *Pushkin in Life*:

> Scourge of gendarmes, god of students,
> Plague of husbands, delight of wives . . .
>
> (. . .)
>
> With saucy eyes and ready grin . . .
>
> (. . .)
>
> Stretching out his feet to warm them
> And jumping on the table in
> The presence of the Emperor
> This wilful African –
>
> A laughing matter for our ancestors . . .?

Pushkin is portrayed as the great-grandson of Peter the Great's Arab and the true heir to Peter the Great himself ("Peter and Pushkin"):

> The last – posthumous – immortal
> Gift to Russia – from Peter.

He is portrayed not as a man of inspiration – perhaps because that is a secret to be kept hidden from the uninitiated – but as someone who, like her, worked hard at his poems:

> To an ancestor – a workmate:
> In the same workshop!
> Every mark of a pencil
> As though by his hand.

She is not embarrassed to call herself Pushkin's direct descendant: she has won this right through her labours and her inspiration.

We see Pushkin caught in the tenacious grip of Nicholas I, who disliked and feared him:

> Pitiful gendarme
> Of Pushkin's fame.
>
> Faulting the author,
> Pruning the manuscript . . .

Tsvetaeva described "Poems to Pushkin" as "terribly abrupt, terribly free, having nothing in common with the canonized Pushkin, but in every way antithetical to the canon". This is Pushkin "through the eyes of someone who loves him", not Pushkin "through the eyes of the mob". Tsvetaeva's polemical fervour, however, has the adverse effect of making her portrait of Pushkin somewhat external, more a portrait of his life than an evocation of the spirit of his poetry.

Her sketch, "Natalya Goncharova", contains an interesting observation on the repetition of themes in Goncharova's work. She begins by asking why particular themes keep returning in the artist's work. Goncharova herself answers that it is a matter of "getting rid of something", that "to do something definitively means to get rid of it". Tsvetaeva then asks, "What is it, in general, that one returns to?" and answers: "To what has not been completed (and is hateful) and to what one cannot bear to part with (and is loved), i.e. to what has not been completed by you and to what has not been perfected within you." A little further on she writes: "The repetition of themes is the development of a problem, its growth". It is curious that Tsvetaeva relates this idea solely to artists, "to an alien art", and denies its application to poetry. Her own poetry, of course, contains many examples of repeated themes and images: Orpheus, the Sibyl, trees – to name just a few . . . And one of the themes which "flowed without interruption, like an underground river, appearing here and disappearing there" through Tsvetaeva's writings of the thirties was Pushkin himself.

303

His figure appears, each time from a different point of view, in all her works on poetry. It is as though Pushkin lived within Tsvetaeva, accompanying all her later reflections on poetry and literature; as though he compensated for the absence of contemporaries equal to herself.

In "Art in the Light of Conscience", which was begun soon after the completion of "Poems to Pushkin", Tsvetaeva takes a further step in her understanding of Pushkin. Prose allowed her to deliberate in a way that seemed impossible in poetry. In her analysis of Walsingham's song from *Feast in Time of Plague*, Tsvetaeva penetrates into the psychology of poetic creativity. Now she immerses us in Pushkin, writing about him "from the inside", just as Pushkin himself had created Walsingham, just as all poetic images are created. She identifies Pushkin with Walsingham in order to demonstrate to the reader the process through which "the elements" act on, and are then "overcome" by, the poet. Tsvetaeva uses Walsingham's song as evidence for the main thesis of her article: that art is outside morality. Song – like Poetry in general – is the highest manifestation of enchantment, a glorification of the elemental and so – from a religious point of view – can only be seen as blasphemy. By overcoming the enchantment through song, by ridding himself of it and thus saving himself, the poet "aims" the enchantment at the reader. It is impossible to resist the temptation of true poetry and, in particular, that of these lines from Walsingham's song in Pushkin's *Feast in Time of Plague*:

> All, all that threatens ruin,
> Promises for the mortal heart
> Pleasures indescribable . . .

"Art is a test,"* claims Tsvetaeva, "perhaps the last, most refined, most insuperable of earth's temptations . . ." In her analysis of *Feast in Time of Plague* Tsvetaeva develops the idea, first expressed in "The Poet on the Critic", that "the thing [or: the work] uses me to write itself". This idea was one of her deepest and most unchanging convictions. After speaking of the genius Pushkin showed in not balancing "Hymn to Plague" by a prayer, thus leaving the reader still under the power of the enchantment, Tsvetaeva adds: "It is unlikely that Pushkin thought about any of this. One can only think a thing through in reverse, from the last step taken to the first, walking with sight the path you first walked blind." It is this subjection "to the elements", this independence of the work – "which writes itself" – that will justify the poet at the "Last Judgment of the Word". The danger for the

---

* Tsvetaeva plays on the very similar words *iskusstvo* (art) and *iskus* (test; or – temptation; or – novitiate).

poet is to allow "the hand to outrun the ear", to escape momentarily from the power of inspiration. This can happen even to the greatest of geniuses. Tsvetaeva then shows how the last two lines of the "Hymn" not only fail to add anything to the preceding lines, but even contradict them, falling from the height of inspiration to the level of "merely authorial" composition. Further on, with a similar lack of reverence, Tsvetaeva says of Pushkin's famous "Bird of God", "who knows neither cares nor labour", that no such birds exist, that "the lines were clearly written about a butterfly" and that "Pushkin's bird is poetic licence". She was indeed writing of "her Pushkin" – someone she knew, read, loved and learned from but was never awed by. Her prose confirms what she had already written in verse:

> I squeeze Pushkin's hand,
> But do not lick it.

Tsvetaeva felt the spirit of Pushkin to be constantly beside her. After hearing the news of Pasternak's marriage, she wrote in the letter to Lomonosova that I have already cited: "I keep living. I had put my last stake on the man. But I still have my work, my children and Pushkin's lines: 'There is no happiness in the world, but there is peace and *freedom*' . . .". Her work, her children and Pushkin – in that order – are what will remain with her till the end.

Tsvetaeva's theoretical constructions form an indissoluble whole with her analysis of literary texts. Her thinking is remarkably logical. The three short chapters of the essay "Art in the Light of Conscience", make up one integral unit. Tsvetaeva's logic is so powerful that, through her analysis of the "Hymn", she is able to say all that needs to be said both about *Feast in Time of Plague* and about Pushkin's inner world. Towards the end of the essay, after brief references to Goethe, Tolstoy, Gogol and Mayakovsky, she returns to Pushkin – almost as though to advertise her future essay, "Pushkin and Pugachov". In a meditation on what "belongs" to a poet and what is "alien" to him, she refers to Pushkin's example in "appropriating even miserliness" in "The Miserly Warrior" and "even untalentedness" in Salieri (in "Mozart and Salieri").

Five years later Tsvetaeva wrote "Pushkin and Pugachov" – Pushkin had indeed brought her and Pugachov together. This was to be the last piece she wrote on Pushkin, the last piece she wrote on her own childhood and in fact her last work on any literary theme. In my view, it is Tsvetaeva's finest prose-work, the beginning of what could have been a new stage in her development as a prose-writer.

In the first place, "Pushkin and Pugachov" is written in a genre that is new for Tsvetaeva. Her concern is not with some philosophical or theoretical problem, not with the work of a particular poet as a whole, but with two individual works by Pushkin: *The Captain's Daughter* and *A History of the Pugachov Uprising*. Her engagement in the details of the text does not in any way narrow the breadth of her vision or interfere with her freedom to generalize. The reader – and especially a reader brought up in the Soviet Union – is astonished by the boldness with which Tsvetaeva refers to Pugachov as one of the most romantic heroes of world literature and defines *The Captain's Daughter* as "the purest romanticism, the crystal of Romanticism". The reader is even convinced by the initially implausible comparison between Pugachov and Don Quixote.

Tsvetaeva's writing is now guided by a different logic, the logic of art rather than the logic of thought. In a passage about how, unrecognized by the author, the adolescent Grinyov – the narrator of *The Captain's Daughter* – is gradually replaced by Pushkin himself, with all the wisdom he has acquired over the years, she writes: "It is not an 'I' that makes a work autobiographical, but the essence of this 'I'. Pushkin did not realize, as he began the story with a conditional, borrowed 'I', that this 'I' would soon become real, would become Pushkin himself, his own flesh and blood." Her thoughts about the transformation of the Pugachov of *A History of the Pugachov Uprising* into the Pugachov of *The Captain's Daughter* are guided by the same order of logic, as is her explanation – based on "Hymn to Plague" – as to why it was impossible for Pushkin not to fall under the spell of the uprising.

As in "My Pushkin", Tsvetaeva is able to recapture the experience of reading Pushkin for the first time, as a child, without help or interference from adults. But now, instead of effacing herself in the subtext, the adult Tsvetaeva is allowed to appear more openly, interrupting the child's story with her own thoughts and judgements. Despite all I have said, however, I would not say that "Pushkin and Pugachov" marks a new stage in Tsvetaeva's career were it not for a remarkable change in her style.

Tsvetaeva herself defined the style of *The Captain's Daughter* as "Narrative calm and literary restraint". It is precisely these qualities that characterize the prose of "Pushkin and Pugachov". She had of course been gradually developing these qualities as she wrote her other essays, gradually sloughing off her excessive complexity and her tendency to let words run riot on the page. But "Pushkin and Pugachov" clearly shows the influence of Pushkin's own prose. Tsvetaeva's "narrative calm and verbal restraint" do not exclude either passion, logic or persuasiveness; they can perhaps best be understood as manifestations of a new wisdom that has no need for anything excessive but is sufficient to itself. Unfortunately, instead of leading to new possibilities, it was here that Tsvetaeva's "my" Pushkin broke off.

As well as her articles, Tsvetaeva wrote essays or memoirs on Valery Bryusov, Osip Mandelstam, Andrey Bely, Maksimilian Voloshin and Mikhail Kuzmin. These essays are not so much literary portraits as portraits of souls – both her own and that of the poet in question.

To write about someone, Tsvetaeva needed "the sign of *Kinship*". From her letters to G. P. Fedotov, the philosopher and an editor of the journal *New City*, we can see that "Epic and Lyric of Contemporary Russia: Vladimir Mayakovsky and Boris Pasternak" was originally intended as an article about Pasternak in relation to Soviet poetry as a whole. The idea of comparing Mayakovsky and Pasternak arose only after she had read a considerable amount of Soviet poetry and found most of it entirely alien to her. She also abandoned her plans – made soon after hearing the news of his suicide – for a long poem or drama about Sergey Esenin; probably she had come to feel that he too was alien to her. Neither politics or personal relations had anything to do with all this – all that mattered to Tsvetaeva were her feelings about the poetry. Her apostrophe to Mayakovsky is especially revealing: although all three words in "My beloved enemy!" are emphasized, "my" qualifies both the others and is clearly the most important word of all. Mayakovsky is Tsvetaeva's "enemy" because she cannot accept the ideas to which he is devoted; and he is "beloved" [also translatable as "kindred"] because their affinity as poets is more important than any political differences.

Tsvetaeva never wrote a whole article about Mayakovsky, although she did intend to. She found herself unable to forget about him; her thoughts kept returning to him – as though there were something about both his poetry and his death that she had failed to understand. She touches on these themes in three consecutive articles: "The Poet and Time", "Art in the Light of Conscience" and "Epic and Lyric of Contemporary Russia". In the first of these articles Tsvetaeva emphasizes his uniqueness: "A poet's marriage with his time is a forced marriage. A marriage which, like any violence to which he has been subjected, he feels ashamed of – and from which he tries to escape . . . Mayakovsky alone – an ascetic devotee of his conscience, a forced labourer of the present, has fallen in love with the present day; that is, he has overcome the poet in him." Tsvetaeva believed that Mayakovsky had attached more importance to his personal conscience – which demanded that he serve his time – than to his conscience as a poet –

which demanded that he free himself from any concerns except those of poetry.

Tsvetaeva considered Mayakovsky's ability to overcome the poet in him as his most distinctive peculiarity. In "Art in the Light of Conscience" she went so far as to call this ability an achievement. She then says: "For twelve years on end Mayakovsky the man killed Mayakovsky the poet, in the thirteenth year the poet rose up and killed the man." This is very different from the claim she had made in her poem-cycle: "The dead man shouted to the pioneers: Fall into line!" Tsvetaeva no longer imagines that Mayakovsky's death could have been any kind of appeal or summons. His tragic life – a constant battle between the man and the poet – had ended in a tragic death.

It was, of course, rumoured among the émigrés that Mayakovsky's suicide might have sprung from his disillusionment with the Soviet system. Khodasevich had strongly attacked this view, stating – somewhat crudely – that: "the singer of louts in revolt was becoming a singer in the pay of successful louts." Without directly confronting Khodasevich or anyone like him, Tsvetaeva continued to assert Mayakovsky's greatness in fulfilling his mission as the Poet of the Revolution. The reasons for his death seemed to her not completely clear. She returns to this question in the third of these articles, "Epic and Lyric", but her claim that "Mayakovsky finished himself off, like an enemy" is still somewhat ambiguous. One possible interpretation is that Mayakovsky destroyed the poet in him when he realized that this poet – as can be seen from his late satirical verses and his plays – was hostile to the cause he considered it his duty to serve. But whatever the reasons for his death, he remained "an ascetic devotee of his conscience" – and so it was impossible for Tsvetaeva to look on him simply as an enemy.

Even Tsvetaeva's highly critical essay on Valery Bryusov, ironically entitled "A Hero of Labour", was only written because Bryusov was in some way close to her. It was uncharacteristic of Tsvetaeva to attack a fellow poet, and this essay is the only one of its kind that she wrote. At one level it is a passionate and eloquent retort to the ill will that she believed Bryusov had shown her; the impulse behind it, however, is not only her sense of personal hurt, but also her disillusion with his poetry. She had passionately admired him in her youth, and this adolescent enthusiasm now seemed to her to be entirely unjustified. One remarkable quality of this essay is that, however much one enjoys Tsvetaeva's indignant and sarcastic debunking of Bryusov, it does not in the end make one feel any hostility towards him. At the same time as being an attack on Bryusov, the essay is also a hymn to his intelligence, erudition and diligence

– qualities that triumphed over the fact that he was not a born poet and so enabled him to become a writer, a translator, a teacher of poets and the organizer of the most important literary movement of the century. For all her hostility, Tsvetaeva is unable at times to restrain her admiration of Bryusov.

Mandelstam and Voloshin, on the other hand, were poets to whom she was bound by friendship and shared memories. "History of a Dedication" was written in 1931 in order to "defend" Mandelstam. Georgy Ivanov, in an article in his series "Chinese Shadows", had given a vulgar and inaccurate account of Mandelstam's youth and of life in Koktebel; more important, he had claimed that Mandelstam's poem "Not believing in the miracle of resurrection" was dedicated to some improbable female doctor and had recounted an entirely fictitious story of the relationship between her and Mandelstam. Tsvetaeva read Ivanov's article some time after its publication and immediately leapt into battle. After finishing her own article she wrote to Salomeya Andronikova: "the second section portrays the *living* Mandelstam – and he is portrayed well, with magnanimity, with – if you like – maternal honour." By this time, of course, her indignation about *The Noise of Time* had died down and she had come to speak of the book as "still-born" rather than "vile". In any case, as someone who had loved Mandelstam, she had the right to be indignant with him – whereas Ivanov was alien to that world, knew Mandelstam only by hearsay and tended to lie about everyone with the same carefree cynicism. What she was defending from Ivanov's vulgarity were "her own" Mandelstam poems, Max, Pra, and the whole world of Koktebel.

"Not so many people have addressed good poems to me, and, above all: not so often is one poet inspired by another that I can allow this inspiration to be ceded, just like that, to some imaginary girlfriend of some imaginary Armenian. A possession like *this* is something to which I must stake my claim." Tsvetaeva stakes her claim with great success; she really does portray the "living Mandelstam" – he comes over as someone unique, somewhat eccentric, impractical, uncompromising and not entirely of this earth, as a child and a sage, as a poet. Tsvetaeva does indeed write with humour and irony but, more important, she writes of him with love – and with tolerance and understanding for human weaknesses she sees as of little importance beside his enormous talent. It is of course "her" Mandelstam; nevertheless, it is Mandelstam, the Mandelstam whose poems we love. Reading Tsvetaeva's article about Mandelstam – and also her article about Voloshin, written a year later – I feel that Tsvetaeva enjoyed this chance to return to the Koktebel of her youth, to its atmosphere of gaiety and obsession with art. My only sorrow is that she was never able to publish these articles.

The nature of Tsvetaeva's relationship with the émigré world as a whole, and with her publishers in particular, is a complex matter. The émigré world was far from monolithic – it was composed of individuals some of whom joined together for political reasons, others of whom were simply continuing friendships from long before. Tsvetaeva, for example, had been on friendly terms with both Volkonsky and Balmont long before she emigrated, just as Efron had been a friend of the Bogengardts. The view that Tsvetaeva was entirely isolated in the émigré world, that she had no circle of friends and no audience, is mistaken – even if some of her own published remarks appear to support it. Her friendships, naturally, had their ups and downs, sometimes she herself lost interest in people and so antagonized them, but she did have a circle of friends – people she knew from Russia, people she knew from Prague and people she had first met in Paris itself. Irina Coll, Margarita Lebedeva's daughter, has described Tsvetaeva's friendship with her parents as follows: "Marina Ivanovna's friendship with my parents was, in my opinion, her only normal friendship – free of sudden tensions, ruptures and disenchantments. M.I. used to visit us frequently, very frequently, she often brought what she had been writing and read it to Mama and Papa . . . and would then discuss it for hours with Mama. Sergey Yakovlevich [Efron] seldom visited – Papa disliked him as a 'White Guard', and later on he began to 'disappear'. Alya lived with us for days on end, weeks on end . . . Our friendship was absolute and full of love, although on the surface we just 'cackled' (Marina Ivanovna's word), went to the cinema and wandered around Paris . . .". A casual glance through Tsvetaeva's published letters reveals that she met, and exchanged ideas with, a huge number of people, including such important figures as Lev Shestov, Nikolay Berdyaev, Sergey Prokofiev, Vladislav Khodasevich and Evgeny Zamyatin . . . And she herself was a known figure. She may only have been a modest success in the émigré world, but then – because of both her own nature and that of her poetry – she would have been no more than that in the Soviet Union. What must be remembered is that she did have both readers and admirers.

The question of Tsvetaeva's relationship with her editors is equally complex. There were, of course, a huge number of émigré newspapers, journals and almanachs, many of which folded after only two or three issues. There were some, though – *Latest News, Renaissance, Days, The Will of Russia* and *Contemporary Notes* – that lasted for years or even decades. Most of these at one time or another published Tsvetaeva. Nevertheless, Tsvetaeva constantly complained – and with reason – at the lack of understanding shown by editors and the difficulty of getting her work into print. I have already mentioned that *Latest News* refused to publish Tsvetaeva after 1928 because of her attitude towards Mayakovsky. In summer 1933, after friends interceded on her behalf, they agreed to publish her once again and it was hoped that she would be able to write for them regularly – every week, every month, or even just every three months. Difficulties, however, kept arising. Firstly Tsvetaeva was refused a promised advance, then the manuscript of "Two Forest Kings" – a comparison of Goethe's ballad "The Erlking" with Zhukovsky's translation of it – was returned with the words: "this interesting piece of philological research is quite unsuited to a newspaper", then "Mother's Tale" was printed with so many changes and abridgments that Tsvetaeva "wept" as she read it. The final crisis arose over "A Posthumous Present", an article in memory of Nikolay Gronsky that she wrote at the request of his father – who was himself a well-known public figure and a regular contributor to *Latest News*. This article, written in two parts to comply with the newspaper's demands, "lay around" at the office for over three months. In spring 1935, indignant at the lack of respect shown to her work and to the memory of the dead poet, Tsvetaeva took back the manuscript. And that was her last contribution to *Latest News*.

"My affairs are quite desperate", Tsvetaeva once wrote. "I *don't know* how to write so as to please Milyukov" (a historian, politician, and the chief editor of *Latest News*) "Or Rudnev. *They* don't please *me!*" The people who managed the literary world were for the main part people who had no direct relationship to literature – professors, politicians and public figures, people who were both educated and worthy of respect but who were not themselves writers. In Tsvetaeva's own words, "literature is in the hands of illiterate people". Rudnev, a trained doctor and a public figure, was one of the editors of *Contemporary Notes*, the most weighty of the émigré journals. As such he was Tsvetaeva's "curator". He was in no way ill-disposed towards her, he simply failed to understand her importance. His principal concern was with the average reader. If he considered that the average reader would be unable to understand a manuscript, then he would either abridge it or throw it out. Naturally enough, Tsvetaeva thought him incompetent. She found it difficult to get him to publish her poetry, still more difficult to get him to publish her prose. She herself valued her prose no less than her poetry and once explained to Rudnev: "A poet's prose is something different from the prose of another writer – in it the unit of effort – of zeal – is not the sentence but the word, and often even the syllable. You can find confirmation of this in my rough drafts." Any editor, however, considers himself a competent judge of prose, and Rudnev had other concerns than Tsvetaeva's attention to syllables and her rough drafts. He corrected and abridged as best he could while Tsvetaeva, needing the money, for the main part put up with it.

Some readers of Tsvetaeva's correspondence have expressed surprise at the harshness with which she speaks of *Contemporary Notes* and of Rudnev in particular. But it is not true that she only criticized him behind his back. It is clear from her letters to him that she did often complain to him directly. One letter, written during a disagreement over the manuscript of "The House at Old Pimen", is of particular interest. It is both an ultimatum and a statement of her principles as a writer. I quote it with abridgements:

Dear Vadim Viktorovich,
    (This letter is also addressed to the editorial board as a whole)
    I have worked on Old Pimen too long, too passionately and in too much detail to agree to any abridgements whatsoever . . .
    I am unable to break up an artistic and living unity, just as I would not be able – out of external considerations – to add even a single additional line at the end. I would rather let it wait for some other, more fortunate occasion; I would rather leave it to Mur, to be published after my death (he will be RICH WITH ALL MY POVERTY AND FREE WITH ALL MY BONDAGE) – yes, let it be inherited by my *rich* heir, together with a good half of my writings as an émigré – writings for which the émigré world, in the person of its editors, has found no need, in spite of all the constant complaints about the lack of good prose or poetry.
    During these years I have eaten and drunk more than enough bitterness. I was first published in 1910 (there is a copy of my first book in the Turgenev library) and yet now, in 1933, people *here* still consider me to be either a beginner or an amateur, or some kind of casual worker. I say *here* because in Russia my poems are included in anthologies as examples of concise and graphic speech. I have held one such book in my hand myself, full of delight – since I have not only done nothing to win such recognition, but seemingly everything to avoid it . . .
    It is not in my nature to speak of my rights and merits, just as it is not in my nature to translate them into money – even though I do know the worth of my work; I have never asked for more but have always accepted what is given – and if now, for the first time in all my life, I do speak of my rights and merits, then it is only because what is at issue is the essence of my work and its future possibilities.
    This *essentially* is my answer – *once and for all* . . .

By abridging my "Art in the Light of Conscience", you made it incomprehensible, depriving it of continuity and turning it into mere fragments. [. . .] You will be doing exactly the same if you throw out the middle of Pimen, i.e. Ilovaysky's children, without whom – whether or not he really is Ilovaysky – the image of the old scholar is incomplete . . .

My "Pimen" could have been made into an entire novel; what I give is just a brief lyrical representation: a POEM. It has already been shortened, and by a more powerful force than that commanded by any editor – the force of inner necessity, the force of an artist's intuition . . .

"The House at Old Pimen" was eventually published without abridgement, though not necessarily as a result of this letter. In a letter to Vera Bunina, Tsvetaeva wrote: "Pimen was only saved by my sudden shower of tears – the result of indignation and a sense of injury. Rudnev took fright – and yielded . . .".

And yet . . . In many letters to this same Rudnev Tsvetaeva expresses her gratitude for careful proof-reading, timely advances or friendly advice. And yet . . . thirty out of seventy issues of *Contemporary Notes* include prose or poetry by Tsvetaeva – sometimes more than one work in the same issue. And yet . . . Tsvetaeva also appeared not only in *The Will of Russia*, which published everything she sent them ("They took everything, and for that I will be grateful to them till the grave – and beyond the grave, if there is a beyond"), but also in *Meetings, Window, New City, Numbers* and many other journals and anthologies.

If you turn to the bibliography of Tsvetaeva's work, you will probably be surprised – in view of her own indignation – at the amount of her émigré writing that was in fact published. Of her major works only "Perekop", the Poem on the Tsar's Family, *The Bus* and *Poems to Bohemia* were never published – the first two for political reasons, the last two on account of the entanglements of her own life at the time. The cycles "Poems to Pushkin", "Poems to my Son" and "Desk" were never published in full; and a number of short poems were never published at all – though we do not know whether they were rejected or whether Tsvetaeva never submitted them. She even managed to publish a considerable amount of what she had written in Moscow during the time of the Revolution, including over a third of *The Camp of the Swans*. I am certain that, with these exceptions, Tsvetaeva published everything she wished to publish. There were certainly no discoveries among her posthumous publications of the order of, say, Mandelstam's "Voronezh Notebooks". As for her prose, all of that was published except "History of a Dedication" – which was accepted for publication by the *Will of Russia* just before the journal folded, and the second half of "The Story of Sonechka" – which was accepted by *Russian Notes* but never published, probably because Efron had just (at the end of 1937) been unmasked as a Soviet agent.

I do not wish to make out that Tsvetaeva was particularly fortunate in her relations with the literary world, that she was surrounded by understanding and good will. But in regard to the somewhat fruitless debate as to whether or not Tsvetaeva would have been better off if she had remained in the Soviet Union, I cannot help thinking of the stories of Mikhail Bulgakov and Osip Mandelstam. Many of their most important works were still unpublished decades after their death. Tsvetaeva at least lived in the free world – even if this only made it all the more painful for her to feel she was an outcast.

During her fourteen years in Paris Tsvetaeva published just one book – *After Russia 1922–25*, published in 1928 with the help of a rich admirer. Tsvetaeva had great hopes for this book, but in the end it attracted surprisingly little attention. In 1931 she attempted to publish "The Rat-catcher" as a separate book, with illustrations by Alya; a subscription was announced, but nothing came of the project. In terms of the number of books she published, Tsvetaeva was indeed one of the most "unnoticed" of all the émigré writers. And this was certainly not for lack of material – the New York collected Tsvetaeva runs to two volumes of prose and five volumes of poetry.

Tsvetaeva was, however, level-headed enough to understand that if she had chosen to adapt to the demands of her time, she could have been as famous and successful as anyone. In a letter to Lomonosova she wrote:

> . . . I could have been the first poet of my time, I know that, because I have everything, everything necessary but I do not *love* this time, I do not recognize it as my own.

> > . . . For I was born
> > *Outside* time. To no purpose and in vain
> > Do you fight! Time, you're Caliph for an hour:
> > I pass you by.

> And again – more precisely: I could have been a rich and recognized poet, either *here* or *over there*, without even having to act against my conscience – if I had just pretended to some qualities that are alien to me. Qualities that are irrelevant to me, not a part of my essence. (Nothing is really alien!) And I am so incapable of this, I so profoundly *ne daigne*, that I have never, not for one moment of my life, seriously asked myself: what if? The question has already been decided within me, there never has been, never can be, such a question.

Tsvetaeva felt an equal sense of duty to poetry and to her family. She tried to earn money during the thirties by entering the mainstream of French literature, reconstituting herself in French without forfeiting her "essence" or betraying her principles. Her first work in French was the translation of "The Swain" that had been prompted by Natalya Goncharova's illustrations. Tsvetaeva plunged with typical eagerness into the arduous task of learning a foreign poetic language. She admitted that she was learning as she went along – her ear helped her – but she was writing correct verse in French after only one chapter. She worked on this translation for six months, insisting on working alone, refusing the help of a French poet recommended to her by Salomeya Andronikova. She even became absorbed in the question of the nature of translation. "The thing is going well," she wrote to Andronikova, "I could now write a theory of verse translation – to the effect that one must transpose or change the tonality while preserving what is fundamental. Not only by using different words, but by using different images. In a word, in another language one has to write something anew. Which is what I am doing. And which is something only an author can take it upon herself to do." Tsvetaeva believed that she had succeeded in recreating in French the folkloric style of her Russian: "Something *new* . . . A translation into verse, from within a popular and archaic French which no one any longer uses – which no one ever did use, since a lot of it is entirely my own." Pasternak praised the extracts Tsvetaeva sent him and put her in touch with Charles Vildrac, a well-known French poet and verse theoretician. A reading of the poem was arranged for her in a French literary salon. "Everyone is full of praise . . ." – but no one helped her to publish any of it. It appears, however, that this was the result of something more than indifference. Tsvetaeva's attempts to preserve in French the sonority and rhyme system of the Russian was evidently not considered acceptable in French poetry – though no one said anything about this to Tsvetaeva herself. Alec Brown's English translation, unfortunately, was no more successful. None of this, however, lessened Tsvetaeva's determination both to translate into French and to write in French herself. In the years 1932–36 she wrote in French – "Letter to the Amazon", "Miracle with Horses", "Florentine Nights" (a short story based on her correspondence with Vishnyak), and an essay "Mon père et son Musée", at the same time as she was working on her Russian autobiographical prose. She also translated her favourite poems of Pushkin in the hope of publishing a small volume to coincide with the centenary of his death in 1937. None of these works, however, were published except for a small number of the Pushkin translations.

Throughout her years in Paris Tsvetaeva struggled desperately to find ways of earning money from her writing. One possibility was to arrange literary evenings. Every year Tsvetaeva put on at least one, some years she put on two or three, and in 1932 she put on four. There was, of course, a considerable amount of preparation to be done for these evenings: a hall had to be found, announcements had to be made in newspapers and tickets had to be both printed and distributed. Usually the whole family took part in these preparations; Alya and Efron would distribute tickets in advance and Alya would also sell tickets on the evening itself. The financial success of an evening hinged on the expensive tickets; there were always plenty of takers for the five-franc tickets, but the proceeds from them were very meagre. The expensive tickets had to be offered, either directly or through friends and acquaintances, to possible patrons. Buying tickets was, in effect, an act of charity and Tsvetaeva was not especially adept in cultivating the literary ladies on whom the success of the evening depended. If, however, the evening was a success, it would pay either for a few months' rent, for Mur's school, for clothes for him and Alya, or even for a summer holiday.

I have already mentioned that Tsvetaeva initially invited singers, musicians and sometimes other writers to perform at these evenings. In 1931, however, she performed alone for the first time, reading "History of a Dedication" in the first half and her poems addressed to Mandelstam, together with his poems addressed to her, in the second. The evening was a success and from then on Tsvetaeva always appeared alone. She sometimes read her own poems, but more often she would read some of her most recent prose, sometimes completed only just in time for the evening. She herself said that it was easier to read prose with feeling than to read poetry.

The following, quoted from an old newspaper, is a typical example of the announcements through which Tsvetaeva advertised her evenings:

AN EVENING OF MARINA TSVETAEVA

On Thursday, 29 December, in the Maison de la Mutualité (24 rue St Victor) there will be an evening of poems by Marina Tsvetaeva – "Poems of Childhood and Youth" (My childhood poems about children. My childhood revolutionary poems. High-school poems. Youthful poems.) The evening will begin at 9 p.m. Tickets at the door.

This announcement is of especial interest for its reference to Tsvetaeva's "revolutionary poems"; these have never been published and would appear to have been irrecoverably lost.

Tsvetaeva's literary evenings were not enough to save her from poverty; after all, she had two children and very little in the way of regular income. Efron earned a little money now and then, but his only real interest was Russian politics. While the Eurasian movement still had a publishing house in Paris, he earned a small regular sum from his work there – Tsvetaeva used to call him "the Eurasian camel". He also acted from time to time in crowd scenes in films. In 1928 they were able to spend the summer by the sea and even to invite the daughter-in-law of a friend to come with them and help look after Mur. In autumn 1929, however, the Eurasian publishing house closed down and Efron was left without work. At this time he was also suffering from severe over-exhaustion and a recurrence of his tuberculosis. With financial help from Svyatopolk-Mirsky and the Red Cross he was sent for nine months to a sanatorium in Savoie. Tsvetaeva spent the summer in a peasant's cottage close by.

Tsvetaeva's main source of income – apart from the Czech government – was her friends, and the friends of her friends. Throughout her years in Paris she constantly had to ask for money. In a letter that begins with the words, "We are utterly perishing", she describes a meeting with Boris Pilnyak who was then on his way to America via Paris; she asked him for ten francs and he gave her a hundred. Her main source of financial support, however, was Salomeya Andronikova. From 1926 until at least 1934 she sent Tsvetaeva a monthly sum of 300 francs of her own together with another 300 francs (sometimes less) that she had collected from friends. She always sent her own 300 francs even if she had been unable to find anyone else to contribute. Tsvetaeva's letters to Andronikova are filled both with requests for help and with expressions of gratitude. For example: "Dear Salomeya! A big, big request: could you possibly give me 80 francs for some shoes – my own are completely worn out . . ." Four days later: "Dear Salomeya, Thank you with all my heart! I have bought some wonderful shoes – they're going to last for 100 years. I embrace you. A WELL-SHOD M.Ts." Andronikova appears to have refused Tsvetaeva nothing. She helped to find a publisher for *After Russia*, gave her furniture, clothes and shoes, found work for Alya, distributed tickets for Tsvetaeva's evenings . . . But Andronikova was not alone in her generosity. Many other people, some of whom had never even met Tsvetaeva, were also of considerable help to her. A few names I should mention are: Svyatopolk-Mirsky, Anna Tesková, Raisa Lomonosova and, of course, Margarita Lebedeva.

In the mid-thirties there was even established a Marina Tsvetaeva Benefit Committee. As well as Salomeya Andronikova, this included a number of very well-known writers. I have been unable, however, to find out exactly what was achieved by this committee.

A little money also found its way to Tsvetaeva from the yearly charity balls held by the Union of Russian Writers and Journalists in Paris. The following is the text of a letter that Tsvetaeva wrote to the Secretary of the Union to accompany one of her official "petitions":

Dear Vladimir Feofilovich!

I *beg* you to allow me something from the Pushkin evening. I enclose a petition. Together with a stamped and addressed envelope – don't be offended! It's just for speed and simplicity – knowing how busy you are – with the earnest request that you dash off a few words to me: is there any hope of money and when should I come for it? I'm not able to telephone and it's impossible for me to come on the off-chance.

With warmest greetings!

M. Tsvetaeva

Life was a constant struggle to save money. She was always moving to cheaper apartments; she did her own cooking, washing and darning, she altered her own clothes; she economized on food, heating and public transport; the only thing on which she did not economize was her childrens' education. Alya was a competent artist; at one time or another she studied with Natalya Goncharova, at the Shukhaev studio and the École du Louvre, and at Art et Publicité. In one letter, in a list of her joys in life, Tsvetaeva includes: "Mur reading in Russian, Alya's successes in drawing and my own poems." She was proud of her son's fine command of Russian, his interest in French – which he learnt by himself at the age of six – and his "wonderful", "splendid" successes at school, for which he even received a school "order". Until she reached the end of her teens, Tsvetaeva was also equally proud of Alya – of her intelligence, her diverse abilities and her willingness to help.

Tsvetaeva's life was also made bearable by such small joys as family visits to the cinema and her own love of photography. From time to time they would have guests and Tsvetaeva would serve them tea or cheap wine as she read them her poems. She would make pancakes for Shrove Tuesday and traditional cakes for Easter. There would be presents – albeit extremely modest ones – every Christmas, and there would always be a tree. Alya delighted her mother by being awarded the institute prize for the best illustration – a prize that included a free course in engraving. Tsvetaeva was equally delighted when Alya bought some wool with a little money given to her by Margarita Lebedeva and knitted fine sweaters for Marina and Mur. And the family enjoyed their walks in the Meudon woods and their occasional summer trips to the sea or Savoie . . .

Life became more difficult as the years went by. Autumn 1930, after they came back from Savoie, appears to have been a turning point. This was probably largely due to the general economic climate of the time: her Czech "maintenance" was reduced, her friends were less able to help and it was now more difficult to earn money from writing. Efron was earning nothing and had no profession. It is difficult to judge how much he ever attempted to help his family as this is not something Tsvetaeva ever mentions in her letters. Mark Slonim, however, has written: "Sergey Yakovlevich had few needs himself, he was somehow unaware of poverty and he hardly did anything to provide for his family in any way. He did not know how to earn money – he had no abilities that way, he had no profession or practical skill and he made no particular effort to get himself work – he just wasn't interested." After Savoie he studied in a cinema photography school – something as impractical as all his other undertakings. In March 1931 he was awarded a diploma as a cameraman. Tsvetaeva looked on him as a great expert in both the theory and the practical techniques of the cinema, but he was still unable to find work. Towards the end of the year he took on a job as a physical labourer, but he soon lost that too. Alya, meanwhile, earned a little money from making toy hares and teddy bears out of cloth, but Tsvetaeva was still the main bread-winner. She had to do nearly all the housework as well, since Alya was now absent more and more of the time. Like any young girl, Alya wanted to have fun; she wanted her own life and had begun to feel oppressed by the atmosphere at home, by her mother's constant demands and reproaches. What Tsvetaeva wanted was something impossible – a daughter who was an exact copy of herself. And she felt that Alya's generation was incomprehensible and alien.

> You're not to be one of the young
> Nothings, nor harmful!

as she wrote in "Poems to a Son".

I have written earlier that Tsvetaeva was a bad mother. Now I come to the most difficult period of her life, I feel less certain of this. Perhaps she was just a mother like any other mother. Her children were an enormously important part of her life. She took great care of their health, their education and their general upbringing. What concerned her most of all – in view of their heredity – was their health. Alya's "complete emancipation", about which Tsvetaeva complained to Andronikova in spring 1934, was especially upsetting in view of her apparent tendency to neglect her health: "What distresses me most of all is her health: the obstinacy with which she goes about its obvious destruction . . .". Needless to say, Tsvetaeva was unable to remember herself at Alya's age: her endless cigarettes, her sleepless nights, her interminable conversations and poetry readings – all without any concern whatsoever for her health!

Alya's "emancipation" was not only a matter of her spending less time at home; it was also – much more painfully for her mother – an emotional and intellectual estrangement. All her life she had tried to direct her daughter – and now she was losing her. Alya was following in her father's footsteps, moving in an opposite direction to Tsvetaeva herself. The disagreements between Alya and her mother were overtly about politics, but were almost certainly aggravated by the family's material circumstances. If it had been easier for Alya to find interesting work, to earn money, to move into an apartment of her own, she might have been less tempted by "post-revolutionary currents", might not have gone along with her father's view of the Soviet Union as the embodiment of an ideal and might not have thought of returning to Soviet Russia. The long-running political disagreement – in which Tsvetaeva was isolated – resulted in repeated family quarrels. Tsvetaeva believed that "a lot of harm was done by various mutual acquaintances who had been undermining everything for years". To some extent this is true. The people who were to accuse Tsvetaeva, after her death, of turning her daughter into a housemaid, had no doubt already said the same kind of thing to Alya herself. In any case the atmosphere became increasingly strained, mutual misunderstandings became increasingly frequent and everyone began to feel more and more hurt. The following passage from a letter to Vera Bunina was omitted from the published volume of her correspondence:

> 22 November 1934: Vera, this is the latest episode. S. and Alya shut themselves away from me in the kitchen and begin to talk in hushed voices (arranging her future). I hear: ". . . and then, maybe your relationship with your mother will improve." Me: "It won't." Alya: " 'Mother' is listening." Me: "How dare you say 'mother' like that? Why the inverted commas? Of course it's your mother listening and not your father!" (You should have heard that "Mother" and the triumphant mockery in it.) Me to Sergey: "Well, have you heard now? What do you feel when you hear something like that?" Sergey: "*Not a thing.*"
>
> S. even says in Alya's presence that I'm the living image of Aleksandra Ilovayskaya, that that is why I could describe her so well . . .

Even if Tsvetaeva is exaggerating, even if she herself was to blame, this episode is enough to give one a sense of how isolated she felt. There were many other episodes:

> 11 February 1935: . . . I am now physically enslaved and emotionally liberated: Alya has gone and with her I have lost what little (and during

the last two years – somewhat constrained!) help that I have had, but this is also the end of a constant mockery and opposition that had become intolerable . . .

She left suddenly. In the morning I asked her to go and fetch some medicine for Mur – it was the day of my talk on Blok and I hadn't even read the manuscript through. She just sulked and said: "Yes, Yes . . ." Ten minutes later it was the same thing again: "Yes, yes . . ." I can see her – first she just sat there and darned her stockings, then she read the newspaper, she just *wouldn't go*. "Yes, yes . . . When I've done this and that, then I'll go . . ."

From then on it just got worse and worse. When I said it was disgraceful to treat me like that on the day of my talk, she just said: "You're already a disgrace." "What?" "It can't get any worse. You should just listen to what people say about you."

But it did get worse: after warning her ten times that I'd slap her in the face if she didn't stop, after the eleventh time, after she'd said, "Everyone knows how deceitful you are," I finally did slap her. "Yes, that's what I'd do to anyone who speaks to me like that – not just to my grown-up daughter. I wouldn't care if you were President of the Republic" (which I swear is true).

Then S.Ya., who was in a furious rage (WITH ME) told her she shouldn't stay for another minute and gave her some spending money . . .

My daughter is the first person who has ever treated me with CONTEMPT. And probably the last person. Unless her own children are the same.

I have no idea where Alya went or when she returned. I only know that she and her mother did not cease to love one another, however much their political disagreements, together with their terrible poverty, may have distorted their relationship. Nothing of all this, however, is especially surprising. The one truly surprising fact about this period in Tsvetaeva's life is that she continued to work.

In her articles about poetry Tsvetaeva always focuses on the nature of inspiration, on the poet's subordination to a higher force. For some reason she writes very little about the next stage in the composition of a poem, about what happens when the poet finds himself alone, not with inspiration, but with a rough draft in need of revision. She did, however, work extremely hard and extremely conscientiously at her poems – as can be seen from her rough drafts, from her notes and plans, and from her countless variants of single lines. Sometimes she mentions this kind of work in her letters: "I search all *day* (at my desk, *without* my desk, in the sea, washing the dishes, washing my hair, and so on) for an epithet, i.e. for one word, all *day* – and sometimes I don't find it." During the period I am now writing about, however, inspiration was less often able to break through the confusion of everyday life. This is part of the reason why Tsvetaeva wrote more prose during the thirties; she herself once said that her mind still functioned while she did the housework, but that her feelings slept. Yet the need to write poetry did not fade away. "I desperately want to write. Poems. Anything. It's painful," she wrote in 1934; and in 1935, during a summer holiday, she wrote, "for me my work *is* my holiday. If I don't write, I'm just unhappy, and no seas can make any difference." And Tsvetaeva did write – 1937 is the only year she wrote no poetry at all – even though she often had no chance to finish what she had begun and would suddenly recollect that her notebooks were full of unfinished work. She would then seize the notebooks and attempt to put them in order. "I have to do this," she wrote, "in order that something should be left from *these years*."

The poems she wrote during her last years in Paris mark a further development in her work. They are distinguished by a greater degree of restraint, external simplicity and – at least apparent – objectivity. They are wise rather than passionate – poems of estrangement, of solitude, sometimes of loneliness. Tsvetaeva's concern is now less with people than with the non-human world. She writes about a house or a desk, a bush or an elder, about a garden, about trees . . . With them she feels at ease, on equal terms. She personifies them and expects understanding from them.

> Yes, there was a man beloved!
> And that man was – a desk
>
> Of pinewood . . .

The cycle "Desk" marks an anniversary about which it is possible that no one else was aware – thirty years of her own writing. It is a unique poem – a hymn to her desk – seen as a constant and faithful working companion. At the same time it is an all-embracing settling of accounts: through her praise of her desk she defines her own "place in the universe": herself and her duty ("You took me away from non-eternal blessings"); herself and God ("You've hurt me and left me out? Thank you for giving me a desk [stol] . . . Thank you, Carpenter [Stolyar] . . ."); herself and her poetry (". . . writing – and you won't find any finer in the entire kingdom!"); herself and other people ("You'll be laid out on the dining-table, but I'll be laid out on my writing desk . . .", "I'll be laid out naked, with two wings for covering"). It is interesting to note the degree to which Tsvetaeva endows this idealized writing desk with characteristics of her mother; it is as though the desk has become for her writing what her mother once was for her music. As the mother once sat her down at the piano, so the desk also makes her sit down, teaches her, forces her to work and protects her from the joys, temptations and baseness of the world . . . Just as a bush can shelter her from the noise people make . . . Just as a garden can shelter her . . . All these things awake in Tsvetaeva a sense of God; she thanks him for the desk and begs him for a garden:

> Just say: enough of torment – take
> A garden – lonesome like myself.
> (But do not stand nearby, Yourself!)
> A garden, lonesome, like Myself.

There is little of Tsvetaeva's rebelliousness in these verses; her outlet for that was now through her letters. Rather than struggling against it, Tsvetaeva now appears to accept her fate, to sink ever deeper into herself. If she never published such poems as "I opened my veins . . ." and "Solitude: retire . . .", it may be because she didn't want strangers to look so deep into her being:

> Solitude: retire
> Into yourself, as our ancestors into fiefdoms.
> Solitude: in your heart
> Seek and discover freedom.
>
> (. . .)
>
> Solitude in your heart.
> Solitude: retire,
>
> Life!

And then, quite unexpectedly, a man appeared in her life, a man who needed her – or so, at least, she imagined:

> At long last I have met
> The one I need:
> Someone has a desperate
> Need of me.

This poem, indeed the whole cycle, "Poems to an Orphan", is addressed to Anatoly Shteiger, a young poet whom Tsvetaeva lived for during the summer of 1936. It would have been difficult for her to find anyone more unsuitable towards whom to direct her feelings: in the first place he was homosexual, secondly he was close to Georgy Adamovich and his "Parisian note", and thirdly he was a member of the Fascist/neo-Bolshevik organization, "Young Russia". What appealed to Tsvetaeva, however, was the fact that he was seriously ill and spent most of the time either in hospital or in a sanatorium; this meant that he was both inaccessible and in need of care, sympathy and love. And they were separated by a frontier: Shteiger was undergoing medical treatment in Switzerland while Tsvetaeva was spending the summer in Savoie . . .

Several years earlier Shteiger had given Tsvetaeva a copy of his book, *This Life. The Second Book*, with the dedicatory inscription: "To Marina Ivanovna Tsvetaeva, a great poet. From a profoundly devoted A. Shteiger. 1932." They had met once: Shteiger had introduced himself to her at one of her evenings. The short-sighted Tsvetaeva couldn't even remember his face. And then he suddenly contacted her from his sanatorium and sent her a copy of his latest book. Something about him touched her, probably his helplessness ("tuberculosis . . . is the illness that is closest to me," she wrote in a letter), his youth (he was just twenty-nine), and his need for support. And she had had no one for eight years, since her "non-meeting" with Gronsky. In one of her letters she wrote: "Maybe you have done me a poor favour, calling out to me and so depriving me of my psychic balance. Or maybe it is the only favour anyone can do for another person?" These lines are a key to their relationship, to the letters Tsvetaeva wrote to Shteiger (her last epistolary romance) and to "Poems to an Orphan" (her last cycle of love poems). Tsvetaeva's need for Shteiger was infinitely more important than anything she herself could offer him. In the real world she could only offer him some old postcards of St Petersburg, a jacket for which he probably had absolutely no need, and her dreams of a meeting . . . And in some other world she could offer him her soul, her poems and letters – and a refuge in the cave of her own womb:

> If I could, I would
> Take you into the womb of the cave:
> Into the cave of the dragon,
> Into the lair of the panther.
>
> Into the paws of the panther
> If I could, I would.
>
> (. . .)
>
> But the cave's not enough
> And the lair's not enough!
> If I could, I would take you
> Into the cave of the womb.
>
> If I could, I would.

Thirteen years before she had longed in a similar way to take Bakhrakh – not into a cave, but into a "shell" – except that she had only wanted to take Bakhrakh for a short time, to bring him up and then let him go, whereas she wanted to take Shteiger in order to keep him there and preserve him forever. The other difference is that, after suffering so many disappointments, Tsvetaeva looked on a meeting with the man she needed as an event of quite extraordinary, almost infinite importance. It is because of this that the "Poems to an Orphan" are so full of hyperbole:

> With the crest of granite of cliffs.
>
> (. . .)
>
> . . . And with the river, swelling in two,
> To create and to embrace an island.

Shteiger was necessary to Tsvetaeva as an excuse for her "to respond with her whole being"; this does not, however, mean that she was not entirely sincere in her readiness to adopt him, to care for him and cherish him. Unfortunately, Shteiger found Tsvetaeva's extreme emotionality oppressive and said so quite boldly in one of his letters. Their single meeting in Paris was the end of their "relationship". Tsvetaeva wrote of this "separation": "I believed there was someone to whom I was necessary – like bread. And it turned out he needed not bread but an ashtray full of fag-ends. Painful. Stupid. Sad." She was left with her arms wide open, ready for an embrace but encountering only emptiness:

> I embrace you with the sweep . . .
>
> (. . .)
>
> . . . With the round of a flower-bed and of a well,
> Where a stone will fall – quite grey!
> With a mutual pledge of orphanhood,
> With my loneliness, utter loneliness!
>
> (. . .)
>
> With all of Piedmont and all of Savoie,
> And – slightly indenting the ridge –
> I embrace you with the pale blue horizon
> And embrace you with my own two arms!

She is on her own with the hills, the trees, the streams and the horizon, on her own in a vast world where she feels as lonely as a ripened poppy. In the final poem she glimpses summer, a field of poppies and death . . .

HOMESICKNESS

Nostalgia for the Motherland!
A nuisance long since exposed
I am utterly indifferent
As to where I am utterly
Alone . . .

This all appears quite straightforward, though one might perhaps wonder why, if homesickness is such nonsense, Tsvetaeva needs to write about it at such length. But the poem's conclusion overturns everything that has come before:

But if along the road a bush
Should rise, especially a rowan-tree . . .

Tsvetaeva breaks off in mid-sentence; the reader is left to understand for himself what follows after. And he does indeed understand, he understands that the whole poem is an expression of immeasurable pain. Tsvetaeva's exclamation marks and enjambments are like sobs, and the function of the words is to hide these sobs. The words in the first five lines are an attempt at indifference, but the rhythm conveys the fact that this indifference is only a pretence.

"Everything is forcing me towards Russia," Tsvetaeva wrote to Tesková as early as the beginning of 1931, after discussing her difficulties in the èmigré world, "but I am *unable to go there*. Here I am *unnecessary*. There I am *impossible*." It is interesting that she writes, "I am *unable* to go"; does this imply she would have considered returning if she had believed it possible? I do not know Tsvetaeva's feelings as she left Moscow, but she wrote later that she had not expected to return for at least ten years. And it is quite clear, from a letter she wrote to Bulgakov in 1926, that she saw no possibility then of returning to a still-Bolshevik Russia. What then was it that changed? Why did Tsvetaeva choose to return to the Soviet Union? Had her attitude towards the Soviet régime changed? Or was there simply "no choice"?

I have already quoted a letter Efron wrote to Voloshin from Prague, where he dreams of "returning soon to Russia". This hope gradually grew stronger at the same time as he began to reevaluate his "White" past. In 1925 he wrote:

For me, returning is associated with capitulation. We suffered defeat thanks to a number of political and military errors, maybe even crimes. I am ready to admit to both the one and the other. But what the Volunteers died for is something deeper than politics. And I cannot give up this truth of mine even if it means I never find my motherland. And it is not fear of the Cheka . . . that stops me, but fear of capitulating to the Checkists – of renouncing my own truth. Between me and the embassy lies an insurmoutable obstacle: the grave of the Volunteer Army.

Gradually, however, this obstacle came to appear less insurmountable. According to Tsvetaeva, by the time she herself was writing "Perekop", Efron had already "grown cold towards Perekop", had ceased to acknowledge that there was any truth to the ideals for which the Whites had fought. He began both to feel guilty towards Russia and to imagine that he somehow had to win her "forgiveness". It was at this time that he first became attracted to the Eurasian movement.

This is not the place to expound the theories of this movement. I will just say that Russia was seen as some kind of special continent, a unique world, both Europe and Asia, whose historical landmarks were Genghis Khan, Peter the Great and Lenin. The Eurasians rejected Communism but did not reject the Revolution itself, searching instead for ways of "overcoming" it. One of the central points of their philosophy was the Messianic destiny of Russia-Eurasia . . . By the end of the twenties the movement had split; Efron naturally aligned himself with the "left" wing, those who were no longer content to theorize but who were searching instead for a path of political action. These "left" Eurasians were interested not only in Russia's historical past, but also in its Soviet present; they approved both of some Soviet writers and of some aspects of contemporary Soviet life. Efron was an editor of *Mileposts*, a journal sympathetic to the Eurasians, and also the editor of *Eurasia*, the Eurasian newspaper and publishing house in Paris. Tsvetaeva herself was on friendly terms with many of the Eurasians and once wrote that if she were to consider joining any Party, it would be theirs . . . This was probably at least in part because she was impressed by Efron's own role in the movement. She did not notice the first portent of the tragedy that was to come:

Professor Alekseev (and others) claim that S. Ya. is a Chekist and a Communist. If I should meet them – I'm afraid of myself . . . Professor Alekseev is a scoundrel, believe me . . . Personally I am glad that he is leaving, but I do very much suffer on S.'s behalf – he is so pure and his heart is so ardent. Leaving aside just two or three others, he alone is the *moral strength of Eurasianism.* Believe me – he is even called the "Eurasian conscience", and Professor Karsavin has referred to him as "the golden boy of Eurasianism". If the movement is saved, then it will be on his shoulders (or bones).

In this letter, written in early 1929, Tsvetaeva still speaks of her husband with the same rapture, still shows the same faith in his utter impeccability, as in the first poems she wrote to him.

Eventually Efron did indeed become a Chekist – as a result of his love of Russia, his sense of guilt ("We have fought against our own people") and his heightened interest in the changes that were taking place in the Soviet Union. It was clearly not a step he took suddenly. Konstantin Rodzevich, who was to become a Chekist himself, said to me that "Seryozha" was too weak, that he was not made for such complex and dangerous business; as he said this he was unable to conceal his own sense of superiority . . . I myself am more inclined to agree with Tsvetaeva: that Efron was too pure, that he was not devious enough.

During the late twenties and early thirties Soviet agents began to penetrate the Paris Eurasian movement, to subsidize the movement and to direct its activities . . . Rodzevich claims that Efron was first "entangled" and then "recruited". Efron would have been difficult, if not impossible, to frighten; most probably he was "bought" with the promise of being helped to return to Russia. He first became one of the organizers of the Paris Union for Return to the Motherland, an organization originally conceived by the NKVD. To Efron the words "return to the Motherland" had a magic power. Once again he was "serving Russia" – and with the same conviction as when he had been a Volunteer in the White Army. Did he know that he was working for the NKVD? It is possible that for a long time he did not know. His motives were idealistic – as is clear from the fact that it was some time before anyone could persuade him to accept any payment for his work. It is equally clear that he did not talk to his wife about the main part of his work; their lives had grown more and more apart and he may anyway have preferred not to trouble her with such a burden. Not long before the end he evidently told Bogengardt that he was working for the NKVD. Bogengardt's daughter has informed me that one evening, when she was lying in bed, she heard Efron confess to her father in the next room. Many years later she asked her father whether this really had happened or whether she had just dreamed it. Bogengardt confirmed that Efron really had confessed that he worked for the NKVD and that that had been their last meeting. It is possible that Bogengardt was the only person apart from his "colleagues" who knew about Efron's work. The Château d'Arcine in

Savoie, where he spent most of 1930, was apparently a nest of Soviet agents. He spent two weeks there in August 1931, and probably paid other visits as well. Rodzevich also went there . . .

The idea of returning to the Motherland was a popular one, especially among the young, the generation who had lived most of their lives abroad. Many people believed that a new life was being built in the Soviet Union. The successes of the system were exaggerated, its horrors never mentioned. Those who returned, or wished to return, were motivated primarily by love for Russia, faith in Russia and – perhaps most important of all – by a deep sense of being out of place, unneeded, in the countries where they lived. Even Tsvetaeva appears to have yielded for a while to this mood, at least as far as her son was concerned. This is the only way I am able to explain her "Poems to a Son", written in January 1932:

> It is neither here nor there –
> Go, my son, to your own country –
> To a land, where all is topsy-turvy!
> Where to go *back* is to go *forward*
> For you, particularly,
> Who have not seen your Russia,
> My child . . .

Mur was not yet seven and was clearly unable to travel anywhere, Tsvetaeva would certainly never have let him be separated from her, so what do these lines mean? The Soviet Union was not in any particular need of being defended, so why did Tsvetaeva, who usually only sang the defeated, write poems like these?

> . . . Understand: he is blind
> Who leads you to a requiem
> For the people, which eat bread
>
> And which will give it to you, as soon
> As you leave Meudon and go to the Kuban.
> Our quarrel is not your quarrel!
> Children! You yourselves must fight the battle
>
> Of your own days.

One might imagine that Tsvetaeva really was thinking of returning to the Soviet Union, that she had been taken in by her husband's propaganda, except for the fact that she wrote to Tesková, in the same month: "Go to Russia? There this same Mur will finally be taken away from me, and whether that would be a good thing for him I don't know. And I won't be gagged merely by being unable to publish my work, I won't even be allowed to write it." Later in the same year she wrote, also to Tesková: "S.Ya. has completely buried himself in Soviet Russia, can see nothing else, and sees in Russia only what he wants to see." In view of these statements, I am unable to understand why she wrote "Poems to a Son". Of the three poems, incidentally, only the last, the most characteristically "Tsvetaevan", was published. In it she affirms, "You are not to be a Frenchman" and then admits:

> I have instilled into you – all Russia,
> All Russia – as if by a pump!

The first two poems, the most "ideological", were not published during Tsvetaeva's life. But whether or not she ever tried to publish them, she did write them; and quotation from them can seem to establish that she was indeed sympathetic towards the Soviet Union.

> Then let us not revere the words!
> Rus'* is for our forbears, Russia for us,
> For you – enlighteners of caves –
> The summons: USSR, –
> Is no less a summons in the
> Darkness of the heavens than: SOS.

These poems, however, are more than outweighed by Tsvetaeva's numerous expressions of an entirely opposite point of view. She remained true to herself; what she had seen during the first years of the Soviet regime was enough to turn her against Bolshevism for ever. In all probability "Poems to a Son" are a reflection of the arguments that were tearing her family apart. Efron had already made up his mind; he was prepared to pay any price in order to return to the Soviet Union. In one of her letters Tsvetaeva quotes him as saying, "I am in debt to my country"; I would imagine he said this more than once. He was desperate to expiate his guilt, to be of service to his country, to return there and be accepted as a worthy citizen. He wanted the whole of his family to accept his views and to return with him. Tsvetaeva, however, was convinced that not only was there no reason to return, but also that there was no place to which she could return:

> With a lantern search through
> The whole world under the moon.
> That country exists not
> On the map, nor yet in space.

* An old, nostalgic, name for "Russia".

> Drunk up as though from the
> Saucer: the bottom of it shines!
> Can one return to a
> House, which has been razed?

As she wrote these lines, she must have thought of the day when she went with Alya into Tryokhprudny Lane and found that the house where she had been born had been replaced by a patch of wasteland . . . The next two lines are clearly spoken by Efron himself:

> Be born again!
> Into a new country!

They are followed by what must be Tsvetaeva's answer:

> Well then, mount up again
> Onto the back of your steed
>
> Which threw you! (Bones
> Intact – at least?) . . .

These lines return us to the year 1921, to the poem she wrote on Seryozha's name-day ("25 September, Sergey's day"), when he was a fugitive from a defeated army:

> Your trace is not known,
> Your forelock a tousle.
> Rock-foil and willow-herb
> Crunch under the hooves.
> An untrodden path,
> A ne'er-do-well flame.
> Oh, motherland, Rus',
> Steed without shoes!
>
> (. . .)
>
> If you mount, you must jump!
> Once up, don't grumble! . . .

Then she had written that Mamay (Lenin) was the only rider who could ride the wild horse that was Russia; now she was convinced "that Russia is no longer". Efron, however, was determined to look on Mamay's Russia as the realization of his dream. Lydia Chukovskaya, in her volume of memoirs, has recorded a story that Tsvetaeva told her a few days before her death: "Sergey Yakovlavich once brought home a newspaper – pro-Soviet, of course, – which included photographs of a workman's canteen in a provincial factory. The tables were covered with crisply starched tablecloths, the cutlery shone and there was a pot of flowers in the middle of each table. I just said: "And what's on the plates? And what's in their heads?"

By 1932 Efron had evidently made up his mind and applied for a Soviet passport. In October 1933, however, Tsvetaeva wrote to Salomeya Andronikova:

> S. is here, he doesn't yet have a passport – which makes me very happy. The letters we have had from people who've gone back (I saw them off and waved them goodbye myself) are eloquent: some people are always asking for transfers of money so they can use the hard-currency shops; while someone else, the wife of a qualified engineer who went back to a factory job that had been arranged for him in advance, describes in great detail how, every evening, instead of supper, they drink tea at the house of a friend – with sugar and bread. (Petersburg.) In that case all S. will get is tea – without sugar and without bread – and maybe not even that . . .

Even if Efron believed such letters, they clearly had no influence on him; such mundane and material matters simply didn't mean anything to him. Tsvetaeva went on to say: "I am definitely not going – which means we must separate. And that (however much we bicker!) is – after twenty years of living together – extremely difficult. And the reason I am not going is that I have already *left the country* once. (Salomeya, we once saw a film, *Je suis un évadé*, about a convict who chooses to return to his forced labour – that's just what it would be like!)" The tone of this letter is still relatively genial; as time went by, however, the conflict became more and more bitter.

Both the children shared the aspirations of their father. Alya worshipped and adored him. Her first image of her father came from her mother's poetry and she held to this image throughout her entire life. She spoke of her father in the same tone even in the late sixties and early seventies – we never, of course, dared question her about his work for the Cheka or his tragic end. As an adolescent she had believed unconditionally in her father's ideals and had always seen her own future in Soviet Russia. And then of course there were the difficulties of émigré life, unemployment, the extreme poverty of her family and her mother's difficult and demanding character. Alya needed to escape into an independent life ("Be born again! Into a new country!"), to construct her own life as she thought fit. Tsvetaeva herself believed that life was not something one could "construct", that it took on its own form according to some inner but unknown principle. Alya, in any case, became an active member of the Union for Return. She began working – as an illustrator and translator – for a journal, *Our Union*, published by the Soviet embassy. Like her father, she was evidently infuriated by Tsvetaeva's obstinacy, by her refusal to sympathize with their aspirations. Both Alya and Efron saw Tsvetaeva as an anachronism, someone who lived according to outdated laws, unable to comprehend either the present or the future. Mur was also on Efron's side; he had treated his mother with a kind of patronizing irony ever since he was a small child – something that was only encouraged by his mother's impetuous love and adoration.

Tsvetaeva's sorrows included not only the lack of understanding shown by her family and her own sense of powerlessness in the face of their delusions. She was also deeply pained at appearing to be the cause of her family's constant discord. 1934: "S.Ya. is torn between *his* country and his family: I am *definitely not* going, and it is difficult to break up an association (Tsvetaeva no longer used the words "love" or "marriage" – V.S.) that has lasted for twenty years – even if you do have 'new ideas'. So he tears himself apart." 1935: "Mur is torn apart between my own humanism and his father's near-fanaticism . . ." – this at a time when Mur was only ten years old. 1936: "Everything comes down to one question: to go or not to go. (If you do go, then it's for ever.) In short: S.Ya., Alya and Mur are all dying to go." It was as though she alone were preventing her family from attaining happiness, as though she were standing between them and a door to which they had already found the golden key. Her husband and daughter were by now leading a separate life – and she herself was no longer included; she had no conception of the nature of her husband's life.

In the letter to Vera Bunina from which the following passage is excerpted, Tsvetaeva writes about her love for Rodzevich and how she had been unable to join him because of her family:

> . . . But I was given a terrible gift in the cradle – the gift of conscience: the inability to stand by while others suffer.
>
> It *may* be, (I was a fool!) that they would have been *happy* without me: much happier than with me! Now I can say this for sure. But who could have convinced me *then*?! I was so sure (and they assured me!) that I was *irreplaceable*: that they would die without me.
>
> But now all I am to them is a burden, a divine punishment. Above all to S. – Alya's already shaken me off. Our lives are quite separate. Mur? I can only answer by repeating the question mark. I don't know *anything*. They all want to *live*, to act, to *communicate*, to "construct life" – or at the very least their own lives.

Gradually Tsvetaeva began to yield, to waver. She came to feel that she had no right to hold her family back, to prevent their happiness. Not realizing that Efron had yet to "earn" this right, she thought it was her fault that he had not yet gone back to Russia. Her letters begin to include remarks to the effect that she is not holding him back, that she wouldn't dare to hold him back any longer . . . She even writes that she would go with him – "so as not to be separated" – if only he would say straight out that he was going. "But he doesn't take this upon himself, he waits for me to burn my boats *voluntarily* (or as he would put it: 'to set all sails')." And that was something she felt incapable of: "*and I shall feel the same till I die.*"

Efron's politics made Tsvetaeva's position in émigré society extremely difficult. Her strong moral code, together with her independence of the various political groupings, had in most circles won her a certain respect. In one of her letters she describes an occasion when a group of "Young Russians" called Mark Slonim a *yid* while he was giving a talk on Hitler and the Jews. She herself fearlessly abused the "Young Russians" and then left the hall. For the main part Tsvetaeva appears to have enjoyed her independence – though there was always a price to pay. Efron had once been refused work in a left-wing publishing house after an interview with Tsvetaeva had appeared in a monarchist journal. The left-wing *Latest News* – as we have seen – refused to accept contributions from Tsvetaeva after the publication of her open letter to Mayakovsky. Now that her husband and daughter wanted to return to Soviet Russia, it was assumed that she herself must be a Bolshevik sympathizer. It is possible that *Latest News* broke with her for the second time not because of her article about Gronsky, but because of Efron. Tsvetaeva's position "outside politics" was becoming more and more difficult to maintain. "My position is ambiguous", she wrote to Tesková. "Today, for example, I am reading at a big evening of émigré poets (everyone in Paris, even the ruins of Merezhkovsky – who once wrote poems himself). And another day (I don't know when) I am reading – at the request of my family – at an evening for people returning to the Soviet Union (the same poems at both evenings and I'm not being paid). It could all look rather ugly." It was at this time that she began a never-completed poem with an epigraph taken from [the nineteenth-century poet] Fyodor Tyutchev:

> Not a warrior of two camps, but – if by chance a guest –
> Then a guest, like a bone in the throat, like a nail in a shoe.
>
> I was given a head – two hammers beat on it:
> Self-interest of some, malice of others.
>
> (. . .)
>
> Not a warrior of two camps – judge, plaintiff, hostage,
> An adversary of both! Spirit is adversary.

One of the ironies in all this was that Tsvetaeva loved Russia and missed Russia more than anyone else in her family. What she loved was neither a memory nor a hope, neither an old idea of Russia nor a new idea. The spirit of Russia was simply a part of her, it was the spirit of the language in which she wrote. "Homesickness" was not the product of a momentary frenzy, but one of Tsvetaeva's most important statements, the confession of a love she had kept almost secret for years on end. She had previously divulged this love only in such lines as

> Irrevocable like our
> Russian glory . . .

from the poem "In exchange for a stirrup". Or, from a poem addressed to Pasternak:

> Greetings from me to the Russian rye,
> To cornfields which overshadow a peasant woman.

Or, from her poem-cycle in memory of Voloshin:

> In a country, which alone
> Of all countries was called the Lord's . . .

Thoughts about the motherland inevitably give rise to thoughts about the Russian language:

> Neither shall I be seduced by
> My native language, its milky call.
> I don't care in which language I am
> Misunderstood by those I meet!

Maybe it was all the same to her in what language she was misunderstood, but she did care what language she thought in, what language she felt and wrote in, what language she and her children spoke together. During her first years as an émigré Tsvetaeva had said that the motherland "is an absolute of memory and blood". Now it is the "milky" call of her mother tongue that betrays the poet: language is more important than either memory or blood, it is the only thing about which she is unable to ironize.

In those first years she had written: "You can only be afraid of leaving Russia or forgetting her if you think of her as outside yourself. If Russia is inside you, then she is yours until the end of your life." Now, however, Tsvetaeva was no longer the self-confident and hopeful young woman who had left Prague for Paris. Her recollection of the unforgettable evening when she had read poetry "to all Petersburg" now ends in a cry of despair: "And they are all dead, dead, dead . . ."

On March 15 1937 Alya Efron left Paris for the Soviet Union; she had been granted her Soviet passport. Her dream had been realized. She had no doubt that she was returning with her eyes open. The following is an extract from her last letter to Vladimir Lebedev, who was then living in America:

27.1.37
(. . .)
A process has been underway during the last year which will finally be completed *there* – the process of my "becoming human" – something slow, difficult, painful and *good*. [. . .] My eternal obstinacy has developed into a quality I very much lacked – persistence. In the best sense of the word. You know, life here could work out very well for me *now* – as a journalist. Even my "France – USSR"* quite seriously suggested I remain here at least for a while – to work for them seriously, and even to earn money fairly seriously . . . I have no doubt that I could get excellent work here now – I have a lot of new left-wing French friends – but none of that is what really matters to me. What I am escaping now is "the good life" – and I think that is something more worthwhile than escaping unemployment or a feeling of being unneeded.

Je ne me fais point d'illusions about my life and work there, about all its great difficulties and great mistakes, but all that – life, work, difficulties, mistakes and all – will be *mine*. And "ease" here weighs on me more than thousands of tons of difficulties there. There might be work for me here – well and good! But there I will find work that I have earned – if one can put it like that – and it is so good that there is a country which is constructing itself in spite of such enormous difficulties, that is growing and creating, and that this country is my own . . .

Alya left Paris full of enthusiasm and hope. Her friends all showered her with presents and she was dressed in smart new clothes. Tsvetaeva had given her daughter a gramophone and when they were on board the train, she also gave her a "last present – a silver bracelet, a cameo brooch and – just in case – a small cross". Tsvetaeva wanted to believe in the general atmosphere of joy but was unable to. "It was a very joyful departure", she wrote in a letter to Tesková. "People only set off like that when they're going on honeymoon – and by no means everyone even then."

After a period of silence letters began to arrive from Alya. She was living with "Aunt Lilya" Efron in Merzlyakovsky Lane. She had been offered work by the *Revue de Moscou* – just as in Paris, she was working as a translator and illustrator. There was a possibility that she would be offered permanent work. She was content but was missing her family.

* A society for which Ariadna Efron worked.

Alya's departure cleared the air. A decision about whether or not the rest of the family should return was postponed. Tsvetaeva's life appeared to have grown somewhat easier. She and Mur were able to spend the summer by the sea, together with the Lebedevs.

One of Alya's letters contained the news of the death of Sofia Gollidey; Alya had tried, at her mother's request, to track her down. Shaken by this news, Tsvetaeva spent the summer writing "The Story of Sonechka" – something that took her back to her youth and to Russia. She also revised and copied out her "Poems to Sonechka"; it was almost twenty years since she had first written them. *Russian Notes* accepted both the story and the poems.

It was just then, when Tsvetaeva appeared to have been granted a breathing space, that the catastrophe occurred: Efron was accused of complicity in the murder of Ignaty Reyss, a Soviet agent who had refused to return to the USSR. Efron had helped to organize the shadowing of Reyss (it later emerged that he had done the same a year earlier to Trotsky's son, L. Sedovoy). Reyss was murdered in Switzerland during the night of 4/5 September 1937. The Swiss police had asked for assistance from the French and the trail had led to the Union of Friends of the Soviet Motherland – and to Efron in particular. It also emerged that the Union – and Efron in person – had recruited volunteers for the International Brigade in Spain – something forbidden by French law. Efron was summoned for interrogation by the Paris police.

After the first interrogations Efron disappeared – it was probably one of the conditions of his employment that he should disappear if things went wrong. It is reasonable to suppose that, if he had been handed over to the Swiss courts, he would have been sent to prison and would thus have remained alive. In the Soviet Union, on the other hand, he was sure to be either shot or sent to a camp. But even if Efron realised this, he had no choice but to return: in the person of Alya the NKVD now had a hostage.

I do not know whether Tsvetaeva first heard about what had happened from Efron himself or from the newspapers. It is clear, however, that they did talk, that Efron did not leave France without first saying goodbye to his wife and son. According to one account, Tsvetaeva and Mur were intending to take him to Le Havre by car; somewhere near Rouen, however, Efron took fright at something, jumped out of the car and disappeared. All this took place some time between 27 September (it is clear from a letter Tsvetaeva wrote to Tesková that she knew nothing then) and 29 October – when an article about his escape was published in *Renaissance*. This article included the lines: "As is well known, he is married to the poetess Marina Tsvetaeva. Tsvetaeva comes from a Moscow professorial family, she

337

formerly held right-wing views and even intended to write a long poem about the Tsar's family. Now it appears that her views must have changed – she knew very well about her husband's open Bolshevism . . .".

We know that Tsvetaeva was herself interrogated by the French police: she is supposed to have said: "His trust may have been abused, my trust in him remains unchanged." Tsvetaeva was so astonished and shaken by the questions put to her, even beginning to read out some of her translations into French, as to leave no doubt that she knew nothing whatsoever about her husband's affairs. She was cleared of suspicion and released; nevertheless, she was a broken woman.

Tsvetaeva had long ago understood – during the family arguments about returning to Russia – that it would be impossible for her to remain alone in Paris with Mur. Her dream then – as she wrote in a letter to Tesková in spring 1936 – had been to return to Czechoslovakia: "I would like a lair – for the rest of my life." There appears even to have been discussion of practical arrangements: "We were always dreaming that one day Marina would suddenly appear and that we'd give her the room by the kitchen (*we'd already begun to get it ready for her*) . . .", Tesková wrote to a friend after hearing the news. Now, however, Tsvetaeva's only choice was to return to the Soviet Union. It was certainly impossible for her to remain in France: all but her closest friends had turned away from her after the revelations about Efron and she could no longer publish her work there and earn money. She and Mur had to leave the flat where they had spent the previous four years . . . Mur also had to leave his school – apparently because of his outspokenly pro-Soviet opinions – and study with a private tutor.

Had Tsvetaeva and Efron agreed that she would apply to return to the Soviet Union as soon as she had received news of him? Did she come to this decision on her own? Or did Soviet "representatives" somehow "suggest" this to her? The latter is more than likely – Tsvetaeva was after all the wife of a failed agent and as such could have been a dangerous witness. So at least the NKVD may have thought. Alla Golovina heard from Tsvetaeva not long before her departure that she received a small allowance from the Soviets and was not supposed to contribute to émigré publications.

Soon after Efron's flight, in any case, Tsvetaeva began preparations for her departure. No doubt it took a considerable amount of time to arrange the necessary documents and visas and to have her Soviet citizenship restored. What concerned her most of all, however, were her own papers. Sorting out her personal archive was an enormous task. In March 1938 she wrote to the Bogengardts: "I'm now earnestly going through my archives: 16 *years* of correspondence – I start at 6.30 in the morning and there's no end in sight yet. I want to deposit everything somewhere – everything, that is, of any value. The times are too uncertain and I won't be able to look after it all myself. And it is all history. It's hard work: line after line – sixteen years of my life – I really am looking through everything. (I'm also burning a lot – tons and tons!)" As well as her and her husband's letters, Tsvetaeva went through all her manuscripts, revised some of them and copied out all the poems she had written since *After Russia* into a separate exercise book. She also copied out *The Camp of the Swans* and "Perekop" and annotated some of her earlier poems. All this was like living her life once again and it turned out to be a year's work. At the same time she either sold or gave away her books, household utensils and furniture. On 1 June 1938 she and Mur left their flat and spent the summer in a village by the sea; they returned in the autumn to a small and cheap hotel.

Tsvetaeva appears to have left the main part of her archives to the Lebedevs. But they had to leave Paris as the Germans invaded. The archive was left in the cellar of a French neighbour and was then apparently destroyed during a severe flood. Mark Slonim has written that a part of it, including the Poem on the Tsar's Family, was taken by some Socialist Revolutionary Friends to the International Socialist Archive in Amsterdam, but no trace of it has yet been discovered there. The only safe place turned out to be Switzerland: in spring 1939 Tsvetaeva gave a small parcel of manuscripts and corrected proofs to Professor E. Mahler of Basel University; these manuscripts are still kept by the University.

"Like a cuckoo I have stuffed my children into other people's nests", Tsvetaeva remarked bitterly.

Immersed as she was in her own affairs, Tsvetaeva learned about world events only from Mur. It was a shock for her to learn that Germany, the country she had always loved, was now threatening the whole of Europe – and Czechoslovakia in particular.

GERMANY

No country is more magical or wise
Than you, country of fragrance.

Tsvetaeva remained true throughout her entire life to the views she expressed in her adolescent poem "Germany". The poetry, philosophy and landscapes of Germany were always of central importance to her. In 1925

Tsvetaeva published an essay, "On Germany", that was drawn mainly from her diary entries for the year 1919: the ruined and defeated Germany of that time was still the land of spiritual aspirations to which she had been introduced in childhood by her mother. The essay begins with the words: "My passion, my motherland, the cradle of my soul!" As the years passed, she was to grow still more conscious of this sense of spiritual kinship. And of course she did herself have German blood – her grandfather, Aleksandr Meyn, was a Baltic German. "I have many souls", she once wrote. "But the most important of them is the Germanic. There are many rivers within me, but my most important river is the Rhine." I myself consider this an exaggeration – Tsvetaeva was primarily and centrally Russian. It is true, however, that Germany was her second country. It wasn't simply a matter of having learnt German as a child, of having sung German songs and listened to German fairy tales. What was more important was that her mother had imbued her with her own love for Germany – just as Tsvetaeva herself had "pumped" "all Russia" into her own children.

Tsvetaeva not only loved German culture herself; she also saw it as having a profound kinship with Russian culture as a whole. In an article about Voloshin she wrote:

> Our closest kin, our relative, is Germany, our modest and unprepossessing neighbour whom our finest minds and hearts may have loved for many years, but with whom we have never fallen in love. Just as you don't fall in love with yourself. It is not a matter of history – "In the eighteenth century we loved France, but in the first half of the nineteenth century we loved Germany" – but of pre-history; not a matter of transient moments, but of the blood we share with Germany, of our shared origins, of the wine sung by the Russian poet Osip Mandelstam at the height of the war:
>
> > And I sing the wine of ages –
> > The origin of Italic speech –
> > And Slavonic and Germanic flax
> > In the proto-Aryan cradle.
>
> This is a brilliant formula to describe the union we have always had, and always will have, with Germany.

What Tsvetaeva loved most of all was German literature, everything from the epics and legends to the most recent poetry. In the mid-thirties, in an attempt to explain her indifference towards Tolstoy and Dostoevsky, she wrote: "What I love is not the deepest things in the world but the highest things – and this is why I value Goethe's joy more highly than Russian suffering, their solitude more than Russian agitation . . .". Hölderlin and

Rilke were the "German Orpheus", and Tsvetaeva's whole view of the
world was deeply coloured by the discoveries of German Romanticism. A
compilation including "The Rat-catcher", the brilliant essay "Two Forest
Kings" and her various uncollected remarks about Germany and German
literature would constitute a volume of great interest and would fully bring
out the importance of Germany to Tsvetaeva. My aim here, however, is
more modest: to enable the reader to imagine how profoundly Tsvetaeva
was shocked by the first rumblings of the impending war.

Unlike in 1914, when Tsvetaeva was barely aware of the beginning of
the war, Tsvetaeva was now desperately frightened of war. In spring 1934
she wrote to Tesková: "I am terrified by the future war (Russia – Japan,
they say it's inevitable), I'd rather die." Her terror was intensified by the
fact that her son was now growing up: any future war or revolution would
be a direct threat to his life. Slonim once commented, with justice, on
Tsvetaeva's lack of a sense of history: "she failed to understand the movement of events." It is for this reason that the Munich agreement in 1938 was
such a shock to her: even though she listened to the radio, even though she
couldn't not hear conversations between other people, even though she had
heard Slonim's talk on "Hitler and Stalin", she had failed to take in what
had been happening in Europe during the last decade.

A day after the announcement of a general mobilization in Czechoslovakia Tsvetaeva wrote to Tesková: "I think of you continually – and I yearn
and feel pain, and indignation, and *hope*, together with you. *I feel Chekhia* [i.e.
Bohemia] *to be a free spirit over which bodies have no power.*" From then on
Tsvetaeva followed everything that related to Czechoslovakia, reading all
the newspapers – for the first time in her life – listening to the radio and
watching any films that were shown.

Tsvetaeva saw the Munich agreement itself – which allowed Hitler to
take the Sudetenland – as an act of betrayal. Two days later she wrote to
Tesková: "I love Bohemia infinitely, and I am infinitely grateful to her, but I
don't want to *weep* over her (one doesn't weep over someone in good health
and she is the only country who is still healthy – it is the others that are
sick!), I don't want to weep over her, but to *sing* her." Tsvetaeva soon got
down to work. "Poems to Bohemia [Chekhia]" was the last poem-cycle she
was to write. It was the second time in her life she had turned to civic poetry
– and "Poems to Bohemia" is at least equal to *The Camp of the Swans* in its skill
and power. As always when she was engaged in a major work, Tsvetaeva did
her research diligently, studying Czech history, culture and folklore. She
wrote to Tesková more frequently than ever, asking for books, photographs
and details of history, geography and everyday life.

"Poems to Bohemia" is composed of two different cycles: "September", written in November 1938, and "March", written in spring 1939. The mood of the two cycles is not identical. In September 1938 there was still hope that Hitler might be content with the Sudetenland and that Czechoslovakia would continue to exist as an independent state. Tsvetaeva was evidently of that opinion herself. The first three poems of "September" contain no mention of Germany or the Germans and are simply a song of praise to Bohemia and its people, to their love of work, their friendliness and their ability to make good use of their freedom. These poems show what it is about Czechoslovakia that had made Tsvetaeva dream of it throughout her years in Paris:

> Happiness was woven in the villages
> In red and blue and motley.
> What has become of you,
> Czech lion with two tails?
>
> *Foxes* have overcome
> The forest warrior!
> Three hundred years of bondage,
> Twenty years of freedom!

By foxes Tsvetaeva means all the countries that had betrayed Czechoslovakia, that had allowed her to be divided. Wanting to support her Czech friends, Tsvetaeva continues in prophetic tone:

> All your misfortune will last
> But an hour – no more!
> After one night of bondage –
> The white day of freedom!

Tsvetaeva was able to send these first poems to Tesková and was thanked "for the understanding, the ardent feeling, the nobility, strength and beauty of your poems to *Bohemia*".

I have not been able to read Tesková's letters to Tsvetaeva and so I am unable to judge to what degree Tsvetaeva drew upon them for her poems. One point, however, is worth mentioning. In a letter she wrote to Valentin Bulgakov on 23 December 1938, Tesková lamented: "As a pacifist you are probably glad that there has been no war!! We, however, are weeping that our soldiers were not allowed to defend a just cause with all their might...". She may well have said something similar to Tsvetaeva: two of the poems are devoted to the Czechs' defence – if not of their country – at least of their honour. "One Officer" and "They Took" both have epigraphs taken from newspapers – as though to confirm their factual truth – and are both connected to the fact that the Czechs were forbidden to shoot at the occupying army. The first relates an episode when a single Czech officer opened fire on the German troops:

> . . . The good news
> Has been brought,
> That Czech honour
> Is spared!
>
> It means – the land
> Has not given in,
> It means that for
> All that – there *was* war!

"One Officer", which contains Tsvetaeva's first direct mention of the Germans, was begun in October 1938, but completed only in 1939, at a time when she was already working on "March".

March 1939 destroyed Tsvetaeva's last hopes and forced her to return to work. On 14 March the Germans began to occupy Czechoslovakia, and on 15 March they entered Prague. Tsvetaeva now had to admit that the Germans she so loved had turned into barbarians:

> O tears in the eyes!
> The sob of love and anger!
> O land of the Czechs in tears!
> The land of Spain in blood!
>
> O black mountain,
> Eclipsing all the light! . . .

The structure of "March" is extremely musical. The poem begins with the quiet, even notes of "Lullaby", follows a gradual crescendo to the scream of "Germany", breaks off and then crescendoes again from the quiet tone of "March" up to the howl of the final poem. Strikingly absent from the poem is any sense of hatred. For all her grief over Czechoslovakia, Tsvetaeva cannot bring herself to hate Germany – only to feel sorrow for the way Germany has betrayed herself. The first lines of "Germany" are in fact almost a confession of love:

> O maiden, rosier than them all
> Among the mountains green –
> Germany!
> Germany!
> Germany!

This lyrical beginning is interrupted by the single word:

Shame!

Not hatred, but shame and bewilderment. And perhaps an attempt to bring Germany to her senses:

> O mania! O mummy
> Of grandeur!
> You will burn,
> Germany!
> Madness,
> Madness
> You are committing!

In a letter to Tesková, Tsvetaeva wrote: "I think that Bohemia is my first grief of this kind." Grief over both Czechoslovakia and Germany. What had happened was a catastrophe for Germany, a catastrophe for Bohemia and a catastrophe for Europe. Tsvetaeva was now living only out of inertia, only out of her inordinate sense of duty. "Poems to Bohemia" ends with one of Tsvetaeva's most tragically artless poems, a declaration to God that she no longer wants to take part in the game that we call life:

> O black mountain,
> Eclipsing all the light!
> It's time, it's time, it's time
> To return the Creator's ticket.
>
> I refuse – to be.
> In the Bedlam of non-people
> I refuse – to live.
> With the wolves of the squares
>
> I refuse – to howl.
> With the sharks of the plains
> I refuse to swim –
> Down stream with the crowds.
>
> I need no ear-holes
> Nor prophetic eyes.
> I make but one reply
> To your mad world – refusal.

These lines were completed exactly a month before Tsvetaeva left Paris. It was now all the same to her where she *didn't live*.

*

Tsvetaeva's bags had been packed for a long time; her decision had been made and there was no going back on it. Was there anyone who tried to dissuade her from returning to the Soviet Union? Quite possibly not. The majority of people who knew her were not in the least interested, a few gloated, and her closest friends – people like Lebedeva and Tesková – understood the impossibility of her position. People with pro-Soviet views, of course, sympathized. Salomeya Andronikova has told me how she went to Paris from London in order to say goodbye to Tsvetaeva. "And you didn't try to dissuade her from leaving?" I asked. "Why should I?" she replied. "I thought she was doing the right thing – Russia is our motherland." I felt that Andronikova had failed to understand that Tsvetaeva was returning not to Russia, but to the Soviet Union. In any case it is unlikely that anyone could have dissuaded Tsvetaeva. She had thought obsessively for years about the possibility and even necessity of returning and had given herself this warning: "Before putting out to sea, before selling and giving away all your goods and chattels, before saying goodbye to everyone and everything – weigh up carefully whether or not the country you are intending to go to is worth that price, and whether it can be considered a country." She herself understood better than anyone what it was she was returning to: "an abomination to which I will not submit *anywhere* – just as I will not submit to any organized violence . . .".

In 1936, in a letter to Tesková, Tsvetaeva had listed the pros and cons of returning to Russia. The pros included "sister Asya, who loves me . . ."; and "All the same there is a circle of real writers there, not just debris. (The writers here don't love me, they don't look on me as one of their own.)" She did not know that she would never again see Asya, who had already been arrested – nor could she know that it was a long time since there had been any "circles" whatsoever in Moscow, that everyone just wanted to hide away and make themselves as invisible as possible. Nevertheless, Tsvetaeva did have an understanding of the nature of Soviet life – as we can see from a letter she wrote about Alya to Vladimir Lebedev: "There are constant letters from Alya . . . She is very satisfied with life, even though there have already been small disappointments – nothing surprising, but it is the first time she has met them – since 'one can never display enough vigilance' (I would say 'display enough *trust*'). I can't see any circle of people around her: she writes only about relatives and doesn't mention a single new name; knowing her, I doubt if there *are any. In general* she is satisfied, work will sort itself out (so far she has only had temporary work), and she will soon get acclimatized to everything (she will indeed – to *everything*)." Tsvetaeva's irony is at the expense of her daughter's attempts to justify things that can never be justified. Tsvetaeva had no such ability herself, she knew very well that she would never get "acclimatized" to Soviet life, and yet she had no choice: as she wrote to Tesková five days before her departure, "I cannot abandon someone in trouble, that's the way I was born."

Tsvetaeva knew that Efron was in trouble, that his life "in a village", "in complete isolation, like on an island", was far from idyllic, and she may even have understood that he was already under something not so very different from house arrest. But she had renounced her own life; it was only her husband and her son who mattered. Tesková, who knew Tsvetaeva better than anyone, wrote after her death: "But for Mur, she would never have gone back to Russia." Or as Tsvetaeva herself wrote: "And so I'll go – like a dog . . .".

Mark Slonim has described how Tsvetaeva and Mur came to say goodbye to him. They talked about Prague and about the fate of Tsvetaeva's papers. She read Slonim her last poem, "The Bus". Slonim was ecstatic about it, but "Mur listened with a bored look. Tsvetaeva said at one point that she didn't know what awaited her in Moscow and whether she would be allowed to publish her work. Mur had been yawning, but at this he woke up and declared: 'What do you mean, Mama? You never believe anything – it will all work out fine.' M.I. paid no attention to her son but just repeated an old phrase of hers: 'the best place for writers is where people least interfere with their writing, i.e. their breathing.'" It is important to remember that Mur was only fourteen years old.

Tsvetaeva continued to say goodbye to everything and everyone – both the living and the dead. She went to a requiem for her old friend Prince Volkonsky. Nina Berberova has described her standing alone on the porch while the crowd appeared to flow around her. She visited the grave of the Efrons and arranged for a modest tombstone in Montmartre cemetery for Elizaveta Petrovna, Yakov Konstantinovich and Kostya [Sergey's parents and brother]. As always, Tsvetaeva thought of herself last of all. Three letters she wrote to N.I. Tukalevskaya during these last days have been published. "If you wish to give me anything for the journey, I beg you to make it some *coffee*: one can take a lot and all I have left is a packet I have already begun and I have no money at all. And if you can – a shirt – as simple as possible . . . all I have to wear are *rags*." Her two last letters were written the morning and evening before her departure, when she was sitting on her luggage and waiting to go. It is clear that nothing any longer depended on her, that someone else – doubtless the Soviet consulate – was now in charge. "Yesterday we sat here the *entire* day, waiting for a telephone call. In the evening it emerged that we weren't leaving. Today will be the same –

maybe we'll go, maybe we won't . . . If we *don't* go, then Mur will call round tomorrow. If he doesn't, then we've left. We don't know anything until the last moment and we can't go anywhere because they only telephone a short time in advance." On the afternoon of 11 June Tsvetaeva finally learned that they would be leaving the next morning.

It was perhaps because of all this uncertainty that no one saw them off. This may indeed have been the purpose of the uncertainty around the date of their departure. In the train to Le Havre – where they were to catch the boat to the Soviet Union – Tsvetaeva described her last minutes in the hotel: "Before we left, Mur and I sat down for a moment in the old way and crossed ourselves beneath where the icon had been (it has found a good home . . .)" She finished this letter to Tesková with the following words:

Goodbye! What comes now is no longer difficult, what comes now is fate.

CHAPTER 6

THE RETURN HOME

Can one return
To the home that's razed?

(. . .)

That Russia where my youth
Is on the coins
Has gone.

Neither am I the same.

ON 18 JUNE 1939, AFTER SEVENTEEN YEARS as an émigré, Tsvetaeva returned to her country of birth. She had entered a strange world, a country that she would have to get to know all over again. The newspapers gave the impression that life was in full swing, but it was an unknown life, quite unlike the life she had left behind her seventeen years before. Everything was different: concepts of human values, and personal relationships, the new, now established, way of life, the language itself. She recorded this date on a photograph taken two years later: "On the second anniversary of my ingress. 18 June 1941." Tsvetaeva's use of the word "V'ezd" (ingress) is, to say the least, surprising – it is more often used in relation to a Tsar or to a general returning in triumph. Tsvetaeva's return, by contrast, was an event that passed quite unnoticed. She returned to Russia not as the well-known writer, Marina Tsvetaeva, but as the wife of Sergey Efron, a Soviet agent who had been exposed. Unlike the case of Aleksandr Kuprin – whose return in 1937 had been marked by articles and interviews in both *Pravda* and *Izvestia* – there were no official celebrations. Tsvetaeva and Mur joined Efron and Alya in their dacha that belonged either to the NKVD or to the Peoples' Commissariat for Internal Affairs, in the village of Bolshevo not far from Moscow. Alya, however, only visited now and again; she spent most of her time in Moscow, where she had her work and her friends. She also had a lover. The dacha was on a grand scale, but without any modern comforts: a large hall with a huge fireplace, but an outside lavatory. The oil-stoves and the cellar made it seem as though Tsvetaeva had returned to village life in Prague. The Efrons shared the dacha with the Sezeman-Klepinins – the family of another Soviet agent who had recently returned to Russia. I learned about their life in Bolshevo from Lidia Brodskaya, a friend of Nina Sezeman who paid frequent visits. Lidia Brodskaya said what a nice man Efron had been, how interesting he had always been to talk to, how much he had looked forward to the arrival of his wife and son, and how proud he had been of Mur and his letters. When I asked what it was that had made murderers out of Efron and her husband, she replied: "They wanted to serve their motherland. There was a lot of romanticism in it all . . .". She had got the impression that Efron was unwell and something of a hypochondriac; she had noticed that there were always a lot of medicines beside his bed.

Life in the dacha was far from easy. Tsvetaeva wrote: "my hands are always full . . . I visit the cellar 100 times every day. When can I write??" This notebook entry is important since it shows that Tsvetaeva did at least wish to write. Tsvetaeva also found it difficult to share the dacha with another family. D. Sezeman, who was then a young man, wrote: "I don't know if it is necessary for me to say how difficult it was to share a 'communal apartment' with M.I. Like someone with a missing skin . . . she reacted exaggeratedly to everything . . .". It should be said that Nina Sezeman showed remarkable restraint. Lidia Brodskaya remembers saying to her in regard to one "disagreement": "Well if I'd been in your place, I'd have hit that Tsvetaeva over the head with a saucepan!" Nina Sezeman just answered: "No, Lilya, Tsvetaeva is a genius – one can pardon her everything . . .".

For all this, the months she spent in Bolshevo were a relatively happy and peaceful time. D. Sezeman remembers evening conversations by the fireside and Tsvetaeva reading her poems and translations of Pushkin. But this sense of peace was deceptive. A year later, Tsvetaeva was to write of these months: "There is always an overtone, an undertone, of horror. They promise a partition – and time passes. They promise a school for Murik – and time passes. And I am unused to the wooden landscape – the absence of stone, of a foundation." Tsvetaeva's life at this time was in fact profoundly unstable – there was no foundation beneath anything. She still had no Soviet documents ("I live without papers") and Efron was without work. He was either still registered with the NKVD or was receiving a pension from them. It slowly dawned on Tsvetaeva that she and her husband were both entirely helpless: "There is no one to hold on to. I am beginning to understand that S. is powerless, absolutely powerless, in everything."

During these first months Tsvetaeva saw only relatives, neighbours and a few acquaintances. She appears to have made no attempt to find work or to make herself known in the literary world. She did, of course, want to see Pasternak. We do not know the details of their first meeting, but it was preceded by an episode I was told about by Elena Efimovna Tager: "Suddenly there was a telephone call. It was Pasternak saying: 'Marina Ivanovna has come back and she wants me to go and see her. But I met Kaverin and . . . (another writer whose name Elena Tager had forgotten – V.S.) and they warned me not to go on any account. It's dangerous. I didn't go.' " Elena Tager remembered being shocked by Pasternak's "cowardice" and expressing her indignation on the telephone. Immediately after putting the receiver down, she began to worry: maybe it really was dangerous to have any dealings with Tsvetaeva, maybe something awful would happen to Pasternak if he did go to see her . . . It is possible that Pasternak either knew or guessed about Efron's involvement with the NKVD. Nevertheless, he did eventually meet Tsvetaeva – though not in Bolshevo but at Elizaveta Efron's room in Merzlyakovsky Lane. He also sent Vera Zvyagintseva there, saying that Tsvetaeva wanted to see her. "I remember how I rushed along," Zvyagintseva reminisced. "Marina was sitting there, a quite different woman, like a lady. In a proper dress, sleek, tidy, grey-haired. And her son looked as though he'd been carved out of pink soap." I asked Zvyagintseva whether they had greeted one another warmly or not; she answered, "Guardedly". Tsvetaeva had not, of course, in any way become like a lady. It was probably more a matter of the contrast between Tsvetaeva's sense of tragedy and Zvyagintseva's joyful and all-embracing approach to life. Tsvetaeva's guardedness was probably linked to the "sense of horror" which she confided only to her notebooks. No intellectual understanding could possibly have prepared her for what she found in her motherland and – above all – for the degree to which people themselves had changed. Zvyagintseva remembered Tsvetaeva saying something about "my contemptible daughter"; it is possible that Tsvetaeva blamed Alya for not warning her in her letters. Tsvetaeva attempted to see several of her old friends, but most of them were unwilling to take the risk of meeting her. Tsvetaeva understood all this and with her usual exaggerated sensitivity refrained from pressing herself on anyone.

The "breathing-space" afforded by Bolshevo was not to last long – Alya was arrested on 28 August, in the small hours. Tsvetaeva and Alya had evidently remained on somewhat frosty terms, possibly because each of them found it difficult to hide their anxiety from the other. One entry in Tsvetaeva's notebook reads: "Alya is enigmatic with her false gaiety . . .". Alya's arrest must have put an end to their misunderstandings. Tsvetaeva described it as follows: "Alya was very bright and gallant. Laughing it off . . . She was leaving without saying goodbye! 'What do you mean, Alya? How can you not even say goodbye to anyone?' She just looked over her shoulder, in tears, and gave a wave of the hand. The commandant (an old man with a certain kindness) said: 'She's quite right. Long farewells mean too many tears . . .'".

Tsvetaeva was now one of the millions of Soviet women who spent long hours in prison queues, waiting to hand in parcels to loved ones who had been arrested. Efron himself, as Tsvetaeva must have expected, was not to remain free for long: he and Sezeman were arrested together on 10 October 1939. Tsvetaeva herself did not write anything about this in her notebook, but the housemaid told Lidia Brodskaya that she made a large sign of the cross over her husband as they took him away . . . Tsvetaeva was never again to see either her husband or her daughter. Alya was sentenced by a Special Commission to eight years in the labour camps – for espionage. Efron himself was shot in 1941 after being sentenced by a Military Tribunal. They were both eventually rehabilitated after the death of Stalin "because of the absence of corpus delicti".

Tsvetaeva, Mur and Sezeman's family were ordered to leave the dacha – which was then sealed up. Tsvetaeva was now alone with Mur, with no home and nothing to live on. She had, at least, finally acquired her Soviet passport – without which life would have been still more difficult. It is difficult to imagine what she must have felt at this time. Her notebook contains only a few words: "I unwrap the wound. Live meat." Some time later she remarked to a friend: "if *they* come for me, then I'll hang myself."

Tsvetaeva and Mur were taken in by Sergey's sister Elizaveta, who was living in one small room in what had once been her own apartment. Tsvetaeva herself referred to it as "a burrow, or rather, a quarter of a burrow – with no window and no table and the main thing is that one can't smoke." She did nevertheless have a roof over her head and Elizaveta Efron was extremely brave to show them such generosity.

It was imperative for Tsvetaeva to find work and somewhere more permanent to live. From the viewpoint of official Soviet literature she had long ago ceased to exist – it was as though she were attempting to begin her career for a second time. In 1940, revising a poem she had written twenty years earlier, "To you – after a hundred years", she changed the words "have forgotten" to "don't remember":

> Friend! Look not for me! Another fashion!
> Even old men no longer remember me.

In spite of these lines, Tsvetaeva was still remembered both by readers of poetry and by other poets of her generation who knew her only from her first editions. Semyon Lipkin said in answer to a question of mine:

> I was born in 1911. My contemporaries and I are the last generation who remained civilized. We knew everything, we knew and loved Russian poetry, the Symbolists, and what came after them – Mandelstam, Tsvetaeva. I became interested in poetry around 1925, one could still buy collections of poetry then and I had my own *Mileposts* (I lost it during the war). To us Tsvetaeva was a sacred name, we knew she was a remarkable poet. Copies of a few of her works were circulated, odd poems got through from abroad. We knew that Tsvetaeva hadn't disappeared over there . . .

Lydia Chukovskaya also knew Tsvetaeva by *Mileposts*. Some friends of Vera Zvyagintseva told me that during the years 1927–29 she used to arrange evenings at her home when an actress friend would read poems by Tsvetaeva, including "The Rat-catcher". Another friend of mine, someone who spent thirty-one years in prisons, camps and exile, remembers his fiancée visiting him in 1928 and bringing him a typed copy of "The Rat-catcher".

Tsvetaeva was not entirely unknown, but she was a former émigré and a member of a family of "enemies of the people". Either of these factors alone would have been enough to terrify most Soviet officials and institutions. There was no conceivable place for Tsvetaeva in Soviet literature as it was then understood. Socialist Realism had for a long time been the only acceptable method. The private and cooperative publishing houses that had flourished immediately before and after the Revolution had all long ago disappeared; it was now impossible for a writer to earn money except from the State itself. Most of those who were to be destroyed had by then already been destroyed; most of those who were to survive were actively striving to become "necessary writers" – to use a phrase of Osip Mandelstam's.

On 1 February 1939 *Izvestia* published a decree that 172 writers were to be awarded medals "for outstanding successes and achievements in the development of Soviet artistic literature". It happened to be on the very same day that a parcel was returned to Nadezhda Mandelstam from the camps "on account of the death of the addressee". . . In response to the awards the All-Moscow Congress of Writers addressed comrade Stalin as follows: "Dear Iosif Vissarionovich! While celebrating this joyful day of honours for Soviet writers, we remain aware how much is demanded from us, how much still remains to be done . . ." Their message ended with the words: "We wish, comrade Stalin, for each line of ours to help the cause to which you have devoted your life – the cause of Communism."

Official sources combine to give the impression that life in the Soviet Union at this time was one continuous festival. Events and anniversaries that were celebrated during the first few months after Tsvetaeva's return include: a Congress of Popular Storytellers in Moscow, the thousandth anniversary of the writing of the Armenian epic poem *David of Sassun*, the fiftieth anniversary of the death of Chernyshevsky, and the "liberation" by the Red Army of Western Ukraine and Western Belorussia. Writers were expected to respond to these celebrations with large quantities of poems, stories and articles.

In spite of these varied celebrations, everyone lived in a state of terror. The more intense this terror, the more they tried to suppress it through a frenzied search for comfort and luxury . . . A splendid "House of Writers" had already been set up in Lavrushinsky Lane, the writers' dacha village of Peredelkino was still expanding in size, "Houses of Creativity" were springing up one after the other. The Moscow Writers' Club prided itself on having the finest chef in Moscow . . . One witness was later to describe New Year's Eve 1939 in the Writers' Club as a "feast in time of plague".

In 1920 Tsvetaeva had declared to Anatoly Lunacharsky, then the Commissar for Enlightenment:

> I will not rush into the red round-dance
> Around the May tree . . .

Now, a lifetime later, she was still in the same position, adamantly refusing to join the "red round-dance". Not, of course, that there was any place for her there anyway. Nevertheless she did have to look after her son; she had to earn enough money to find somewhere to live, to feed him and to send prison parcels to her husband and daughter. It was at this moment of desperate need that Pasternak came to her aid.

Pasternak would probably have had nothing to do with Tsvetaeva if her life in the Soviet Union had gone well for her. He was no longer interested in her as a woman, and it seems unlikely that he was still interested in her poetry – soon after her death he described her merely as a poet "of brilliant *potential*". Tsvetaeva wrote with bitter irony of both Pasternak and Aseev, the two fellow poets on whom she had placed her hopes. Aseev – whom she remembered as a comrade of Mayakovsky's – was now a member of the literary élite, someone who might be compromised by any association with Tsvetaeva. He received her once, but was clearly frightened and treated her with extreme coldness. Erenburg likewise preferred to have nothing to do with Tsvetaeva. Pasternak, on the other hand, did what he could to help. Olga Ivinskaya has written that he attempted to interest Fadeev, the head of the Writers' Union, in Tsvetaeva's fate, but that nothing came of it. Vera Zvyagintseva has told me that "Pasternak put her in touch with Goltsev, who gave her some translations". Viktor Goltsev was an important figure in the area of translations into Russian from the various other literatures of the Soviet Union. Lipkin remembered Tsvetaeva's account of a dinner arranged for her by Pasternak with various Georgian poets. There had been fine food and wine and a considerable amount of florid Eastern eloquence: Tsvetaeva had simply been amazed that people could spend an entire day at the table . . . She and Pasternak no longer exchanged poems, and nothing remained of their former intimacy. Some people have said – perhaps unfairly – that this was because he was afraid of his wife's jealousy. In any case it is clear from Tsvetaeva's account to Lipkin that Pasternak treated her not as an intimate and an equal, but as a poor relative who had fallen upon hard times. This, of course, distressed Tsvetaeva; nevertheless, there was hardly anyone other than Pasternak who had the courage or desire to help her at all.

In December 1939 Tsvetaeva moved to the dacha village of Golitsyno – one and half hours by train from Moscow along the line to Minsk. This village contained one of the new "Houses of Creativity" for writers. This move was probably arranged by Pasternak – no one in Tsvetaeva's position would have been admitted to a writers' home without strong support from someone of influence. Not that Tsvetaeva was ever fully admitted to it. Under the pretext that she was with Mur and that "children" were not accepted, Tsvetaeva was merely given coupons. This meant that they could eat in the writers' home, but had to live elsewhere in the village – and pay for a room and find firewood. S. I. Fonskaya, the director of the House, rented a room for Tsvetaeva in a winter dacha close to the writers' house, at the end of the street. Once again Tsvetaeva had to accustom herself to extreme cold, a strange room and a general feeling of instability . . . A note she wrote to Marietta Shaginyan has been preserved: a cry for help in obtaining wood. She took breakfast back home in a saucepan and ate lunch and supper in the Home together with Mur. She was also able to use the telephone there. She stayed in Golitsyno for over five months. During that time a large number of other writers came and went; Tsvetaeva became acquainted with many of them and became friends with a few.

There are few reliable accounts of how other people saw Tsvetaeva at this time. O. A. Mochalova, a poet who was introduced to Tsvetaeva in summer 1917 by Balmont, has left us this account:

> M.Ts. was thin and exhausted, and her face was grey and colourless. She had a greyish curl over her forehead, small pale-blue eyes, and an expression that was anxious and unfriendly. She was like some hobgoblin

that was about to make a sideways jump, play some trick, scratch you and perform a somersault. She spoke quickly and irritably, in spasms, often interrupting the other person: "In the physical world I am very undemanding, but in the spiritual world I am intolerant!" She was dressed very poorly; everything was thrown together any old how. She wore a beret and a cold fur coat with a little grey collar . . .

Mochalova's description of a visit paid to her by Tsvetaeva is in a similar vein:

> . . . she took off her coat, sat down at the desk and began to write something. I thought inspiration must have descended on her and timidly asked what she was writing.
>
> "What does that matter to you?" M.Ts. replied angrily. This is my notebook, you have one too. I wouldn't have had time to note anything down at home, but I can do it here."
>
> I obediently began to make some tea, hoping her writing wouldn't go on for too long. Finally M.Ts. laid down her pen with a satisfied look and put her notebook away in the cloth bag that she took with her wherever she went . . .

Elena Tager and her husband, on the other hand, wrote about the same thing with pride: when she came round, Tsvetaeva sometimes sat down at their desk and wrote – she must have felt at home with them! . . . Semyon Lipkin remembered Tsvetaeva as an intelligent conversationalist, full of laughter and vitality, "anything but a cry-baby". She was slim, perhaps a quarter of her hair had turned grey, she spoke quickly and was always turning her head from one side to another; "she was dressed poorly and in a way that was foreign to us". It may be that it was this "foreignness" which some people found so irritating. Marietta Shaginyan, for example, wrote:

> Some of my contemporaries were captivated not only by the "foreign", "Western", sonorities of her verse (what *does* this mean? – V.S.), but even by what was foreign in her appearance, or at least by what remained of this foreignness – a worn-out scarf round her neck with an unusual design, an unusually shaped comb in her hair and even her cheap frayed notebook with the thin metallic pencil she held in her fingers – my heart sank with pity when I caught sight of these miserable traces of her recent past – it was as though dirty water off her shoes had left a mark in the room.

T. I. Kvanina, on the other hand, was furiously indignant when I read this passage to her. She saw Shaginyan's account as the view of a petit bourgeois and went on to say that everything about Tsvetaeva was so unusual that you really didn't notice what she was wearing – except for her silver bracelets which really did suit her . . . No doubt Shaginyan treated Tsvetaeva with the same condescension when they met in Golitsyno: bereft of her husband and daughter, with no knowledge of Marxist philosophy, without "a place in the sun", Tsvetaeva could hardly have been of any interest to her.

Far more important than any of this is the fact that Tsvetaeva spent several hours on two consecutive days in June 1941 with Anna Akhmatova. Akhmatova had come to Moscow to petition on behalf of her son, who had recently been arrested for the second time. This was their only meeting. All Akhmatova said of it in her account to Lydia Chukovskaya is that: "She came and sat there for seven hours." It is as though she is talking of a boring and unwanted guest. In the notes she wrote in the sixties for a planned book of memoirs Akhmatova wrote: "I want to recall those *Two Days* simply, without any legends." Unfortunately, she never did. She has, however, said that either she herself, or Tsvetaeva – or perhaps each of them – was shadowed when they met at the home of [the literary scholar] N. I. Khardzhiev on the second day. She has also written that she read Tsvetaeva the beginning of "Poem without a Hero": "When, in June 1941, I read M.Ts. part of the poem (the first draft), she said, rather caustically: 'One must be very bold to write of harlequins, columbines and pierrots in 1941.' Evidently she saw the poem as something stylized and fin de siècle, in the spirit of Benois and Somov, i.e. as being like the old-fashioned junk she had struggled against as an émigrée." Tsvetaeva for her part gave – or perhaps read to – Akhmatova "Poem of the Air", one of her most important, most complex and metaphysical works, a poem that aspires like "New Year's Greeting" towards another world. It is probably this poem that Akhmatova had in mind when she said in regard to Tsvetaeva's suicide: "Some people say that there were also other reasons for her death, reasons to do with her work, that she had written an entirely Futurist [*zaumnuyu*] poem, made up of quite separate lines without any connection between them . . . One can only, of course, write one poem like that, one cannot write a second . . .". It is upsetting to hear this kind of thing from Akhmatova. Tsvetaeva never wrote *zaumnuyu* poems, she never wrote a single meaningless line. It is, however, perhaps not so very surprising that they should each have had reservations about the other's poetry: their lyrical "I"s are of a very different nature. Each of them is an egocentric and each of them is concerned with the problem: "I and the world". But if Akhmatova's "I" is first and foremost a woman, Tsvetaeva's "I" is that of a poet. This is the difference between their respective views of the world, between the sense they had of their own place in it. I would say that Akhmatova's world is more intimate and limited than Tsvetaeva's: in the first place it is filtered through the sensibility of a woman, and in the second place it is closer to the earth, to physical reality than Tsvetaeva's world.

> *. . . from*
> The earth, *above* the earth, away
> From the worm and grain!

Akhmatova, like many other people, clearly saw Tsvetaeva's timeless romanticism as an affectation. In 1944, according to O. Mochalova, even Pasternak was to say: "Akhmatova screws up her eyes cunningly, whereas Marina is bombastic. The kitchen primus spilt and flared up near her son – she saw it as the ring of fire round Siegfried." He now saw as bombast what he had previously considered to be an inborn tendency towards hyperbole, a sublimity of feeling and of attitude towards the world.

What Tsvetaeva writes bears only an indirect relation to her personal life, it relates to her only in so far as she is a poet. The reality behind Tsvetaeva's hyperboles is her concept of the poet, the reality behind Akhmatova's hyperboles, on the other hand, is her own fate. There are real events and people behind these lines from "Poem without a Hero":

> He will not be my beloved husband,
> But he and I shall earn such merit
> To put to shame the twentieth century.

Behind these lines is the spectre of the 1946 Central Committee decree relating to the journals *Star* and *Leningrad*, a decree which played a cruel role in Soviet literature as a whole and in Akhmatova's life in particular. But it is a great exaggeration to suppose, as Akhmatova did, that the decree was provoked by events in her personal life or that the twentieth century, the century of Hitler and Stalin, would "be put to shame" because of it. This is a hyperbole as extreme as any of Tsvetaeva's.

Unfortunately, Tsvetaeva never saw any of Akhmatova's later poetry. In autumn 1940 she read the recent collection *From Six Books* and was extremely disappointed: "old and weak . . . But what was she doing between 1917 and 1940? *Inside* herself. This book is an irremediably blank page . . . A pity."

Tsvetaeva wanted a glimpse of Akhmatova's path – and the censored volume she had read did not afford such a glimpse. In reality Akhmatova had already written "Requiem", "A Wreath for the Dead" and "A Late Answer" – a poem addressed to Tsvetaeva herself. Akhmatova never wrote these poems down and she evidently considered it safer not to read them to

Tsvetaeva either. She herself said that she didn't read "A Late Answer" to Tsvetaeva because of the "terrible line about her loved ones":

> The abyss swallowed up my loved ones,
> And the home of my parents is pillaged . . .

Had Tsvetaeva had the opportunity to read these poems, there is no doubt that she would have valued them extremely highly.

Akhmatova, however, was never to value Tsvetaeva's poetry – even though she was to survive her by many years. Even twenty-five years later she was still writing about her with a certain condescension. Noting down her intention to describe their meeting in 1941, Akhmatova added: "It's terrifying to think how Marina herself would have described these meetings if she had remained alive and if I had died on 31 August 1941. It would have become a *fragrant legend* – as our grandfathers used to say." And her libretto for a ballet, thematically related to "Poem Without a Hero", contains the lines: "Marina Tsvetaeva, who had arrived from Moscow for her 'Otherworldly Evening' and who confused everything in the world." There is no point in arguing with Akhmatova; one can only regret that, at a time when they each needed support, these two poets failed to recognize one another.

Akhmatova was not alone in being irritated by Tsvetaeva. I am inclined to think that the true reason for this general irritation relates to the fact that Tsvetaeva had chosen – or appeared to have chosen – to return to the Soviet Union. Her scarfs, her notebook, her zip handbag (unobtainable in Moscow) – everything about her was Parisian . . . How could she have returned to a country where no one had anything at all and everyone lived in constant fear of arrest? . . . People who met Tsvetaeva must have wondered. In literary circles the word went round that: "The White Guard Lady has returned!" And on top of all this, Tsvetaeva was destitute. "She's come back – so what does she want now? She's still unsatisfied!" So people may well have thought – at least unconsciously. It would have been unlike Tsvetaeva to explain that there was no *purpose* behind her return, that she had only returned because of the sense of duty that she felt towards her husband. It was also impossible for her ever to really understand Soviet people – she was divided from them by seventeen years spent in a different world.

Tsvetaeva's poetry was as alien as she was herself. All Tsvetaeva's contemporaries – those at least, who had a voice of their own and their own view of the world – had been erased from literature. All poetry at this time was tending towards song, towards the hymn and the ode. Everyone wrote on the same themes and in the same tone of elated cheerfulness. It was barely possible, in these years, to tell one Soviet poet from another. As Ilya Ilf wrote, "they all write in the same way and even in the same handwriting". Everything "decadent" had been officially expelled from poetry. Concerned as she was with such themes as the soul, poetry, love, homesickness, death and immortality, Tsvetaeva must have seemed like a Martian . . . And of course, Tsvetaeva's complex metaphors and unusual rhythms must have seemed the height of affectation. People who remembered Tsvetaeva, and who still valued her, knew only her pre-revolutionary poems. Tsvetaeva wanted recognition for her new poems, but when she read them – at private homes, needless to say – they attracted little response. Zvyagintseva twice told me that "no one liked" the poems Tsvetaeva read. Lipkin admitted that Tsvetaeva's reading had made no impression on him. People who had never encountered Tsvetaeva's poetry before were no more impressed: Arseny Tarkovsky thought that "many of her poems seemed excessive"; M. S. Petrovykh was quite untouched by them; and Tatyana Kvanina has said to me that she still prefers her prose. The Tagers, who were profoundly impressed by her poetry, were in a distinct minority. This sense of a "non-meeting" with her reader (she had once said that her reader had remained in Moscow) still further intensified her sense of isolation. Tatyana Kvanina, then a very young teacher of Russian language and literature, first became friends with Tsvetaeva in Golitsyno. In a letter to her husband in late 1940, she wrote: "I have a very ambivalent feeling about Tsvetaeva: on the one hand I feel very shy of her, and on the other hand I feel myself to be more experienced. The years of ruin and so on – they have weaned me of many things and taught me many things. There is one thing I understand clearly: she is as alone here as if she were on Mars, in an incomprehensible world and among incomprehensible people – or rather beings. Everything around her – in its turn – refuses to accept her (something, alas, that is so familiar!). Life goes on, but she has been sent off down some side-road . . .".

Nevertheless, Tsvetaeva had achieved some degree at least of stability. She was able to earn her living through literary work and Mur was able to attend the village school. He was also having lessons with a private tutor in order to help him adapt to the Soviet system. Tsvetaeva worked hard. During her months in Golitsyno she translated three long poems by the Georgian poet Vazha Pshavela, two English ballads about Robin Hood and a number of Bulgarian poets – over two thousand lines in all. The longest and most difficult poems were those by Vazha Pshavela. It was the first time Tsvetaeva had worked from an interlinear crib – apparently a somewhat inadequate one – and the poems did not appeal to her. This was one of the few times her work afforded her no satisfaction. Nevertheless she worked on doggedly and painstakingly: "all through the winter, *every* day I translated the Georgians – great slabs of inscrutable cribs". She handed in her translation of the long poem "Etera" at the beginning of June, on the agreed date. A surviving copy of the manuscript – with comments by the editor and Tsvetaeva's final corrections – gives us an idea of the final stages of work. Individual words and sentences have been underlined by the editor and the margins contain remarks like "Where is this from?", "That's not it", "Very free", "An addition" . . . Tsvetaeva made around a hundred final corrections, changing individual words, lines and sometimes entire paragraphs. Some of the editor's comments reflect the spirit of the time. In one passage, for example, the viziers address the Tsar as "Great Leader!" It is unlikely that Tsvetaeva was intending any irony, but these words could not possibly have been allowed to pass: no one except Stalin could be addressed by those words. The editor simply entered an expressive "?!" in the margin and Tsvetaeva altered the offending words to: "O Tsar and Leader!"

In spite of all these difficulties, however, Tsvetaeva was somehow able to bring herself and her own creativity into these translations. Whether one is reading poems from Georgian, Robin Hood ballads or German folk songs, it is impossible not to recognize the spirit of Tsvetaeva herself. If she wrote nothing of her own at this time, it is not because her creativity was exhausted but because working to commission was the only possibility open to her.

Golitsyno was the most intimate of the writers' homes. Nine or ten writers lived there at a time and they all ate round a large table in a comfortable dining room. Tsvetaeva and Mur stood out sharply from the rest of the company. Tatyana Kvanina gave me a vivid account of her first meeting with Tsvetaeva:

My husband and I were living in Golitsyno. I had only recently got married and it was the first time I had moved in these circles. Every writer there made me think of Lev Tolstoy and I looked up to all of them. And then once, when we were all chattering away at the table, the door opened and . . . no, she didn't even come in and it was as though no one had opened the door . . . a slim woman wearing silver jewellery appeared in the doorway. A tall, handsome boy who turned out to be her son was walking (just walking in an ordinary way!) a few steps behind her. They went to their places in the middle of the table and sat down. The whole atmosphere immediately changed. The usual servile gossip immediately came to an end, and they all lost their glamour. I no longer thought of them as Lev Tolstoys . . . The general level of conversation improved. Gossip, meanness and vulgarity were impossible in Tsvetaeva's presence. The content of what she said was always interesting and elevated, and even her manner of speech was very unusual; to me it seemed old-fashioned and bookish. Everyone appeared stupid in the presence of Marina Tsvetaeva; no one there was her equal.

After supper, for some reason, we all saw her back to her room. I wouldn't have gone myself, but my husband went along with everyone else and so I did too. But I wasn't quite at home in the group and I was walking a little apart from them; when we all passed by a tree, I went up to it and stroked it. It was a very fine tree. Tsvetaeva noticed this and marked me out. When we were all saying goodnight, she invited us in – just me and my husband for some reason. We went round again that same evening. We began to visit her . . .

Kvanina was not the only person to be struck by Tsvetaeva's manner of speech. Lipkin, who had somehow imagined she might have forgotten how to speak Russian, was also impressed by her fine use of language – as was Evgeny Tager. Tsvetaeva, needless to say, had not forgotten how to speak Russian. The more important point, however, is probably that she still spoke a pre-revolutionary Russian, unaffected by the changes in idiom that had taken place over the last twenty years. This is probably why Kvanina found her language "old-fashioned and bookish".

In spite of everything, Tsvetaeva was still the same woman – and she still searched for friendship and intimacy. For a while she thought that "Tanechka" Kvanina could offer her the understanding she needed. Kvanina is probably the only person to deny having been a friend of Tsvetaeva's – since her death a remarkable number of people have claimed to have been friends with her at this time. "How could I have been a friend of hers?" Kvanina asked me. "The difference between us was too great – not just a difference in age but a difference in everything. Who am I beside her?" Aware that Kvanina felt there was a gulf between them, Tsvetaeva once wrote: "Tanya, don't be afraid of me. Don't think that I am clever, or anything else (substitute whatever it is that you're afraid of)! What you can give me is infinitely large – the only person who can give me anything is someone who makes my heart beat. That gives me back my heart, my beating heart. If I have no one to love, then I am not myself. It is such a long time since I have been myself. But with you I do feel myself." Kvanina, however, in spite of her obvious interest and sympathy, found it difficult to be a friend of Tsvetaeva's. In one letter to her husband, she wrote: "She talked about her husband and her daughter, about Mur, about Paris, about Pasternak. It all came out jumbled and superficial. She read some poems about Mayakovsky (I don't think they could be published) . . . Her conversation was very disconnected and spiced with a considerable amount of (all too understandable) bitterness. Quite unexpectedly she suddenly asked me: 'And what joy do you get from all this?' and 'What would you most like from life? And what century would you most like to have lived in?' She hardly gave me any time to answer. And questions like that are difficult to answer. I probably wouldn't have told her everything anyway. We are very different. She is up in the clouds and quite outside time. I was only like that myself up to the age of twenty . . .".

For all her sympathy and good will, Kvanina was unable to live up to Tsvetaeva's demands. Like everyone else, she found it difficult to accept Tsvetaeva's extraordinary openness. She also felt that there was something ambiguous about this openness: "You know, I never quite fully believe her in anything," Kvanina wrote to her husband. "It may only be very slight, but there is an element of pose in everything she does. It's as though she invented herself long ago and just carries on as this invented person . . . And what I shall never understand is why she needs me." Lipkin told me in the same tone of surprise how Tsvetaeva used to phone him up to ask ridiculously simple questions about her translations. It was only as he was talking to me that it suddenly occurred to him that she might just have wanted to hear a human voice. Kvanina also took decades to understand why Tsvetaeva needed her: "she was so lonely that she enjoyed attention even from someone she didn't know very well". At the time it had seemed as though Tsvetaeva had a number of important friends, people like Pasternak, Aseev and Erenburg . . .

During this period Tsvetaeva accepted whatever work she could find; she even edited a French translation of the Kalmyk poem "Dzhangar". Whatever she took on, she did to the best of her ability. T. A. Fish, a literary consultant for *Red Virgin Soil*, remembered Tsvetaeva's internal reviews of unknown poets. She had been astonished at how seriously Tsvetaeva took this work and had once asked her why she spent so much time on it. Tsvetaeva had replied that it was impossible to do otherwise – they were, after all, talking about Poetry. Fish went on to tell me that the letters Tsvetaeva had written to aspiring poets had always been much more interesting and inspired than their poems were.

Tsvetaeva received the average pay of a translator, around three or four roubles a line. This was clearly not enough to live on. During a five-month period of 1940 when she was doing more work than usual, she was paid an average of 770 roubles a month. Meanwhile, she was paying 830 roubles a month for her meals, and 250 for lodging. During other months she earned less – and sometimes nothing at all. After giving these details in a letter, Tsvetaeva went on to lament: "I apologize to everyone for working so well (i.e. slowly, carefully and consistently) and for earning so little . . . I am convinced that people would respect me infinitely more if I worked badly and earned more . . .". One of Tsvetaeva's notebooks contains details as to how she divided up her time: every moment that she wasn't standing in prison queues, or visiting institutions to petition on behalf of her family, was devoted to her work. I can no longer remember the figures, but they were impressive.

On 28 March S. I. Fonskaya, the director of the House of Creativity, told Tsvetaeva that from then on she would have to pay double for her coupons – as a result of a new decree from the Literary Fund regarding people who had lived in Houses for over three months. This was clearly not a decision taken by Fonskaya in person: she would no more have decided to throw out a "White Guard" on her own initiative than she would originally have decided to take her in without instructions. Tsvetaeva had nowhere else to go and she didn't want to take Mur away from his studies in the middle of the school year. In the end she decided to stay in Golitsyno and pay for meals for one person only. She went hungry herself and kept most of the food for Mur. Elena Tager, incidentally, told me how surprised people were in Moscow by Tsvetaeva's habit, as a visitor to someone else's home, of taking something nice to eat from the table and putting it in her zip handbag. Tsvetaeva and Mur remained in Golitsyno till the end of the school year and then moved back to Moscow on 7 June.

They spent the summer in a flat near the University belonging to [the art historian] Aleksandr Gabrichevsky and his wife Natalya. Much of the summer was taken up by dealings with officialdom: Tsvetaeva's baggage had finally arrived from Paris. It had been addressed, however, to Alya, and this created complications. When she finally took possession of her baggage, Tsvetaeva immediately either sold or gave away a large proportion of her belongings. Her other – more important – concern was to find somewhere to live – the thought of another winter in the country appalled her. Finding a room in Moscow, however, was not easy, especially for a woman with a son: people always preferred single men who were less likely to use the kitchen, wash clothes and otherwise take part in the life of the communal flat. Tsvetaeva answered numerous advertisements and put up advertisements herself – but all to no effect. On 30 August, when the Gabrichevskys returned, Tsvetaeva and Mur moved in again temporarily with Elizaveta Efron. She then applied for help from the Union of Writers. N. K. Trenyova, the widow of the deputy head of the Writers' Union, once read me over the phone a letter written to the Writers' Union by Pasternak in support of Tsvetaeva's application for help in finding accommodation in Moscow. Pasternak began by saying that he had not read Tsvetaeva's own letter, but that he knew what she was writing about. Her reason for applying was one that he himself disapproved of: "so that people won't say afterwards that she didn't apply to the Union." Pasternak went on to say that he knew Tsvetaeva as someone "intelligent and steadfast" and that if she made any threats, they were not to worry – she wouldn't carry them out. Pasternak put it considerably more delicately, but the above is the sense of his words: the implication is clearly that anything she might say about suicide would be merely an empty threat. He then, somewhat more supportively, said that Tsvetaeva was in an extremely difficult position, "more difficult than she can describe to you", and begged them to accept Tsvetaeva and somehow encourage her – "even though I know you will not be able to help her in any way". At the end of his letter Pasternak mentioned some room or other and said that its tenant was going to be away for a long time. For all its ambiguities, Pasternak's letter appears to have helped: Tsvetaeva was given a temporary room and a residence permit for Moscow. Apparently she had to pay the owner something like three years' rent in advance.

By the end of October Tsvetaeva was living on the Pokrovsky Boulevard, in a room in a communal flat on the seventh floor of a large building, where she was so afraid of the lift that she always chose to use the stairs instead. Once more she appeared to have been granted a breathing-space: she was working as a translator and Mur had been accepted by a good school where he had already made some friends. Her parcels for Seryozha and Alya were still being accepted – which meant that they were still alive and not far away. Horror had gradually become part of the fabric of everyday life. Tsvetaeva was even able to afford to pay a woman who came once a week to clean up the communal flat.

Now that her luggage had arrived from Paris, Tsvetaeva began to go through her manuscripts – those she had decided to bring to the Soviet Union – with the aim of compiling a new collection of poems. This is not a task she appears to have undertaken on her own initiative. At one point she wrote: "Here I am compiling a book, adding things, checking everything, paying for the typing, checking through it all again – and I am almost certain that they will *not* accept it, I would be amazed if they did. But *I have done my bit*, I have shown the best of good will (I have been obedient)." Someone close to her, perhaps Pasternak himself, had evidently persuaded her to attempt to publish a book. If she had succeeded, a book would not only have brought her some money, but would also have served as a much-needed testimony that she had finally been judged politically reliable. She understood the protection such testimony would afford to herself and to Mur.

A book would also have been important in its own right. It was eighteen years since she had last published a book in Moscow and twelve years since her last collection had been published in Paris. Tsvetaeva clearly gave considerable thought as to what to include in this volume. Not only do we still have lists of poems and exercise-books full of poems copied out by hand, but also the final version of the book as it was delivered to a publishing house. Studying all this material, one gets the impression that Tsvetaeva was torn between two contradictory desires: to get the book published no matter what, and to put together a book "for herself". On the one hand she renounced her unshakeable principle never to "make things easy for the reader", by adding titles to a number of poems: "Thus they floated by, the head and the lyre", for example, was entitled "Orpheus". On the other hand she dedicated the first poem, "I was writing on a slate", "To S.E." – i.e. to Sergey Efron. This was an act of considerable courage, expecially as the poem included the lines:

> And finally – let it be known to all!
> That you are loved! loved! loved! loved!

In 1920, when she first wrote the poem, Efron had been fighting in the White Army; in 1940, when she added the dedication, he was in prison. Both then and now Tsvetaeva had no certainty that he was even alive. One manuscript is dated: Moscow, 1920–40. Almost thirty years had passed since their first meeting and she was saying in verse for the first time: "I love you." It was important for her to make this declaration; she wanted everyone to know that she loved him and that nothing would make her renounce her love. At the same time she is repeating in verse what she declared in 1937 to the French police: "His trust may have been abused, my trust in him remains unchanged."

The well-known critic Kornely Zelinsky was commissioned by Goslitizdat to write an internal review of Tsvetaeva's collection. His review was to all intents and purposes a denunciation. It contained such passages as: "For almost two decades (and what decades!) the poet was outside her motherland, outside the USSR. She was surrounded by our enemies. She offers us a book composed for the main part of poems written when she was an émigré and already published . . . in the émigré press . . . . The author's thesis about the political neutrality of the pen is, alas, contradicted by the facts. A whole sequence of Tsvetaeva's poems were dedicated to the poeticizing of the struggle against the USSR." A review such as this could not only easily have prevented the book from being published – which it did – but also have led to her being charged with carrying out anti-Soviet propaganda. Tsvetaeva, however, was angered and hurt not so much by the political slur as by Zelinsky's accusation that she was a formalist: "Marina Tsvetaeva's true tragedy is that, gifted as she is with the ability to write verse, she has nothing to say to people. This is why Marina Tsvetaeva's poetry is anti-humanist and empty of any genuinely human content. And it is for this reason that, in order to satisfy her need to versify, she has to heap up complex, enciphered constructions inside which there is only emptiness, an entire lack of content."

After six pages, the review ends with the words: "From all I have said it must be clear that M. Tsvetaeva's book cannot, in its present guise, be published by Goslitizdat. Everything about it (the tone, the language, the range of interests) is alien to us and in contradiction to the direction of Soviet poetry as the poetry of Socialist Realism. From the entire book one could only select five or six poems which are worthy of being shown to our readers." Zelinsky was an influential figure and it was no chance that the book had been allocated to him; Tsvetaeva could not have failed to understand from the review that this was the end. She may, however, have understood that Zelinsky was at least being consistent: where Socialist Realism blossomed, there could be no place for her own poetry. She replied to Zelinsky on the fair copy of the "assassinated" book: "P.S. Someone who could classify these poems as *formalism* is simply unscrupulous. I am saying this *from the future*. M.Ts."

What still perplexes me is why Tsvetaeva did not make more of an attempt to make the book "acceptable". This would not have been impossible. She could not have included her "Poems to Bohemia" as Germany was at that time a "friend" of the Soviet Union. She could, nevertheless, have included such poems as "Motherland", "Poems to a Son", "Desk", "Homesickness", "In Praise of the Rich" and "Poem of the Barrier". She must have been able to understand that these poems would have allowed a well-meaning reviewer to talk of her love for her motherland, her longing to return there, and her fierce criticisms of capitalism and the bourgeoisie . . . It is possible that Tsvetaeva herself had little idea what she was doing. I think, though, that it was partly a matter of her sense that it was impossible to go on living. While she was compiling her collection, she once wrote: "My *difficulty* (my difficulty in writing poems and perhaps the difficulty other people experience in reading them) is that I have set myself an impossible task: for example, to convey a *groan* (a-a-ah) through *words* (i.e. through meanings)." She also wrote: "Nobody sees, nobody knows, that I have been looking round for a hook for approximately a year . . . I have been trying on death *for a year*." Close to death as she was, she may have felt it absurd to lie, to attempt to accommodate herself to Soviet reality.

On the surface, in the presence of other people, Tsvetaeva gave the impression that she was bearing up well. Everyone remembers her as someone calm, measured and friendly. Few people had any idea of her true feelings — but then Tsvetaeva had no close friends during these last two years. It was only in her diary entries and her letters that she showed her true feelings; in such passages as: "Everyone looks on me as courageous. But I don't know anyone more *timid* than I am. I am afraid of everything." Her fears, needless to say, had their basis in reality: "once again I am not sleeping at night — I am afraid — there's too much *glass* — loneliness — night-time sounds and fears: one moment it's a car carrying God knows what, then it's some inhuman cat, then it's a tree creaking and I jump up." It is not that she pretended when she was with other people; it is simply that she kept herself going as long as she remained alive and considered it necessary to stay alive.

Can one write poetry under such conditions? We know from the example of Akhmatova and Mandelstam that it is possible, that one can use poetry to contend with one's fears. Tsvetaeva herself had always used poetry as a way of coping with her various difficulties. Writing, for Tsvetaeva, was the most natural thing in the world. It was, in fact, a greater achievement for her to have succeeded, on her return to the Soviet Union, in giving up writing, than to have managed — in spite of the seemingly insuperable demands of everyday life — to continue writing for so many years beforehand.

Not long before she left Paris, she wrote to Margarita Lebedeva: "if I can't write there, I shall do away with myself." She continued to write almost until the last day: the last of the "Poems to Bohemia" was written less than a month before she arrived in Moscow. I am certain that Tsvetaeva stopped writing on her return to the Soviet Union not because of some writer's block, but as a result of a conscious choice. After complaining about the difficulties of life in Bolshevo, she asked herself: "When can I write?" It is as though poems were knocking at the door but she didn't let them in. She twice wrote in letters to friends that she wasn't writing anything "of her own": "I've already written what I have to write. I could, of course, write more, but I can quite freely choose not to . . ." It has recently emerged that Tsvetaeva did write five poems during these years but, although they are recognizable as her own, they are of no real intrinsic interest and do not touch on any of her real concerns of this time. Four of them are love lyrics addressed to particular individuals. Does this mean that Tsvetaeva was not concerned by what was happening to her family and in the country as a whole? Does it mean that other poems were not asking to be written? In September 1940 she wrote: "What a lot of lines have passed me by! I don't write anything down. I'm finished with all that."

It is impossible to say for sure why Tsvetaeva decided on this act of renunciation. The most probable explanation, in my view, is that there was simply nothing she could have written about. It would have been impossible for her to become one of the vast choir of Soviet poets singing endless eulogies. She did publish one poem – a poem written twenty years earlier – in a Soviet periodical but even this, in spite of the omission of a stanza about death, attracted hostile attention from critics. It would have been equally impossible for Tsvetaeva to write "for the drawer" – there was no safe place where she could have kept such poems. She had already had some experience of searches and arrests. Unlike Akhmatova and Mandelstam she had no one close to her who could have committed her poems to memory. And so she just did not allow herself to write anything. This act of renunciation may have been conscious but this does not mean that Tsvetaeva ever reconciled herself to it; it was a stage in her eventual suicide.

There were, nevertheless, moments when she rose up from the ashes:

> – It is time! For *this* flame –
> I'm too old!
> > – Love is older than I!
> – A mountain!
> Of fifty Januaries
> – Love is older still . . .
>
> (. . .)
>
> But the pain, which is in the breast,
> Is older than love, older than love.

Tsvetaeva treasured this pain as a sign that she was still truly alive. And, in spite of everything, she remained truly alive until the end. I was recently told a striking story by the poet, artist and translator, A. A. Steinberg:

> I saw Tsvetaeva only once in my life . . . But the true beginning of this story is many years after her death. I was told that I *must* see Galina Ulanova, that she would soon be retiring, and that I couldn't not see her. And so I went to *Giselle*. One scene is of a village festival. Giselle is just one of a crowd of girls, not conspicuous in any way. And then she suddenly sees the prince and walks up to him. All she did was to walk across the stage, but she did it perfectly. She was transformed. It was Woman, Love, Expectation walking towards a man . . .

I have an unusual visual memory. I remember everything I have ever seen. And I remembered that I had already seen this somewhere else. An image surfaced in my mind . . .

It was before the war. I was standing at Goslitizdat in a queue for money, but there wasn't any money and we were waiting for it to arrive. There were a lot of people. Suddenly someone prodded me in the side and pointed to a woman he said was Tsvetaeva . . . I caught sight of an old woman whose stockings were all twisted, someone who obviously no longer cared about her appearance. Her face looked closed and she seemed very alienated from everyone around her. And then her face was suddenly transformed; suddenly it became feminine, happy, expectant. She stretched out with the whole of herself to meet someone who had just come in. I looked round and saw Tarkovsky . . . I remembered this picture with absolute clarity when I saw Ulanova playing Giselle.

Tsvetaeva was in love with Arseny Aleksandrovich Tarkovsky, a young, handsome and talented poet and translator to whom she wrote her last poem, dated 6 March 1941:

> I keep repeating the first verse
> And I keep on correcting a word:
> "I have laid the table for six . . ."
> You have forgotten one – the seventh.
>
> (. . .)
>
> . . . No one: not brother, nor son, nor husband,
> Nor friend – and still I do reproach:
> You who laid the table for six – *souls*
> But did not seat me at the table's end.

No one . . . She so badly needed someone who would look at her not just as a name, but as a soul. But not one of her passions of these years ever came to anything! "*I have no friends*, and without friends *I shall perish*."

As is clear from Steinberg's story, Tsvetaeva was growing old and tired. "Mama," cried Mur indignantly, "you look like some terrible old woman from a village!" Tsvetaeva's response was to feel pleased that he saw her as a peasant. All that was left of the earlier Tsvetaeva was her slim figure, her flying walk and her silver bracelets – together with her sense of responsibility and unyielding inner strength. But for the war, maybe she would have lived on . . .

Tsvetaeva spent the night of 21/22 June 1941 with Tarkovsky and a group of other translators at a party on Telegraph Lane. On her way back home in the morning, she suddenly said to Tarkovsky: "But maybe war has already begun . . .". The official announcement came only a few hours later.

Tsvetaeva was naturally appalled. The war appeared to be following on her heels; she had only just left Paris in time to escape it, now it was pursuing her and Mur in Russia. The German army was advancing deep into Soviet territory. The triumphant poems and songs in the newspapers and on the radio seemed like the blackest of irony. On the fifth day of the war there was an article in *Pravda* saying that the Red Banner Ensemble of Red Army Song and Dance was learning "new military songs":

> "If tomorrow there's war" – so we sang yesterday,
> But today the war has begun,
> And when the time comes for the fight to be fought
> We'll sing out our vigorous song.

All this only intensified Tsvetaeva's feeling of terror.

Mur looked almost adult. He was tall, handsome, intelligent and unusually well-educated for his age. He was also polite. Kvanina writes: "I liked the fact that Mur was respectful: when I came in, he never sat down himself before I did. If I stood up while I was talking to him and moved towards him, he would always stand up too." There is no doubt that Mur was very conspicuous among his contemporaries; nevertheless he was still only sixteen and he had only just been given his first passport.

Mur had dreamed of the Soviet Union, he had insistently begged his mother to return, he had assured her before their departure that "everything will be fine" – he must have been profoundly disillusioned when he got there. As often happens in such situations, he managed to convince himself that everything that had happened was his mother's fault, that she had "taken" him back to the Soviet Union. Probably for this reason – and also because of his age – he appears to have been constantly rude and irritable with his mother and to have treated her with extreme selfishness. This is something on which all the various accounts agree. Kvanina wrote to her husband: "His adolescence reminds me of my own. The same unhealthy atmosphere of exaggerated sensitivity. It will be difficult for him to stand firmly on the ground. And that makes everything else difficult . . .". According to one account, "Mur's attitude towards Tsvetaeva's poetry was negative and contemptuous". Unlike Alya during her own childhood, he appears not to have understood that Marina was "not like everyone else", that it was impossible for her to be "like everyone else". Although she does not spell everything out, Kvanina's description of Mur at this time is probably the most accurate: "Everything, of course, was extremely difficult for him at this period. Everything was new: the country, the way of life, his school, his comrades. He had to learn everything all over again, he had to find a place for himself. On top of all that he was at a transitional age with everything that that entails: an exaggerated irritability, an intolerance of advice (and – God forbid – of orders!), a desperate insistence on being independent and so on, and so on . . . Marina understood what was going on in Mur extremely well, she knew him and understood his character (she and I spoke about all this)".

It is possible, however, that the better Tsvetaeva understood her son, the more frightened she felt on his behalf. She must have been aware that people were interested by Mur – with his fine knowledge of languages and literatures and his unusual breadth of experience – but that they didn't like him. Mur was intelligent enough to realize this himself. After his mother's death, when he was doing his military service, Mur wrote to some people he knew:

> For me letters are simply a kind of hygiene: I feel a need to write, a wish not to be forgotten about completely and so, not having any friends *de facto*, I keep up an illusion of friendship by writing letters here, there and everywhere, generously sending out news of myself for which no one has any need. "You are just being modest," someone will say, "you know very well that it is not true that nobody needs you." But are you so sure of that? Few people will remember me with a good word; I've never done anything "good" to recommend myself and, if I cease to be, everyone will forget me – and with a sense of slight relief – even if they don't forget me immediately. At first they will say, "How terrible!" A little later they'll say, "Maybe it's a good thing after all. He never really found a place for himself. Everyone knows that . . ."

This cool self-assessment was to prove sadly accurate: everyone remembered Mur as intelligent, talented and well-read but nobody really ever has said a good word about him. Tsvetaeva knew very well that her son was a rare bird, someone like herself who would never easily fit into the world. The war only intensified her already considerable worries.

At the beginning of the war, Tsvetaeva was apparently quite out of her mind with fear. M. S. Petrovykh remembered: "Tsvetaeva was very nervous, desperate to be evacuated. The secretary wrote out some certificate for her." According to Tarkovsky, Tsvetaeva's suicide was directly linked to her fear of a German victory. She had parted with her pro-German illusions in "Poems to Bohemia" and no new illusions had appeared to take their place. She had no hopes whatsoever of Russia. A few days before her death, in Chistopol, she had a conversation with Lydia Chukovskaya about whether or not it was worth going on living: Tsvetaeva's view was that it wasn't:

> "But how can you fail to see that everything's finished? Both for you, and for your daughter, and in general."
> We turned into my street.
> "What do you mean – everything?" I asked.
> "Just everything!" Tsvetaeva traced a large circle in the air with her strange little bag. "Russia, for example!"
> "The Germans?"
> "Yes, the Germans too."

Tsvetaeva's last words in this dialogue are an expression of complete despair. She clearly believed that Russia was finished long ago, that the Germans were only the last straw. There was nothing left to hope for; all she wanted was to escape from the war. Ivinskaya wrote that, as she was saying goodbye to one of the editors at Goslitizdat, Tsvetaeva "half-jokingly said that all her relatives had been arrested, that the Germans were advancing and that – if she didn't leave Moscow herself – she would be accused of waiting for the Germans." The irony in this "half-joke" is that a large number of "politically unreliable" citizens were indeed arrested at the beginning of the war, and Tsvetaeva could easily have been one of them.

Tsvetaeva's only concern was Mur's life. During the air-raid alarms Mur and the other boys kept watch on the roof of their home on the Pokrovsky Boulevard. Tsvetaeva was convinced that every bomb and tracer-bullet was aimed directly at him. During these last days in Moscow Zvyagintseva once met Tsvetaeva at the House of Writers: "Marina arrived in a very hysterical state. She immediately began: 'One can't live in agony all of the time. Mur is climbing onto the roofs . . .' I asked: 'What about your poetry, Marina?' 'It's two and a half years since my poetry has been of any help. From the moment I stepped onto the ship's gangway, I knew that everything was finished . . .'". Not even poetry was of any help to her, the ground was slipping away from beneath her feet, but she had to think of Mur. Being an evacuee seemed the only way out. Except that Tsvetaeva did hope Pasternak might suggest that she and Mur came to live with him in his dacha at Peredelkino; there probably wouldn't be any bombs there and there certainly weren't any high and dangerous roofs. Pasternak tried to dissuade her from leaving Moscow, but he didn't say anything about his dacha. On 8 August he saw Tsvetaeva and Mur off at the Khimki river port. They had found places on a boat going to Tatarstan . . .

*

After the event, Pasternak was to speak more than once about his feeling of guilt with regard to Tsvetaeva. After hearing the news of her death, he wrote to his wife in Chistopol:

> Last night Fedin told me that Marina has done away with herself. I don't want to believe it . . . If it is true, then how terrible! Try and look after the boy then, find out where he is and what's happened to him. If it's all true, then I really am to blame myself. One can't talk about 'other concerns' after something like this! This is something I will never be forgiven for. I haven't shown any interest in her during the last year. She was very highly thought of in intellectual circles and was becoming fashionable among people with real understanding; some of my own friends – Garrik, the Asmuses, Kolya Vilyam, and even Aseev – had all come to take an interest in her. People felt very proud to be considered a close friend of hers and for that reason, and for many others, I moved away from her and didn't intrude on her, and during the last six months I almost completely forgot her. And now this. How terrible.

No one could have accused Pasternak of indifference. He did more for Tsvetaeva than anyone. He had no need to justify himself – and certainly not before other people. His attempt to convince himself that things were all right with Tsvetaeva, that she was surrounded by friends and even "becoming fashionable", does, however seem somewhat naïve – to say the least of it. From his bitter confession that he had almost completely forgotten her during the last year we can see that he must have considered he had accomplished his mission by helping to find her a room and that he can have had no real wish to have anything more to do with her. When Aleksandr Gladkov once asked who was responsible for Tsvetaeva's desperate plight after her return to Russia, Pasternak, without a moment's pause for reflection, said: "I am!" He then added: "All of us. I and the others. I and Aseev, and Fedin, and Fadeev. All of us."

Mur did not want to leave Moscow. He had just completed his first year at a Moscow school, he had just settled down and made friends – and now he would have to begin all over again in some unknown place. Once again – or so it seemed to him – he was being taken somewhere against his will, like a little boy. Elabuga must have especially depressed him. He insisted that his mother try to leave. For his sake she applied to move to Chistopol. At a Literary Fund committee meeting – to decide whether Tsvetaeva was to be given a residence permit – she was asked why she wished to leave Elabuga. It seems she "answered in a mechanical voice, repeating over and over again a phrase that she had learnt by heart: 'There is nothing in Elabuga except a vodka factory. I want my son to study. In Chistopol I can send him to a trade school . . .' ". Tsvetaeva's last concern before her death was for Mur. This concern was the only thing that still bound her to life . . . How then could she have allowed herself to die, to leave him alone?

Tsvetaeva did not commit suicide because she no longer had the strength to go on living. She had an inexhaustible reserve of vitality. If there was a reason to go on living, her strength always returned to her. It is not for nothing that she wrote, in her last poem:

I am life, which has come to supper!

No, if Tsvetaeva chose to die, it is because she could no longer see a reason to go on living.

Tsvetaeva had been dying for several years. She had always known that she was returning to the Soviet Union in order to die, that she would be unable either to write or to make any real life for herself there. Her return was itself a kind of suicide. The reality of life in the Soviet Union must have surpassed her worst expectations. What kept Tsvetaeva alive was the sense that she was needed by her family, that it was important that she write petitions on behalf of her husband and daughter, that she send them regular parcels. All her life had been a search for someone who truly needed her:

At long last I have met
The one I need:
Someone has a desperate
Need of me . . .

As the eye needs a rainbow
And grain needs black earth
So each person needs
Another to need him.

Now Tsvetaeva truly was needed. She was the one thread that still connected Seryozha and Alya to the outer world. On one occasion, after considering the possibility of suicide, she stopped herself with the words: "Nonsense. For the time being I am *needed* . . . but God, how small I am, really I can do nothing!" She did, of course, do everything possible (it will be interesting to find out if her letters "to comrade Stalin in person" have been preserved). And when she found out that Alya was in a camp, she made plans to visit her, to bring her everything that she could.

In the letter she wrote to Mur before her death, she wrote: "If you should ever see Seryozha and Alya, tell them that I loved them until the last minute." When she was removed from the noose and taken to the morgue, the undertaker found a tiny (1 × 2 cm) blue morocco-bound notebook in one of the pockets of her apron. There was a very slim pencil attached to the notebook, but to all intents and purposes the notebook was too small to write in. The undertaker kept this notebook, kept it for more than forty years and, on his deathbed asked for it to be given back to Tsvetaeva's relatives. In it, like a message from the other world, was one word in Tsvetaeva's handwriting: Mordovia. Alya had been sent to a camp in Mordovia . . .

With the war everything had changed. There was no longer anything Tsvetaeva could do for her family. It had become impossible to send letters or parcels to prisons or camps. All she had left was Mur. His life mattered more to her than her own, and she imagined he needed her. Their evacuation from Moscow destroyed even this illusion. Mur wanted to live life his own way, free of her constant anxious protectiveness. They had loud quarrels in French, he swore at her and appears even to have threatened suicide. Tsvetaeva understood that her son wanted to get away from her, that her very presence was a burden to him, and that it would be dangerous for him to remain in Elabuga with no other company except her own (she kept repeating that in Chistopol "there are people"). She was clearly terrified. She wrote to Chistopol with an application for a residence permit. As there was no immediate answer, she decided to go there herself. She was grasping at a straw – her very life seemed to depend on whether or not they could move to Chistopol.

On the basis of the notes she made at the time Lydia Chukovskaya has given us a very detailed account of Tsvetaeva's last days. According to Chukovskaya, Tsvetaeva had entirely lost her former lightness, her keenness and impetuosity. She seems to have become all eyes: they were "yellowy-green, always peering obstinately. Her gaze was heavy and inquiring." If her gaze was heavy – the first time anyone has ever described it as such – this was no doubt because it was hiding a single obsessive thought: the thought of suicide. While she was waiting for a decision, she said to Chukovskaya: "Now my fate is being decided . . . If they don't give me a permit for Chistopol, then I shall die. I feel as though they're bound to refuse me. I shall throw myself into the Kama."

In the event Tsvetaeva's application was accepted. In addition, she was almost promised the job she had asked for – as a washer-up in the writers' canteen that was about to open. All she had to do was to find a room in

Chistopol and then move. She would have found people ready to help her in both these tasks. Chukovskaya, however, writes that "Marina Ivanovna did not appear in any way to be pleased at the successful outcome of her application." Residence permits, rooms, moves, work – none of this any longer meant anything to her. "As I left Moscow," she said on her way back from the Council meeting where her permit had been granted, "I clearly understood that my life was finished."

Chukovskaya's account led me to understand that Tsvetaeva's journey to Chistopol was her final settling of accounts with life, and perhaps the final push towards death. From the moment she left Moscow, events had carried her along quite independently of any will or efforts of her own. Like everyone else, she had been uprooted from her everyday life and had been transported from place to place almost as if in a dream. For all the general chaos, the life of the writers' colony in Chistopol had taken on its usual official forms; there were the same Boards, Councils and meetings, the same division between the general "mass" of writers and those who were in a position of authority. It was as though she had returned to Moscow, but without any solid ground beneath her feet, without a residence permit, without her room on the Pokrovsky Boulevard and without translating work. She also knew that her problems were simply an irritation to other people, that she was forcing them to take possibly dangerous decisions, to risk their own wellbeing for her sake. Not that anyone said this. Chukovskaya remembers several people who showed real concern on her behalf. In particular she remembers the warm welcome shown to Tsvetaeva by the Shneiders, the way Tsvetaeva visibly came to life in their home. But all this was too late. And if, as Chukovskaya says, Tsvetaeva was so quick to leave the Shneiders, it may have been because their relaxed good will and cordiality struck a note that was discordant to her own deepest feelings.

Could Tsvetaeva possibly have failed to see how little other people needed her? Could she have failed to see how helpless and excessively importunate she must have appeared, how absurd she must have looked trying to sell her little fluffy skeins of French wool? Could she have failed to see that she was preventing Chukovskaya from going to the chemist's, from finding some honey in the market, from looking after her sick nephew, from helping her daughter with her English lessons? . . . And for all her respect for Tsvetaeva, for all her sympathy and her attempts to be fair, Chukovskaya was unable to hide the fact that she had disliked Tsvetaeva from the moment she first set eyes on her. Unconsciously she couldn't help comparing her with Akhmatova – whom she worshipped. She was unable to restrain herself from expressing her relief that Akhmatova was not in

Chistopol: "Here she would be sure to have perished", "she is unable to do anything". In reply, Tsvetaeva had cried out in fury: "And do you think I can? Akhmatova can't do anything, but you think I can?"

Tsvetaeva's practical affairs were sorting themselves out; even Aseev, who didn't attend the meeting, had written a note in support of her application for registration. Tsvetaeva may have thought that everything would go still better without her, that Mur would do better on his own. With his father already "isolated" and his mother no more, he would no longer be weighed down by the burden of his émigré past. He would be clean in the eyes of the Soviet régime. He would be free to begin life again. "I only make things worse for him," she once said to Chukovskaya. She could no longer help Mur, the best she could do was to get out of the way.*

Mrs Brodelshchikova, Tsvetaeva's landlady during her last days, thought that Tsvetaeva had been in too much of a hurry. She didn't condemn what she had done, she just said to me: "She could have kept going longer. There'd have been time enough after we'd all had something to eat . . .". Ilya Erenburg said much the same: "If she had kept going for another six months, everything would have sorted itself out for her . . .". Six months after Tsvetaeva's death, Boris Pasternak lamented: "If she had only kept going for another month, Konstantin Aleksandrovich (Fedin – V.S.) and I would have arrived and we would have provided her with the same living conditions as ourselves. She would have managed to find work, she would have taken part in the literary conferences we set up and she would have lived in Chistopol." This is entirely probable. But Tsvetaeva didn't want to wash dishes or to translate or to take part in literary conferences. There was no reason for her to keep going, no one to keep going for. Only Mur could have held her back, only Mur could have said that what he needed was her presence – not the money she earned or a residence permit for Chistopol. And he did none of this. Tsvetaeva knew that it was time:

> It is time to take off the amber,
> Time to change the words,
> Time to put out the lamp
> Above the door . . .

She had written these infinitely sad lines in February. She had thought about suicide for a long time; nevertheless it still seemed something frightening and ugly. "I don't want to *die*, I just want *not to be*," she wrote a

---

* After his mother's death Georgy Efron (Mur) was evacuated to Tashkent, where he completed secondary school. He returned to Moscow and entered the Literary Institute. He was drafted into the army. There is no information about him after 1944.

year before her death. She would have preferred to die in some other way, but it is only in verse that one can do it by

> Falling apart, leaving no ashes
> For the urn . . .

Tsvetaeva had no way out. On 31 August 1941 she killed herself in Elabuga.

Her grave does not exist – and perhaps this is a fulfilment of her real wishes? Long before her death, contemplating the fact that she was unlikely to be buried in her beloved Tarusa, she had asked for a stone with an epitaph to be placed there. In this epitaph she wrote not "Here lies . . ." but:

> Here Marina Tsvetaeva
> would have liked to lie.

CHRONOLOGY

1892   Marina Ivanovna Tsvetaeva born in Moscow, 8 October (26 September old style).

1894   Birth of sister, Anastasia (Asya).

1898   Writes first poems (not preserved).

1902   As a result of mother's illness the family moves abroad; Nervi, Italy.

1903   At the Pensionnat Lacaze, Switzerland.

1904   At the Brink boarding school, Freiburg, Germany

1904–5   Russo-Japanese War; Tsvetaeva's growing "sense of her motherland".

1905   Family returns to Russia; Yalta, Crimea.
Revolution in Russia; Tsvetaeva's enthusiasm for it; revolutionary poems (not preserved).

1906   Family goes to the dacha in Tarusa; mother dies; family returns to Moscow.

1909   First major literary work: a translation of Rostand's *L'Aiglon* (not preserved).
Studies Old French literature at summer school in Paris.
Affair with V. O. Nilender; separation.

1910   Finishes High School; spends summer with Asya with a pastor's family near Dresden.
Poet and translator, Ellis, introduces her to the Moscow literary world: Musaget, the Society of Free Aesthetics.
Publication of *Evening Album*; first meeting with Maksimilian Voloshin.

1911   Spends summer with Voloshins in Kotebel; first meeting with Sergey Efron.

1912   Marries Sergey Efron, 27 January (old style); publication of *The Magic Lantern*; honeymoon in Italy, France and Germany.
Official opening of the Emperor Alexander III Fine Arts Museum, founded by Ivan Tsvetaev.
Birth of Tsvetaeva's daughter, Ariadna (Alya) Efron, 5 September (old style)

1913   Publication of *From Two Books*.
Death of father, 30 August (old style).

1914   Affair with Sofia Parnok.

1915   First poems addressed to Akhmatova.

1913–15   Composition of poems constituting "Youthful Poems" (first published 1976).

1916   Travels to St Petersburg and meets the literary world of the capital; affair with Mandelstam.
Composition of poems constituting *Mileposts: I* (including poems addressed to Akhmatova, Blok and Mandelstam).

1917   Sergey Efron joins the army.
Revolution in Petersburg, 27 February (old style).
Nicholas II abdicates, 2 March (old style).
Birth of Tsvetaeva's daughter Irina, 13 April (old style).
The Bolsheviks seize power in Petrograd, 25 October (old style); Sergey Efron takes part in Moscow streetfighting; after the Bolshevik victory Efron leaves for the Crimea.

1918   Tsvetaeva meets members of the E. Vakhtangov studio.
Efron enrols in the White Army.
Tsvetaeva travels to the province of Tambovsk "to find millet"; sees revolutionary Russia.
Works in the Information Department of the Peoples' Commissariat for the Affairs of Nationalities.
Writes the romantic drama *Knave of Hearts* (published in 1974) and *Snowstorm*.

1919   Writes romantic dramas *Adventure, Fortune, Stone Angel* (published in 1976) and *Phoenix*.
Resigns from job at Peoples' Commissariat for the Affairs of Nationalities.

1920   Younger daughter, Irina, dies of hunger in an orphanage, 2/3 February.
Poems by Tsvetaeva are published in the first issue of Russian Paris journal, *Contemporary Notes*; continues to write for them until 1938.

1917–20   Writes the poems constituting *The Camp of the Swans* (first published 1957).

1921   Three years after she last hears from him, Tsvetaeva learns that Efron is still alive.
Death of Blok; execution of Gumilyov; rumours that Akhmatova has committed suicide (August).
Publication of *Mileposts* (poems 1917–20).

1922   Leaves Soviet Russia, 11 May; arrives in Berlin, 15 May; friendship with Bely; joined by Efron in Berlin after four years of separation.
Beginning of epistolary romance with Boris Pasternak.
Publication in Moscow of *The End of Casanova, Mileposts: I, Mileposts: II* and *The Tsar Maiden*.
Publication in Berlin of *Separation, Poems to Blok* and *The Tsar Maiden*
Moves to Czechoslovakia, 1 August; lives in the suburbs of Prague; begins to work for journal *The Will of Russia*.

1923 Publication in Berlin of *Psyche* and *Craft*.
      Affair with and eventual separation from Konstantin Rodzevich.
      Writes "Poem of the Mountain".

1924 Writes "Poem of the End".
      Publication in Prague of the verse fairytale, *The Swain*.
      Works on the editorial board of the anthology *The Ark*.

1925 Birth of Tsvetaeva's son, Georgy (Mur) Efron, 1 February.
      Writes lyrical satire, *The Rat-catcher*.
      Moves to Paris, 1 November.

1926 First poetry reading in Paris, 6 February.
      Efron becomes involved with the Eurasians; works on editorial board of
      Mileposts.
      Tsvetaeva writes for journals *The Loyal* and *Mileposts*.
      Travels to London, where she makes a public appearance.
      Spring and summer in St Gilles-sur-Vie; correspondence with Pasternak and
      Rilke.
      Moves to Bellevue on the outskirts of Paris; death of Rilke.

1927 Moves to Meudon; poems and prose addressed to Rilke: "New Year's
      Greeting", "Your Death" and "Poem of the Air".

1928 Summer in Pontaillac with group of Eurasians; Efron becomes one of the
      organizers and editors of the weekly journal *Eurasia*.
      Attends public reading by Mayakovsky in Paris; publishes a "greeting" to
      Mayakovsky in the first issue of *Eurasia* – as a result *The Latest News* refuses
      to publish any more of Tsvetaeva's work.
      Writes the *poema* "The Red Steer".
      Publication of *After Russia*, the last book to be published in Tsvetaeva's
      lifetime.

1929 Friendship with the artist Natalia Goncharova; writes essay "Natalia
      Goncharova: Her Life and Work".
      Poema on the White Army, "Perekop" (first published in 1957).
      Begins work on long poem about the Tsar's family.
      Split in the Eurasian movement; *Eurasia* folds; Efron, sick and unemployed,
      receives finanical help from the Red Cross in order to recuperate in the
      Château d'Arcine in Haute Savoie.

1930 Mayakovsky commits suicide; Tsvetaeva writes "To Mayakovsky".
      Summer in Haute Savoie; translates *The Swain* into French (illustrated by
      Natalia Goncharova; not published).
      Return to Paris; Efron attends school of cinematographic art.

1931 Writes "History of a Dedication" (essay, first published in 1964).
      Writes "Poems to Pushkin" (first published 1937).

1932   Moves to Clamart.
Literary-philosophical essays: "The Poet and Time", "Art in the Light of Conscience", "Epic and Lyric of Contemporary Russia: Vladimir Mayakovsky and Boris Pasternak".
Voloshin dies in Koktebel; poem cycles: "Ici-haut", "In Memory of Voloshin".
Writes "Poems to a Son"; "Nostalgia for the Motherland".
Efron grows increasingly sympathetic towards the Soviet Union.

1933   Autobiographical prose: "The House at Old Pimen", "The Museum of Alexander III", "The Opening of a Museum" etc; and the articles: "A Living Word about a Living Man (Voloshin)", "Poets with History and Poets without History" (published in Serbian in 1934); writes poem-cycle "The Desk".
Efron applies unsuccessfully for a Soviet Passport.

1934   Moves to Vanves.
Death of Bely; writes essay "A Captive Spirit (My Meeting with Andrey Bely)".
Efron begins to work for the Union for the Return to the Motherland, an organization inspired by the NKVD.

1935   The Paris Congress of Writers in Defence of Peace; meeting – or non-meeting – with Pasternak.
Relationship with family disintegrates, everyone except her wishing to return to the Soviet Union.

1936   Translates poems by Pushkin into French; completion of poems about the Tsar's family (manuscript not preserved).
August in Haute Savoie; correspondence with Anatoly Shteiger; poem-cycle "Poems to an Orphan"
Ariadna (Alya) works for the pro-Soviet journal *Our Union*.
Family disagreements about whether or not to return to Soviet Russia.

1937   Completion of "My Pushkin".
Alya leaves for the Soviet Union, 15 March.
Tsvetaeva writes for the journal *Russian Notes*.
Summer in Lacanau Ocean; completion of "Pushkin and Pugachov".
Alya informs her mother of the death of Sofia Gollidey in Moscow; writes "Story of Sonechka".
Former Soviet agent Ignaty Reyss murdered, 4 September; Efron implicated and interrogated by French police; Efron escapes to Soviet Union, between 27 September and 28 October; Tsvetaeva interrogated by police.

1938   Tsvetaeva moves to Paris; summer in Dives-sur-Mer.
Begins preparations for her return to the Soviet Union, sorting through her archive, copying out manuscripts, giving away her household belongings,

entrusting most of her archive to Margarita Lebedeva in Paris (it is lost during the German occupation).

The Munich Agreement; starts work on "Poems to Bohemia".

1939   Hitler occupies Czechoslovakia; "Poems to Bohemia" ("September" is published in several parts in 1956, 1961 and 1965).

Tsvetaeva entrusts part of her archive to E. Maler, professor at the University of Basle.

Tsvetaeva and Mur leave France for the Soviet Union, 12 June; arrive 18 June; family live together in an NKVD dacha at Bolshevo, just outside Moscow.

Alya arrested, 28 August; translation into French of poems by Lermontov; Efron arrested, 10 October.

Tsvetaeva moves to Golitsyno, not far from Moscow.

1940   Petitions on behalf of her husband and daughter; long hours in prison queues.

Translations of classic Georgian poems by Vazha Pshavela (published 1947).

Moves to Moscow; lodges in various rooms.

Preparation of a volume of poems for a Soviet publishing house (not accepted).

Allocated temporary accommodation in a communal flat (autumn).

1941   Tsvetaeva's only meeting with Anna Akhmatova.

Outbreak of war between Soviet Union and Germany; Tsvetaeva and Mur evacuated; they arrive in Elabuga on the Kama River, 17 August.

Tsvetaeva commits suicide in Elabuga, 31 August.

BIOGRAPHICAL NOTES

ADAMOVICH, *Georgy Viktorovich* (1894–1972): poet and literary critic, who was originally one of the circle of young poets in Petrograd centred upon Nikolay Gumilyov. His first volume of poems, *Clouds*, was published in 1916. He emigrated in 1923, and lived in Paris, where he was involved with the most important émigré publishers and wielded considerable influence. The originator of the so-called *Parisian Note*, he was a strong opponent of Tsvetaeva.

AKHMATOVA (Gorenko), *Anna Andreevna* (1889–1966): major Russian poet who lived most of her life in St Petersburg/Leningrad. She married Nikolay Gumilyov and founded the poetic school of Acmeism with him and other young poets in 1910. She divorced him in 1918. Her first book, *Evening*, appeared in 1912, but it was her second, *Rosary* (1914), that established her popularity. Three further collections, *White Flock* (1917), *Plantain* (1921) and *Anno Domini MCMXXI* (1923), appeared in the early years of the Revolution. In 1935 her son, Lev Gumilyov, and third husband, Nikolay Punin, were arrested. Punin died in a camp in 1953; Lev Gumilyov, after fighting for his country in the Second World War, was arrested for a third time in 1949, sent to a labour camp and only finally released in 1956. During this period, Akhmatova wrote "patriotic" verse in an effort to protect her son. However, apart from these enforced eulogies, between 1923 and 1940 (when wartime conditions allowed greater leniency towards writers) and between 1946 (when she was expelled from the Union of Soviet Writers following Zhdanov's denunciation) and 1965 (when a major new edition of her work, *The Flight of Time*, finally appeared) she was unable to publish anything at all in the Soviet Union. In 1965 she was permitted to travel to Oxford to receive an honorary D. Litt. She died in Leningrad the following year. Her two greatest works, *Requiem* and *Poem without a Hero*, were originally published abroad. They have now, at long last, been published in Russia.

ANDREEVA, *Anna Ilinichna* (1885–1948): émigrée, and the widow of the famous Russian writer, Leonid Andreev. Her friendship with Tsvetaeva began during the latter's years in Prague and continued until her return to the Soviet Union. Tsvetaeva considered Andreeva an exceptionally interesting and unusual person, and Andreeva was a friend to all of Tsvetaeva's family.

ANDRONIKOVA (Halpern), *Princess Salomeya Nikolaevna* (1888–1982): friend of several poets, including Tsvetaeva; Mandelstam and Akhmatova wrote poems to her; she lived in Paris, then London.

A N T O K O L S K Y , *Pavel Grigorievich* (1896–1978): poet, critic, publicist; and director at the theatre of Vakhtangov. In the thirties, forties and fifties he conformed to the prescribed Socialist Realism and (in the war years) Soviet patriotism; he won a Stalin prize.

A S E E V , *Nikolay Nikolaevich* (1889–1963): Futurist poet, influenced by Khlebnikov and Mayakovsky, who became a Socialist Realist under Stalin. He was awarded the Stalin Prize in 1941. After Stalin's death he helped some of the younger poets, but was very conformist in his public utterances.

B A K H R A K H , *Aleksandr Vasilievich* (1902–1985): literary critic and writer of essays and memoirs, who emigrated in 1920, first to Berlin, and then to Paris. He was published in almost all of the Russian émigré periodicals, and was the author of two books – *Bunin in a Dressing Gown* (1979) and *From Memory, from Notes* (1980). The latter includes an essay on Tsvetaeva.

B A L M O N T , *Konstantin Dmitrievich* (1867–1942): until the First World War he was one of the most famous and popular of the Symbolist poets. He had a perfect command of twelve languages and translated a large number of world poets into Russian. He emigrated in 1920. Tsvetaeva's friendship with Balmont began in Moscow in 1917 and continued until her final return to the Soviet Union. In April 1936, on the fortieth anniversary of the beginning of his career as a poet, Tsvetaeva gave a talk, "A Word about Balmont". Balmont drank too much, was mentally ill and died in Paris in extreme poverty.

B A L T R U S H A I T I S , *Yurgis Kazimirovich* (1873–1944): Russian and Lithuanian poet associated with the Symbolists. From 1921 to 1939 he was the Lithuanian ambassador in Moscow and helped many people to emigrate from Soviet Russia. From 1939 on he was Councillor to the Lithuanian Legation in Paris.

B E L Y , *Andrey* (Boris Nikolaevich Bugaev) (1880–1934): major Symbolist poet, novelist and critic. His novels, notably *The Silver Dove* (1909) and *Petersburg* (1913), were a new departure in Russian prose and their experimental manner was influential in the early Soviet period. Like other Symbolists, he was at first inclined to see the October Revolution as an event of mystical significance – indeed, as the Second Coming of Christ. He became the leading Russian disciple of the anthroposophist Rudolf Steiner. He wrote important memoirs of literary and intellectual life in the first years of the century.

B E R D Y A E V , *Nikolay Aleksandrovich* (1874–1948): religious philosopher of European fame, also a historian and the author of works on theology, art and literature. His philosophical views evolved from Marxism to Orthodoxy. He was exiled from Soviet Russia in 1922, and was on good terms with Tsvetaeva, living not far from her on the outskirts of Paris.

B L O K , *Aleksandr Aleksandrovich* (1880–1921): the leading poet of Symbolism. His first volume of verse (1904) celebrated the semi-mystical "Beautiful Lady", partly inspired by

Vladimir Solovyov's vision of the Holy Sophia. In later verse Blok bitterly mocked his own romantic delusions, but in his great poem about the Revolution, "The Twelve" (1918), he reverted to his visionary manner. In the first years after the Revolution he was very active in the various cultural enterprises started by Maksim Gorky under the aegis of Anatoly Lunacharsky, the People's Commissar for Enlightenment. But he died broken and disillusioned.

B O G E N G A R D T , *Vsevolod Aleksandrovich* (1892–1961): his friendship with Sergey Efron began during the Civil War and continued in Constantinople, Prague and Paris. Efron describes his first meeting with Bogengardt, who had been wounded, in a lost chapter of "Notes of a Volunteer". Tsvetaeva remained on good terms with him and his wife Olga Nikolaevna (1893–1967) until her return to the Soviet Union.

B R Y U S O V , *Valery Yakovlevich* (1873–1924): major poet, editor, translator and theoretician of the Symbolist movement, who joined the Communist Party in 1919 and published some 80 books in his lifetime.

B U L G A K O V , *Sergey Nikolaevich* (Father Sergy) (1871–1944): religious philosopher and theologian who was originally drawn to Socialism but became a priest in 1918. He was expelled from Soviet Russia in 1922. In Prague he came to know Tsvetaeva's family and he christened her son. He later became a professor in Paris at the Orthodox Theological Institute.

B U L G A K O V , *Valentin Fyodorovich* (1886–1966): Lev Tolstoy's last secretary, the author of several books about him and an active follower of his philosophy. He was expelled from Soviet Russia in 1923. He was chairman of the Union of Russian Writers and Journalists in Prague, and a member of the editorial board of the anthology *Ark*. Later he organized the Prague Russian Cultural and Historical Museum. He was seized by Soviet troops at the end of the Second World War and deported to Russia. From 1948 he lived and worked in the Lev Tolstoy Museum in the latter's former home at Yasnaya Polyana.

B U N I N A (Muromtseva), *Vera Nikolaevna* (1881–1961): wife of Ivan Bunin, a writer who won the Nobel Prize for Literature in 1933. She lived in Paris and on the Côte d'Azur. As a young woman, Bunina was a friend of Valeria, Tsvetaeva's elder stepsister. Her volume of reminiscences, *By Old Pimen* is similar in its themes to Tsvetaeva's *The House at Old Pimen*. Bunina and Tsvetaeva kept up a close correspondence for many years.

C H I R I K O V , *Evgeny Nikolaevich* (1864–1932): well-known writer before the Revolution, who emigrated in 1921. Tsvetaeva was close to Chirikov's large and friendly family throughout her years in Czechoslovakia: Chirikov's wife was present at the birth of her son; her daughter Lyudmila illustrated Tsvetaeva's poem *The Tsar-Maiden*.

C H U K O V S K A Y A , *Lydia Korneevna* (1907–   ): daughter of the eminent writer Korney Chukovsky. She was an editor at Detgiz (Children's State Publishing House), and is the author of a number of books including two novels, *Sofia Petrovna* and *Going Under*. Her friendship with Akhmatova began in 1938 and she became her confidante, writing a three-volume memoir, the first volume of which is to be published in English, in London and New York, in 1993 as *The Akhmatova Journals, 1938–41*. Her essay, "Predsmertie", concerns the last days of Tsvetaeva's life. She was expelled from the Union of Writers in 1974, but was reinstated in 1989.

D E R Z H A V I N , *Gavrila Romanovich* (1743–1816): classical Russian poet.

E L L I S , (Lev Lvovich Kobylinsky) (1879–1947): one of the "younger" Moscow Symbolists, he played an active role in the literary battles of the beginning of the century. Mystic, poet, translator and critic, he was a regular contributor to the journal *Scales*, and the author of the volume *The Russian Symbolists. (K. Balmont. V. Bryusov, A. Bely)* (1910). He left Russia before the First World War, converted to Catholicism and died in Switzerland. A book he wrote in German, *Alexander Puschkin. Der religiöse Genius Russlands* (1948) was published after his death.

E R E N B U R G , *Ilya Grigorievich* (1891–1967): novelist and journalist. He was imprisoned briefly for Bolshevik activities in 1906; lived in Paris 1909–17; became anti-Bolshevik; returned to Paris from Russia in 1921 and after some wavering became increasingly pro-Soviet. Until 1941, however, he managed to live mainly abroad (as European correspondent for *Izvestia*), making only brief visits to the Soviet Union. He produced numerous novels, stories and essays, as well as memoirs which give a fascinating picture of the fate of the Russian intelligentsia in Soviet times. A sardonic, gifted, ambivalent figure, he did much after Stalin's death to promote the cultural values destroyed by the regime to which he had long paid lipservice as a novelist, journalist, and public figure. His novel *The Thaw* (1954) was of great importance as the first breach to be made in Stalinist mythology, and in his memoirs and essays after Stalin's death he championed freedom of expression in literature and art. Katya, the heroine of his novel *The Life and Downfall of Nikolay Kurbov* (Berlin, 1923), is endowed with many traits characteristic of Tsvetaeva.

E S E N I N , *Sergey Aleksandrovich* (1895–1925): popular lyric poet of peasant origin noted for his lyrical descriptions of the Russian countryside. He married the dancer Isadora Duncan in 1922 and travelled to Western Europe and to America with her. In the twenties his popularity was rivalled only by that of Mayakovsky. After his initial acceptance of the October Revolution, he became disillusioned and came under increasing attack for his riotous behaviour. In 1925 he hanged himself in a Leningrad hotel.

F E D O T O V , *Georgy Petrovich* (1886–1951): philosopher, church figure, critic, columnist and specialist in mediaeval history. A member of the Social-Democratic movement at the beginning of the century, he twice had to flee abroad. He emigrated in 1925, and became a Professor at the Orthodox Theological Institute in Paris. He published articles on historical, philosophical, cultural and political matters in most of the serious émigré journals, and was one of the editors of the religio-philosophical and socio-historical journal *The New City*.

G A B R I A C , *Cherubina de* (Elizaveta Ivanovna Dimitrieva) (1887–1928): poet from the circle around the journal *Apollon*. Her pen-name was Voloshin's invention, who dreamed up for her the role of a passionate Catholic and recluse who was preparing to retire to a monastery. The last literary duel in Russia, between Nikolay Gumilyov and Maksimilian Voloshin, took place on her account in St Petersburg in 1909 – against a background of complex personal relationships. Dimitrieva retired from literary life after Voloshin's mystification had been exposed.

G E R T S Y K , *Adelaida Kazimirovna* (1874–1925): poet, translator and critic, who was closely involved with literary and religio-philosophical circles in Petersburg and Moscow.

G I P P I U S (Hippius), *Zinaida Nikolaevna* (1869–1945): poet, prose writer, playwright, essayist, critic. She was active in the religious and philosophical societies of St Petersburg at the turn of the century, and advocated an apocalyptic Christianity. She emigrated in 1919 and became prominent in émigré literary life in Paris.

G O L L I D E Y , *Sofia Evgenevna* (1894–1934): actress, and student of E. Vakhtangov. In Moscow in 1919 she achieved considerable renown for her one-woman play based on Dostoevsky's "White Nights". Tsvetaeva dedicated poems to her and also a prose narrative, "The Story of Sonechka".

G O N C H A R O V A , *Natalya Sergeevna* (1881–1962): artist and one of the organizers, during the period 1910–1913, of the avant-garde artistic groupings "The Knave of Diamonds", "Donkey's Tail" and "Target". She lived in Paris from 1915, and was particularly well known as a theatre designer for Diaghilev.

G U M I L Y O V , *Nikolay Stepanovich* (1886–1921): poet, and co-founder of the poetic school, Acmeism. Before the First World War he travelled to Abyssinia and his poetry and tales were influenced by his travels, his distinguished military service in the war and his monarchist beliefs. After the Revolution he did translations for Gorky's World Literature Publishing House and taught poetry in the House of Arts. He was shot in August 1921, after he proudly confessed his involvement in a rather confused anti-Bolshevik conspiracy.

I V A N O V , *Vyacheslav Ivanovich* (1866–1949): poet and leading figure in the Symbolist movement. His fifth-floor apartment in St Petersburg, "The Tower", was, until he moved to Moscow in 1913, the main gathering place for the Symbolists and the most renowned literary salon in the capital. Influenced by Vladimir Solovyov and Nietzsche, he believed that a combination of Christianity and the cult of Dionysus could be fertile in new myths to be created by the whole of mankind. In 1924 he emigrated to Italy, where he became a Catholic.

I V A S K , *Yury Pavlovich* (1907–1986): poet and critic. During the twenties and thirties he lived in Estonia, and from 1949 he taught Russian Literature in the USA. His article about Tsvetaeva (1934) aroused her interest and was the beginning of a friendship and correspondence of great literary importance.

K A M E N S K Y , *Vasily Vasilievich* (1884–1961): poet, novelist and playwright; also a travelling actor and an aviator. He joined the Futurist movement at its beginning, experimenting with transrational neologisms.

K H L E B N I K O V , *Velimir* (Viktor Vladimirovich) (1885–1922): Futurist poet noted for his linguistic experimentation. His poetry was suppressed for many years. He died of malnutrition in 1922.

K H O D A S E V I C H , *Vladislav Felitsianovich* (1886–1939): poet, critic and literary historian, who published his first poems in 1908 but won general recognition only after publication of his post-revolutionary books, *The Way of the Grain* (1920) and *The Heavy Lyre* (1923). His poetry expresses the contradiction between the freedom of man's immortal soul and its slavery to matter and necessity. He emigrated in 1922, lived in Paris and became a brilliant literary critic and an expert on Pushkin.

K O L B A S I N A - C H E R N O V A , *Olga Eliseevna* (1886–1964): literary figure and writer of memoirs. She was the wife (although she had been divorced by the time she met Tsvetaeva) of one of the leaders of the Socialist Revolutionary Party, V. M. Chernov. Tsvetaeva and the Chernov family had common literary interests and were friends for several years.

K O R O L E N K O , *Vladimir Galaktionovich* (1853–1921): writer, best known for his stories and autobiography; he was also a publicist, critic and social activist.

K R U C H O N Y K H , *Aleksey Eliseevich* (1886–1968): Futurist poet noted for extreme linguistic experimentation.

K U Z M I N , *Mikhail Alekseevich* (1872–1936): poet whose work influenced the transition from Symbolism to Acmeism.

L A N N (Lozman), *Evgeny Lvovich* (1896–1964): lawyer by training, but also a writer, translator and literary critic. At the time of his brief friendship with Tsvetaeva he was beginning to write poetry; she overrated his poems. He was later to become well known as a translator and biographer of Charles Dickens.

L E B E D E V , *Vladimir Ivanovich* (1883–1956): professional soldier, who took part in the Russo-Japanese war of 1904–5; a member of the central committee of the Socialist Revolutionary Party; and a professional journalist. He emigrated in 1908, but returned to Russia after the February Revolution. He was Admiralty Minister in the Provisional

Government and in charge of military operations on the Volga during the Civil War. In 1919 he returned to Paris. He was a leading figure in the Slavonic movement and in Russian émigré circles. He was a member of the editorial boards of the journals *The Will of Russia* (Prague) and *Russian Archive* (Belgrade, in Serbo-Croat), both of which published Tsvetaeva. He moved to the USA in 1936. During her years as an émigrée, Tsvetaeva and her children were friends with him and his wife – Margarita Nikolaevna (1885–1958), also a member of the Socialist Revolutionary Party, a doctor and a woman of unusual kindness – as well as with their daughter Irina (1916–   ).

LERMONTOV, *Mikhail Yurevich* (1814–1841): great Russian Romantic poet, somewhat Byronic, whom Tsvetaeva loved from childhood. After her return to the Soviet Union, Tsvetaeva translated some of his poems into French for the *Revue de Moscou*.

MANDELSTAM, *Osip Emilievich* (1891–1938): major Russian poet, and an Acmeist. His collections of poetry include *Stone* (1913), *Tristia* (1922), and *Poems 1928*. He also wrote very fine prose, including, *The Noise of Time* (1925), *The Egyptian Stamp* (1928) and *Journey to Armenia* (written 1931). A satirical poem about Stalin led to his exile in 1934 to Voronezh, where he filled three notebooks in a last creative burst. He returned to Moscow in 1937, but was re-arrested. The story of his life and of the ordeal which ended in his death in a camp near Vladivostok in the winter of 1938 has been told by his widow, Nadezhda Mandelstam (see Bibliography).

MAYAKOVSKY, *Vladimir Vladimirovich* (1893–1930): Futurist poet and playwright. He combined powerful poetic gifts with a romantic anguish which could find relief only in total service to the Revolution – at the cost of suppressing in himself the personal emotions evident in his pre-revolutionary work (such as *The Cloud in Trousers*, 1913). After the Revolution he wrote many agitprop pieces on topical themes, as well as long epic glorifications of the new order, such as *Mysteria-Bouffe* (1918), *150,000,000* (1921) and *Vladimir Ilich Lenin* (1924). His concern at the loss of revolutionary momentum is reflected in two plays, *The Bedbug* and *The Bathhouse*, written not long before his suicide. Before the Revolution he had been one of the leading figures of the Futurist movement: after it, from 1922, he headed a group known as LEF ("Left Front of Art"). He was "canonized" in 1935 by Stalin who proclaimed that he "was and remains the best and most talented poet of our Soviet epoch", adding that "indifference to his memory is a crime".

MEYERHOLD, *Vsevolod Emilievich* (1874–1940): theatre director, and a revolutionary figure in the Russian and Soviet theatre, whose own theatre was liquidated by decree in early 1938. Meyerhold defiantly and publicly confronted his persecutors in January 1939. He was arrested the following day; and a week later his wife, the actress Zinaida Raikh, was found dead in their flat from stab wounds, her eyes gouged out.

NAKHMAN, *Magda Maksimilianovna* (1891–19??): artist, a student of L. Bakst, M. Dobuzhinsky and K. Petrov-Vodkin. She left Soviet Russia in 1922. Tsvetaeva knew her from Koktebel. In 1913 Magda Nakhman painted the only portrait of Tsvetaeva to be painted during the poet's lifetime.

N E K R A S O V , *Nikolay Alekseevich* (1821–78): poet, writer, publisher, and the leading representative of the "civic" or "realist" school in nineteenth-century Russian poetry.

N I L E N D E R , *Vladimir Ottonovich* (1883–1965): poet and translator associated with the Symbolists.

P A R N O K , *Sofia Yakovlevna* (1885–1933): poet, critic and translator. She belonged, with Khodasevich and others, to a "neo-classical" group. Her main model from ancient Greece was Sappho. Between 1907 and 1928 she published five collections of poetry.

P A S T E R N A K , *Boris Leonidovich* (1890–1960): major poet and prose writer. The volume of poems which first made him famous and which was very important to Tsvetaeva, *My Sister – Life*, was written in 1917 and published in 1922. Though mainly a lyric poet, Pasternak attempted longer poems, in which he treated revolutionary themes in an epic manner: *The Year Nineteen Hundred and Five* (1925–26) about the first Russian revolution; and *Lieutenant Shmidt* (1926–27). These were followed in 1931 by an ambitiously conceived "novel in verse", *Spektorsky*, about the whole era of war and revolution. Despite a certain ambivalence in his attitude to the Revolution, these works made it clear that Pasternak could never accept revolutionary violence, and that he believed in the absolute autonomy of art. Other prose works of Pasternak are *The Childhood of Lyuvers* (1922), the autobiographical *A Safe Conduct* (1931), and the unfinished play, *The Blind Beauty*. Pasternak wrote one novel, *Doctor Zhivago*, which in many ways he had been working towards all his creative life. Its rejection by Soviet publishers and its publication in the West, the award of the Nobel Prize for Literature in 1958 and the subsequent persecution of Pasternak by Soviet press and literary institutions in the last two years of his life, made him extremely famous.

P U S H K I N , *Aleksandr Sergeevich* (1799–1837): universally regarded as Russia's greatest poet. Among his works (in addition to the large body of lyric poetry) are narrative poems such as "Poltava" (1828) and "The Bronze Horseman" (written 1833), prose fiction including "Tales of Belkin" (1831), "The Queen of Spades" (1834) and *The Captain's Daughter* (1835), verse dramas such as "Mozart and Salieri" (a short drama, 1831) and *Boris Godunov* (a full-scale play, 1831) and the novel in verse *Evgeny Onegin* (1833). He also wrote a work of history, very important to Tsvetaeva: *A History of the Pugachov Uprising* (1834).

R I L K E , *Rainer Maria* (1875–1926): regarded as the greatest German poet since Goethe. He dedicated his life to poetry. He was very moved by the spirituality of Russia, which he visited in 1899 and 1900, and later he called Russia his true homeland. Among his main collections of poetry are *Das Stundenbuch* (The Book of Hours) (1905), *Neue Gedichte* (New Poems) (1907–8), *Duineser Elegien* (Duino Elegies) (1923), and *Die Sonette an Orpheus* (Sonnets to Orpheus) (1923).

R O D Z E V I C H , *Konstantin Boleslavovich* (1895–1988): Russian émigré. During the Civil War he fought first in the Red Army and then for the Whites. Afterwards he emigrated to Prague and studied at the university together with Sergey Efron. In Paris he became a member of the Soviet-inspired Union for Return to the Motherland. During the Spanish Civil War he commanded a Russian battalion. Later he became a member of the French Communist Party. There is very little doubt that he worked as an agent for the KGB from the late twenties or early thirties.

R O S T A N D , *Edmond* (1868–1918): French playwright, idealistic and non-political who wrote *Cyrano de Bergerac* (1897), and *L'Aiglon* (1900) about the ill-fated son of Napoleon.

R O Z A N O V , *Vasily Vasilievich* (1856–1919): Russian philosopher, essayist and critic, who had mystical religious views and highly original ideas on sex, which he presented in a new prose style.

S H A G I N Y A N , *Marietta Sergeevna* (1888–1982): Soviet novelist and (before the Revolution) a minor poet on the fringes of the Symbolist movement. During the 1920s she was known mainly for her attempt to write thrillers and detective fiction in Western style.

S H A K H O V S K O Y , *Prince Dmitry Alekseevich* (Archbishop John of San Francisco) (1902–89): poet who published several volumes of poems (after taking vows he published under the name "The Wanderer"). He was the founder and editor of the literary-philosophical journal *The Loyal*, to which Tsvetaeva and Efron were both contributors.

S H E S T O V , *Lev Isaakovich* (1866–1938): philosopher and religious thinker of European fame, who emigrated in 1920. Together with Tsvetaeva he was involved with the journal *Mileposts*.

S L O N I M , *Mark Lvovich* (1894–1976): Russian émigré and active member of the Socialist Revolutionary Party. He was also a literary critic and literary historian, the author of *Modern Russian Literature: from Chekhov to the Present* (New York, 1953), and the literary editor and chief literary critic for the journal *The Will of Russia*. In 1928 he organized a literary society in Paris, "Nomad Encampment", to which Tsvetaeva was invited as a much-respected guest. One of the first literary critics to show an interest in Soviet literature, Slonim attempted to evaluate it objectively (*Portraits of Soviet Writers*, Paris, 1933). He was a devoted friend of Tsvetaeva and her most serious and profound critic. His memoirs of her are of great interest.

S T A K H O V I C H , *Aleksey Aleksandrovich* (1856–1919): actor and teacher at the Arts Theatre. A member of an aristocratic family, he abandoned his career as a military diplomat for the theatre.

S V Y A T O P O L K - M I R S K Y , *Prince Dmitry Petrovich* (1890–1939): literary historian and critic. After serving in the White Army, he emigrated in 1920 to Greece, then to

England, where he joined the British Communist Party in 1931. In 1932 he returned to Soviet Russia, where he was arrested; he disappeared in 1937. His *History of Russian Literature* (1926) is still a standard work.

T E S K O V Á , *Anna Antonovna* (1872–1954): writer, translator and public figure. She spent her childhood in Russia, but was educated in Czechoslovakia where she then worked as a teacher in girls' schools. She was one of the founders in 1919 of the Czech-Russian Union; for many years she continued to chair this organization which carried out cultural and charitable work among the Russian émigrés.

T Y U T C H E V , *Fyodor Ivanovich* (1803–73): important Russian poet of the nineteenth century.

V I S H N Y A K , *Abram Grigorievich* (1895–1943): émigré and the owner of Helicon, a Berlin publishing house. He published two volumes by Tsvetaeva: *Separation* (1922) and *Craft* (1923). A number of Tsvetaeva's Berlin poems were addressed to him, as well as the letters which eventually formed part of the story she wrote in French, "Florentine Nights".

V O L K O N S K Y , *Prince Sergey Mikhailovich* (1860–1937): grandson of the Decembrist of the same name and of the Maria Volkonskaya to whom Pushkin wrote poems. A ballet and theatre critic and writer, for a short period before the Revolution he was director of the Imperial theatres. He was close to the "World of Art" group. Tsvetaeva remained a friend of his until his death. It was to her that Volkonsky dedicated his book, *Everyday Life and Inner Being* [Byti bytie] (1924). Tsvetaeva wrote an article, "Cedar. An Apology" about his book *Motherland*.

V O L O S H I N , *Maksimilian Aleksandrovich* (1877–1932): poet, painter of water-colours, translator, art critic and literary critic. Voloshin played an extremely active role in the literary and artistic life of pre-Revolutionary Russia. He was involved with the journal *Apollon*, with "The World of Art" and "Free Aesthetic" groups, and with the publishing houses, Scales and Musaget. In their house in Koktebel (Eastern Crimea) Voloshin and his mother Elena (Pra) Ottobaldovna Voloshina (1850–1923) created a special world, a centre for the literary and artistic intelligentsia; it became a refuge for many creative people, no matter what their politics, and had a considerable influence over several generations of poets, writers, artists and actors. The friendship between the Voloshins and Tsvetaeva and her husband continued until the early twenties. The Voloshins' home in Koktebel is now a museum.

Z H U K O V S K Y , *Vasily Andreevich* (1783–1852): lyric poet, noted particularly for his translations of German Romantic poetry, and of Gray's "Elegy".

Z V Y A G I N T S E V A , *Vera Klavdievna* (1894–1972): poet, translator and (in her youth) actress, who lived in Moscow. She was of great support to Tsvetaeva during the Civil War and also after her return to the Soviet Union.

BIBLIOGRAPHY

I STANDARD EDITIONS OF THE WORKS OF MARINA TSVETAEVA

Stikhotvorenia i poemy v pyati tomakh [Lyric and narrative poems in five volumes] compiled and edited by Alexander Sumerkin (preface by Joseph Brodsky; biographical essay by Viktoria Schweitzer), New York, 1980.
    Four volumes published so far: I (1980) Stikhotvorenia 1908–1916; II (1982) Stikhotvorenia 1917–1922; III (1983) Stikhotvorenia, perevody 1922–1941; IV (1983) Poemy.

Izbrannye proizvedenia [Selected works] ed. Ariadna Efron and Anna Saakyants. Biblioteka poeta, Moscow–Leningrad, 1965.

Neizdannoe. Stikhi, Teatr, Proza [Unpublished works. Poems, Theatre, Prose] Paris, 1976. (Includes "Yunosheskie stikhi" [Youthful poems].)

Izbrannaya proza v dvukh tomakh 1917–1937 [Selected prose in two volumes 1917–1937] ed. Alexander Sumerkin (preface by Joseph Brodsky), New York, 1979.

Sochinenia v dvukh tomakh [Works in two volumes] ed. A. Saakyants, Moscow, 1980.

Sochinenia v dvukh tomakh ed. Anna Saakyants, Moscow, 1988.

Teatr ed. A. A. Saakyants, Moscow, 1988.

Proza ed. A. A. Saakyants, Moscow, 1989.

Stikhotvorenia i poemy ed. E. B. Korkina, Biblioteka poeta, Leningrad, 1990.

II INDIVIDUAL WORKS

a) Books published during her lifetime:

Vecherny albom. Stikhi [Evening Album. Poems] Moscow, 1910.

Volshebny fonar. Vtoraya kniga stikhov [The Magic Lantern. Second book of poems] Moscow, 1912.

Iz dvukh knig [From Two Books. (Selections from two earlier books.)] Moscow, 1913.

Versty. Stikhi [Mileposts. Poems] Moscow, 1921 and 1922.

Versty. Stikhi. Vypusk I [Mileposts. Poems. Part I] Moscow, 1922.

Konets Kazanovy. Dramatichesky etyud [The End of Casanova. A dramatic study] Moscow, 1922.

Razluka. Kniga stikhov [Parting. Book of poems] Moscow–Berlin, 1922.
   (Includes the long poem "Na krasnom kone" [The Red Steer].)
Stikhi k Bloku [Poems to Blok] Berlin, 1922.
Tsar'-devitsa. Poema-skazka [The Tsar Maiden. A tale in verse] Moscow, 1922 and Berlin,
   1922.
Psikheya. Romantika [Psyche. Romanticism] Berlin, 1923.
Remeslo. Kniga stikhov [Craft. A book of poems] Berlin, 1923.
   (Includes the long poem "Pereulochki" [Sidestreets].)
Molodets. Skazka [The Swain. A Tale] Prague, 1924.
Posle Rossii. 1922–1925 [After Russia. 1922–1925] Paris, 1928.

b) Books published posthumously:

Lebediny stan. Stikhi 1917–1921 [The Camp of the Swans. Poems 1917–1921] ed. G. P.
   Struve, Munich, 1957.
Perekop [Perekop] New York, 1967.
Mon frère féminin: Lettre à l'Amazone (note by Ghislaine Limont), Paris, 1979. (N.B. The
   first part of the title was added by the publishers.)

c) Longer works published during her lifetime in anthologies and journals:

This list is designed to give an idea of the amount and range of work Tsvetaeva
published during her émigré years. Only the place and year of publication are given;
for further details see Karlinsky 1966 (4a below) and *Bibliographie des œuvres de Marina
Tsvetaeva*, compiled by Tatiana Gladkova and Lev Mnukhin (introduction by
Véronique Lossky), Paris, 1982. The latter work should also be consulted for details of
individual poems published in journals and anthologies.

1 PLAYS
"Metel" [The Snowstorm] Paris, 1923.
"Fortuna" Paris, 1923.
"Priklyuchenie" [An Adventure] Prague, 1923.
"Feniks" [Phoenix] Prague, 1924.
"Tezej. Tragedia" [Theseus. A tragedy] Paris, 1927.
"Fedra" [Phaedra] Paris, 1928.

2 LONG POEMS
"Poema kontsa" [Poem of the End] Prague, 1926.
"Poema gory" [Poem of the Mountain] Paris, 1926.
"Krysolov. Liricheskaya satira" [The Rat-catcher. Lyrical satire] Prague, 1926.
"Lestnitsa. Poema" [The Stairs. A narrative poem] Prague, 1926.
"Popytka komnaty. Poema" [Attempt at a Room. A narrative poem] Prague, 1928.
"S morya" [From the Sea] Paris, 1928.

"Novogodnee" [A New Year's Greeting] Paris, 1928.

"Poema vozdukha" [Poem of the Air] Prague, 1930.

3 PROSE WORKS

"Otkrytoe pismo A. N. Tolstomu" [An Open Letter to A. N. Tolstoy] Berlin, 1922.

"Svetovoi liven" [Downpour of Light] Berlin, 1922.

"Iz knigi *Zemnye primety*" [From the book *Omens of the Earth*] Prague, 1924.

"Kedr. Apologia (O knige kn. S. Volkonskogo *Rodina*")" [Cedar. An Apology. (On Prince S. Volkonsky's Book *Homeland*.)] Prague, 1924.

"Cherdachnoe (Iz moskovskikh zapisey 1919–1920gg)" [Garret Words (From Moscow notes of 1919–1920)] Berlin, 1924.

"Volny proezd. Vospominania" [Free Transit. Recollections] Paris, 1924.

"Iz dnevnika" [From a Diary] Paris, 1925.

"Moi sluzhby. Vospominania" [My Jobs. Recollections] Paris, 1925.

"O Germanii (Vyderzhki iz dnevnika 1919g)" [About Germany (Excerpts from a diary of 1919)] Berlin, 1925.

"O lyubvi (Iz dnevnika 1917g)" [About love (From a diary of 1917)] Berlin, 1925.

"Balmontu" [To Balmont] Prague, 1925.

"Geroy truda (Zapiski o Valery Bryusove)" [Hero of Labour (Notes on Valery Bryusov)] Prague, 1925.

"Otvet na anketu zhurnala *Svoimi Putyami*" [Reply to a questionnaire from the journal *Our Own Ways*] Prague, 1925.

"Vozrozhdenshchina" [Renaissanciana] Berlin, 1925.

"O blagodarnosti (Iz dnevnika 1919)" [On Gratitude (From a diary of 1919)] Brussels, 1926.

"Iz dnevnika (Smert Stakhovicha)" [From a diary (The Death of Stakhovich)] Paris, 1926.

"Poet o kritike" [The Poet on the Critic] together with *Tsvetnik* [Flower Garden] Brussels, 1926.

"Oktyabr v vagone" [October in a Railway Carriage] Prague, 1927.

"Tvoya smert" [Your Death] Prague, 1927.

"Natalya Goncharova" Prague, 1929.

"O novoy russkoy detskoy knige" [On Recent Russian Children's Books] Prague, 1931.

"Iskusstvo pri svete Sovesti" [Art in the Light of Conscience] Paris, 1932.

"Poet i Vremya" [The Poet and Time] Prague, 1932.

"Zhenikh" [The Intended] Paris, 1933.

"Epos i lirika sovremennoy Rossii: Vladimir Mayakovsky i Boris Pasternak" [Epic and Lyric of Contemporary Russia: Vladimir Mayakovsky and Boris Pasternak] Paris, 1933.

"Bashnya v plyushche" [The Ivy-Covered Tower] Paris, 1933.

"Zhivoe o zhivom (Voloshin)" [A Living Word about a Living Man (Voloshin)] Paris, 1933.

"Plenny dukh (Moya vstrecha s Andreem Belym)" [A Captive Spirit (My Meeting with Andrey Bely)] Paris, 1934.

"Dom u starogo Pimena" [The House at Old Pimen] Paris, 1934.

"Otkrytie muzeya" [The Opening of the Museum] 1934.

"Khlystovki" [Women of the Flagellant Sect] Paris, 1934.

"Dva lesnykh tsarya" [Two Forest Kings] Paris, 1934.

"Strakhovka zhizni" [Life Insurance] Paris, 1934.

"Kitaets" [The Chinaman] Paris, 1934.

"Pesnici sa istorijom i pesnici bez istorije" [in Serbian translation: Poets with History and Poets without History] Belgrade, 1935.

"Pesnik alpinist" [In Serbian translation: The Poet Mountaineer] Belgrade, 1935.

"Skazka materi" [Mother's Tale] Paris, 1935.

"Mat i muzyka" [Mother and Music] Paris, 1935.

"Chort" [The Devil] Paris, 1935.

"Nezdeshny vecher" [An Otherworldly Evening] Paris, 1936.

"O knige N. P. Gronskogo *Stikhi i poemy*" [On N. P. Gronsky's book, *Lyric and Narrative Poems*] Paris, 1936.

"Reč o Baljmontu" [In Serbian translation: A Word about Balmont] Belgrade, 1936.

"Pushkin i Pugachov" [Pushkin and Pugachov] 1937.

"Moy Pushkin" [My Pushkin] Paris, 1937.

"Povest o Sonechke" [Story of Sonechka], first half only, 1938.

NB The original Russian text of the three essays published in Serbian translation is not extant.

d) Works published posthumously:

PLAYS

"Chervonnyi valet" [The Jack of Hearts] New York, 1974.

"Kamennyi angel" [The Stone Angel] Paris, 1976.

LONG POEMS

"Egorushka", Moscow, 1971.

"Avtobus" [The Bus] Moscow, 1965.

"Pevitsa" [The Singer] Moscow, 1981.

"Charodey [The Enchanter] New York, 1971.

Additionally, Tsvetaeva wrote several short works in French, in 1936, which were not published at the time but were published in 1970, in *Zvezda*, no.10, in Leningrad.

PROSE WORKS

"Istoria odnogo posvyashchenia" [History of a Dedication] *Oxford Slavonic Papers XI*, 1964.

"Povest o Sonechke" [Story of Sonechka] part two, Paris, 1976.

"Volshebstvo v poezii Brusova" [Magic in the Poetry of Bryusov] Moscow, 1979.

III ENGLISH TRANSLATIONS

a) Prose

Marina Tsvetaeva. *A Captive Spirit: Selected Prose* Edited and translated by J. Marin
King, Ann Arbor, 1980; London, 1983 (with introduction by Susan Sontag).
[Contains: A Living Word about a Living Man (Voloshin. Koktebel. Max and
the Folk Tale.); A Captive Spirit; An Otherworldly Evening; My Father and his
Museum; Charlottenburg; The Uniform; The Laurel Wreath; The Opening of the
Museum; The Intended; The Tower of Ivy; The House at Old Pimen; Mother and
Music; The Devil; My Pushkin; Two Forest Kings; Pushkin and Pugachov.]
(N.B. A revised edition of these translations and the accompanying notes is in
preparation by J. M. King.)
Art in the Light of Conscience: Eight Essays on Poetry by Marina Tsvetaeva. Translated with
introduction and notes by Angela Livingstone, London, 1992.
[Contains: Downpour of Light; The Poet on the Critic; History of a Dedication
(in part); The Poet and Time; Epic and Lyric of Contemporary Russia; Two
Forest Kings; Poets with History and Poets without History (in part); Art in the
Light of Conscience; Also twelve poems by Tsvetaeva in translation.]

b) Poetry (collections)

Selected Poems of Marina Tsvetayeva Translated by Elaine Feinstein, with a foreword by
Max Hayward, Oxford, 1971, then Harmondsworth, 1974.
Selected Poems of Marina Tsvetayeva (Revised edition.) Edited, translated and introduced
by Elaine Feinstein, Oxford, 1981, London, 1986.
Marina Tsvetayeva. *Selected Poems* Translated by David McDuff, Newcastle-upon-Tyne,
1987.
Demesne of the Swans [The Camp of the Swans]/*Lebediny Stan* Translated by Robin
Kemball, Ann Arbor, 1980. (A bi-lingual edition.)
After Russia Translated by Michael Naydan. (A bi-lingual edition.) Ann Arbor, 1992.

IV   BIOGRAPHIES, MEMOIRS AND LETTERS IN ENGLISH

a) Biographies

Simon Karlinsky. *Marina Cvetaeva. Her Life and Art.* Berkeley and Los Angeles, 1966.
Simon Karlinsky. *Marina Tsvetaeva. The Woman, her World and her Poetry.* Cambridge,
1985.
Elaine Feinstein. *A Captive Lion. The Life of Marina Tsvetayeva.* London, 1987. Reprinted
as *Marina Tsvetaeva* 'Lives of Modern Women' Series. Harmondsworth, 1989.
Jane A. Taubman. *A Life Through Poetry. Marina Tsvetaeva's Lyric Diary.* Columbus,
Ohio, 1989.

Bibliography

Tsvetaeva. A Pictorial Biography. Edited by Ellendea Proffer. Introduction by Carl
Proffer. Ann Arbor, 1980. Third edition 1989.

b) Memoirs

None of the works listed below is devoted to Tsvetaeva, but all contain passages in
which she is recalled. Page numbers given are to these passages.

Boris Pasternak. *An Essay in Autobiography.* Translated by Manya Harari, London, 1959.
pp 104–110 (first part of the chapter "Three Shadows").

Ilya Erenburg. *First Years of Revolution 1918–1920* (Volume 2 of *Men, Years, Life*).
Translated by Anna Bostock, London, 1962. pp 22–28.

Nina Berberova. *The Italics are Mine.* Translated by Philippe Radley, London, 1969.
pp 204–208.

Olga Carlisle. *Poets on Street Corners, Portraits of Fifteen Russian Poets.* New York, 1970.
pp 166–172 (followed by some of Tsvetaeva's poems in translation).
    This includes (pp 166–167) the short description of Tsvetaeva given by Ilya
Ehrenburg in his *Portrety russkikh poetov* [Portraits of Russian Poets] Berlin, 1922,
and also (pp 170–172) part of that given by Boris Pasternak in *An Essay in
Autobiography* (see above).

Nadezhda Mandelstam. *Hope Abandoned.* Translated by Max Hayward, London, 1974.
pp 459–468 (in the chapter "Old Friends").

Olga Ivinskaya. *A Captive of Time. My Years with Pasternak* Translated by Max Hayward,
London, 1978. pp 170–185 and 188–192.

c) Letters

Letters, Summer 1926: Boris Pasternak, Marina Tsvetayeva, Rainer Maria Rilke. Edited and
introduced by Yevgeny and Yelena Pasternak and Konstantin Azadovsky.
Translated by Margaret Wettlin and Walter Arndt, New York, 1985, and London,
1986.

INDEX

Index

Kleyn, R. I., 18, 42
Klodt, Mikhail, 14
Kobylinsky, Lev Lvovich. *See* Ellis
Kobylyansky, Vladislav Aleksandrovich, 34–5
Kogan, P. S., 178
Koktebel, 21, 67–9, 71, 77–80, 82, 88, 95, 100,
   102, 120, 122, 131, 136, 143, 146, 148, 244,
   288, 309, 394
Koktebel Echo, 95
Kolbasina-Chernova, Olga Eliseevna, 390n
Korolenko, Vladimir Galaktionovich, 24, 390n
Kozlov, 51
Kostroma, 1
Krachkovsky, D., 255
Krakht, E., 57
Kruchonykh, Aleksey Eliseevich, 122, 390n
Kudrova, Irma, 45–6, 47, 50
Kuntsevo, 188, 189
Kuprin, Aleksandr, 348
Kuzmin, Mikhail Alekseevich, 116, 117n, 158,
   171, 307, 390n; "Alexandrian Songs", 251
Kuznetsova. *See* Grinyova, Maria Ivanovna
Kvanina, Tatyana I., 355, 359, 360, 361–2, 370

Lacaze, Pensionnat, 35, 36
La Motte Fouqué, 24n 29
Lann (Lozman), Evgeny Lvovich, 198, 199–
   200, 206, 390n
Latest News, 261, 262, 290, 310–11, 334
Lausanne, 35, 36
Lauzun, Duc de, 151, 157
Lay of the Host of Igor, The, 123n, 196, 210
Lebedev, Vladimir Ivanovich, 230, 336, 345,
   390–91n
Lebedeva, Irina (Coll), 230, 310
Lebedeva, Margarita Nikolaevna, 230–31, 310,
   376, 318, 339, 345, 367
Lenin, Vladimir Ilich, 163, 211, 327, 331
Leningrad, 357
Lermontov, Mikhail Yurevich, 391n
Lesbos, 101
Letters, Summer 1926 (Pasternak, Rilke,
   Tsvetaeva), 289n
Lichtenstein (Hauff), 37
"Lieutenant Shmidt" (Pasternak), 281
Lipkin, Semyon, 295, 352, 354, 355, 359, 362
"Literary Moscow" (Mandelstam), 171
Litfond (Literary Fund), 5
LITO (Literary Division), 189
Lomonosova, Raisa, 282, 284, 295, 296, 314,
   317
London, 263–4, 274, 345

Lorelei, 24, 24n
Loyal, The, 261, 262, 273
Lunacharsky, Anatoly, 113, 353, 387
Luzhenovsky, General, 42n

Mahler, Professor E., 339
Malot, Hector, *Sans famille*, 24
Mamay, 211, 331
Mandelstam, Nadezhda, xv, 124, 126, 127,
   169, 191, 199, 280–81, 352; *Hope Abandoned*,
   135, 199n, 281n; *Hope Against Hope*, 281n
Mandelstam, Osip Emilievich, 7, 9, 45, 78n,
   105, 117–36, 144, 158, 169, 171–3, 199,
   221–4, 264–5, 266, 270, 281, 288, 307, 309,
   314, 316, 340, 352, 367, 368, 390n;
   "Badger's Lair, The", 134; "Dithyramb to
   Peace", 120–21; "Egyptian Stamp, The", 9;
   "François Villon", 131; "Half turned away,
   O grief", 117; "Humanism and the Present
   Age", 172; "Hymn", 172, 173;
   "Interlocutor, An", 131; "Like a Black
   Angel in the Snow", 126; "Literary
   Moscow", 171; "Menagerie, The"
   ("Dithyramb to Peace"), 120–21; Moscow
   poems, 133; *The Noise of Time*, 264; "Not
   believing in the miracle of resurrection",
   121, 129, 131, 309; "On a country sleigh,
   laid out with straw", 133; "On
   Contemporary Poetry", 117; "Pushkin and
   Skryabin", 131; "Pyotr Chaadaev", 131;
   relationship with MTs, 103, 119–36;
   "Sleeplessness", 78, 217; *Stone*, 120, 126;
   Tristia, 135; "Twilight of Freedom", 172;
   "Voronezh Notebooks", 313
Marie Antoinette, 157
Marx, Karl, 164
Masson, Frédéric, 52
Matrimonial Gazette, 62
Mayakovsky, Vladimir Vladimirovich, 41, 91,
   105, 139, 153, 154, 170–71, 223, 270, 278,
   286, 289–93, 299–300, 305, 307–8, 311,
   334, 353, 354, 361, 390n; compared with
   Pasternak, 307; "Emperor, The", 294;
   "How to Make Poems", 270; "Man", 291;
   suicide, 290–93, 308, 388
Medvezhatkin, 26
Meetings, 313
Merezhkovsky, 334
Mérimée, Prosper, 159
Meyerhold, Vsevolod Emilievich, xv, 153, 154,
   198, 390n
Meyn, Aleksandr Danilovich (MTs's

Index